A
Handbook
for
Horticultural Students

Peter Dawson

Written, illustrated and published by:

Peter Dawson
Chestnut Cottage
South Harting
Nr. Petersfield
Hampshire
GU31 5LR

Telephone: 01730 825376
Email: bigredbook@btinternet.com

This book can be obtained directly from Peter Dawson at the above address. There is no charge for delivery, and a discount is available for 5 or more copies. Please telephone or email for current prices.

To provide a comprehensive teaching package there is a set of illustrations available, designed for use by tutors in the classroom, and which can also be used as student handouts. These are available in a PDF file that can be obtained from Peter Dawson..

for Sunny, Tiffany, Emma and Jonathan

ISBN 0-9525911-1-1

Introduction

This book is for new students of horticulture.

The book is based on the syllabus of the Royal Horticultural Society's Level 2 theory-based qualification, which is a popular and widely recognised qualification. A summary of the syllabus is included in the book.

The book is also suitable for other courses and examinations for new students, such as City and Guilds, BTEC, and NVQ levels 1 and 2.

I have tried to cover the syllabus of the examinations thoroughly but concisely, and to present the information in a form that is clear, and suitable for reproduction in the examination room.

The information in the book is deliberately limited in some areas to avoid students learning details which are not likely to increase their chances of examination success. For example, there are no long lists of plants included, although there are examples of plants of all types and for all uses.

The Level 2 qualification covers a very wide range of horticultural topics, and anyone using the book will, therefore, acquire a sound and comprehensive base of theoretical and practical knowledge.

My aim is to make the book the best single source of information for the new student, and I welcome comments or suggestions for improvement.

Peter Dawson
August 2011

Table of contents

Table of contents

Table of contents

Plants

This section is about plants as a whole. You may think that there is little in common between an oak tree and a poppy, but in fact all plants have a number of things in common which enables us to consider them as a group.

Plant types

Introduction

Let us start with something you probably already know.

When discussing plants we tend to classify them in some way. Doing this gives us certain information about the plants without having to specify it in detail. For example, if we say a particular plant is a 'tree', then that immediately defines certain characteristics of the plant such as it is a woody perennial plant that has a trunk.

The groups that we commonly use are either based on the growth habit of the plant or on what we use it for. For example, a 'tree' is based on the growth habit whereas a 'vegetable' is based on usage.

Note that this method of grouping plants is not the same way in which botanists will group them. As we will see in **Topic A-2 'Plant names'**, the botanist is interested in classifying them according to how they have evolved.

Main plant types:

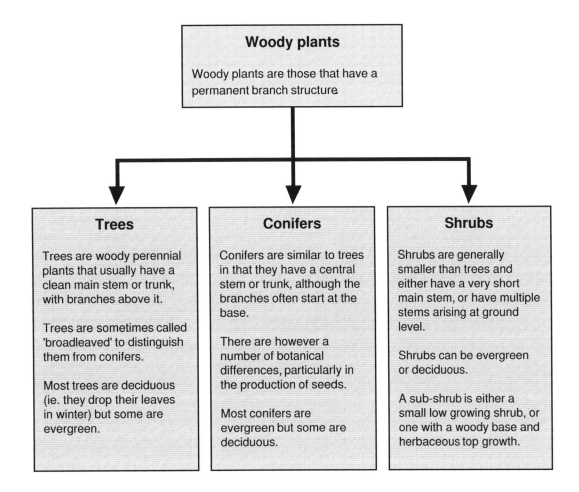

Woody plants

Woody plants are those that have a permanent branch structure

Trees

Trees are woody perennial plants that usually have a clean main stem or trunk, with branches above it.

Trees are sometimes called 'broadleaved' to distinguish them from conifers.

Most trees are deciduous (ie. they drop their leaves in winter) but some are evergreen.

Conifers

Conifers are similar to trees in that they have a central stem or trunk, although the branches often start at the base.

There are however a number of botanical differences, particularly in the production of seeds.

Most conifers are evergreen but some are deciduous.

Shrubs

Shrubs are generally smaller than trees and either have a very short main stem, or have multiple stems arising at ground level.

Shrubs can be evergreen or deciduous.

A sub-shrub is either a small low growing shrub, or one with a woody base and herbaceous top growth.

Herbaceous plants

Herbaceous plants do not develop a woody structure, and their stems and leaves usually die in winter.

Annuals

An annual is an herbaceous plant that completes its life cycle in 1 year.

Annuals are divided into 'hardy' and 'half hardy'. Half hardy annuals will not tolerate frost and cannot be planted in the garden until the danger of frost is over.

Biennials

A biennial is an herbaceous plant that completes its life cycle in 2 years, making vegetative growth in the first year, and flowering in the second year.

Perennials

A perennial is an herbaceous plant that has a life of more than 2 years.

The term 'perennials' usually means hardy perennials which are those that can survive outdoors, although some perennials are tender.

Some perennials retain their leaves over winter.

Bulbs, corms and tubers

These are herbaceous plants that are collectively called 'bulbous' plants. The differences between them will be covered later in this book.

The characteristic they share is that they have a mechanism for storing food that enables them to survive through their dormant season.

Other groupings

There are a number of other ways in which we group plants that may include plants of more than one type.

Evergreens	An evergreen plant retains its leaves in all seasons. Most conifers, some trees and many shrubs are evergreen. A few perennials are also evergreen, mostly retaining leaves at the base of the plant. Some plants are described as semi-evergreen which means they may retain their leaves in mild winters.
Hedges	Hedges are trees or shrubs planted close together to form a continuous row. They are usually cut to maintain a regular size and shape.
Ground cover	Generally dense, low growing and spreading shrubs that can cover a large area, suppress weeds, and need little attention.
Climbers	Plants, usually shrubs, that have a natural adaptation for growing up vertical structures.
Alpines	Plants, usually small shrubs or perennials, that grow naturally in mountainous areas and which are often used on rockeries.
Water plants	Plants, usually perennials, that have a natural adaptation for growing in water (aquatics) or wet soil. (bog plants).
Vegetables	Plants that are grown to provide food. The edible part may be roots, stems or leaves. To complicate matters some vegetables like tomatoes and marrows are botanically fruits.
Fruit	Plants that are grown for their fruit. These plants can be trees, shrubs or perennials.

All the types of plants and groupings in this section are covered in more detail later in this book.

Plant names

Common name

The common name is the one known and used by most people to refer to the plant. The origin of the common name will in most cases date back to the time the plant was first known or cultivated.

Examples of common names are:

Poppy
Heather
Beech

The common name has two main disadvantages;

1. The common name in a country is in the language of that country and is unlikely to be the same as the common name in another country with a different language.

    This makes effective communication between different countries difficult.

2. The common name does not necessarily uniquely identify the plant. In the above examples there are a number of different variations of each plant within each of the common names.

Botanical name

The botanical name overcomes the disadvantages of the common name. The names are recognised in all countries and there is a method of ensuring that each plant is uniquely identified. Relationships between plants are also identified so that ones with a common ancestry can be traced.

The method used for botanical names was devised by a Swedish botanist named **Linnaeus** in the eighteenth century.

The botanical name is made up of at least two parts. The first part is called the **GENUS** (plural GENERA) and the second part is called the **SPECIES**.

As an example we will take the botanical name for a type of poppy:-

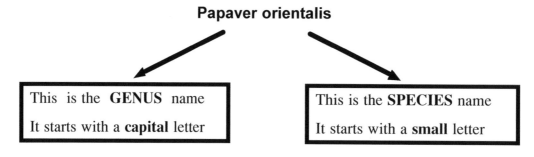

Papaver orientalis

This is the **GENUS** name

It starts with a **capital** letter

This is the **SPECIES** name

It starts with a **small** letter

Genus name

● The genus name represents a group of plants with similar characteristics.

- In evolutionary terms the genus name represents a common ancestor for all the plants contained in the genus.

Species Name

- The species name represents a sub-group of one or more plants within the genus. As with the genus, the species name represents plants with similar characteristics.

- There can be many species within a genus. For example the genus representing oaks contains around 450 species.

- **One characteristic of plants within the same species is that they can reproduce with each other.**

- In previous examination papers the RHS have used the term **specific epithet** rather than **species name**, but the two terms mean the same thing.

The genus name and species name are in Latin, and although this may at first appear difficult and cumbersome to understand, it is important to get used to referring to plants in this way. In fact many common names are the same as the genus name and are used without difficulty. Clematis, hydrangea and phlox are all genus names.

The names can provide information about the plant, and the meaning of some of the species names is included at the end of this topic.

The genus name and the species name can be likened to the surname and christian name used to identify people and the relationship between genus and species is often shown in the form of a family tree.

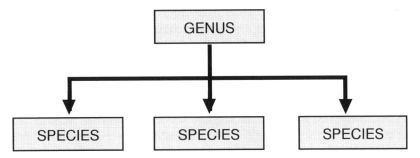

The rule when writing the botanical name is to start the genus name with a **capital** letter and the species name with a **small** letter. Also it is normal practice to write these names in *italics*.

This method of naming plants is called the **binomial** method because there are two names. However even these two names are not enough in all cases to uniquely identify a plant.

Variety names

Within a species there can be variations which require to be separately identified. The variations can occur either naturally through the cross fertilisation of plants or they can occur though the deliberate breeding of plants in an effort to produce better and more attractive varieties.

A naturally occurring variety is referred to as a **variety** and a bred variety is referred to as a **cultivar** (an abbreviation of cultivated variety).

The rule when writing a variety name is to start it with a **small** letter, and when writing a cultivar name to start it with a **capital** letter and enclose it in **single quotation marks**. The variety name is also written in *italics* where it forms part of the full botanical name, but the cultivar name is not.

The cultivar name will be chosen by the breeder and will therefore be in the native language. One cannot help suspecting that the cultivar names are chosen with a view to attracting potential buyers! 'Silver Carpet', 'Pink Diamond' and 'Rose Queen' are all examples of cultivar names.

In the remainder of this book the term variety is used to include both natural and bred varieties.

The following table lists some botanical names, and analyses them to show the genus, species and variety names.

Common Name	Botanical Name	Genus	Species	Variety/ Cultivar
Poppy	*Papaver orientalis* 'Mrs Perry'	*Papaver*	*orientalis*	'Mrs Perry'
Heather	*Erica carnea* 'Vivellii'	*Erica*	*carnea*	'Vivellii'
Beech	*Fagus sylvatica purpurea*	*Fagus*	*sylvatica*	*purpurea*

Another way in which plant names are sometimes written is with a combination of common name and variety name. In fact this is more usual when referring to fruit and vegetables, eg.

Raspberry 'Glen Cova'

Potato 'Majestic'

Hybrid names

A hybrid plant is one produced by sexual reproduction between different varieties, species or genera.

This is comparatively rare for different species and even more rare for different genera. When this is done a new species or new genus is created and a special method is used to indicate this within the name.

A plant that is a hybrid between two different species has an 'x' placed in front of the species name, eg.

Magnolia x *soulangiana*

Clematis x *jackmanii*

A plant that is a hybrid between two different genera has an 'x' placed in front of the genus name, eg.

x *Cupressocyparis leylandii*

x *Osmaria burkwoodii*

The genus name in this case is formed from the genus name of its parents.

Cupressocyparis is a hybrid between the genera *Cupressus* and *Chamaecyparis*, and *Osmaria* is a hybrid between the genera *Osmanthus* and *Phillyrea* .

Family names

All plants belong to a family which is a higher level of grouping than the genus. A family can therefore be made up of a number of genera.

The family name is not necessary to make the plant name unique and is not therefore written as part of the plant name.

We can now redraw the family tree structure to show both the family and the variety. We will put on the tree, details of the poppy we have used in earlier examples. The poppy is in a family called **Papaveraceae.**

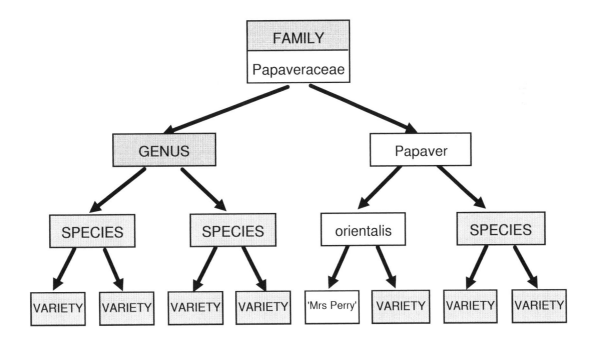

For the botanist, knowing the family a plant belongs to can be very useful because he will know the common characteristics of that family.

For the horticulturist, and certainly for the amateur gardener, it is of less use. Although the plants within a family share common characteristics it is not always apparent and the plants may be very different in appearance. The same family can include trees, shrubs and perennial plants.

Remember that the botanists classification is based on the evolution of the plant. In determining the evolution the structure of the flower is of particular importance and a description of a family usually goes into great detail in this area.

Plants (1) Types and names

Examples and meanings of species names

Colour

alba	white	*aureus*	gold
cardinalis	red	*cyaneus*	blue
nigra	black	*purpurea*	purple

Habitat

alpinus	alpine	*campestris*	field
montana	mountain	*pratensis*	meadow
sylvatica	forest	*saxitile*	rock

Countries

arabis	Arabia	*chinensis*	China
japonica	Japan	*occidentalis*	America
orientalis	Orient	*sibirica*	Siberia

Growth habit

columnaris	columnar	*compressa*	closely packed
dentata	toothed	*fruticosa*	bushy
lanata	woolly	*repens*	creeping

There are a number of books available that contain comprehensive lists of the meaning of both genus and species names.

Plant classification

Botanic classification

This topic is concerned with the way in which botanists classify plants.

This is done within a framework of classification that includes all living things. It is a major task as the number of different species runs into millions. Classifications are also subject to change as more information is obtained about the origin of plants, and this is the reason why plant names sometimes change. The use of DNA analysis is likely to lead to a higher rate of change.

The science of classification is called taxonomy.

We have looked at part of the system as it affects horticulturists, and have seen that plants can be grouped into species, genera and families. There are a number of further groupings above the level of family. These other groupings represent some degree of commonality in terms of evolution just as the genus and family groupings do.

It is not necessary to know all these other groupings but there are some major groups of plants identified at these higher levels that should be known.

They can best be identified in the form of a family tree.

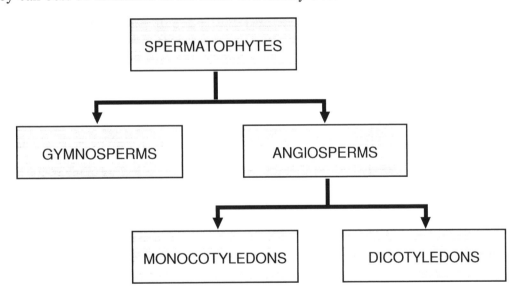

- Spermatophytes

  This group includes all seed producing plants.

- **Gymnosperms**

  This group produces seeds that are not protected by being enclosed in a ovary. The word gymnosperm means 'naked seed'. They are considered to have evolved before angiosperms.

  All conifers are included in this group and comprise the majority of it.

  Gymnosperms do not produce flowers or fruit.

- **Angiosperms**

  This group comprises all flowering plants. They produce their seeds within a ovary that develops into a fruit.

  Angiosperms account for the majority of all plant life.

- **Monocotyledons** (often abbreviated to monocots)

  This name is derived from the fact that they have one seed leaf within their seed (a cotyledon is a leaf).

  Grasses, including both lawn and agricultural grasses such as wheat and barley, are in this group, and so are ornamental plants like irises, tulips, daffodils and orchids.

- **Dicotyledons** (often abbreviated to dicots)

  Dicots have two seed leaves within their seed.

  These are the most common flowering plants and include most trees and shrubs.

In the following topics on plants the assumption is that the plants are dicotyledons although in **Topic A-11** the differences between the two are summarised.

Parts of the Plant

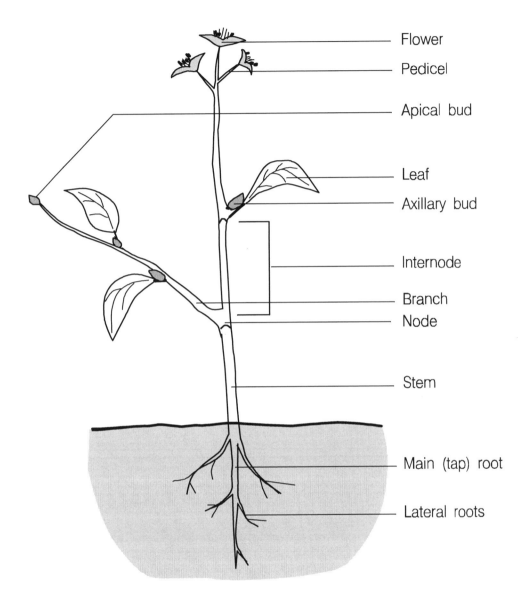

Major organs

The major organs of the plant are the roots, stems, leaves and flowers. These will be considered in more detail in later topics and here we will provide only brief definitions

- **Roots**

    The roots hold the plant firmly in the soil, and enable it to take up water and nutrients from the soil.

    Many roots have a branched structure with a main (or tap) root, with lateral roots branching from it.

- **Stems**

    The stems provide the above ground support of the plant to which the leaves and flowers are attached.

The botanical meaning of stem includes such terms as trunks, branches and shoots.

- **Leaves**

  Leaves contain the cells in which photosynthesis takes place, which is the process that produces food for the plant.

- **Flowers**

  Flowers are the organs of sexual reproduction. The fact that flowers are often very beautiful is not for our enjoyment but is to increase the attractiveness of the plant for pollinating insects.

Other parts

- **Node**

  A node is the point on a stem from which a leaf grows.

- **Internode**

  This is the space on a stem between two nodes.

- **Bud**

  A bud is an undeveloped stem or flower, which given the right stimulus will develop and form a new stem or flower. In form it is like a very compressed stem, with its leaves overlapping and wrapped tightly around it. The outer leaves protect the bud and are called **bud scales**. As it develops it elongates, and the leaves are spaced out along it.

  There are two types of bud:

  → **Apical bud**

    This is the bud at the end of a stem, and is where new cells are generated to lengthen the stem.

    The apical bud produces a hormone that inhibits the development of the axillary buds below it. The term for this is **apical dominance**. It is because of this that the growing tip of some plants, (eg. Chrysanthemums and pinks) is removed to encourage the axillary buds to develop into sideshoots and make the plants more bushy.

  → **Axillary bud**

    These buds are formed in the angle (axil) between the stem and leaf. These buds may remain dormant, or develop if given the right stimulus. If they develop the leaf is shed leaving a scar on the stem.

  Either apical or axillary buds may develop into flowers rather than stems. A flower bud can often be distinguished from a stem bud by being plumper and more protruding.

- **Pedicel**

  A pedicel is the stalk which supports a flower.

Plant cells

Discovery of cells

Cells are the building blocks of nature. All plant and animal life is made up of cells.

Individual cells are not visible to the naked eye, and it was not until after the invention of the microscope in the 17th century that the cell structure was discovered. It was made by Robert Hooke, an English physicist in 1665 when examining a slice of cork. It was he who used the word 'cell' which was probably derived from the Latin name for a small room.

The invention of the electron microscope in the 20th century, with its capability of magnifying many thousands of times, revolutionised the study of cells and significantly increased the knowledge of what they contain and how they work. Nevertheless scientists still do not fully understand the process by which a single cell, invisible to the naked eye, can transform itself into so many different forms, from a delicate orchid to a mighty oak.

Parts of a plant cell

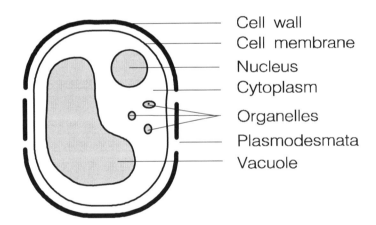

Cell wall
Cell membrane
Nucleus
Cytoplasm
Organelles
Plasmodesmata
Vacuole

- **Cell wall**

    The cell wall surrounds and contains the cell. It is made from a substance called cellulose which is permeable and will allow liquids and gases to pass through it.

    During the life of a plant the cell wall can change becoming thicker and more rigid. In woody plants a substance called **lignin** is added to it which gives it strength. As the walls thicken the protoplasm is forced out until the cell eventually dies. As we will see later the dead cells still perform an essential function.

- **Protoplasm**

    The protoplasm is the living contents of the cell and includes all the items within the cell wall which are listed below.

- **Cell membrane**

  Also known as the cytoplasmic membrane. This is a thin sheet within the cell wall that encloses the cytoplasm and controls the movement of substances in and out of the cell.

- **Cytoplasm**

  The cytoplasm is a jelly like substance that fills the cell within the cell membrane and surrounds the other contents of the cell.

- **Nucleus**

  The nucleus is the control centre of the cell. It contains the genetic information (DNA) that determines the characteristics of the plant, and it initiates cell division which is the primary way in which plants grow.

- **Vacuole**

  The vacuole is a sac surrounded by its own membrane that contains water, minerals and waste products of the plant.

  The pressure of the liquid against the membrane contributes to the structural stability of the plant rather like the air in a balloon. If a plant loses too much water then the soft growth of the plant like new shoots and leaves will wilt as this pressure is lost.

- **Organelles**

  There are many other small bodies suspended in the cytoplasm which are known collectively as organelles. At this level of study we will identify just two:

  → **Chloroplasts**

    Chloroplasts exist in great numbers in the cells of leaves and, to a lesser extent, of stems. They contain a pigment called chlorophyll which gives plants their green colour, and are the part of the plant where photosynthesis takes place. This is a fundamental process of plants and is discussed further in **Topic A-14 'The engines of growth'**.

  → **Mitochondria**

    These exist in all parts of the plant and are where another fundamental process called respiration is carried out. Respiration is also discussed further in **Topic A-14.**

- **Plasmodesmata**

  These are strands of cytoplasm that pass through the cell walls and provide a connection to adjacent cells. This allows substances to be passed between cells.

Cell types

Cells are broadly grouped into three types:

- **Parenchyma**

  These are the most common cell type, found in all parts of the plant, and are characterised by having thin cell walls and intercellular spaces. They are used both for storage of plant nutrients and for photosynthesis and respiration.

- **Collenchyma**

These are more specialised cells with thickened cell walls and whose basic function is to provide support. They are most commonly found at the growing points of the plant and they can elongate to accommodate the growth.

● **Sclerenchyma**

These cells also provide support through the lignin in the cell wall and are found in stems, roots and leaves. Unlike the other cell types these cells perform their function when they are dead.

Cell division

All plants that are created by sexual reproduction start life as a single cell. Growth of the plant is by:

1.   **Cells replicating themselves by dividing into two.**

2.   **Existing cells increasing in size.**

Of these by far the most significant is the replication of cells by dividing into two.

The process of replication starts with the division of the nucleus and then extends to the whole cell.

Between the two cells there is a thin wall called the middle lamella which tends to bind the cells together.

Although cells are packed together there are some cavities and channels between them which are vital for the movement of liquids and gases through the plant.

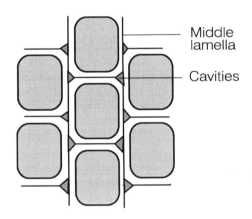

Middle lamella

Cavities

Plant growth by cell division

New cells are not produced randomly or haphazardly. They occur in specific parts of the plant and in response to certain stimuli.

As new cells are produced they are grouped into **tissues** which have a common purpose and the tissues are grouped to form the **organs** of the plant such as roots, stems and leaves.

An area of active cell division is called a meristem.

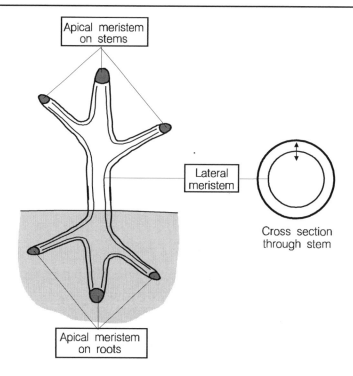

Meristems occur in two areas:

1. Apical meristem

An apical meristem occurs at the tips of roots and stems. It is these meristems that cause the lengthening of these organs.

2. Lateral meristem

The lateral meristem runs like a tube through the roots and stems of the plant. It produces cells on either side of it that cause the organs to thicken. This is necessary so that as the plant increases in length it also becomes broader so it can support the increased length.

Primary and secondary growth

Primary growth is that which takes place at the apical meristems.

Secondary growth is that which takes place at the lateral meristem.

In simple terms it is the primary growth that makes the plant **longer**, and the secondary growth that makes it **wider**. The secondary growth is very important in providing the structural stability of the plant, and in trees it can produce trunks of considerable girth.

Bits and pieces

1. Cells vary in size. A typical range is between 0.01 to 0.05 of a millimetre. At 0.05, a cubic centimetre would contain 8 million cells.

2. Living plants may contain a large number of dead cells. In a woody plant such as a tree over 90% of the cells may be dead. It is in fact the dead cells that constitute the 'wood'. The dead cells perform a vital function: they provide the structural stability of the plant and the channels along which liquids are transported.

Roots

Function of roots

1. They hold the plant firmly in the soil

2. They take up water and nutrients from the soil

3. In some plants food is stored in the roots, eg. carrots and parsnips

External form of roots

There are two basic types of roots

1. **Tap roots**

   These are comprised of a main root with smaller roots branching from it. Tap roots can extend to a considerable depth, and draw up water from deep in the ground.

   Most trees and shrubs have tap roots.

2. **Fibrous roots**

   With a fibrous root there is no main root. All the roots are multi-branched and originate at the base of the stem.

   The roots occupy a large area of shallow soil around the base of the plant and are effective in preventing soil erosion. They rely on water draining from the surface of the soil and are therefore the first plants to suffer in periods of drought.

   Grass is the best example of a plant with fibrous roots.

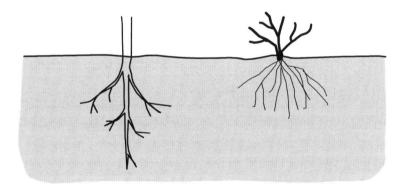

Tap root   Fibrous root

Internal form of roots

Although the exact form of roots will vary from plant to plant the following is a generalised representation that shows the main parts.

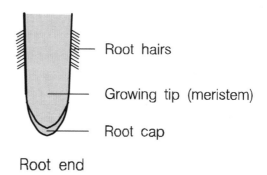

Root end

- **Root cap**

  The root cap is a layer of cells on the surface of the root tip that protect the tip as it grows and pushes through the soil. The cells can be destroyed by this but they are replaced by new ones.

- **Growing tip**

  The root meristem where division of cells takes place.

- **Root hairs**

  A growth from the epidermal cells close to the growing tip. The hairs significantly increase the surface area of the roots. This brings them into contact with more water and nutrients and therefore assists in the take-up of those substances.

  It is the root hairs that are mainly responsible for the uptake of water and nutrients rather than the main root body.

  The root hairs are very fine and there may be 200-400 per square millimetre.

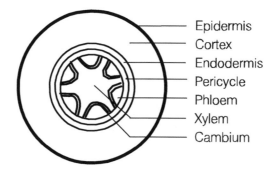

Cross section through root

- **Epidermis**

  The outer layer of cells. It provides some protection to the root and is the equivalent to the skin of animals.

- **Cortex**

  The cortex is usually a fairly thick layer of cells. It is these cells that produce the energy for the growth of the root and which are used for the storage of food.

  Water and nutrients can pass through and between the cells of the cortex.

- **Endodermis**

  The innermost cells of the cortex that control the movement of water and nutrients from the cortex into the phloem and xylem.

- **Pericycle**

  The pericycle is a band of cells from which new roots are generated. The new roots push their way through the cortex and other cells to reach the soil.

- **Phloem**

  The phloem is the part of the plant that transports food from where it is manufactured in the leaves to all other parts of the plant. It can be considered as a tube connecting to all parts of the plant and is therefore present in all organs of the plant.

  Together with the xylem it is known as the **vascular system** of the plant. It can be considered as performing in a similar way the the system of veins and arteries in humans.

  The transport system in plants is covered in more detail in **Topic A-15 'Transport systems'**.

- **Xylem**

  The xylem performs a similar function to the phloem except that it transports water and nutrients absorbed by the roots to all other parts of the plant.

- **Cambium**

  This is a thin layer of cells between the phloem and xylem and which produces new phloem and xylem cells. It is therefore the meristem that causes secondary growth.

  It is more correctly called **vascular cambium** as, when we consider stems, we will see that there is another type of cambium.

Stems

Function of stems

1. Provide support for leaves and flowers

2. Provide structural stability

3. Provide the means of transporting water, nutrients and food around the plant

External form of stems

Stems come in all shapes and sizes. Trunks, branches and shoots are all forms of stem.

Stems are formed from buds; either the apical bud or an axillary bud. Newly formed stems are usually green although other colours, such as red or yellow, are possible. On woody plants the stems usually turn brown as the plant ages.

Newly formed stems are usually smooth, but they can be hairy or downy, usually to provide some form of protection.

Although it is usually easy to distinguish the stem there are some special adaptations where this is not so easy:

● A **bulb** has a compressed stem that stays underground

● A **stolon** is a stem that runs along the ground and can root at its nodes

● A **rhizome** is a stem that develops underground and can root at its nodes

● The **tendrils** of some climbing plants are modified stems

Internal form of stems

Although all stems contain similar tissues, the arrangement of them differs between young, herbaceous (non-woody) growth and older, woody growth.

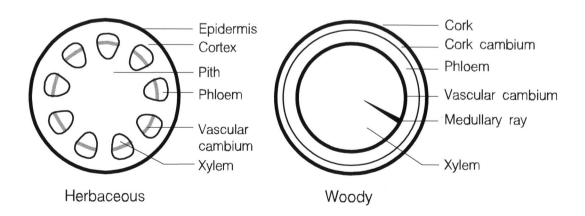

Herbaceous   Woody

Herbaceous stems

The main difference between woody and herbaceous stems is in the positioning of the phloem, xylem and cambium (the **vascular bundles**). In herbaceous stems there are several vascular bundles arranged around the stem. In woody stems they spread to form complete rings around the stem.

The same plant may contain both woody and herbaceous growth. The new growth on a tree or shrub is herbaceous and it only becomes woody with age. The herbaceous growth can be distinguished because it is green, soft and pliable, turning darker, and getting harder and more rigid as it ages.

- **Epidermis**

  The epidermis is the outside layer of cells on herbaceous stems, and is usually only one cell in depth. Its function is to protect the stem and control the loss of water from the plant. It is often covered with a waxy layer called a **cuticle** to increase water retention even further.

- **Cortex**

  As in roots

- **Pith**

  These are loosely packed cells at the centre of the stem whose main function is to store food.

- **Vascular cambium**

  As in roots this is a layer of cells between the phloem and xylem.

  This cambium is particularly important as it produces the phloem and xylem that constitute the secondary growth of the plant. This cambium will go on producing phloem and xylem cells for the life of the plant, which for a tree can be over a hundred years.

- **Phloem**

  As in roots.

- **Xylem**

  As in roots.

  The xylem in woody plants is the 'wood'. Up to 10 times more xylem cells are produced than phloem cells, so that the bulk of woody plants is made up of these cells.

  The xylem cells are produced during the growing season and are larger in spring than in summer. It is this uneven production that produces the 'rings' that can be seen on a cross section of a tree trunk, and which can be used to calculate a tree's life span.

Woody stems

The additional tissues in a woody stem are as follows;

- **Cork**

  This is the equivalent of the epidermis in herbaceous stems. It consists mainly of dead cells and serves to protect the stem.

- **Cork cambium**

  This is a layer of cells that produces the cork as the stem expands due to the secondary growth.

- **Medullary rays**

  These are groups of cells that originate from the vascular cambium and run at right angles to the stem, rather than parallel to it. Their purpose is to transport water and nutrients across the stem.

- **Lenticel**

  The lenticel is a pore in the cork cells on the outside of the stem which allows oxygen, carbon dioxide and water vapour to enter or leave the plant. As you will see later there are similar pores on leaves called 'stomata'

  On some stems it is possible to see these as small white or raised marks.

  The lenticel can be an entry point for diseases.

Other common terms in connection with trees

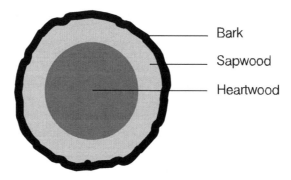

- **Bark**

  The bark comprises the cork, cork cambium and the phloem. If the bark is removed the tree will die, as food can no longer be supplied to the roots. Rabbits often strip the bark from young trees with this result.

- **Sapwood**

  Sapwood is made up of the outer layers of the xylem which are active in transporting water and nutrients (the sap) through the plant.

- **Heartwood**

  Heartwood is made up of the inner layers of xylem which are dead and used to contain a lot of waste products of the plant, such as resins, which give the heartwood its characteristic dark colour. They do not transport water and nutrients but still serve a useful purpose in providing structural support.

Leaves

Function of leaves

1. Produce food by the process of photosynthesis.

2. Release excess water from the plant by the process of transpiration.

3. Allow carbon dioxide and oxygen to enter and leave the plant. These gases are used in the processes of photosynthesis and respiration which are covered in a later topic.

External form of leaves

The form of leaves is almost unlimited, and must tax the ingenuity of botanists in devising names to describe them.

Here we will consider the main differences in form and shape.

How are leaves attached to stems

They can be attached by a stalk (called a petiole) or directly to the stem.

- A **petiolate** leaf is attached by a petiole
- A **sessile** leaf is directly attached to the stem

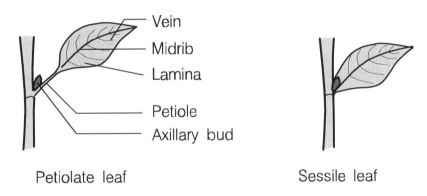

Petiolate leaf   Sessile leaf

Parts of the leaf

- **Petiole**

  The advantage of a petiole is that it provides some flexibility in positioning the leaf to gain the maximum light.

- **Lamina**

  This is the whole of the leaf, also called the blade.

- **Midrib**

  The main vascular bundle of the leaf that runs along the centre of the leaf.

- **Veins**

  The web of vascular tissue that spreads from the midrib to all parts of the leaf.

- **Axillary bud**

  The bud between the leaf and stem.

Arrangement of leaves on stem

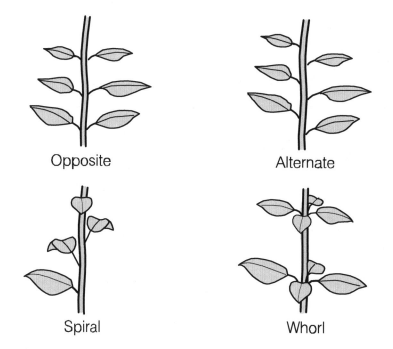

Opposite   Alternate

Spiral   Whorl

The most common arrangement is either opposite or alternate.

When is a leaf not a leaf

A leaf may be divided into leaflets. A leaflet can have the same shape as a leaf but several leaflets make up the complete leaf.

- A **simple** leaf is one without leaflets
- A **compound** leaf is one divided into leaflets

Compound leaves can have their leaflets arranged in different patterns. For example, a **pinnate** compound leaf has them arranged along a central stem.

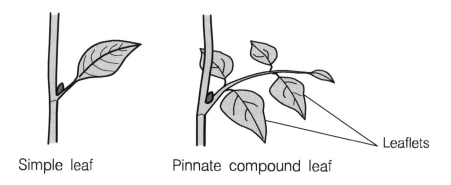

Simple leaf   Pinnate compound leaf   Leaflets

In some case it is not easy to distinguish a leaflet from a leaf, but the distinguishing factor is that only the leaf has an axillary bud.

Leaf shapes

There are numerous different leaf shapes each with their own name. Some of the more common shapes are:

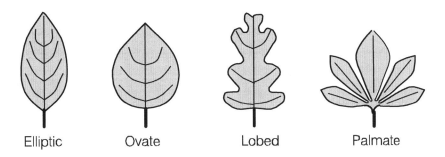

| Elliptic | Ovate | Lobed | Palmate |

Inside the leaves

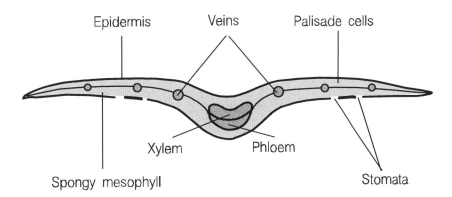

Cross section through leaf

- **Epidermis**

  This is a single layer of cells that cover the surface of the leaf. It provides some protection to the leaf and helps to prevent loss of water from the plant. The protection is increased by a thin waxy layer over the surface of the cells called the **cuticle.**

- **Mesophyll**

  The mesophyll comprises the palisade cells and the spongy mesophyll cells.

- **Palisade cells**

  These cells are directly below the epidermis and are specially adapted for the process of photosynthesis by having many chloroplasts in them.

- **Spongy mesophyll**

  These are loosely packed cells which allow gases (carbon dioxide, oxygen and water vapour) to pass freely between them.

- **Stomata**

  In the epidermis there are many pores called stomata. There can be many thousands of stomata within one square centimeter of leaf.

The pupose of the stomata is to:

1. **Allow carbon dioxide and oxygen to enter and leave the plant**

2. **Allow excess water to leave the plant**

Most of the stomata are located on the underside of the leaf where they are less likely to be clogged with dust or affected by sunlight.

The stomata have a mechanism that enables them to close the pores. This is achieved by having two cells either side of the stomata called **guard cells**.

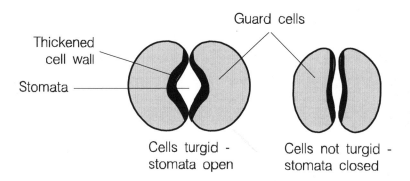

The guard cells have one wall that is thicker and less elastic than the other. When the cell is turgid (full of water) the thinner wall stretches more than the thicker one, and this pulls the cell into a semi-circular shape and opens the stomata. The reverse happens when the guard cells water content decreases.

Therefore the water loss through the stomata can take place when the plant is full of water but is reduced when the plant loses its water.

The stomata also close at night since no carbon dioxide is needed as no photosynthesis can take place at night.

● **Xylem & phloem**

As already covered.

Adaptation of leaves

Leaves are a good example of how plant organs are adapted to perform specific functions.

1. The mainly broad shape offers a large area to the light to achieve the maximum photosynthesis.

2. Many leaves are shaped to shed water so that the stomata do not become blocked. Conversely some leaves are shaped to trap water, where the survival of the plant depends on this.

3. The cells containing the most chloroplasts are situated just below the upper epidermis.

4. The large spaces in the spongy mesophyll allow free movement of gases.

5. There are large numbers of stomata to allow gases to enter and leave the plant.

6. The network of veins brings water close to all the cells.

Flowers

Function of flowers

Flowers are the organs of sexual reproduction. In order to fulfil this function it is necessary to have male and female organs. These can exist in the same flower, in different flowers on the same plant, or in different plants.

● A **hermaphrodite** plant has male and female organs on the same flower.

● A **monoecious** plant has male and female organs on separate flowers on the same plant.

● A **dioecious** plant has male and female organs on different plants.

The flowers develop at the end of a shoot and cause the shoot to stop growing.

Parts of the flower

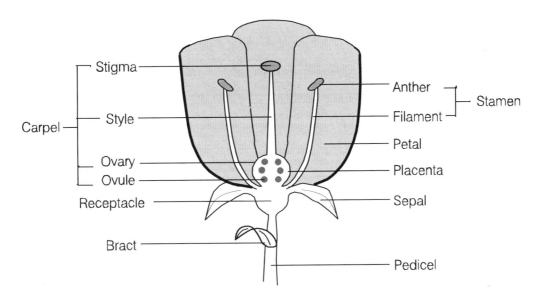

● **Pedicel**

The flower stalk.

● **Bract**

A leaf like structure at the base of a flower. In some plants it can be large and more prominent than the petals.

● **Receptacle**

The top of the pedicel that supports the other parts of the flower.

● **Sepal**

A leaf like organ, usually green, that protects the flowerbud prior to it opening. After the flower has opened its function is finished and it may fall off.

- **Calyx**

  The collective name for all the sepals.

- **Petal**

  A thin leaf like organ, often brightly coloured, that surrounds and partially protects the sexual organs.

  The size and colouring of flowers is to attract pollinating insects. Wind pollinated flowers have much less significant flowers as they do not need to have the same visual attraction.

- **Corolla**

  The collective name for all the petals.

- **Perianth**

  The collective name for the calyx plus the corolla.

- **Stamen**

  The male sexual organ made up of:

  ➜ **Anther**

     The part of the stamen in which pollen is produced.

  ➜ **Filament**

     The stalk of the stamen which attaches to the receptacle.

  The anthers are held on a filament to increase the chances of pollen being transferred to pollinating insects.

  There can be a number of stamen and they are usually arranged in a ring around the carpels.

- **Carpel**

  The female sex organ made up of:

  ➜ **Stigma**

     The receptive surface at the end of the style on which the pollen grains must land if they are to pollinate the plant. The surface is often sticky to retain the grains of pollen.

  ➜ **Style**

     The organ joining the stigma to the ovary. The purpose of the style is to place the stigma where it is likely to be brushed against by pollinating insects thus transferring the pollen.

  ➜ **Ovary**

     The part of the carpel that contains the ovules. The ovary has a thick wall which, after fertilisation has taken place, develops into the fruit.

  ➜ **Ovule**

     The ovary may contain many ovules which contain the female sex cell (called ovum or egg-cell). When fertilised these cells will develop into seeds.

→ **Placenta**

The tissue within the ovary surrounding the ovules.

There may be more than one carpel within a flower although one is common.

Inflorescence

Flowers are sometimes produced in clusters called inflorescences.

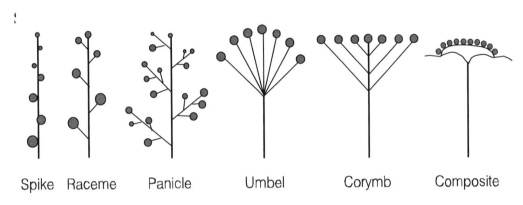

Spike   Raceme   Panicle   Umbel   Corymb   Composite

Spike	Flowers attached without stalks eg. Acanthus
Raceme	Flowers attached by short stalks to a central shoot eg. Hyacinth
Panicle	Many branches each with the form of a raceme eg. Gypsophila
Umbel	Flower stalks originate from one point and are the same length eg. Agapanthus
Corymb	Flowers are on stalks of different lengths so that the flowers are all at the same level eg. Hydrangea
Composite	Many small flowers grouped together giving the appearance of one flower eg. Sunflower

Fruits and seeds

Fruits

Fruits and seeds form as a result of fertilisation. The **process** of fertilisation will be covered in a later topic, and in this topic we will just cover the **parts** of the fruits and seeds.

After fertilisation most of the flower parts will wither and die, but the ovary will grow and form the fruit, with the ovules forming the seeds. The purpose of the fruit is to protect the seeds, and the seeds cannot germinate until the fruit has been broken down and disposed of in some way.

Fruits come in many shapes, sizes and consistencies, and not all are edible. The broadest distinction is between those that are fleshy such as a berry, and those that are dry such as a pea pod. There are different terms to define the different types and some of the most common are:

Berry	A fleshy fruit usually containing many seeds eg. Tomato, grape
Drupe	A fleshy fruit with a single seed contained in a hard coat eg. Cherry, olive
Pome	A fleshy fruit derived from the receptacle rather than the ovary eg. Apple, pear
Legume	A dry fruit usually containing multiple seeds arranged in a line eg. Pea, bean
Nut	A hard fruit usually containing one seed eg. Chestnut, acorn

Another distinction can be made between **dehiscent** seeds that burst or split open to release their seed as they mature such as a poppy, and **indehiscent** seeds which remain intact such as an acorn.

Parts of the fruit

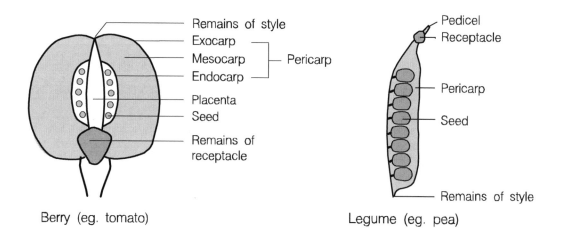

Berry (eg. tomato)   Legume (eg. pea)

These are examples of a **simple** fruit formed from one ovary. There are also **aggregate** fruits formed from many ovaries (eg. strawberry) and **multiple** fruits formed from many ovaries which have fused together (eg. pineapple).

Most of the terms in the above diagrams have already been covered. The new ones are:

● **Pericarp**

> The pericarp is the whole of the fruit that develops from the ovary, and surrounds the seed(s).
>
> In some fruits it consists of three identifiable parts:
>
> → **Exocarp**
>
> > This is the outside layer, forming a skin. It can be soft as in a berry, or hard as in a nut.
>
> → **Mesocarp**
>
> > This is the fleshy part and is often edible.
>
> → **Endocarp**
>
> > This is the part immediately surrounding the seed(s). It can also be soft, as in a berry, or hard, as in a drupe.

In some cases what we regard as the fruit is not formed from the ovary but from the receptacle. This is called a **false fruit** and an example is a strawberry, where the receptacle swells and becomes red and the real fruits are imbedded in it.

Some fruits develop without seeds and these are called **parthenocarpic**. These can occur naturally although it is regarded as a fault since without seeds the plant cannot reproduce. However pathenocarpic plants can be attractive to the consumer since the seeds may detract from the taste or texture of the fruit, and grapes, tomatoes and cucumbers have been deliberately bred to be parthenocarpic.

Seeds

Seeds are formed from the female ovules as a result of fertilisation and are the prime method by which flowering plants reproduce.

The seeds are able to survive in adverse conditions that may kill the parent plant. For example, annual plants will produce seeds in late summer and die with the onset of winter. The seeds however are able to survive the winter and germinate when the weather gets warmer in the following spring.

Seeds are very hardy and can survive in a dormant state for many years if conditions for germination are not right. This is why weeds can come up in a garden year after year, particularly if the garden is cultivated as this brings fresh seeds to the surface.

Parts of the seed

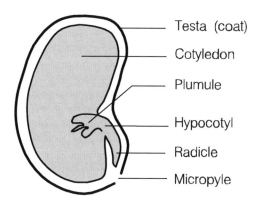

- **Testa**

  This is the seed coat that protects the seed, and it can be very tough. It may be necessary for the testa to be damaged in some way before the seed will germinate. This can be done naturally by soil organisms or soil particles, or artificially by soaking the seed or nicking the testa.

- **Cotyledon**

  This is a small leaf, known as a seed leaf, that provides a store of food for the germinating seed. There can be one seed leaf (monocotyledon) or two seed leaves (dicotyledon).

  Sometimes these leaves stay beneath the surface of the soil but in some cases (eg. runner bean) they emerge with the new shoot.

- **Plumule**

  This is the part of the seed that will form the first shoot.

- **Hypocotyl**

  This connects the plumule to the radicle.

- **Radicle**

  This is the part of the seed that will form the first root.

- **Micropyle**

  This is a small hole in the testa where the pollen tube entered the ovule at the time of fertilisation. It can be the point at which water enters the seed to start the germination process.

- **Endosperm**

  This is not shown in the diagram as it is not present in all seeds. It is formed at fertilisation time and is used as a source of food for the embryo as it grows to form the seed.

Dicotyledons & monocotyledons

In **Topic A3 'Plant classification'** we mentioned that flowering plants could be subdivided into dicotyledons and monocotyledons.

Throughout this section the text and diagrams have assumed we are discussing dicotyledons although there is a lot that is common to both.

In this topic the main differences between the two are summarised.

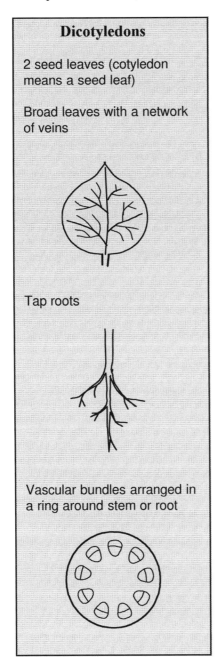

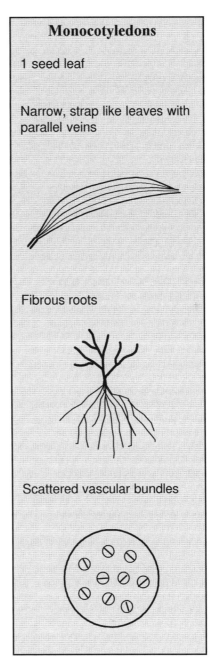

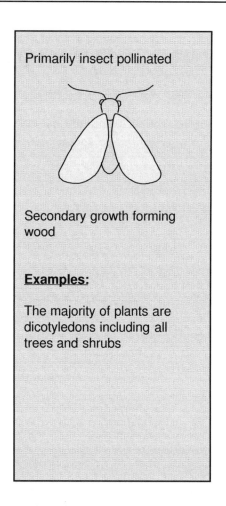

Primarily insect pollinated

Secondary growth forming wood

Examples:

The majority of plants are dicotyledons including all trees and shrubs

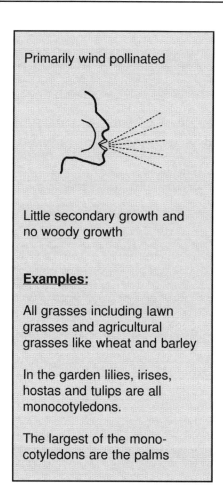

Primarily wind pollinated

Little secondary growth and no woody growth

Examples:

All grasses including lawn grasses and agricultural grasses like wheat and barley

In the garden lilies, irises, hostas and tulips are all monocotyledons.

The largest of the mono-cotyledons are the palms

Monocotyledons do not grow as big as the dicotyledons but they are more flexible, and the ratio of stem length to width can be much higher, (100:1 in some cases). It is this flexibility that enables palm trees to withstand hurricanes when more rigid plants would be snapped off.

A little bit of chemistry

Most of the information in this topic is not part of the examination syllabus and there will be no questions on it. It is included as background information that may give a better understanding of the plant growth processes.

The exception is the part dealing with osmosis. You should try to understand this and remember the formal definition.

Atoms

All matter is made up of atoms. An atom is the smallest unit of matter and cannot be divided (an atomic bomb relies on splitting the atom but this is a rather special case!).

Atoms are exceedingly small and cannot be seen even with an electron microscope. As an example it would take 4 million hydrogen atoms to stretch across 1 millimetre.

There are a limited number of different atoms, and the same or different atoms group together to form the substances we are familiar with.

A substance made up of atoms of the same type is called an element and some of these are familiar to us. For example oxygen is an element made up from oxygen atoms. Similarly copper, iron, hydrogen and nitrogen are elements. Note that the element can be a solid or a gas and, in fact, it can also be a liquid. As we will see later there are a number of elements that are essential to plants.

In order to identify a particular type of atom letters are used as a shorthand notation. An oxygen atom is identified by an 'O', a copper atom by 'Cu' and a nitrogen atom by 'N'. You may be familiar with the NPK specification on fertilisers which shows the percentage content of nitrogen(N), phosphorus(P), and potassium(K).

Molecules

Atoms of one element can combine with atoms of other elements, to form different substances. These substances are called compounds and can be things that we are familiar with in everyday life. Water, salt and chalk are all substances made up from combinations of atoms. The combining can be done in different ways and it is more than just mixing the atoms together. You can think of it conceptually as the atoms having hands with which they will hang on to other atoms.

A group of atoms combined together is a molecule.

The molecule is identified by a formula which specifies the atoms it consists of. For example water is made up of molecules that consist of 2 atoms of hydrogen and 1 atom of oxygen and has the formula 'H_2O'. The subscript $_2$ means there are two atoms of hydrogen. Similarly carbon dioxide, a gas that is used by plants, is made up of molecules that consist of 1 atom of carbon and 2 atoms of oxygen and has the formula 'CO_2'.

These are fairly simple molecules but it is possible to get ones that are more complex and consist of more than two types of atom.

A **chemical reaction** occurs where bonds between atoms and molecules are either formed or broken.

Sometimes chemical reactions involve more than a quantity of 1 of an atom or molecule. For example:

$6CO_2$ + $6H_2O$ means 6 molecules of carbon dioxide plus 6 molecules of water.

Ions

An ion is an atom or molecule that has a positive or negative electric charge. An ion with a positive charge is called a **cation** and one with a negative charge is called an **anion.**

Just how they acquire such a charge is beyond the scope of this book. The significance is that ions with opposite charges are attracted to each other and will cling together. This can be compared with the action of magnets.

Where this interests the horticulturist is in its effect within the soil. As we will see later the workability of the soil, and the availability of nutrients to the plant, is affected by the cations and anions within the soil.

Diffusion

Diffusion is a very important process to plants. It is the mechanism by which plants absorb and release water, oxygen and carbon dioxide. A significant point about it is that it is a natural process that takes place automatically without the plant having to use any of its own energy.

The principle of diffusion is that where atoms or molecules are free to move, as they are in gases and liquids, they move so that they are evenly distributed. The effect of this can be seen if some colouring agent is added to water. The molecules of the colouring agent spread through the water until it is evenly coloured.

Let us take another example. If we place some pure water in one half of container, and water containing salt in the other half then we will have a situation in which there are more molecules of water on the side containing pure water and more molecules of salt on the other side.

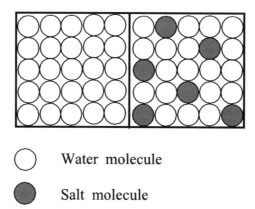

○ Water molecule

● Salt molecule

If the divider separating the two liquids is removed then water molecules from the pure side will move to the impure side and salt molecules from the impure side will move to the pure side until there is an even distribution through the whole liquid.

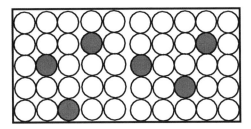

Put more technically, atoms or molecules will move from an area of high concentration (where there are most) to an area of low concentration (where there are least).

Osmosis

Osmosis is a process that uses the principles of diffusion and is how plants take up water.

Water in the cells of a plant usually contains more dissolved substances than water in the soil. This gives a higher concentration of water outside the cell, just as in the above example there were more water molecules in the pure water. The water molecules outside the cell therefore move into the cell by diffusion to try and make the concentration equal.

You might think that by the same process the dissolved substances in the cell would try and move out of the cell just as the salt molecules in our example moved. This would be the case but for the fact that the cell membrane stops them being moved. Because the cell membrane allows water through but not the dissolved substances it is said to be semi-permeable.

A formal definition of osmosis is:

> **Osmosis is the process by which water moves across a semi-permeable membrane from a solution with a higher concentration of water molecules to a solution with a lower concentration.**

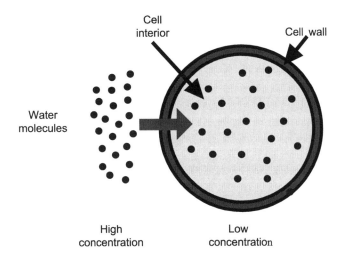

Requirements for growth

In order to grow a plant needs **material** from which to make new cells, an **environment** in which this can take place, and **energy** to cause it to happen.

The following table summarises all requirements which will be covered in more detail in following topics.

Requirement	Source	Comments
Carbon dioxide	Atmosphere	Required for photosynthesis. Carbon is incorporated in new cells
Oxygen	Atmosphere	Required for respiration
Water	Soil	Required for cell turgor, for photosynthesis and as a means of transport through the plant
Nutrients	Soil	Nutrients are the chemicals required by the plant, and they have many uses within the plant. The nutrients are derived from the weathering of rock or the breakdown of organic matter.
Light	Sun	Light is essential for the process of photosynthesis
Temperature	Sun	Plants will only grow successfully within certain temperature ranges (not the same range for all plants)

Plants require these things in balance. The growth will be limited by the resource which is least available.

The resources can be manipulated by the grower to some extent in order to provide the best possible conditions. This is done commercially to produce plants out of their normal season.

Photosynthesis and respiration are covered in **Topic A-14 'The engines of growth'**.

Stages in the growth cycle

However long the life of a plant is, it goes through some definite stages which are important to the gardener and horticulturist.

The stages are:

Juvenile

The juvenile stage covers the initial growth period of the plant. The actual time this takes can vary from days in the case of a annual up to years in the case of a tree. The time appears to vary with the size of the plant. The characteristics of a plant in its juvenile stage are:

- Plants do not flower in the juvenile stage.

- Propagation is often easier from juvenile growth, due to a high concentration of growth hormones.

- Plant form, in terms of leaf shape and growth habit, can be different from adult growth.

How these factors are exploited will be covered later in this book.

Adult

This stage follows the juvenile stage and it is probably triggered by a change in the plant's hormones. The adult stage of a plant will cover the longest period in its growth cycle, varying from several weeks in the case of an annual to many years in the case of a tree. The plant will continue to grow in size during its adult life.

Senescence

Senescence is the process during which the plant starts to deteriorate leading eventually to death.

The engines of growth

For any living organism to grow it requires food, which it uses to produce energy to fuel the growth process.

$$FOOD \longrightarrow ENERGY \longrightarrow GROWTH$$

Plants produce food by a process called **photosynthesis**, and convert that food to energy by a process called **respiration.**

Photosynthesis

Photosynthesis is the process by which plants use the energy from light to convert carbon dioxide and water into carbohydrates (food) and oxygen.

The chemical equation for this:

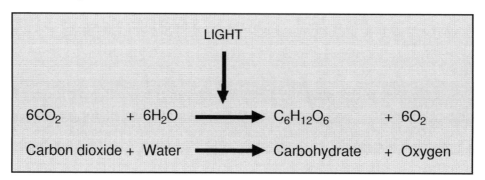

Photosynthesis takes place primarily within the **chloroplasts** in the **palisade cells** of the leaves.

The carbon dioxide is obtained from the atmosphere through the stomata, and the water is obtained from the soil and transported to the leaves through the xylem.

The carbohydrates are transported through the phloem to other parts of the plant where they may be:

- **Used in the process of respiration to provide energy for growth.**
- **Stored as starch for future use. They are often stored in the cortex cells of the root.**
- **Used to construct other plant material such as cellulose and proteins.**

The oxygen released in the process may be reused in the process of respiration or released through the stomata.

The photosynthesis takes place in two stages:

1. **Light stage**

    The water molecules are split to release the hydrogen. This is called the light stage because it only takes place in the presence of light.

2. **Dark stage**

The hydrogen molecules combine with the carbon dioxide molecules to form the carbohydrates. Although this is called the dark stage it takes place in light or dark.

Factors affecting the rate of photosynthesis

- **Light intensity**

  This is the most significant factor. Light is the energy source that fuels the process and without it photosynthesis will not take place. In reduced light levels the rate will reduce. It is possible to use artificial lights but these have to be of the correct wavelength.

- **Temperature**

  Temperature can also affect the rate, although the light intensity may override the effect. The optimum temperature for photosynthesis is 25-35° C, with a minimum of about 5° and a maximum of 45°.

- **Water availability**

  If there is insufficient water available in the plant, the stomata will close and inhibit photosynthesis.

- **Carbon dioxide levels**

  Carbon dioxide will not normally be a limiting factor, although it could in a closed environment like a glasshouse, since the carbon dioxide used by the plants will not be being replaced. It is possible to buy equipment that will generate carbon dioxide in these circumstances.

The importance of photosynthesis

- **It is the basic process that captures energy from the sun and utilises it for building living things.**

- **All life depends on this process since all animal life depends directly or indirectly on plant life.**

- **By absorbing carbon dioxide and releasing oxygen it balances the process of respiration.**

Respiration

Respiration is the process by which cells release energy contained in carbohydrates in order to fuel the growth of the plant.

Do not confuse respiration in this context with the more common use meaning breathing. Use of respiration here is sometimes called **cellular respiration** to avoid any confusion.

The chemical process is the reverse of that for photosynthesis.

$$C_6H_{12}O_6 \quad + \quad 6O_2 \quad \longrightarrow \quad 6CO_2 \quad + \quad 6H_2O$$

Carbohydrate + Oxygen → Carbon dioxide + Water + Energy

Respiration is carried out in the mitochondria of the cells.

The carbohydrate is produced by the process of photosynthesis, and the oxygen is obtained from the atmosphere through the stomata or from the output of photosynthesis.

The carbon dioxide is released into the atmosphere through the stomata or used in the process of photosynthesis. The water is released as water vapour through the stomata.

Gaseous exchange

During the processes of photosynthesis and respiration the gases oxygen, carbon dioxide and water vapour all play a part, and are at various times being taken in by the plant, given off by the plant, or being reused within the plant.

The gases diffuse in or out of the plant through the stomata on the leaves or the lenticels on the stems.

The following diagram shows the movement of gases between the atmosphere and the plant and within the plant. The shaded area represents activity within the plant.

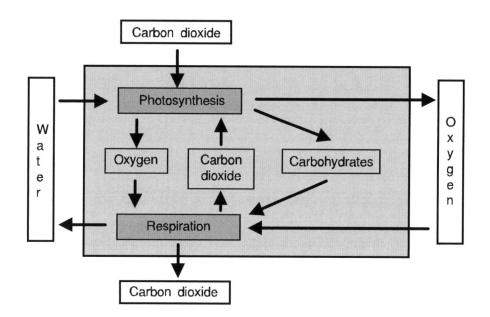

Transport systems

In previous topics we have discussed the function of the **xylem** and **phloem** which together make up the plant's vascular system.

The xylem transports water and nutrients (dissolved minerals) from the roots where they enter the plant to all other parts of the plant.

The phloem transports food from the leaves where it is manufactured to all other parts of the plant.

What we have not covered so far is the mechanism by which these substances are transported and this is what we shall do in this topic.

Transport of water and minerals through the xylem

In general terms water enters the plant through the roots, is transported through the stems, and is lost by transpiration through the leaves.

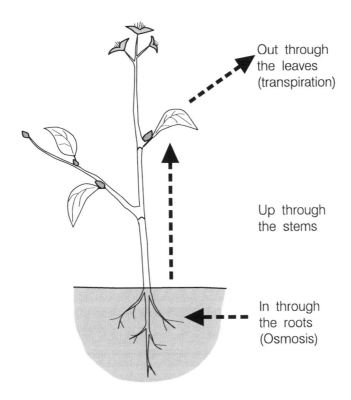

Out through the leaves (transpiration)

Up through the stems

In through the roots (Osmosis)

Water uptake by the roots

Water enters the roots by osmosis, primarily through the root hairs.

Under some circumstances the concentration of dissolved substances in the soil water can be higher than the concentration in the cells. In this case water will move from the plant into the soil which, if it continues, can seriously damage the plant. This condition is known as **PLASMOLYSIS**. You can simulate this by placing a carrot in a strong solution of water and salt. After a while the carrot will lose its firmness as water is lost from its cells.

Having entered the cells of the epidermis by osmosis the water is pushed across the cortex as more water enters the plant. The word 'osmosis' comes from the Greek word for push.

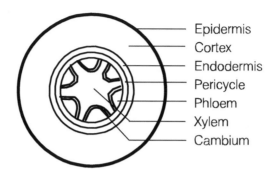

The cells of the cortex are loosely packed and the water tends to move between them.

On the inside of the cortex the cells of the endodermis again push the water by osmosis into the cells of the xylem. The cells of the xylem through which the water is conducted are dead and are called **vessels**. The vessels are elongated with open ends and holes in the side called **pits**. This enables the water to be carried as a continuous stream through the plant.

The pushing effect of the epidermis and endodermis is called the **root pressure**. This root pressure can push the water a certain way up the stem of the plant but it cannot alone account for water reaching to the top of a large tree.

Transpiration

Transpiration is the loss of water from the plant by evaporation, mainly through the stomata on the leaves.

Of the water taken up by the plant only a small proportion is retained. Over 95% is lost by transpiration.

The loss of water by transpiration creates a pulling effect, known as **transpirational pull**, that together with the root pressure and the property of water that causes it to cling together, enables the water to reach the heights required. The effect can be likened to sucking water up through a straw.

The amount of water lost by transpiration can be considerable. A mature tree can transpire 1000 litres in a day.

The rate of transpiration can be affected in a number of ways:

- **Light**

   The stomata close at night preventing transpiration.

- **Temperature**

   The loss of water is greater in higher temperatures. In areas of very high temperature plants are adapted to minimise the water loss by such things as few stomata, or a thick cuticle.

- **Humidity**

  Less water will be lost if the area around the leaves is kept humid. This is the principle behind mist propagation units.

- **Wind**

  Wind can increase the water loss by removing humid air from around the leaf.

- **Water uptake by roots**

  If the plant is short of water the stomata will close.

Osmosis and transpiration are independent processes although both are affected by the water content of the plant and are therefore normally kept in balance. It is however possible at times for them to get out of balance. On a hot day, for example, the loss by transpiration may be greater than the rate at which water can be absorbed by the roots and temporary wilting may occur.

Transport of food through the phloem

Food is manufactured in the leaves by the process of photosynthesis and has to be transported to the parts of the plant that require it. This includes roots, stems and flowers. The food may be stored in other parts of the plant such as the cortex in the root, (this is what happens in root vegetables such as carrots).

The cells of the phloem are tubular with perforated ends, called **sieve plates**, through which the food can be transported. Unlike the cells of the xylem, the phloem cells are living.

The mechanism by which the food is transported is not fully understood. It is generally accepted however that it is not by the process of diffusion since it may move the food to an area which already contains a higher concentration. The plant therefore has to take specific action, entailing the use of energy, to move it around. This is given the general name of **active transport** to distinguish it from diffusion which is passive, (ie. does not require energy from the plant).

Control systems

The need for control

We have established that plants grow by cell division and cell enlargement. We also know that the energy to do this comes from a process called **respiration** which uses food manufactured by a process called **photosynthesis.**

However, we also know from simple observation that plants do not grow at random times but follow a definite timetable from germination, through vegetative growth, through flowering, through dormancy in some cases, and to eventual death.

If a plant were not to follow a timetable then its existence could be threatened. If for example, it germinated in winter when frost would kill the emerging plant, or if it flowered when the insects required for pollination were not available.

There therefore have to be some external factors that stimulate the plant, and some factors in the plant that respond to that stimulus.

External factors affecting growth

1.   Day length

Of all the environmental factors this is the one that has been constant for millions of years and it is the one that acts as the plants biological clock.

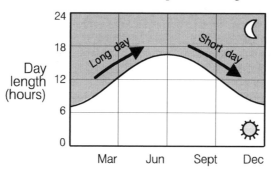

The reaction of the plant to day length is called **photoperiodism.** It affects a number of the functions of the plant but particularly flowering and dormancy.

Not all plants react in the same way and we can distinguish three groups:

Short day plants	React when the day length is below a specified figure. In general these will be the later flowering plants.
	eg. Chrysanthemum
	        Dahlias
	        Poinsettia

Long day plants	React when the day length is above a specified figure. In general these will be spring and summer flowering plants.
	eg. Petunia
	        Gypsophila
	        Helenium

Day neutral plants	These plants are unaffected by day length and will flower after a specific period of growth. eg. Begonia Cucumber Viburnum

In addition to the day length being correct, the plant must be of such a size and state to be ready to flower. In annuals this state is reached in the first growing season, but in some trees and shrubs it may be several years before the plant reaches this state.

2.   **Temperature**

In general an increase in temperature increases the rate of growth whereas a drop in temperature decreases it. Many plants are dormant over the winter when very little growth takes place.

An optimum temperature for growth is 25-35^0 C, with a minimum of 5^0 and a maximum of 45^0, as shown in the following chart.

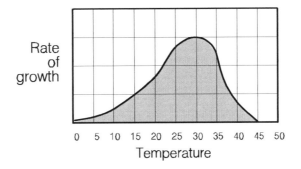

In some plants a period of low temperature is required before growth or flowering can be initiated. In the UK winter provides this period but if plants are moved to another country it may have to be provided artificially. For example, in some warmer countries tulips have to be dug up each year and artificially chilled in order for them to flower the following year.

Where vegetative growth takes place but flowering is dependent on a cold period this is called **vernalisation**. The common example of this is with biennials, such as wallflowers, which grow one year and flower the next.

An increase in the soil temperature is the trigger for a number plants to commence growth. This is the case, for example, with spring flowering bulbs.

Internal factors controlling growth

Within the plant it is the hormones that control the growth.

The hormones are chemicals, produced mainly in the apical meristem, and transported to other parts of the plant where they affect the growth.

The way in which the hormones act is complicated.

- **In some cases a high concentration of the hormone can produce the opposite affect of a low concentration.**

- **Some hormones encourage activity while some inhibit activity.**

- **The relative levels of different hormones can produce different results so that as one level drops and another rises the behaviour of the plant changes.**

Five hormones are commonly recognised although it is thought that there are more. They are present in very small quantities which makes their identification difficult.

The following table shows the major effects of each hormone.

Auxin	Promotes cell elongation	Auxin tends to move away from the light. When a plant receives light from one side the auxin moves to the shady side and elongates the cells with the result that the shoot bends towards the light.
	Stimulates cell division	Hormone rooting powders are based on chemicals similar to auxin.
	Inhibits growth in high concentrations	The apical bud on a stem produces a high concentration that inhibits the development of axillary buds below it. Removal of the apical bud will cause the axillary buds to grow.
		This effect is used in pruning plants to obtain a more bushy growth.
		A high concentration also inhibits growth in roots.
	Disrupts normal growth patterns	Synthetic auxins like 2,4-D are used as weedkillers.
	Inhibits abscission (leaf drop)	
Gibberellin	Promotes cell elongation	This causes the distance between nodes to be increased. This hormone has more effect in low light situations, causing the stem to lengthen and therefore reach the light. In extreme situations it can lead to a state called **etiolation** where the stems are long and spindly.
	Stimulates cell division	
	Breaks dormancy of seeds and buds	
	Promotes flowering	Application of gibberellin is used to induce flowering out of normal timeframe.
Cytokinin	Promotes cell division	
	Breaks dormancy of seeds and buds	
	Delays ageing of leaves	This is used commercially to keep the leaves of lettuce looking fresh.

Abscisic acid	Inhibits growth	Closes stomata and inhibits stem growth during drought conditions.
	Promotes ageing of leaves	The dropping of leaves, flowers and fruit is called abscission, and is caused by the weakening of cells called the abscission zone.
	Maintains dormancy in seeds and buds	
Ethylene	Induces flowering and ripening of fruit	Picked fruit can carry on ripening in the presence of ethylene.
	Promotes ageing of leaves	
	Breaks dormancy of buds in some plants	

Manipulation of control systems

Knowing the factors that affect the growth and ageing of plants has led to the manipulation of these factors for our own benefit.

The artificial use of light and temperature is comparatively easy to achieve and some plants are grown in completely artificial conditions, involving regulation of light, temperature, growing medium, water and nutrients.

Many of the plant hormones have been synthesised and are applied to the plants, flowers or fruit to enhance or change the plants natural growth pattern.

The following are some examples of specific manipulation:

1. **Chrysanthemums for cut flowers can be produced all the year round by using artificial lighting to deceive the plant into flowering.**

   Since chrysanthemums are a short day plant they can be induced to flower by cutting out the light for the required period of time (about 15 hours). Similarly they can be stopped from flowering by not letting them have the required period of darkness. In fact the requirement for darkness is that it should be continuous and it is therefore only necessary to interrupt the natural darkness for a short period of time.

2. **Synthetic auxins are used as hormone rooting powder and hormone weedkillers.**

3. **Cytokinins are used to delay the ageing of leaf crops like lettuce after they have been picked to keep them looking fresh.**

4. **Ethylene is applied to tomatoes and citrus fruits to stimulate ripening.**

In addition there are some chemicals not produced naturally by plants that can affect the growth. Growth retardants, that inhibit the effect of gibberellin, are used to produce sturdy, compact plants such as chrysanthemums and poinsettia.

Plant nutrients

Nutrients are the chemicals required by plants and are used in a number of ways.

In nature nutrients come either from the weathering of the rock from which the soil is formed, or from the breakdown of organic matter in the soil. They can all be supplied artificially as compost, manure or fertilisers (See **Topic B-12 'Soil Management (3) Feeding'**).

The nutrients are dissolved in the soil water, absorbed through the roots, and transported through the xylem to the parts of the plant requiring them.

Some nutrients are required in quite large amounts while others are required only in minute amounts. It is therefore convenient to divide them into two groups. The ones required in large amounts are called the **major nutrients** and the others the **minor nutrients** (also called trace elements).

Major nutrients	Minor nutrients
Nitrogen	Iron
Phosphorus	Manganese
Potassium	Boron
Magnesium	Copper
Calcium	Zinc
Sulphur	Molybdenum

It is not always easy to distinguish symptoms of nutrient deficiency from other plant problems, or to determine which nutrient is deficient. It is possible to get soil analysed in the laboratory and this is probably the best way to determine whether any nutrients are lacking.

Major nutrients

Nitrogen (N)
Encourages vegetative growth and is therefore important in lawns and leaf crops. Easily leached from the soil.
Constituent of **p**roteins, nucleic acids and chlorophyll.
Symptoms of deficiency:
Slow, spindly growth.
Yellowing of leaves (chlorosis) - old leaves first.
Flowers and fruit small.

Phosphorus (P)
Important for root growth and the ripening of fruit. Must be present in seeds for germination to take place. Recycled within the plant.
Tends to build up in regularly fertilised soil and deficiences are rare.
Constituent of proteins, nucleic acid and enzymes.
Symptoms of deficiency:
Growth retarded. Leaves dull blue/green and may fall prematurely.
Flowers and fruit delayed and small.

Potassium (K)

Essential for good flower and fruit formation.

Increases the general hardiness of the plant.

Symptoms of deficiency:

Poor quality fruits and seeds.

Leaf scorch on older leaves.

Leaves bronzed and rolled inwards and downwards.

Magnesium (Mg)

Required for correct functioning of photosynthesis, and movement of phosphorus.

A constituent of chlorophyll.

Symptoms of deficiency:

Intervein chlorosis.

Leaf tips curl upwards.

Early leaf fall.

Calcium (Ca)

Required for activity in meristems, and a major constituent of cell walls.

May be unavailable in acid soils.

Symptoms of deficiency:

Weakened cell walls leading to tissue dying.

Inward curling, pale young leaves.

Examples are **'bitter pit'** in apples, **'blossom end rot'** in tomatoes.

Sulphur (S)

Required for production of chlorophyll.

Constituent of proteins and enzymes.

Rarely deficient.

Symptoms of deficiency:

Chlorosis - younger leaves first

Minor nutrients

Minor nutrients are only required in minute amounts (measured in parts per million) and deficiencies are less likely to occur.

The nutrients are usually effective in a narrow concentration range and over fertilisation may give problems.

Iron (Fe)

Required for the production of chlorophyll.

Constituent of enzymes.

Symptoms of deficiency:

Intervein chlorosis - young leaves first.

Failure to flower and fruit.

Manganese (Mn)

Required for the production of chlorophyll.

Constituent of enzymes.

Symptoms of deficiency:

Intervein chlorosis - oldest leaves first.

Boron (B)	Copper (Cu)
Makes calcium available within the plant. Involved with the movement of sugars and synthesis of gibberellin. **Symptoms of deficiency** Leaves misshapen and fruit malformed. Flowering suppressed. Examples are **'corky core'** in apples and **'brown heart'** in turnips.	Involved in the correct functioning of enzymes. Rarely deficient. **Symptoms of deficiency** Varies with species. Dark green leaves becoming twisted and withering - young leaves first.
Zinc (Zn)	**Molybdenum (Mo)**
Involved in the correct functioning of enzymes. Required for pollen production. **Symptoms of deficiency** Varies with species. Poor development of leaves. Examples are **'little leaf'** in citrus fruits and **'rosette leaf'** in apples.	Helps in the uptake of nitrogen and in root nodule activity. Rarely deficient. **Symptoms of deficiency** Chlorosis in older leaves. Suppression of leaf growth. Example is **'whiptail'** in brassicas.

Availability of nutrients

Having the minerals in the soil is not the same as them being available to the plant for three reasons:

1. The acidity or alkalinity of the soil can affect the availability. See also **Topic B-8 'Soil chemistry'**.

Nutrients restricted in acid soils	Nutrients restricted in alkaline soils
Calcium Phosphorus Molybdenum	Iron Manganese Boron

A pH of 6-7 is the best to ensure a balanced supply.

2. The presence of some nutrients can interfere with the availability of others, eg.

➜ **A high potassium level can restrict the availability of calcium and magnesium**

➜ **A high calcium level can restrict the availability of iron**

➜ **A high molybdenum level can restrict the availability of copper**

3. Some nutrients, which are taken up by the plant as positive ions, may be attracted so strongly to soil particles that they cannot be absorbed by the plant roots.

Adaptations

Plants cover almost the whole of the earth's land surface. Only in the very extremes of climatic conditions such as the deserts and the polar regions have plants been unable to flourish.

To survive under a huge range of climatic conditions plants have had to adapt over millions of years to those conditions. For the gardener, a knowledge of the plant's area of origin can give vital information about the cultural conditions he should endeavour to supply in his own garden.

In this topic we will summarise some of the main ways in which plants are adapted to particular conditions or for particular purposes.

Adaptation for heat

The main problem of heat is moisture loss, both from the plant by transpiration, and from the soil by evaporation.

- **Leaves**
  - Thick cuticles
  - Small surface area
  - Covered with wax or hairs
  - Reduced number of stomata
  - Stomata on underside of leaf
  - Water stored in leaf (succulents do this)
  - In extreme cases leaves completely modified and do not perform normal function, eg. spines on cactus are modified leaves
  - Grey leaved plants lose less water which is why many sun loving plants, such as artemesia and lavender, are grey

- **Stems**
  - Water stored in stems, eg. cactus
  - Similar epidermal changes to leaves

- **Roots**
  - Long tap roots to search for moisture in soil

Adaptation for cold

The main problem of cold is the freezing of water within the plant cells. As water expands on freezing this can rupture and kill the cells.

- **Seeds**

  The mechanism of seed production and germination enables some plants to survive. The most obvious example is annuals that produce seed in one year before the plant itself is killed by the winter weather. The seed survives dormant through winter and germinates in the following year.

- **Dormancy**

  Many plants remain dormant over the winter. The growth above ground either dies back as in herbaceous plants or, in the case of deciduous trees and shrubs, leaves are shed.

  The meristems of dormant plants are usually well protected with bud scales (modified leaves).

- **Cold hardening**

  As cold weather approaches some plants accumulate additional sugars in their protoplasm that act as an 'antifreeze' to lower the freezing point.

  In addition water is allowed to 'leak' from the cells into the inter-cellular spaces.

- **Leaves**

  Some of the characteristics which protect the leaves from heat, such as thick cuticles, small surface area, and a covering of hairs, also serve to protect them from cold. Most alpine plants are small leaved.

Adaptation for protection

Plants are at risk from animals, ranging from microorganisms to large grazing animals like cattle.

- **Physical protection**
  - → Thorns which are modified branches, eg. hawthorn
  - → Spines which are modified leaves, eg. cactus, holly
  - → Prickles which are modified epidermal tissue, eg. roses
  - → Hairy leaves, eg. some willow varieties
  - → Prostrate growth, eg. plantains

- **Chemical protection**
  - → Poisonous plants, eg. foxglove, aconite
  - → Irritation - some plants can cause an irritation to the skin, eg, stinging nettles

- **Other protection mechanisms**
  - → Ants - some plants have a symbiotic (mutually beneficial) relationship with ants whereby, in return for providing the ants with some nutrients, they drive off other pests
  - → Colour - it is thought that the red leaves on plants like phormium and the young shoots of pieris may be there to deter or confuse pests.
  - → Camouflage - this mainly applies to seeds which as gardeners will know are often very difficult to see in the ground.

Adaptation for climbing

This type of adaptation has arisen through a plants constant search for light in competition with other plants like trees. Tropical rain forests are home to many climbers.

A variety of mechanisms are used to attach to the surface.

- **Adventitious roots**

  These are roots formed at stem nodes that can penetrate other structures, either living like trees or man-made like walls.

  > eg. *Hedera* (ivy)
  > *Hydrangea petiolaris*

- **Adhesion**

  Adhesive pads attached to short stems.

  > eg. *Parthenocissus quinquefolia* (Virginia creeper)

- **Tendrils**

  Tendrils are modified leaves that twine round their support

  > *eg.* *Vitis* (Vines)
  > *Lathyrus odoratus* (Sweet pea)

- **Twining stems or petioles**

  Stems or petioles naturally coil around other structures.

  > eg. *Lonicera periclymenum* (Honeysuckle)
  > *Wisteria sinensis*
  > *Clematis*

Types of reproduction

1.   **Sexual reproduction**

This is the normal method of reproduction for flowering plants.

It entails male and female sex cells fusing together to produce an embryo, which grows into a seed from which a new plant can grow.

The sex cells are produced by a process called meiosis which is discussed in a later topic. The male sex cell is a sperm held within a pollen grain, and the female sex cell is an egg within the ovary.

2.   **Vegetative reproduction**

This is a form of non-sexual reproduction which entails growing a new plant from part of an existing plant. This can take place naturally or be induced by the gardener or commercial grower.

Many plants are capable of both sexual and vegetative reproduction.

What is the difference between sexual and vgetative reproduction

Sexual reproduction gives the new plant a mixture of the characteristics of its parents so that it can end up unlike either of them.

Vegetative reproduction gives the new plant the same characteristics as its parent plant. It is a copy of that plant called a **clone**.

Advantages of sexual reproduction

1.   **Adaptation**

Over a long period of time plants will adapt to changing conditions. This is because the offspring of plants that are best suited to the conditions will thrive and become more dominant than the offspring that are not so well suited.

This is the basis of Charles Darwin's theory of evolution, known as **natural selection** or, more commonly, **survival of the fittest.**

Without the ability to adapt plants would die out. In fact throughout the history of the earth many have died out, just as many animal species have disappeared.

2.   **Variety**

The mixing of characteristics from two parents gives the chance of new and better varieties.

Plant breeders use sexual reproduction to create 'better' plants, whether it be in terms of size, yield, resistance to disease or any other characteristic deemed desirable.

3.   **Survival**

The production of seed allows the plant to survive harsh conditions that may kill the parent plant.

Seed can remain dormant for many years until conditions are right for germination.

4.   Volume

Many plants produce a large number of seeds, sometimes running into thousands.

This is the plant's way of increasing its chance of survival. Gardeners and commercial growers can use it as a cheap and easy way of increasing their stock of plants.

Advantages of vegetative reproduction

1.   New plants are clones

New plants are identical to the old. To ensure a particularly good variety is perpetuated vegetative reproduction has to be used since sexual reproduction can change the characteristics.

2.   Uniformity

All clones will behave in the same way, such as growing to the same size and flowering at the same time. This can be important in a commercial situation but may be the opposite of what is required in a domestic garden. Do you really want 50 lettuces available at the same time!

3.   Colonisation

Plants can quickly and densely colonise an area of ground. Many grasses reproduce vegetatively which helps to maintain a dense growth.

4.   Sterility

Intensive breeding has, in some cases, made plants sterile so that they can only be reproduced vegetatively.

The different types of reproduction are covered in the following topics.

Sexual reproduction

Stages in the reproductive process

1.   Pollination

2.   Fertilisation

3.   Seed dispersal

4.   Germination

Gametes and zygotes

- **Gamete**

    A gamete is a sex cell. A male gamete is a sperm and a female gamete is an egg. Sexual reproduction takes place when the sperm fuses with the egg.

    The male gamete is held within a pollen grain and the female gamete is held in an ovule within the ovary.

    The sex cells are produced by a special form of cell division called **meiosis** which we will look at in more detail in **Topic A-22 'Heredity and breeding'.**

- **Zygote**

    This is the cell formed by the fusion of the male and female gametes.

    The zygote is the first cell of the new plant and it develops into an embryo plant within a seed.

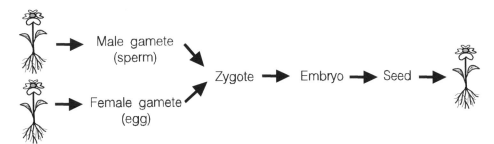

Pollination

Pollen from the male sex organ (stamen) has to be brought into contact with the female sex organ (carpel). Generally only pollen from the same species of plant can pollinate another plant.

Pollination can be:

- **Cross pollination**

    The pollen is from a different plant.

- **Self pollination**

    The pollen is from the same plant. This can happen when a plant is an hermaphrodite or monoecious, (See **Topic A-9 'Flowers'**).

    Although self pollination can produce plants that are unlike the parent, the scope for change is not so great as no new genes can be introduced. Cross pollination is therefore considered preferable, and even on hermaphrodite or monoecious plants, devices may exist to avoid self pollination, eg.

→ Pollen grains from the same plant are rejected

→ Pollen is produced when the stigma is not ready to receive it

→ The anthers and stigmas may be positioned so that self pollination is difficult

The grains of pollen, of which there may be many thousand, are held in pollen sacs in the anther of the stamen. Each grain of pollen initially consists of one cell. The pollen is released at the appropriate time by the pollen sac splitting open.

The pollen grains have a distinctive shape by which they can be recognised when landing on a stigma. They are very resistant to decay and can remain viable for long periods of time.

The pollen may be transferred by insects, by wind or, in a few cases, by water.

Insect pollination

Plants that are insect pollinated tend to have large showy flowers to attract the insect, often complemented by scent or the secretion of nectar. When plants give off a scent in the evening it is likely to be because the pollinating insect is nocturnal. The flowers often have markings on them to lead the insect precisely to where the nectar is located.

The pollen is transferred by the body of the insect coming into contact with the anther and stigma, and the pollen brushing off. The anther and stigma are positioned to maximise the chances of them being touched. The stigma may be sticky to help the pollen adhere to it.

The most common pollinating insect in the UK is the bee, although there are others such as butterflies and moths. In some cases a plant can only be pollinated by one particular type of insect, so that if the insect dies out, the plant may also die out. Cases have occurred where this has happened which indicates the delicate balance of nature.

With the trend to larger and larger fields the pollination of some crops has become difficult, and farmers are having to reinstate hedges or areas of wild growth as a habitat for the insects. In some cases bee hives are imported to ensure crops are adequately pollinated.

Wind pollination

Compared with insect pollinated plants wind pollinated ones tend to have insignificant flowers, but ones that have the anthers and stigma exposed. They also produce very large amounts of pollen to increase the chances of it hitting an appropriate stigma.

The pollen grains tend to be very small so that they can be carried large distances.

Catkins are examples of wind pollinated male flowers and can contain over 2 million grains of pollen.

Summary of differences between insect and wind pollinated plants

Insect pollinated
Large showy flowers often with scent or nectar
Anthers and stigma in position to be touched
Pollen may be sticky or spiky
Stigma may be sticky

Wind pollinated
Insignificant flowers with no scent or nectar
Anthers and stigma exposed
Very large quantities of pollen
Pollen very small, smooth and light

Fertilisation

Fertilisation takes place when the male gamete reaches and fuses with the female gamete forming a zygote.

When the pollen grain lands on the stigma it creates a pollen tube through the style attached to the stigma. This extends down to an ovule in the ovary, containing an ovum.

The male gamete moves down the pollen tube and fertilises the ovum to create a zygote.

In some plants a further fertilisation takes place to create the endosperm.

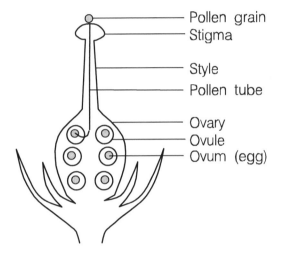

This activity can be happening for many pollen grains and many eggs at the same time within the same plant.

The zygotes grow and form the embryo of the new plant within the seed.

The ovary which contains the seeds enlarges and forms the fruit. The function of the fruit is to protect the seeds and to aid in their dispersal. As we have already seen the fruits can take many forms and are not necessarily edible.

Seed dispersal

Plants use a number of ways to ensure that their seeds have as good a chance as possible to survive, which means distributing them as widely as possible. Some of the agents of dispersal are:

Wind	Some seeds are extremely small and easily carried on the wind, eg. orchids. Some have devices to assist the wind, eg. the feathery growth of the dandelions or the wings of sycamore.
Animals	Some seeds are sticky or have burrs on them causing them to stick to the coats of animals.
	Some seeds are eaten by birds and subsequently

	excreted.
Touch	Some plants eject their seed with some force in reaction to being touched, eg. Hairy bittercress (*Cardamine hirsuta*) - a particularly difficult weed to eradicate because of this habit.
Water	A few seeds are dispersed by water.

Germination

Germination is the growth of a plant from its seed to its appearance above ground.

Requirements for germination

Water	Seeds hold very little water - about 5% compared to 80-90% in a mature plant. It is one of the reasons that seeds can stay dormant for a long time.
Temperature	The requirements of individual seeds will vary within an overall range of 5-35⁰ C. In our climate 10-20⁰ C is typical.
	Heat will speed up the process which is why we use greenhouses and propagators to assist germination.
Oxygen	A supply of oxygen is necessary for respiration.
Food	A supply of food is necessary to fuel the process until the plant is able to photosynthesise. The food is stored in the seed in the cotyledons or the endosperm.
	If seeds are planted too deep they can die by exhausting their food supply before reaching the point at which they can photosynthesise.
Light	Some seeds require light to germinate.
Time	Some seeds have chemical inhibitors which need to diminish before germination is possible.

Special requirements

In some cases special conditions are required before germination will occur. A common one is that a seed must undergo a period of low temperature. This is a safety measure to stop seeds germinating when conditions are unsuitable. For example, seeds produced in summer will often not germinate until the following spring.

This cold period can be simulated by artificially exposing the seed to cold by placing it in a refrigerator. This process is called **stratification**.

Sequence of events

1. Water enters the seed through the testa or the micropyle. This causes the inside of the seed to swell and split the testa. This process can be speeded up by soaking the seeds in water prior to sowing them. Soaking may also help to remove any chemical inhibitors.

   Sometimes the testa is so tough that it requires either some natural breaking down by microorganisms or the abrasive effect of soil particles, or some artificial help like nicking or filing it. This process is called **scarification**.

2.   The radicle is the first part of the plant to emerge and, irrespective of the position of the seed, will grow downwards to form the root and start to take up water and minerals.

3.   The hypocotyl is the next part to emerge. This often emerges in an inverted U shape, dragging the plumule behind it to protect the growing tip. The hypocotyl and plumule will automatically grow upwards towards the light.

      The direction in which a part of the plant grows, according to some external stimulus is called a **tropism**. Growing upwards towards the light is called **phototropism**; growing downwards under the effect of gravity is called **geotropism**.

4.   The growth of the plant is fuelled by food stored in the cotyledons or the endosperm. Sometimes the cotyledons emerge above the soil (**epigeal** germination) but they soon wither and die. In other cases the cotyledons stay in the soil (**hypogeal** germination).

5.   As soon as the first leaves form, the plant is able to photosynthesise and support itself.

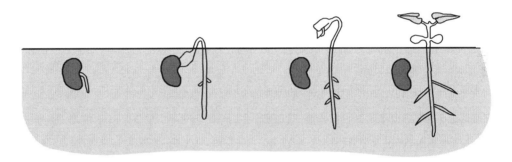

| Radicle emerges and develops into root | Hypocotyl emerges from the soil protecting the plumule from damage | Cotyledons emerge from soil and first true leaves begin to emerge | First true leaves open and start to photosynthesise. Cotyledons will wither and die |

Vegetative reproduction

Vegetative reproduction entails growing a new plant from some part of the old plant. This is possible since each plant cell contains in its nucleus the complete genetic information about the plant.

Horticulturists make use of this capability to reproduce plants in a number of ways that we will cover in a later topic. In this topic we will just cover ways in which plants reproduce naturally by vegetative means.

Methods of vegetative reproduction

*   Bulbs
*   Corms
*   Stolons
*   Rhizomes
*   Root tubers
*   Stem tubers

In addition to reproducing vegetatively some of the forms also serve as a means of ensuring the survival of the plant over winter. This is called **perennation** and it applies to bulbs, corms, some rhizomes, root tubers and stem tubers. In all these cases food is stored in the plant to fuel the initial growth in the following year.

Bulbs

Bulbs consist of a compact stem with fleshy leaves attached to it in which the food is stored.

Shoots and flowers develop from the main bud, and may develop from an axillary bud between the leaves. If two buds develop in this way then each will form a bulb for the following year.

Examples of bulbs are narcissi, tulip and onion.

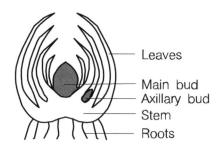

Leaves

Main bud
Axillary bud
Stem
Roots

Corms

A corm is somewhat similar to a bulb but is made up primarily of a short swollen stem in which the food is stored.

Shoots and flowers develop from the main bud, and may develop from an axillary bud between the leaves. If two buds develop in this way then each will form a corm for the following year. The new corm develops on

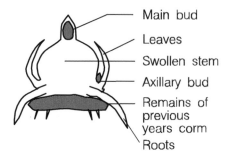

Main bud

Leaves

Swollen stem

Axillary bud

Remains of previous years corm

Roots

top of the old one which eventually withers away.

Examples of corms are crocus and gladioli.

Stolons

A stolon is a stem that grows horizontally close to the ground and puts down roots from its nodes.

The new plant is fed through the stolon until it becomes self sufficient when the stolon will die.

Stolons are also called **runners** although strictly speaking a runner only puts down roots at its tip.

Examples of plants reproduced by stolons are buttercups and strawberries.

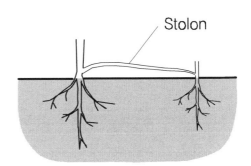

Rhizomes

Rhizomes are similar to stolons but the stems grow under the surface of the soil and put up shoots and develop roots at their nodes.

Some rhizomes are used to store food.

Examples of plants reproduced by rhizomes not acting as a food store are couch grass and stinging nettles.

Examples of plants reproduced by rhizomes and acting as a food store are irises and ginger.

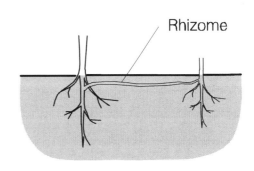

Stem tubers

Stem tubers are organs formed at the end of rhizomes which store food over winter and develop into independent plants in the following year.

Examples of stem tubers are potatoes and artichokes.

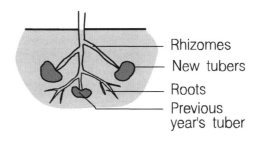

Root tubers

Root tubers are organs formed at the end of roots which store food over winter. Root tubers are usually organs of perennation only and do not develop into independent plants.

Examples of root tubers are dahlias.

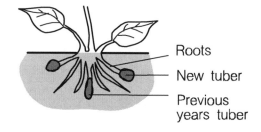

Roots

New tuber

Previous years tuber

Heredity and breeding

Heredity is the inheritance of characteristics by a new plant from its parents.

Breeding is the reproduction of plants to introduce or perpetuate desirable features such as size, colour, scent, disease resistance etc.

We are only concerned here with sexual reproduction as vegetative reproduction retains the characteristics of the parent plant.

Chromosomes and genes

Chromosomes and genes are the vehicles of heredity.

- **Chromosome**

    A chromosome is a thread like structure contained in the nucleus of all cells. It contains the DNA which you may have heard of, and which is used for 'genetic finger-printing'.

    The number of chromosomes is the same in all plants of the same species but can vary between species.

    Most cells have two sets of chromosomes with one set having come from each parent. A cell with two sets of chromosomes is called a **diploid.**

    A cell with one set of chromosomes is called a **haploid**. It is also possible for some plants to have three sets **(a triploid)** or even more.

    The gametes produced for sexual reproduction only contain one set of chromosomes and are therefore haploid cells. The reason for this is that when the male and female gametes fuse, the one set in each gamete join to form two sets again. In this way the same number of chromosomes is preserved from generation to generation.

- **Gene**

    Genes determine the characteristics of a plant, such as size, colour, scent etc.

    The genes are held within the DNA of each chromosome, and there may be several thousand of them. Since there are two sets of chromosomes it follows that there are two sets of genes.

    The genes in one set of chromosomes are paired with the genes in the other set, so that there are two genes for each characteristic.

    When a gamete is produced either gene of the pair may be included in the chromosome passed to the gamete.

Mitosis and Meiosis

- **Mitosis**

    This is the normal method of cell division that plants use to grow. As we have already seen this type of cell division takes place in apical and lateral meristems, (See **Topic A-5 'Plant Cells'**).

● **Meiosis**

This is the cell division that takes place in order to produce gametes.

It is more complex than mitosis and involves many stages. It is outside the scope of this book to cover these in any detail, but the important thing to remember is that it results in cells that contain **one** set of chromosomes, which may contain a mixture of the genes from the chromosomes of the parent cell.

Summary of differences between mitosis and meiosis

Mitosis	**Meiosis**
Normal method of plant growth	Only used for producing gametes
Takes place in all meristems	Takes place only in gamete parent cells
Results in 2 new diploid cells	Results in 4 new haploid cells (4 male cells become pollen; 1 female becomes egg - other 3 discarded)
Chromosomes remain the same	Chromosomes are halved
New cells are genetically the same as old cell	New cells are genetically different from the parent cell and from each other

Determination of characteristics

There is a pair of genes for each characteristic but they do not necessarily say the same thing. One gene of the pair for flower colour may indicate red while the other of the pair may indicate white.

What colour do we end up with in this case ? The possibilities would seem to be red, white or something in between.

In order to determine the answer to this we have to introduce another factor into the equation. This is the fact that one gene of the pair may be dominant so that it always determines the characteristic.

In the case of the flower colour, if the red gene was dominant then all flowers would be red, whereas if the white gene was dominant all flowers would be white.

If there is no dominant gene the flower will be some intermediate colour such as pink.

A **dominant** gene is one that takes precedence over others.

A **recessive** gene is one which is subordinate to a dominant gene.

Distribution of genes

When meiosis takes place, either of each pair of genes may be passed to the gamete. As a large number of gametes are produced, on balance 50% will have one of the pair and 50% the other.

When the male and female gametes fuse there is the possibility of four different combinations for each gene pair in the new plant.

In the following example **AB** is a gene pair in one parent, and **CD** is a pair in the other parent.

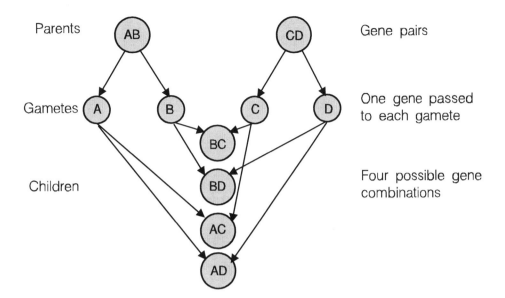

Let us consider an example using the flower colours red and white with the following assumptions:

1. Red is the dominant gene for colour. We will represent this gene with a capital 'R' and the white gene by a small 'r'.

2. Both parents have 1 red gene and 1 white gene (indicated by Rr)

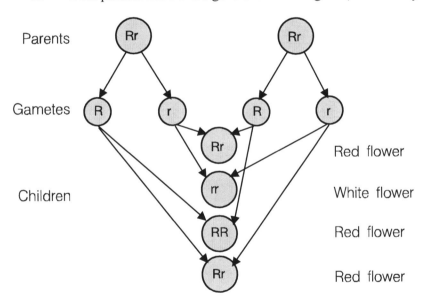

This 3:1 pattern will always exist if both parents have the dominant gene.

If only one parent had the dominant red gene the result would be two red flowers and two white flowers. See if you can work out why.

F₁ hybrids

From a commercial point of view it is desirable that all the characteristics of new plants should be predictable and the same.

This can be achieved if both of the genes within a pair produce the same characteristic.

If we change the assumptions of the previous example so that one parent has the genes RR and the other rr then every combination will give Rr and all the new plants will have red flowers.

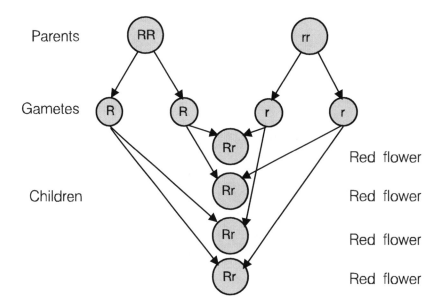

Parents with the same characteristic for each gene of a pair are called **pure bred**. To achieve this the plants are interbred over several generations until all the children produced have the same characteristic. In effect what it means is that each gene in a pair indicates the same characteristic.

The first generation of plants from pure bred parents are called F_1 **hybrids**. These plants are often more robust and vigorous than their parents. This is called '**hybrid vigour**' and is another reason why F_1 hybrids are desirable.

Because of the care needed in pollination F_1 hybrids are more expensive.

Note that plants produced using the F_1 plants as parents will not be all the same.

Breeding programs

You could say that nature has always had a breeding program through the survival of the fittest. It is this that has enabled plants to adapt to changing conditions.

From the earliest days of farming man has also aided this process by choosing the best plants to use from year to year.

Breeding is now extensively carried out to try and produce 'better' plants. Very often what is required is to combine the best of two or more plants. For example, one plant may have a good yield but poor disease resistance, whereas another may be the opposite. The breeder will therefore produce hybrids of these two to try to get a plant with a good yield and disease resistance. Of course some of the hybrids will have a poor yield and no disease resistance!

A problem with conventional breeding programs is that, as indicated above, the results can be hit or miss and take many generations and therefore time to produce a satisfactory result. Also breeders can only work with the genes that already exist within the plants being bred.

Genetic engineering

This is the direct manipulation of genes in the laboratory to bring about a desired result. This is still comparatively new, although activity in agricultural crops has been going on for some years. Some changes that have been implemented or are being tested are:

Production of vitamin A in rice plants
Insertion of an insecticide into maize to reduce insect damage
Production of herbicide resistant maize and oilseed rape
Resistance to blackspot in roses (hooray)

Developments in this area are undoubtedly going to continue. It is not however just a technical problem. There are political and ethical implications. No one can be unaware of the arguments that have surrounded the introduction of GM (genetically modified) crops.

Arguments for GM crops	Arguments against GM crops
Higher yields	'Meddling with nature' - general fear of unforeseen effects
Greater nutritional value	Uncontrolled transfer of genes to non-GM plants creating unforeseen problems, eg. herbicide resistant weeds
Better insect and desease resistance	
Eliminate inherent weaknesses	Inability to guarantee organic crops due to cross fertilisation
Better solution for some problems eg disease resistance than chemical alternatives	Unknown long term effect on consumers
Necessary to meet growing world population	Developing countries may not be able to afford the technology

Mutations

A mutation occurs where something goes wrong in the reproductive process producing an unexpected result. An example could be the occurrence of a variegated shoot on an all green plant.

By propagating from the mutated part of the plant the change can be perpetuated.

In horticulture a plant produced as a result of a mutation is called a **sport**.

Mutations can happen naturally but it is also possible to try to induce them.

Polyploids

We have discussed cells with one set of chromosomes (haploid) and two sets of chromosomes (diploid).

In fact it is possible to have more sets. A cell with more than two sets is called a **polyploid. A triploid** is a polyploid with three sets and a **tetraploid** is a polyploid with four sets.

Very often polyploids are more vigorous and produce bigger yields or larger flowers, and breeders may try to produce them artificially.

The drawback with polyploids is that they can be difficult to fertilise and may need to be propagated vegetatively.

Self test questions

These questions are to enable you to assess how well you have understood and remembered the information in the previous section. No answers are given as these should be apparent from reviewing the relevant topics.

The questions are **not** intended to cover everything you should know.

1   What is the binomial system of plant classification.

2   Identify the errors in the following plant names:
>   Papaver orientalis Mrs Perry
>   Erica carnea 'vivellii'
>   Fagus Sylvatica purpurea

3   What is the difference between apical and lateral meristems.

4   Distinguish between primary and secondary growth.

5   Identify five ways in which dicotyledons differ from monocotyledons. Illustrate your answer where appropriate.

6   Draw a cross section through a dicotyledon root. Label and briefly describe the parts.

7   Briefly describe:
>   Xylem
>   Phloem
>   Vascular cambium
>   Epidermis

8   Distinguish between:
>   Petiolate and sessile leaf
>   Simple and compound leaf
>   Stomata and lenticels

9   Draw a cross section through a dicotyledon leaf. Label and briefly describe the parts.

10   Name the male and female reproductive organs, and the parts that they are comprised of.

11   Describe the process of osmosis.

12   List the basic requirements a plant needs to grow and specify their source.

13   Define transpiration and list four factors that can effect the rate.

14   Describe the process of photosynthesis, (chemical equation not required).

15   Define 'short day', 'long day' and 'day neutral' plants, and give two examples of each.

16   List three hormones that affect plant growth, and briefly describe what affect they have.

17   List the major nutrients required by a plant. Define the use, and symptoms of deficiency, of nitrogen, phosphorus and potassium.

18   Specify the main difference between plants produced by sexual and vegetative reproduction, and the advantages of each.

19 In connection with pollination distinguish between:
    Cross pollination and self pollination
    Insect pollination and wind pollination

20 List the factors required for seed germination.

21 Describe the processes of meiosis and mitosis and the importance of each.

22 Define an F_1 hybrid and specify what special steps are necessary to produce them.

23 With the aid of diagrams distinguish between:
    Bulb and corm
    Stolon and rhizome
    Give two examples of each

Soil

This section deals with the function and properties of soil, and the activities to manage it successfully.

Introduction

In their natural environment plants grow in soil. Well, I know that some grow in water and some grow on other plants, but these are such a small proportion that for our purposes at this stage we can ignore them.

In special situations, such as in intensive cultivation under glass, plants are grown in artificial mediums such as specially formulated composts. However it would be quite impossible to do this for all crops, particularly agricultural ones.

Soil is therefore absolutely vital for supporting life and any loss of soil on a large scale can have catastrophic results. In recent times we can cite two examples where this has happened:

1. In the USA in the 1930's large scale cultivation in the prairie states left the soil unprotected for periods of time and it literally blew away causing storms of dust.

2. The destruction of the rain forests which is currently taking place not only destroys the trees, but because of the loss of the tree canopy it has devastating effects on the ground vegetation. All this leaves the soil vulnerable to erosion and the heavy rains are washing it away.

Soil functions

1. **Provide physical support for the plant.**

2. **Hold the water, air and nutrients that are essential to plant growth.**

3. **Provide a home for all the organisms that play an essential part in making the soil suitable for supporting plant life.**

The formation of soil

Soils have been formed over millions of years. They start with the weathering of rocks which produce mineral particles. Primitive life forms like mosses and lichen establish in the particles and contribute to further weathering of the rocks, and on their death combine with the minerals. Over long periods of time the combination of minerals and organic remains grows deeper and supports more advanced life forms. This cycle continues until the soil supports the forms of life we are familiar with.

The weathering of rocks is key to the formation of soil and this can happen in a number of ways:

- **Physical weathering**

  Heat, cold, wind, rain and ice can all cause the creation of rock particles.

- **Chemical weathering**

  Water in the soil can dissolve some of the minerals in the rocks. This is accentuated by the fact that the soil water tends to be slightly acid.

- **Biological weathering**

  Roots of plants can penetrate tiny fissures and crevices, and as they grow can dislodge mineral particles.

When the plants die they leave channels that were occupied by their roots, which allows water to penetrate giving more physical weathering.

Soil does not necessarily stay in the place where it is originally formed. It is affected by major changes in the earth's crust caused by volcanoes, earthquakes and glaciers. Over long periods of time the earth's crust has been subject to many changes. Things that we regard as permanent, such as mountains and lakes are in fact transient in terms of the evolution of the world.

On a shorter time scale the distribution of soil is affected by the eroding effects of wind and rain. An obvious example is the movement of soil from hilltops into valleys.

The rock from which soils are formed is called the **parent rock** and soils which stay over their parent rock are called **sedentary**. Soils that have been moved away from their parent rock are called **transported**. Those transported by water are called **alluvial**, those transported by gravity (from hilltop to valley) are called **colluvial** and those that are transported by wind are called **loess**.

Types of soil

There are many different types of parent rock and many major and minor changes that can distribute and change the soil. It will therefore be no surprise to know that worldwide there are very many different soil types. In fact as you may have experienced there can be different soil types within a few hundred yards or even within the same garden.

It is also possible to get different soils from the same parent rock. The final soil is dependent on:

Parent rock	The same parent rock can produce different soils depending on the other factors.
Climate	Climate has a major impact on the weathering process.
Topography	The geographic features of the location can impact the formation, eg. altitude.
Organisms	The size and nature of the organisms the soil can support affects its development.
Time	Over long periods of time the soil may be formed, distributed and reformed many times.

Soil classification

There are a number of soil classification schemes which attempt to impart information about the soil, but these are outside the scope of this book.

Soil components

Soil is a complex substance made up in varying degrees from the following components. Some of the components, like the minerals are relatively permanent, but others are subject to constant change which can alter the characteristics of the soil.

- **Minerals**

  Minerals are the particles originating from the parent rocks.

- **Water**

  Water is essential to plant life. The amount held in the soil will vary for different soils and at different times within the same soil.

- **Air**

  Air is essential for the roots of plants to ensure healthy growth. The amount held in the soil will vary for different soils and at different times within the same soil.

  The air and water compete for the same space within the soil so that if the air content is high the water content will be correspondingly low, and vice versa.

- **Organic matter**

  Organic matter is the remains of plant and animal life.

- **Living organisms**

  The soil is host to millions of living organisms, varying from microorganisms like bacteria to comparatively large organisms like earthworms.

A typical soil

It is difficult to define a typical soil but to give some idea of the relative proportions of the components, the following is an example of a cultivated soil in the UK.

	%
Minerals	**50-60**
Water	**5-40**
Air	**5-40**
Organic matter	**1-5**

The above is a **mineral soil** as the major component is minerals, but there are some soils where the major component is organic matter. This occurs in peat soils where, because of the waterlogged conditions, the organic matter does not break down very much. Such soils are called **organic soils**.

Soil profile and soil horizon

In order to determine the characteristics of a soil it is necessary to examine it. The terms **soil profile** and **soil horizon** are used in this context.

- **Profile**

    This is a vertical section through the soil which can show how it is made up.

    Digging a pit is the usual way of looking at the profile although an auger can be used to extract a core of soil.

    A soil may be many centimetres deep, but for normal horticultural purposes 100-150 centimetres will be sufficient depth to examine.

- **Horizon**

    An horizon is a horizontal layer of similar material within the profile.

    There may be few or many horizons making up the full depth of soil. A typical set of horizons would be the topsoil, subsoil and parent rock.

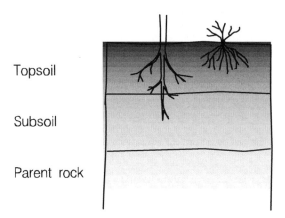

Topsoil

The topsoil is, as its name implies, the uppermost horizon and may exhibit some or all of the following characteristics:

- Consist of small lumps like crumbs
- Be the most fertile part of the soil
- Contain most of the soil organisms
- Contain most of the organic matter
- Be dark in colour due to the presence of organic matter and humus
- Contain most of the plant roots
- Vary widely in depth. A satisfactory depth would be 30-60 cm

Subsoil

The subsoil is the horizon below the topsoil and may exhibit some or all of the following characteristics:

- Consist of large lumps
- Contain some soil organisms
- Contain little or no organic matter
- Be lighter in colour than the topsoil. This is the easiest way to identify where the topsoil ends and the subsoil begins
- Contains some roots, usually of larger plants such as trees or shrubs
- Vary widely in depth

Soil minerals

Function of minerals

In most soils the mineral content comprises the majority of the soil. In the UK a typical soil would contain 50-60% of mineral particles.

The impact of the mineral content is immense. In addition to providing the stability for the plant by firmly anchoring the roots it:

1.   **Largely determines what plants can be grown**

2.   **Provides nutrients for the plant**

3.   **Affects workability of the soil**

The mineral content of soils originates in the weathering of rock and may be further modified by physical, chemical and biological action.

The result is mineral particles that vary both in composition and in size.

In size the minerals vary from stones to minute particles of clay.

Soil texture

The texture of a soil is its composition in terms of particle size.

There are a number of different systems of classifying particle size. All of them divide the particles into gravel, sand, silt and clay, but in some cases the division between them is different, and some have further sub-divisions.

The one used by the Soil Survey of England and Wales is as follows:

Gravel	**> 2.0**
Coarse sand	**0.6 - 2.0**
Medium sand	**0.2 - 0.6**
Fine sand	**0.06 - 0.2**
Silt	**0.002- 0.06**
Clay	**<0.002**

Sizes are the diameter in millimetres

From these figures it may not be too obvious just how different the particle sizes are. If we take the largest size for a sand particle of 2 mm and the largest clay particle size of 0.002 mm then one sand particle is the equivalent of 1000 million clay particles.

The other significant thing about particle size is that as something is divided into smaller and smaller parts then the total surface area increases. If you envisage cutting a cube into two parts then you can see that this has created two new surfaces so the total

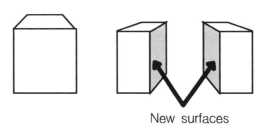

New surfaces

surface area for the same volume has increased. In our comparison of sand and clay particles, the surface area for the clay particles is 1000 times that of the sand particle.

It may seem that undue emphasis is being put on this size difference but it is in fact the most important thing in determining how easy or difficult the soil will be to cultivate.

Soil pores

The particles in the soil have pores between them that link up to form a network of channels through which water and air can circulate, and into which the plant roots can penetrate. The size of the pores reflects the size of the particles so that sand will have large pores and clay will have small ones.

Pore size and continuity has a big effect on the water retention and drainage capabilities of a soil.

Pores that are greater than about 0.1 mm will allow water to drain through them, and will then hold air. Pores that are less than 0.03 mm will be too small for plant roots to extract the water. It is the intermediate pores that are the most useful in retaining water that can be used by the plant.

It follows that a mixture of pore sizes is best for the plant so that the roots have access to both air and water.

Characteristics of sand, silt and clay

Sand	Feels gritty when wet
	Good drainage
	Little water retention capability
	Little nutrient retention capability
	Quick to heat up
	No electrical charge
Silt	Feels silky and soapy when wet
	Fair drainage
	No electrical charge
Clay	Feels sticky when wet
	Poor drainage
	Good water retention
	Good nutrient retention
	Slow to heat up
	Negative electrical charge

Texture classes

Most soils have a mixture of particle sizes, and the mixtures are divided into texture classes so that any soil can be placed in a texture class. The following diagram relates particle size composition to texture classes.

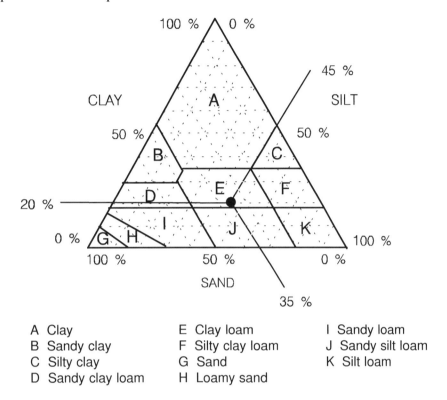

A Clay	E Clay loam	I Sandy loam
B Sandy clay	F Silty clay loam	J Sandy silt loam
C Silty clay	G Sand	K Silt loam
D Sandy clay loam	H Loamy sand	

This is not the easiest diagram to interpret, but the example shows a soil with 45% silt, 35% sand and 20% clay. The point at which the lines through these points converge is in area E which identifies it as a clay loam.

A **loam** is a soil that has a mixture of of sand, silt and clay, and generally speaking is the most desirable soil type since it incorporates some of the advantages of each type.

A simplified version of the above diagram is probably of more practical use.

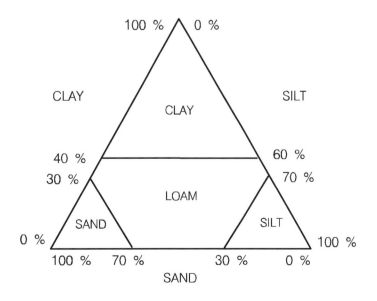

Soil

Determining texture class by feel

Although it is possible to analyse soil in the laboratory, it is also possible to assess the type of soil by feeling it, and trying to form it into threads by rolling it between your palms, and then trying to form the thread into a ring.

In order to do this take a ball of soil that will fit into your hand, and ensure that it is moist.

The following chart shows the characteristics at the extremes of sand, silt and clay.

	Gritty	Soapy	Sticky	Forms threads	Forms rings
Sand	YES	NO	NO	NO	NO
Silt	NO	YES	NO	YES	NO
Clay	NO	NO	YES	YES	YES

Remember that most soils are a mixture of sand, silt and clay, and therefore the assessment of the soil texture will not be as clear-cut as in the above table.

A loam for example is likely to show some degree of all the above characteristics.

Soil water

Function

The water in the soil, together with the minerals dissolved in it, is taken up through the roots of the plant. Within the plant this is what is meant by the sap. The water serves three main purposes:

1. **It provides transport, through the xylem and phloem, for minerals and food in the plant.**

2. **It provides structural stability to non-woody parts of the plant by filling the vacuoles in the plant cells.**

3. **It directly participates in some of the chemical reactions in the plant such as photosynthesis.**

The amount of water in the soil has an impact on what plants can be grown. In areas of little or no rainfall it is very difficult for any plants to survive and those that do are specially adapted to the conditions such as cactus. In extreme cases the landscape becomes a desert.

Rain or irrigation disposition

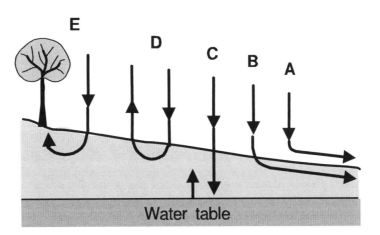

A. Some water may run off the ground before it has any chance to soak in. This will happen particularly with heavy rainfall after a dry spell and can be the cause of floods.

B. Some water may soak into the ground and run off into underground streams before it reaches the water table.

C. Some water may soak through the ground eventually reaching the water table. This is more likely to happen in sandy soils than in clay ones.

    As the ground above the water table dries out some water will be drawn up by capillary action.

D. Some water may soak into the ground but be lost again by evaporation.

E. Some water may soak into the ground and be taken up by the roots of plants. Of the water that is taken up by plants approximately 95% is lost by transpiration.

Water available to the plant

Water that passes through the rooting zone of the plant may be available to it but not necessarily so.

We can identify three types of water:

1.   **Gravitational water**

    This is water that drains through the larger pores in the soil to the underlying water table. Bearing in mind what we have already discussed about pore sizes in different types of soil, sandy soils will lose gravitational water much quicker than clay soils.

    This water is of little use to the plant as it drains from the soil too quickly.

2.   **Capillary water**

    This is water that is held in intermediate pores by what is called capillary action. This is a property of water that enables it to adhere to, and move through, small diameter tubes. The network of pores constitute the tubes and the smaller they are, the further the water can move.

    This water is available to the plant and provides the majority of its needs.

3.   **Hygroscopic water**

    The adhesive property of water causes it to be attracted to particles in the soil and to resist attempts to move it.

    You can see this effect when you wash your hands. When you remove them from the water some of the water falls from them but they will stay wet. Even if you shake them a film of water will remain and if you took no action to dry them the film of water would stay until it evaporated. A characteristic of this adhesion is that as the film of water gets thinner it hangs on even harder.

    The result of this is that some hygroscopic water may be available to the plant but some of it may be held too strongly for the plant to extract it.

Available water and soil types

From a consideration of the above factors we can make some general statements about the behaviour of sand and clay soils

Sandy soil	Loses gravitational water quickly.
	Has few small pores to hold capillary water.
	Holds less hygroscopic water than a clay soil since the total surface area per volume of soil is less.
Clay soil	Loses gravitational water slowly because of very small pore sizes.
	Holds significant amounts of capillary water.
	Holds significant amounts of hygroscopic water.
	Most water is lost by evaporation and transpiration.

- **Sandy soils have a low water holding capacity**
- **Clay soils have a high water holding capacity**

Water and workability

It is the combination of small particle size and high water holding capacity that makes clay soils difficult to work.

When wet, the soil sticks together to make large lumps which are difficult to break down and make into a suitable tilth for planting or cultivating.

When dry, the soil forms hard lumps that are equally difficult to break down. The soil often cracks as the moisture disappears.

For these reasons clay soils are not always workable, and it may be that they can only be cultivated for a part of the year.

In contrast, sandy soils do not differ that much between their wet state and their dry state and they can cultivated for most of the year.

Clay soils are often called **heavy** and sandy soils **light** reflecting the degree of effort to cultivate them.

Other soils will vary between the extremes of sand and clay depending on the exact texture.

Water definitions

There are a number of specific definitions relating to the water content of soils which must be known.

- **Saturation**

  Saturation occurs when all pores are filled with water. This is the condition that exists below the level of the water table. Most plants will not grow in saturated soil.

- **Field capacity (FC)**

  The water that remains in the soil after gravitational water has drained off.

  It consists of capillary water and hygroscopic water, and represents the optimum growing situation.

  Field capacity is higher on clay soils than on sandy soils.

- **Permanent wilting point (PWP)**

  The point at which plants wilt because there is no more available water in the soil.

  Note that there may still be water in the soil but it is not available to the plant as it is in pores too small for the plant roots to penetrate, or is held too strongly to the soil particles.

  Permanent wilting point is likely to be reached more quickly on sandy soils.

- **Available water content (AWC)**

  This is the difference between water held at field capacity and the water held at permanent wilting point.

- **Soil moisture deficit (SMD)**

  This represents the water that needs to be added to restore the soil to field capacity.

The following chart shows the relationship between field capacity and permanent wilting point for different soil types.

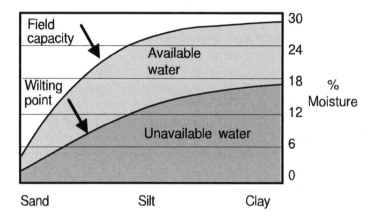

Soil air

Function of air

Air is required to provide the oxygen for:

1. Respiration of the roots

2. Respiration of living organisms

In the absence of oxygen plants will not grow successfully and organic matter will not break down. The soil may have a smell of bad eggs.

Availability of the air

The air in the soil occupies the pore space between particles, and in this respect it competes with water. The pore space may be up to 40% of the total volume of the soil and at any particular time may have more air or more water.

A well structured soil will have a good balance between the two, with water draining out of the large pores by gravity and leaving them occupied by air, but being held in the smaller pores and around the soil particles.

The air in the soil is similar to the atmosphere but has more carbon dioxide which is released during respiration.

The air is refreshed by air in the atmosphere and it is therefore important that the porosity of the soil extends to the surface. If this is not the case the levels of carbon dioxide could reach toxic levels.

Care must therefore be taken to avoid the surface of the soil becoming compacted and therefore impermeable. This can occur by walking or using machinery on the soil, or it can be caused by heavy rain, particularly on fine soils like seed beds.

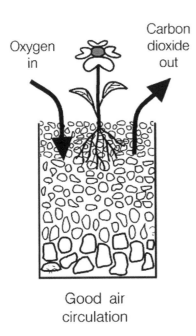

Good air
circulation

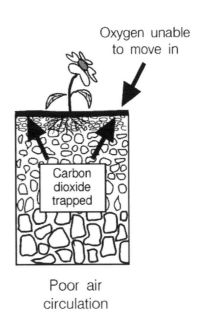

Poor air
circulation

Soil organic matter

What is organic matter

Organic matter consists of the dead and partly decomposed remains of animal and plant life. When the remains are fully decomposed they leave a substance called **humus** which is very important to soil quality.

In a natural situation organic matter is continuously produced as part of the cycle of life and death. In a commercial horticultural, or garden situation, the natural cycle is often interrupted and, unless steps are taken to add organic matter, the quality of the soil will drop.

Humus

Humus is the substance which remains after organic matter has been decomposed.

It consists of very fine particles which are dark in colour and resistant to further decomposition. It has a number of properties that make it very important to soil quality:

- It can hold up to 80-90% of its own weight in water. A small increase in humus can give a large increase in water holding capacity.
- It can attract and hold a large number of plant nutrients, preventing them from being leached from the soil and making them available to the plants.

How does organic matter improve the soil

1. Improves the structure and stability of the soil.
2. Improves the water holding capacity which is particularly useful on sandy soils.
3. Prevents the loss of some nutrients by their adhesion to the humus.
4. Improves the drainage of clay soils.
5. Helps the soil to heat up quicker since soil containing organic matter is darker.
6. Provides a reservoir of nutrients for the plants, particularly nitrogen, potassium and sulphur.
7. Encourages the growth of microorganisms.

How is organic matter broken down

This is a multi-stage operation in which various life forms are involved.

- Larger organisms/animals like worms and moles eat the the organic matter and excrete the remains.
- Fungi grow and feed on the dead material and are important in breaking down woody growth.
- Microorganisms (bacteria) take part in the final decomposition and eventually convert it to the simple chemicals that can be reused by the plant.

Sources of organic matter

Source	Advantages	Disadvantages
Garden compost	- Easy and cheap to produce - 'Green' method of waste disposal	- May contain weeds, pests and diseases
Stable manure	- Good all round soil conditioner - Encourages earthworms	- May contain pests and diseases - May be difficult to obtain - Messy to handle - Must not be applied fresh
Leaf mould	- Excellent soil conditioner	- Some leaves can take a long time to break down
Spent mushroom	- Good soil conditioner	- May be difficult to obtain - Strongly alkaline
Green manures	- Provides organic matter and nutrients	- See Topic B-12 'Feeding'

In addition to the above, there are many processed forms of organic matter available, which are cleaner to handle but tend to be expensive.

Nutrient cycles

All nutrients required by plants are subject to cycles. What this means is that they may exist in different forms, or different environments, at different times, and be reused over and over again as the cycle repeats itself. The cycle for nitrogen is described below.

Within our gardens we try to keep the nutrient supply and demand in balance by adding fertilisers in some form to replace the nutrients lost by the removal of plant growth. Feeding our lawns is a good example: if the clippings are removed the nutrients contained in them are lost, and it will be necessary to feed the lawn to prevent it deteriorating.

Keeping nutrient cycles in balance on a larger scale is a major challenge in agriculture, particularly in developing countries. For example, in Africa, the nutrients exported as part of plants or timber is greater than the nutrients imported as fertilisers, resulting in a net loss of nutrients for the continent as a whole.

The nitrogen cycle

Nitrogen is the one of the important nutrients provided by the organic matter.

Nitrogen is easily leached from the soil so it is one of the nutrients that requires periodic replacement by organic matter or fertilisers.

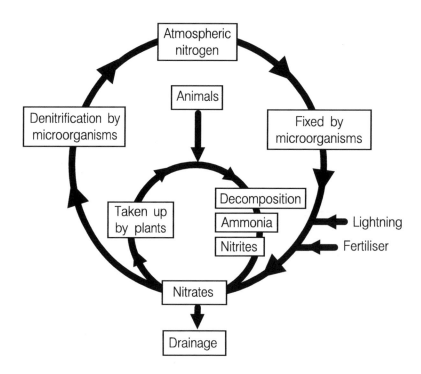

Notes to diagram.

1. Plants absorb the nitrogen in a particular form called nitrates. The decomposition process produces ammonia and nitrites as stages in the production of the nitrates.

2. Some bacteria are able to fix nitrogen in the soil or, in some cases, in nodules attached to the plant roots. Other bacteria are able to transform the nitrates back into atmospheric nitrogen.

3. Lightning can cause a small amount of nitrogen to be washed into the soil by rain.

4. Nitrogen can be added as a fertiliser and be lost by drainage. It is not one of the nutrients that adheres to soil or humus particles and is therefore liable to be washed out.

The carbon/nitrogen balance

The microorganisms in the soil need both carbon and nitrogen in order to grow and as a source of energy. They require about 8 parts of carbon to 1 part of nitrogen.

If there is an imbalance of these nutrients in the soil it can lead to the plants not receiving all they require.

This can happen if organic matter with a high carbon/nitrogen ratio is added to the soil. For example, straw has a ratio of about 60:1. Therefore to fully utilise all the carbon, the microorganisms need 7.5 times more nitrogen (60 divided by 8) than is contained in the straw and they will take it from the soil if possible.

It is partly for this reason that organic matter should be composted or rotted down before being used in the soil. If this is not done extra nitrogen should be added as a fertiliser.

Soil organisms

The soil is host to countless millions of living organisms, ranging from comparatively large ones like earthworms to microscopic ones such as bacteria.

All organisms contribute to the organic matter in the soil when they die.

Function of soil organisms

1. **Structural improvement**

    The larger organisms can help to aerate the soil.

2. **Decomposition**

    The organisms form an essential function in the following ways:

    *   Minerals are broken down to create nutrients.
    *   Organic matter is broken down to provide nutrients and to create humus.
    *   Chemicals used as pesticides and herbicides can be broken down into less harmful substances.

    Many different organisms take part in this activity starting with the larger ones and ending with the smallest. The break down is a cyclic process in which waves of organisms of gradually decreasing size decompose the minerals and organic matter.

3. **Nitrogen fixation**

    Some microorganisms are able to capture and store nitrogen so that it is available to the plant.

4. **Pests**

    Some organisms are pests to certain plants, either directly by eating them (eg. slugs, millipedes, nematodes), or by causing diseases (eg. potato blight)

    Growing the same crop on the same piece of land can lead to a build up of pests which is why crop rotation is practised.

    It should be borne in mind that use of pesticides can affect the beneficial action of the soil organisms.

Types of organism

There are many different types and here we will deal with the major ones.

Small animals

Under this heading we can include animals such as mice, moles, ants, springtails and mites, which all play some part in the decomposition process.

Earthworms

These are one of the most beneficial organisms.

*   They create channels in the soil that have a significant effect on the

aeration and drainage of the soil.

- They drag organic matter (eg. leaves) from the surface of the soil and mix it into the topsoil where it can be further broken down by other organisms.

- They eat and excrete the soil and organic matter and break it down into finer particles.

Earthworms do not like acid conditions and will be much reduced in number in an acid soil.

Fungi

Fungi live on decomposing organic matter and play an important part in breaking down woody matter.

Some fungi grow in close association with plant roots and assist in the transfer of nutrients from the soil to the plant.

They thrive in acid conditions where other organisms do not flourish.

Microorganisms

The main microorganisms are bacteria. They play a major part in the breakdown of minerals and organic matter, reducing them to the simple chemicals that the plants can then reuse.

Although microscopic, it is estimated that the top 15 cm of soil can contain one tonne of microorganisms per hectare.

There are both beneficial and harmful microorganisms. The beneficial ones need oxygen to be present in the soil (aerobic conditions), whereas the harmful ones will flourish if no oxygen is available (anaerobic conditions).

- **Azotobactor** are particularly useful as they are able to extract nitrogen from the air and fix it in the soil.

- **Rhizobium** are also able to fix nitrogen which they do by invading the roots of legumes and fixing the nitrogen in nodules on the roots. This relationship between the legumes and the bacteria where both derive benefit is called a **symbiotic** relationship.

Soil chemistry

Acid and alkaline soils

Soils are classified as acid, neutral or alkaline. This factor has an important impact on what plants can be grown.

What makes a soil acid or alkaline

Technically it is the number of hydrogen ions in the soil that determines its classification. The greater the number of hydrogen ions the more acid is the soil.

The pH scale

This measures the acidity or alkalinity on a scale of 1 to 14. A measurement of 7 is considered neutral: below 7 is acid and above 7 is alkaline.

The neutral value of 7 is based on a measurement of hydrogen ions in pure water.

The scale is a logarithmic one. All this means is that each value on the scale represents a tenfold increase or decrease of the hydrogen ions. To make matters a little more complicated the lower the value on the scale the more hydrogen ions there are. Therefore a value of 6 represents ten times as many hydrogen ions as a value of 7.

Determining the pH value

There are a number of soil testing kits that will provide a pH value.

The simplest entails taking a small sample of the soil, placing it in a tube with some water and a tablet that comes with the kit. The water will turn a different colour depending on the pH and this colour can be matched against a chart to give the pH value.

There are also meters available that come with a probe that is pushed in the soil but these have not proved to be very accurate.

Soils in the UK range from a pH of around 4 up to 8.

Impact of pH on nutrient availability

In **Topic A-17 'Plant nutrients'** we identified the nutrients that could be affected by the pH of the soil. For completeness this is repeated here.

Nutrients restricted in acid soils	Nutrients restricted in alkaline soils
Calcium Phosphorus Molybdenum	Iron Manganese Boron

Impact of pH on plants

As a generalisation most plants will grow best in a pH of 6-7, although many will tolerate a wider band.

Plants that prefer an acid soil are called **calcifuges** and plants that prefer an alkaline soil are called **calcicoles.** Some examples of each are:

Calcifuges	Calcicoles
Rhododendron	Clematis
Camellia	Dianthus (pinks)
Erica	Scabious
Magnolia	Viburnum

It is often possible to gauge the pH of the soil by looking at the plants that are thriving in it.

Changing the pH value

In order to grow particular plants or crops it is possible to modify the pH value to some extent.

Over a period of time soils tend to become more acid because:

1.   **Alkaline nutrients like calcium are leached from the soil.**

2.   **Alkaline nutrients like calcium are used by the plant and removed with it.**

3.   **Microorganism activity releases acids.**

4.   **Rainfall tends to be slightly acid.**

5.   **Some fertilisers are acid.**

Lime is used to raise the pH of a soil. Because of the tendency of soils to become more acid a regular program of liming is often carried out.

Sulphur can be used to reduce the pH of a soil.

Liming

As we have just seen lime can be used to raise the pH of a soil.

It is usually applied to the surface of the soil in the form of calcium carbonate (ground limestone). It does not have an immediate effect and it is therefore better to apply it in the autumn when it can be combined with digging.

Do not apply lime at the same time as manure as the two can react, causing a loss of nitrogen in the form of ammonia. A reasonable program could be to lime and manure in alternate years.

There seem to be a lot of different opinions about the amount to apply. The following guidelines are taken from the RHS website:

	Clay	Loam	Sand
To raise pH by 0.5	**420**	**190**	**140**

Figures are in g/sq m

If the total increase required is greater than 0.5 it is better to do it in stages rather than at one time.

Lime has an important effect on clay soils other than raising the pH. It can cause **flocculation** of the clay particles. What this means is that the individual clay particles will group together to form larger particles. This improves the structure of the soil by making it less dense.

Advantages of liming

1. **Raises the pH**

2. **Provides the nutrient calcium**

3. **Encourages worm and bacteria population**

4. **Discourages some diseases, eg. club root in brassicas**

4. **Makes clay soils more workable by flocculating the clay particles**

5. **Can make other nutrients more available**

Special properties of clay and humus

Both clay particles and humus particles are what are known as **colloids** and as such have certain properties:

1. **They are extremely small** (<0.002 mm).

2. **They have a large surface area relative to their size.**

3. **They have a negative electric charge.**

Because they have a negative charge they will attract and hold positive ions (cations). Amongst the cations held in this way are hydrogen, calcium, magnesium and potassium. The significance of this is that these cations will resist being leached from the soil and therefore remain available to the plant. On the other hand, nitrogen which is held as a negative ion is not attracted to the particles and is therefore easily leached out.

The situation is further complicated by the fact that cations attached to a particle can be exchanged for other cations. Let us take an example of a soil containing many hydrogen ions. As mentioned earlier in this topic a soil with many hydrogen ions tends to be acid. If we add lime which consists mainly of calcium to the soil, the calcium ions will replace some of the hydrogen ions and the soil would become less acid.

The ability to exchange ions is an important factor in soil fertility and is called the **cation exchange capacity (CEC)**.

Soil structure

In previous topics we have looked at the components of the soil and what impact they can have. The end result is a soil with a particular structure.

A well structured soil is the main aim of soil management and is critical to the successful growth of plants.

Definition of structure

The soil structure is the way in which the individual components, such as the minerals, organic matter and humus, are combined into larger groupings known as aggregates or peds.

Things that we would call lumps, clods or crumbs are all forms of aggregates.

When you are digging a soil you will notice that it does not separate into its individual components, but instead hangs together in lumps of various sizes. The extent to which it hangs together will depend largely on the soil texture. Sandy soils have a much greater tendency to to separate into individual components than clay soils. In fact wet clay soils are very difficult, if not impossible, to break down into reasonable sized aggregates.

What binds particles together

- The attraction of clay and humus particles for nutrients such as calcium, magnesium and potassium
- Flocculation caused by the application of lime
- Organic matter and particularly humus
- Plant roots
- Gums secreted by some soil organisms

The ideal structure

The ideal structure is made up of **crumbs** which are small rounded aggregates of 1-5 mm. This is known as a crumb structure.

A soil that will readily break up into crumbs is called **friable**.

A good structure should be capable of withstanding bad weather, particularly heavy rain, and bad treatment, such as cultivation with heavy machinery.

Tilth

This is a term commonly used to refer to the physical state of the soil in relation to plant growth.

Ideally the plant roots require an environment that is warm, moist, friable and porous.

A fine tilth is particularly important for seed sowing so the seed can come into contact with the soil particles.

Fertility

Fertility refers to the state of the soil with respect to the amount and availability of nutrients. It is likely to be better in a well structured soil.

Problems with structure

The problems with sand

● Sand has very little structure.

● Individual grains of sand have no positive or negative charge and are therefore not attracted to other particles and do not hold on to nutrients.

● Organic matter that can help bind soil particles together tends to be leached from the soil.

● Water which can have an adhesive effect drains away quickly.

The problems with clay

● Clay can have a satisfactory structure but it can be difficult to maintain it

● Clay particles are very small and when wet and compressed can become an unworkable mass.

● Water can be slow to drain making the soil sticky and depriving the roots of oxygen.

● To maintain a satisfactory structure heavy machinery must be kept off the soil when it is very wet.

● If clay dries out it tends to crack and form hard clods.

Improving the structure

Sand

1. Add organic matter.
2. Dig or otherwise cultivate if the soil becomes compacted.
3. It is possible to add clay (a process called marling) but is not considered economic on a commercial basis.

Clay

1. Add organic matter.
2. Add lime to cause flocculation.
3. Improve drainage if necessary.
4. Dig or otherwise cultivate.
5. Avoid walking or using machinery on the soil when wet.
6. Keep soil surface covered by plants or a mulch.

Soil texture and soil structure

Explaining the difference between these two terms is a likely examination question so you should be sure you know it.

Soil texture is the composition of the soil in terms of particle size

Soil structure is the way in which the individual components in the soil are combined to form larger aggregates

Soil

Examples of good and bad structure

GOOD
- Crumb structure
- Free draining

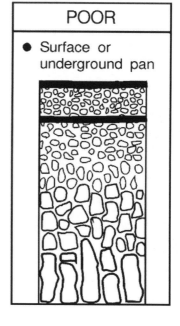

POOR
- Surface or underground pan

POOR
- Shallow tilth
- Block structure

POOR
- Sand - Poor water and nutrient retention

Management (1) What to look for

The first step in determining a program for soil management is to examine and understand what the current situation is. The following are the main points to be considered:

1. **Depth of top soil**

    Topsoil may vary from virtually nothing to a metre or more. It is the most fertile part of the soil and the deeper the better.

    Most roots are in the top 15 cm of the soil but they can extend to several metres.

2. **Texture**

    Most desirable is a medium loam. It is difficult to make significant changes to the soil texture since it is a fundamental characteristic of the soil.

3. **Structure**

    A good structure is the main aim of soil management. Ideal is a crumb structure of 1-5 mm. It is however a delicate thing that can easily be damaged by:

    ● Over-cultivation - there is a school of thought that believes the soil should not be disturbed by cultivation.

    ● Use of heavy machinery.

    ● Heavy rainfall.

    ● Lack of organic matter.

4. **pH value**

    One of the most important factors in determining what plants can be grown.

    A simple test kit will provide a reliable indication.

5. **Fertility**

    The simplest indication of fertility is whether plants grow successfully. Some of the symptoms of nutrient deficiencies were covered in **Topic A-17 'Plant nutrients'.**

    Simple test kits are also available for testing for the main nutrients, but the most reliable method would be to use one of the laboratories that offer a soil analysis service.

6. **Drainage**

    Poor drainage can affect the growth of plants.

    Digging a hole, filling it with water, and seeing how quickly it drains will give an indication of any problems in this area.

7. **Earthworm activity**

    Little activity may indicate infertile or acid soil.

8. **Presence of organic matter**

Organic matter and humus is very important to soil quality. A dark coloured soil indicates the presence of humus.

9. **Root growth**

Healthy roots indicate a good soil.

10. **Areas of compaction**

Compaction can be at the surface or it may occur at a particular horizon within the soil. In either case it impedes the free transport of of air and water and is undesirable.

11. **Colour of soil**

Generally soil colour of red, orange or yellow indicates good conditions whereas blues and blacks indicate problems with drainage or aeration.

Management (2) Drainage

Plants will not grow successfully and seeds will not germinate in a very wet soil.

Symptoms of poor drainage

- Poor plant growth
- Water collecting on the surface (puddling)
- Soil constantly wet
- Types of plant, eg. mosses, sedges
- Blue/black colouring in subsoil

Effect of improving drainage

- Provides better structure
- Soil warms up more quickly
- Improves aeration
- Encourages favourable bacteria
- Increases rate of organic matter breakdown
- Makes nutrients more available

Causes of poor drainage

Cause	Action
Clay & silt soils	Add organic matter Add lime
Poor structure	Add organic matter Cultivate
Surface compaction	Cultivate
Sub-surface compaction	Cultivate Drainage system
High water table	Drainage system

Adding organic matter

Organic matter can improve the structure of heavy soils allowing more freedom for the circulation of air and water.

It can also improve the water holding capacity of sandy soils by acting like a sponge and absorbing the water.

See also **Topic B-6 'Soil organic matter'**

Adding lime

Adding lime to a clay soil will cause the flocculation of the clay particles giving a better structure to the soil and allowing better circulation of air and water.

See also **Topic B-8 'Soil chemistry'**

Cultivation

Surface compaction can be alleviated by spiking (the usual method for lawns), digging, rotavating, harrowing or otherwise breaking up the surface layer.

Care should be taken not to worsen the problem by using machinery which itself causes the compaction.

In heavy soils the cultivation may be only possible at certain times of the year and under certain conditions.

Compaction below the surface may be harder to deal with, and the cause needs to be established. It may be due to cultivation, to a naturally impervious horizon in the soil, or to the leaching of nutrients which then form an impervious layer.

It may be that the same methods used for surface compaction will solve the problem but if not then a sub-soiler may be used to break up the compaction or some form of drainage system may be required above the level of compaction.

Sub-soiler

As its name implies this is a tool that can be used to create drainage channels and fissures within a subsoil.

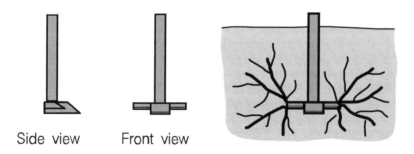

Side view   Front view

It entails pulling a winged tine through the subsoil so that it fractures it and leaves behind a network of fissures. This is best done in the autumn when the soil is dry as it will then fracture more easily.

Drainage systems

A drainage system is unlikely to be necessary in the normal domestic garden, but it may be necessary in a commercial horticultural or agricultural situation. There are also some special situations like sports pitches where drainage is essential.

We will look at four types of drainage system:

Soakaways

> **Ditches**
> **Tile drains**
> **Mole drains**

Soakaways

A soakaway is simply a pit filled with rubble into which surplus water can drain.

It is simple to construct and could be used in a domestic garden.

The pit should be at least a cubic metre and should be sited at the lowest point in the garden or where it is wettest. It could also be used in a level garden with rubble or gravel filled channels draining into it.

Ditches

Open ditches can be used to lower the water table over an area.

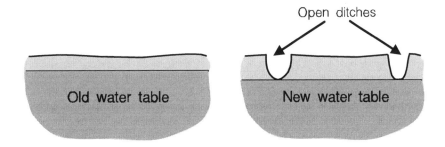

For large areas, ditches will be used in conjunction with drains (see below), with the drain outlet going into the ditch.

Tile drains

Tile drains are a more sophisticated form of drainage often used on agricultural land. They are based on a pattern of adjoining pipes into which the water permeates and down which it is conducted to an outlet. Traditionally the pipes were made of earthenware but they are now usually of some form of plastic.

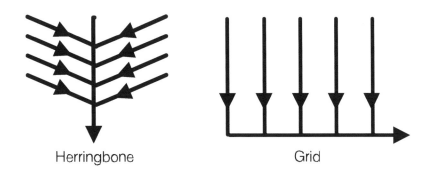

The pipes come in diameters of 10-15 cm. Their depth and proximity will depend on the soil conditions. The depth must be below the level of normal cultivation and will usually be 30-60 cm. The distance apart could be from 2-10 m. The heavier the soil, the higher and closer will be the drains.

Constructing a tile drain

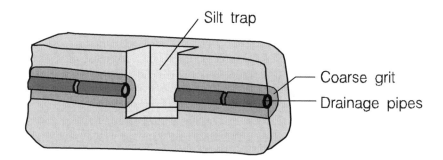

- Plan the layout taking into account any natural slope of the land as the drainage works by gravity.
- Dig trenches 50-150 cm deep and with a slope of at least 1:100.
- Place 10 cm of coarse gravel in the bottom of the trench and place the pipes on top.
- Leave 3 mm gap between the pipes to allow the water to enter.
- Cover the pipes to a depth 10 cm with coarse gravel.
- Fill in the trench
- If draining a large area, silt traps can be built into the system to prevent the pipes silting up.

There are now drain laying machines that draw a continuous length of plastic pipe through the soil without a trench having to be dug.

Mole drains

A mole drain is so called because it creates a tunnel in the soil similar to a mole run. The tunnel is created by pulling a bullet shaped object (the mole) through the soil at an appropriate depth (usually 75-100 cm depending on the type of soil). To work successfully requires a natural slope on the ground.

The soil needs to be quite heavy otherwise the tunnel will collapse. Even so the life of a mole drain is only 3-5 years.

The advantage of a mole drain is that it is cheap and easy to do and does not disturb the topsoil very much. The disadvantage is that it is not long lasting.

Management (3) Feeding

The need to feed

We have already made the point that what is taken out of the soil must be put back, and therefore part of the soil management is the use of compost, manure or fertilisers to maintain soil fertility.

The main inputs and outputs of nutrients are as follows:

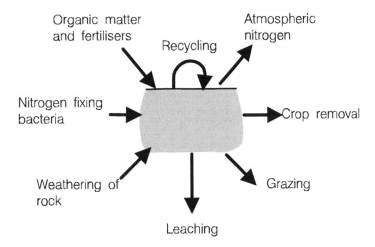

Organic matter is usually some form of **compost or manure**. Its primary benefit is to improve the quality and structure of the soil, although it also provides some nutrients.

Fertilisers are concentrated forms of nutrients that have been produced by some form of processing.

Note that these are not really alternatives. Organic matter is a soil conditioner that improves the quality of the soil, and soils that are only fertilised will deteriorate over a period of time.

Of all the nutrients, nitrogen is the one most likely to be needed, as plants require a significant amount, and it is easily leached from the soil. The others likely to be needed are phosphorus and potassium, and many proprietary fertilisers contain all three.

Remember that an excess of fertilisers can harm the plants and the environment.

Organic matter

The benefits and sources of organic matter have been covered in **Topic B-6 'Soil organic matter'**, and this topic should be reread.

The nutrient content of compost and manure is low compared to fertilisers but because they are applied in bulk the effect can be similar.

Applying compost and manure

They can be incorporated into the soil when it is cultivated or they can be applied as a surface mulch, in which case they will be gradually incorporated by the action of earthworms. A guideline on the amount to apply is a barrowload per 4 sq m.

The best time to apply it to clay soils is in the autumn so that it can be broken down over the winter, but in sandy soils leave it to late winter or early spring to avoid it being leached out.

Green manures

These are different to other manures as they are plants that are grown on the soil to be manured, and are incorporated directly into that soil a few weeks before a crop is to be planted.

The plants are grown and used in one season and should be incorporated into the soil before they start to turn woody. Ones that can be sown in late summer and dug in the following spring are probably the most useful as they cover the bare soil in winter and protect the soil structure.

Advantages of green manures

1.   Provides organic matter and nutrients to the soil particularly when nitrogen fixing plants are used.

2.   Protects the surface of the soil and prevents erosion or the leaching of nutrients

3.   Prevents the proliferation of weeds.

Plants suitable for green manures

1.   **Clover** *(Trifolium pratense)*

Clover has the advantage of fixing nitrogen and can be left to overwinter. Sow from April to July.

2.   **Mustard** *(Sinapis alba)*

A fast growing summer crop. Sow between March and August and dig in before flowering.

3.   **Winter rye** *(Secale cereale)*

Sow from August to October to overwinter.

Fertilisers

Fertilisers can be **organic** or **inorganic**. Organic fertilisers, such as bonemeal, are derived from material which was once living. Inorganic fertilisers, such as sulphate of ammonia, are manufactured or derived from minerals. Inorganic fertilisers are probably more precise in their nutrient content, and may be quicker acting. Also, since the BSE crisis, there is some concern whether all organic fertilisers are safe to handle.

Fertilisers can also be **straight**, which means they contain one nutrient, usually nitrogen, phosphorus or potassium, or **compound**, which means they contain more than one. 'Growmore' and 'Fish, blood and bone' are examples of compound fertilisers.

Fertilisers can come as a powder to be used directly on the soil, or in a solution, or as granules.

Controlled release fertilisers

Most fertilisers are quick acting but a comparatively recent development is the use of controlled release fertilisers which allow the nutrients to be released over a period of time. This is particularly useful for nutrients which are easily leached from the soil such as nitrogen.

Originally aimed at crop production such fertilisers are now available for a wide variety of environments including pot plants and lawns.

These fertilisers are almost certainly the thing of the future. There is already one on the market for use with trees and shrubs which is effective over 2-3 years.

Application of fertilisers

Method of application

- **Base dressing**

  The fertiliser is incorporated in the soil. In a domestic garden situation it would be dug in, but in a commercial situation there are more sophisticated methods of applying it by distributing it with the seed directly into the drill, or applying it as a band alongside the drill.

- **Top dressing**

  The fertiliser is applied to the surface of the soil and relies on rain or irrigation to carry it down to the roots. For this reason the fertiliser must be soluble.

- **Liquid**

  The fertiliser is dissolved in water and applied to the soil surface. This will give a faster reaction than a top dressing.

- **Foliar feed**

  The fertiliser is dissolved in water and applied as a spray to the leaves of the plant. Foliar feeds are quick acting and are particularly useful where the soil conditions prevent the uptake of some nutrients.

Timing of application

Nitrogen fertilisers are best applied 2-4 weeks before planting because of the possibility of them being leached out. Also, since they encourage vegetative growth, they are not applied in late summer or autumn when new growth may be damaged by winter weather.

The application of other fertilisers is not so critical, but as a general rule apply in spring before new growth begins. Some crops may also require additional applications during the growing season.

Whatever the method or time of application it is important to follow the manufacturer's instructions.

Comparison of bulky organic matter with fertilisers

Organic matter	Fertiliser
Bulky	Concentrated
Low nutrient content	High nutrient content
Imprecise control (exact nutrient content not known)	Precise control
Slow effect	Quick effect (unless controlled release)
Effective over longer period	Effect may be quickly lost
Improves soil structure	No impact on soil structure
Will contain pests and diseases	No pests or diseases

Nutrient content of organic matter and fertilisers

N	- Nitrogen	Ca	- Calcium
P	- Phosphorus	Mg	- Magnesium
K	- Potassium	S	- Sulphur

	N %	P %	K %	Ca %	Mg %	S %
BULKY ORGANIC MATTER						
Garden compost	0.6	0.3	0.8			
Animal manure	0.6	0.1	0.5			
Mushroom compost	0.7	0.3	0.3			
ORGANIC FERTILISERS						
Bonemeal	3	20				
Fish, blood and bone	3	8				
INORGANIC FERTILISERS						
Growmore	7	7	7			
Sulphate of ammonia	21					24
Superphosphate		18		20		
Potassium sulphate			50			17
Calcium nitrate	15			20		
Magnesium sulphate					10	

In addition to Growmore, there are many other proprietary compound fertilisers designed for general use or for a specific purpose.

Management (4) Cultivation

By cultivation we mean the preparation of the soil for sowing or planting by digging, rotavating or ploughing.

In a domestic garden digging will usually be the method used. In large gardens or small commercial operations a rotavator may be used while in larger commercial operations a tractor with ploughing and harrowing attachments may be used.

In the rest of this section we will assume a domestic garden situation although the principles apply to any situation.

There is a school of thought that cultivation damages the soil rather than improves it. Without wishing to come down on one side or the other, the advantages and disadvantages are summarised below.

Pre-cultivation tasks

- **Clearing unwanted vegetation**

  This may be just getting rid of weeds or undergrowth, but it could include more major tasks like removing trees.

- **Removing debris or other features not required**

  Anybody who has moved into a brand new house will be familiar with the task of getting rid of old bricks, concrete, or other builder's debris.

  Other things that may need to be removed are paths, walls, fencing or buildings.

- **Ensuring there is adequate topsoil**

  This may be a problem with new houses. The builder may have removed or destroyed the topsoil. If this is the case topsoil will need to be purchased.

- **Contouring the site**

  This could be either flattening an undulating site, or putting undulations in a flat site. In either case the important thing is to protect the topsoil by removing it, making the changes with the subsoil, and then replacing the topsoil.

Advantages and disadvantages of cultivation

Advantages	Disadvantages
1. Prepares an uncultivated area for planting.	1. Disturbs the natural structure built up by organisms such as earthworms.
2. Improves the structure of the soil by improving access for air and water.	2. Can damage the soil structure if done when soil conditions are not suitable, or by using heavy machinery.
3. Exposes clods to the weathering effects of winter. This is still one of the best methods of getting a good structure in a heavy soil.	3. Dormant seeds may be brought to the surface where they will germinate.

Advantages (contd)	**Disadvantages** (contd)
4. Breaks up pans that may prevent free circulation of water and air.	4. Leaving a bare surface may cause erosion or the leaching of nutrients.
5. Allows organic matter or fertilisers to be incorporated into the soil.	5. Moisture may be lost from the soil.
6. Buries crop remains and weeds.	6. Hard work !
7. Exposes pests to weather and predators.	

When to dig

1. When soil conditions are suitable - not wet or frozen or parched. Ideally the soil should be friable.

2. Dig clay soils in autumn to get the benefit of overwintering to break it down

3. Light soils can be dug in autumn or spring

Single digging

Single digging entails digging to a depth of 1 spit (30 cm or spade depth).

In shallow soils do not bring any of the subsoil up into the topsoil even if it means digging to a depth of less than 1 spit. It is however worth breaking up the subsoil and incorporating some organic matter in it.

The normal method of single digging is to dig out the first trench and move the soil close to where the last trench will be. The second trench is then dug and placed into the first trench. This process is repeated until the final trench is filled with the soil from the first trench.

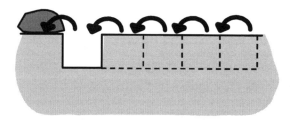

Single digging

Double digging

As its name implies double digging entails digging to a depth of 2 spits. Double dig if:

● The ground has not been cultivated before

● There are pans within the soil profile

● The soil is very heavy

Even if the topsoil extends to the two spits it is still worth keeping soil from the upper spit on top of the soil from the lower spit since it will be the most fertile.

The simplest way to achieve this is to dig the second spit in situ. Organic matter can be incorporated in the second spit as it is dug.

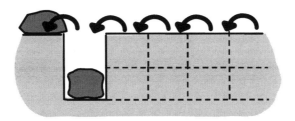

Double digging

No-dig systems

Vegetables can be grown in conditions that require no digging other than the initial cultivation.

● Double dig the soil for the initial cultivation incorporating plenty of organic matter to provide a reservoir of humus and nutrients.

● Use narrow beds separated by permanent paths so that all cultivation and harvesting can be done without treading on the beds.

● If drainage is a problem use the topsoil from the paths to make raised beds.

● If possible run the beds from north to south.

● Make the paths wide enough for a wheelbarrow.

● Keep the ground covered to prevent the structure being damaged by rain and to reduce weeds. This can be done by:

  - **planting close together**
  - **intercropping**
  - **green manures**
  - **mulching**

This no-dig system is also called the **deep bed** system.

Advantages	Disadvantages
1. The natural structure of the soil is preserved.	1. Pests may build up in the soil.
2. Soil organisms are not disturbed.	2. It may be difficult to maintain levels of organic matter in the soil since it can only be applied as a surface mulch
3. Drainage can be improved if raised beds are used.	3. Fertility and structure may be reduced in the long term.
4. Harvesting can be done in any weather.	
5. Weed seeds are not brought to the surface.	
6. Less hard work and time is required.	

Self test questions

These questions are to enable you to assess how well you have understood and remembered the information in the previous section. No answers are given as these should be apparent from reviewing the relevant topics.

The questions are **not** intended to cover everything you should know.

1   List five typical differences between topsoil and subsoil.

2   Describe what is meant by soil texture, and list the main characteristics of sand, silt and clay.

3   By means of a diagram show how water falling on the soil surface may be disposed of.

4   Explain the importance of pore size within the soil, and the effect this has on the water available to the plant.

5   Define the terms;
       Field capacity
       Permanent wilting point
       Available water content
       Soil moisture deficit

6   How can the addition of organic matter improve the soil.

7   Specify three beneficial effects of organisms in the soil.

8   What does the pH scale measure, and what effect can the pH have on plant growth.

9   What effects can the addition of lime to the soil have. In what circumstances would lime be added and what would be the best time of the year to do it.

10   Describe what is meant by soil structure. Explain what problems with structure may occur in sand and clay soils, and what steps can be taken to correct them.

11   List four causes of poor drainage.

12   Briefly describe four ways of improving drainage on wet soil.

13   Describe the advantages and disadvantages of the following forms of organic matter.
       Garden compost
       Stable manure
       Spent mushroom compost
       Leaf mould

14   Compare compost and manure with fertilisers as a source for feeding the soil.

15   List the advantages and disadvantages of cultivating the soil by digging or rotavating.

Plant problems

This section starts by identifying the types of problems and the main methods for controlling them. The later topics identify common weeds and specific pests, diseases and disorders that are common to many plants. Pests and diseases that only affect certain plants are identified in later topics dealing with those plants.

What problems - What solutions ?

We all want to grow healthy plants and we would like to do this without causing any damage to the environment.

Unfortunately there are a whole host of things that do not appreciate our requirements and will do their best to upset them.

One thing that contributes to the problems is that we often grow plants out of their natural environment which may mean that natural predators are absent or that the environment is not suitable.

This section identifies the types of problem that may arise and the ways in which they can be reduced or eliminated.

What problems

1. **Weeds**

    I am quite sure you have all come across the definition of a weed as a plant growing where it is not wanted. Thus daisies in a wild garden may be fine, but growing in a lawn they become a weed.

2. **Pests**

    Pests are animals that have a detrimental effect on a plant. They mainly use the plant as a source of food, either by eating parts of it or sucking out the sap.

    Pests can range in size from a large vertebrate, like a deer or rabbit, to small invertebrates like aphids, mites and nematodes (eelworms).

3. **Diseases**

    Diseases are problems caused by other organisms such as fungi, bacteria or viruses. In severe cases they can cause the death of the plant.

    Diseases are often spread by pests.

4. **Disorders**

    A disorder is a problem caused, not by another organism, but by the environment in which the plant is grown. An example is that there may be insufficient nutrients in the soil to feed the plant.

    These problems are sometimes called **physiological** problems.

5. **Climate changes**

    This is different to the other problems because it is more of a potential problem than a current one. It is included because there is considerable concern in this area and it could become the worst problem of all.

What solutions

1. **Cultural control**

Cultural control embraces all the activities involved in providing a good environment and good growing conditions. Good cultural practices can significantly reduce all types of problems.

Advantages	Limitations
• Traditional method	• Difficult to control all pests
• All plants can benefit	• Difficult to stop some damage
• No damage to the environment	• May be more labour intensive
• No contamination of food crops	• May not be suitable for large scale commercial production
• Sustainable (can be repeated year after year with no deterioration)	

Cultural control is covered in more detail in **Topic C-2**.

2. **Biological control**

Biological control entails using natural methods of control like the introduction of predators for certain pests.

Advantages	Limitations
• Extension of Nature's way of control	• Not available for all pests
• No damage to the environment	• Many biological controls only effective in glasshouses
• No contamination of food crops	• Timing of application is critical
	• Some degree of damage is likely
	• Control may itself become a pest

Biological control is covered in more detail in **Topic C-3.**

3. **Chemical control**

The use of chemicals for control has raised a number of concerns in recent years and there is undoubtedly a move away from them.

Nevertheless they are very effective in a lot of situations and, although the amateur gardener may be able to manage without them, most commercial growers would consider them essential.

Advantages	Limitations
• Most successful single method in many cases	• Some pests are becoming resistant
• Can be applied to a predetermined schedule	• Indiscriminate (beneficial insects may be killed)
• Easiest method of treating large commercial crops	• Public concern about eating chemically treated food
	• Public concern about damage to the environment
	• Cost of applying chemicals can be high

Chemical control is covered in more detail in **Topic C-4.**

4.   Plant breeding

Some plants are naturally more resistant to problems than others. In addition a lot of work is being done by plant breeders to produce more resistant plants.

It has been discovered that most resistance is controlled by genes, and with the advances being made in genetic engineering this is an area that is likely to increase in importance and achievement.

Advantages	**Limitations**
● Permanent benefit	● High cost of research and development
● Automatic benefit for all growers	● Not likely to give complete control
● No additional labour cost	● Concern of public about genetically modified food plants
● No damage to the environment	● Genetic modification may make plant unattractive to humans eg. bitter taste

Integrated pest management

Integrated pest management (IPM) is a comparatively new concept. It means having a planned program of control which may incorporate aspects of all the other control methods.

It has arisen largely because of concern about the widespread and indiscriminate use of chemicals:

1.   **Some pests are becoming resistant to specific chemicals.**

2.   **Chemicals tend to kill beneficial insects (a few are selective).**

3.   **There is increased public concern about eating chemically treated food crops.**

4.   **There is public concern over the damage chemicals can do to the environment, and the risk of getting into the food chain.**

5.   **The cost of applying chemicals can be high and several applications may be needed in one growing season**

There is also concern about the question of **sustainability**. What this means is that whatever methods are used they should be able to be applied year after year, with no adverse affect on the environment, either in terms of damage or the use of non-renewable resources.

In general IPM entails applying the most appropriate control for the type and extent of the problem, and using chemicals as sparingly as possible. For example, small infestations of caterpillars may be controlled by hand-picking them off the plant.

An IPM program needs to be carefully planned and the following list identifies some of the things to be considered.

●   What pests are likely to cause unacceptable damage

●   Choice of resistant varieties

●   Selection of planting date

- Selection and preparation of planting site
- Cultural procedures including aftercare plan
- Biological controls, if any
- Chemical controls, if any
- Pest monitoring procedures
- Damage acceptance level
- Harvest date
- Cost effectiveness of alternative programs

Format of this section

In the next three topics the major aspects of the control methods will be covered.

The remaining topics cover each of the problem areas and specify some of the more common problems that, on the whole, can affect a number of plants. It is not however the intention to produce exhaustive lists of the pests, diseases and disorders that may be encountered, or of the chemicals that can be used against them.

Other problems that only affect a particular type of plant will be included in the topics dealing with those plants.

Cultural control

Cultural control covers all the activities designed to ensure that plants get the best possible growing conditions since the best protection against many problems, particularly physiological ones, is to ensure plants are healthy.

Cultural control is not new. It is only over the last 50 years that the use of chemicals has grown to such an extent that some traditional cultural practices have been abandoned.

Cultural control of weeds

Weeds can seriously affect the growth of other plants through robbing them of moisture and nutrients. Recent trials have shown that keeping an area around a newly planted tree free of weeds was the single biggest benefit to growth, exceeding the effect of adding organic matter or fertilisers.

Whatever method of removing weeds is used, the most important factor is to get them before they seed, since most weeds seed prolifically.

- **Removal by digging or rotavating**

   On uncultivated ground this is probably the only option. If digging, the weeds can be buried which will kill most annual weeds although not their seeds.

   Perennial weeds, particularly deep rooted ones like dandelions, will probably survive. Some also have the ability to regenerate from small pieces left in the soil, such as ground elder.

   In agriculture and large scale horticulture one of the benefits of ploughing is that it buries weeds.

- **Hoeing and hand weeding**

   These are the traditional methods of control and still the most appropriate on cultivated ground and around other plants.

   Hoeing and hand weeding should be done regularly while the weeds are small and certainly before they seed.

- **Mulching**

   See **Topic E-9 'Mulching'**

   This is a good option. Inorganic mulches like polythene and stone chippings are particularly effective at suppressing weeds. Bark is also quite good and looks attractive in the ornamental garden.

- **Ground cover planting**

   See **Topic G-7 'Ground cover'**.

   Ground cover plants can be used in the ornamental garden although it is important to clear the ground of weeds before they are planted.

   In the vegetable garden close spacing of plants and intercropping can reduce weeds.

Plant problems

Cultural control of pests and diseases

This is not always easy, particularly for commercial growers where the public demands unblemished fruit and vegetables. The emphasis should be on preventing problems since this is easier than curing them once they have occurred. It is also important to correctly identify the problem, which is not always easy, as the symptoms from some diseases and disorders can look very similar.

The methods of control available are:

> **Healthy plants in a healthy garden**
> **Encourage natural predators**
> **Physical barriers and traps**
> **Crop rotation**
> **Time of sowing**
> **Companion planting**

● **Healthy plants in a healthy garden**

Just as with humans, healthy plants are best able to resist attacks from pests and diseases.

➔ Ensure there is a fertile and well structured soil.

➔ Only use plants suitable for the conditions.

➔ Buy resistant plants where these are available.

➔ Buy plants certified to be disease free where these are available.

➔ Provide the necessary aftercare.

➔ Take prompt action at the first signs of any problem.

➔ Remove and burn any infected plants.

➔ Remove garden debris and burn or compost it.

➔ Sterilise pots and seed trays before use.

● **Encourage natural predators**

Predators are the main means of natural control and should be encouraged by including suitable features in the garden such as a pond, and including plants that will attract them, such as ones with pollen, nectar, fruit and berries.

If pesticides are used they should be ones that are selective and do not kill the predators.

● **Physical barriers and traps**

There are a number of physical barriers or traps that can be used depending on the pest concerned.

➔ **Fencing** can be used for larger pests, such as cats and dogs.

➔ **Cages** or **netting** can be used for birds and rabbits.

➔ **Collars** around the base of plants can be used for insects that lay their eggs there, such as the cabbage root fly.

➔ **Grease bands** can be used for insects where the larvae hatch in the soil and climb up the plant, such as the winter moth on fruit trees.

➔ **Crop covers** (fleece) can be used to protect against some insects, such as carrot root fly, cabbage root fly and caterpillars.

➜ **Pheromone traps** can be used to lure some pests like the codling moth, and they also will highlight that the pest is present.

➜ **Sticky traps** can be used in the greenhouse to trap insects such as whitefly.

● **Crop rotation**

Crop rotation is a system of growing vegetables where the different families of vegetables are grown on a different piece of ground each year.

For a fuller discussion see **Topic H-1 'General principles'**.

● **Time of sowing**

Some pests can be reduced by choosing the time of sowing.

➜ Sow broad beans in autumn so that they get a head start and are less susceptible to blackfly attack.

➜ Delay the sowing of carrots to June to reduce the chances of attack from carrot root fly.

➜ Sow peas early or late to avoid damage from the pea moth.

● **Companion planting**

There is a school of thought that some pests and diseases can be deterred by companion planting. This entails planting some other plant alongside the crop, which will stop the crop being attacked. Examples are:

French marigolds in a greenhouse to deter whitefly
Garlic under roses to prevent blackspot
Mint around brassicas to deter the cabbage white butterfly

Aftercare

Examination questions often ask for details on the aftercare of particular plants. The following list specifies aftercare tasks, and although not all plants will require all tasks you should memorise the list and be prepared to comment on the tasks applicable to particular plants.

● **Watering**   See Topic E-6

● **Feeding**   See Topic B-12

● **Weed control**   Covered in this topic

● **Pest and disease control** Covered in this topic

● **Pruning**   See Topic E-5

● **Supporting**

Biological control

What is biological control

Biological control is the use of natural enemies to control pests.

Biological control methods have been developed largely because of the concerns about the use of chemical controls.

The use of natural enemies

This method is used by nature to achieve an ecological balance. If it was not we could all find ourselves buried under tonnes of aphids! There are many enemies of aphids, including ladybirds, lacewings and hoverflies. Most pests in fact will have some natural enemy.

As mentioned earlier, one concern with the use of chemicals is that they can kill the natural enemies, although there are some that are selective.

There are a number of reasons why we cannot leave it all to nature:

- Commercial growers cannot afford to have any degree of damage.
- Plants may be grown away from their natural environment and therefore away from their natural enemies.
- Intensive growing may result in a shortage of natural enemies. This is particularly the case where the same crop is grown over a large area. This provides a perfect environment for pests and diseases to spread, while at the same time not providing a good environment for the enemies which may require other plants to breed on and support them.

The enemies fall into three categories:

Predators	**The predator kills the pest**
Parasites	**The parasite lives off the pest and eventually kills it**
Diseases	**The disease attacks the pest but not the plant**

There are a number organisms that can be purchased from specialised firms that are suitable for use by the amateur, and many of these are now available from garden centres.

General considerations

- Many of the biological controls are only really effective in glasshouses where they will not be dispersed and conditions can be controlled. In particular many of the enemies require a temperature of around 20^0 C to thrive.

- Most chemicals used against the pests will also kill the enemies and therefore cannot be used.

- The timing of using the enemies can be quite critical. In general they need to be used when the pest is present in small numbers.

- The enemy may need to be introduced several times within a growing season.

There is always a risk that a biological control may itself turn out to be a pest. A classic example is the introduction of the cane toad into Australia in 1935 to try to control the sugar cane beetle. The cane toad has become a significant pest and is rapidly spreading across Australia.

Examples of biological controls

Pest	Control	Comments
Aphids	Aphidoletes	This is a predatory midge.
		It can lay up to 100 eggs which hatch within 2 days to produce small orange larvae. The larvae can kill many aphids by poisoning them and consuming the body fluids.
		It is supplied in the form of pupae which are sprinkled around the plants.
Caterpillars	Bacillus thuringiensis	This is a bacteria that kills caterpillars without harming other insects.
		It is supplied as dried spores that are mixed with water and applied as a spray.
Slugs	Nematodes	The nematodes are mixed with water and applied around plants to be protected. They enter the body of the slug, killing it within a few days, and reproducing inside it.
		Can be effective outside if soil temperature is above 5^0 C.
		Not effective on snails.
Red spider mite	Phytoseiulus persimilis	This is a predatory mite.
		Each mite can lay 50 eggs which hatch within 7 days. As each mite can eat about 5 spider mites a day it can be an efficient control.
		It is supplied on pieces of leaf or card which should be cut up and distributed among the plants to be protected.
		Control should start after two weeks and be completed in six weeks.
		Crops on which it is effective include tomatoes and cucumbers.
Vine weevil	Nematodes	The nematodes are mixed with water and poured onto pots or around plants. They kill the vine weevil larvae but not the adults.

Whitefly	Encarsia formosa	May be successful outside if the soil temperature is above 10⁰ C. This is a parasitic wasp. It lays its eggs in the scale (larvae) of the whitefly causing it to turn black and eventually produce a new wasp. This cycle takes about 20 days. It is introduced on leaves as blackened whitefly scales and should be distributed evenly through the crop. Its egg laying capacity must exceed that of the whitefly and it requires a temperature of 25⁰ C to achieve this.

Other pests for which there are biological controls are thrips, mealybugs and soft scale.

Pheromone traps and sprays

Pheromones are the sexual attractants produced by some female insects. If a trap is baited with this it will attract and entrap the males. Examples of this are traps for the tortrix moth and codling moth.

The number of insects trapped will give an indication of the size of the problem and whether other control methods like spraying should be used.

Experiments have also been carried out with pheromone sprays to try and disturb the mating pattern of some insects.

Chemical control

Introduction

There is a big difference between the chemicals available to the amateur gardener and those available to the professional. The reason for this is all to do with safety. Those for use by the amateur are less dangerous than those for the professional and do not require the use of protective clothing when using them. They also tend to break down quickly and not leave harmful residues.

This topic only deals with the chemicals available to the amateur. Also in other parts of the book where reference is made to the availability or suitability of chemicals, the comments only apply to those available to the amateur.

When you look at the array of products available in the garden centres you may think there are many chemical controls to choose from. This can be misleading as different manufacturers market the same chemical under different trade names. For example all the following products are based on the chemical 'glyphosate'

Tumbleweed	**The Scotts Company (UK) Ltd**
Super Strength Glyphosate	**Bayer CropScience Ltd**
Weed Buster	**Westland Horticulture Ltd**

In fact the pool of chemicals available to the amateur is contracting. There are a number of reasons for this including safety considerations, economic considerations by the manufacturers and the move to more 'green' methods of control. In addition the crops on which they can be used is becoming more restricted. In fact there are some common problems for which there is no chemical control, eg. potato scab, club root, onion white rot.

The reduction of chemicals may be a good thing if it encourages people to look at 'greener' ways to control problems. The fact remains though that used properly they can be extremely useful, and professional growers are very dependent on them.

There are three groups of chemicals we are concerned with:

1. **Herbicides**   **For controlling weeds**
2. **Insecticides**   **For controlling pests**
3. **Fungicides**   **For controlling diseases**

The term **pesticide** covers all three groups.

There are continuing changes taking place in the pesticides that are available and students should check the current availability. The best way of doing this is through the web site of the Chemicals Regulation Directorate (CRD), which is **'www.pesticides.gov.uk'**,

EU (European Union) Review of Pesticides

In 1991 the members of the EU agreed to standardise pesticide approval and usage across the EU. This review has resulted in an EU directive and any pesticide used in a member country must be on the EU approved list.

As a result of the review a number of pesticides have been withdrawn from use. This is not necessarily because they are dangerous, but can be because they are no longer supported by the manufacturer due to being superseded or not commercially viable. In 2003 eighty-one products available to the amateur were withdrawn due to six chemicals not being approved.

When a pesticide is withdrawn three dates are usually set. The first for stopping selling, the second for stopping using, and the third for stopping holding. This phasing out period can be several years. After the third date has expired it would be illegal to hold the pesticide in your garden shed!

UK Legislation

Chemicals can be hazardous and need to be handled with care. In fact a number of chemicals that have been used in the past are now no longer available. Nicotine and arsenic were used at one time, but probably the best known chemical which has been banned for some time is DDT. This was used extensively as an insecticide during and after the Second World War but it was found to build up within the organisms and got into the food chain with serious results.

The EU Review has resulted in further pesticides being withdrawn and this is likely to continue.

The Plant Protection Product Regulations 2005

These regulations control pesticides for both professional and amateur use. Pesticides are approved by the **Chemicals Regulation Directorate (CRD)**, which is part of the **Department for Environment, Food and Rural Affairs (defra)**. Their registration number appears on the pesticide container and is called the **MAPP** number (Ministerially Approved Pesticide Product).

The regulations apply not only to the manufacturers but also to the users, and it is an offence to use a pesticide in any way other than that specified on the label.

Labelling

The labels are themselves subject to regulations and the following information must be shown and identified as 'Statutory Conditions of Use':

1. Field of use restrictions, eg. 'For use only as a garden insecticide'
2. User restrictions
3. The crop or situation which may be treated
4. Maximum individual dose/application rate
5. Maximum number of treatments or maximum total dose
6. Maximum area or quantity which may be treated
7. Latest time of application, harvest or re-entry interval
8. Operator protection or training requirements if applicable
9. Environmental protection requirements

In addition to the statutory information the label will contain other information including the trade name, the MAPP number, the chemicals (the active ingredient) used and advice on safe use and disposal. Hazard warning symbols common across the EU are also included.

The trade name can be a very significant asset to the marketing company as it is often well known, eg Weedol. Where chemicals are withdrawn a product may be reformulated with different chemicals but retain the same trade name, sometimes with a number or letter following the name, eg Weedol 2.

Safety precautions

1.   Read the label to ensure it is suitable for your requirements, and understand the conditions and precautions for its use.

2.   Store it in a safe place out of the reach of children, and away from food or drink. A storage area should be secure, dry and well ventilated.

3.   Keep it in its original container. In particular never put it in an unmarked container.

4.   Apply the chemical at the rate indicated on the label. Doubling the dosage will not make it twice as effective.

5.   Do not spray when conditions are windy as the spray may seriously damage other plants.

6.   Do not eat, drink or smoke while applying.

7.   Avoid contact with skin or eyes, and wash immediately if contact occurs.

8.   Do not inhale the spray, dust or fumes. The use of a nose and mouth shield is sensible even if not recommended.

9.   Keep children and pets off the area until after treatment.

10. Wash hands after use.

11. Do not store any surplus spray solution or partly used sachets. Dispose of surplus spray on a path, drive or uncultivated ground. Dispose of small quantities of unwanted chemicals, in enclosed containers or firmly wrapped up, in the dustbin.

12. Clean equipment thoroughly after use.

13. Do not pick crops until the harvest interval has expired.

Form of chemicals

Chemicals can be supplied and used in a number of forms:

Concentrated liquid or powders that are diluted with water
Ready to use, non-rechargeable spray guns
Granules
Dusts
Aerosols
Fumigants

Application of chemicals

Liquids are usually applied by a sprayer. These range from a simple hand held atomiser holding up to a litre of spray to a knapsack sprayer holding several litres, and where the pressure is maintained by a hand pump. With the more sophisticated sprayers there are a variety of nozzles to produce the spray in different patterns.

It may be necessary to calibrate the sprayer to ensure the chemical is applied at the correct concentration.

It is possible to apply liquids via a watering can fitted with a fine rose or a sprinkle bar. Where spray drift might be a problem this should be considered.

Granules can be applied by hand although a more even distribution will be achieved using a spreader of some form.

Dust and aerosols are applied direct from their containers.

Fumigants are designed for use in enclosed spaces like a glasshouse. The most common type is the smoke cone that is lit and releases its fumes as smoke.

More detailed information on spraying is covered in **Topic E-7 'Spraying'**.

Herbicides

Herbicides are used for killing weeds. They can be used to:

> **Completely clear uncultivated areas of all vegetation**
> **Keep hard areas like paths, drives and patios free of weeds**
> **Kill weeds within ornamental, vegetable or fruit gardens**
> **Kill weeds selectively in lawns**

Different herbicides act in different ways.

- **Contact**

  These kill or damage any plants that they touch. They are effective against annual weeds but not against perennial ones since they kill the top growth but not the roots.

- **Translocated (or systemic)**

  These are absorbed by the plant and distributed around it in the sap. They thus reach all parts of the plant and are effective against perennial weeds.

- **Residual**

  These are held in the soil and prevent the germination of seeds. They are commonly used on hard areas to keep them free of weeds. If used on soil the soil must not be disturbed after application.

- **Selective**

  These will affect certain plants but not others. Lawn weedkillers are in this category, killing broad leaved weeds but not the grasses.

The following table lists some of the herbicides available.

Diquat	This is a quick acting contact herbicide that can be used for controlling both grasses and broad leaved annual weeds. It will not kill perennial weeds.
	It will kill the green parts of plants but not the woody part and it can therefore be used right up to the stems

	of trees and shrubs.
	It is inactivated on contact with the soil but it is very toxic and should be used with care.
Glyphosate	This is a translocated herbicide that is effective against all plants including perennial weeds. It is the best one to use for clearing uncultivated or overgrown areas.
	It is inactivated on contact with the soil but It may take 2-3 weeks before its effect is apparent.
	A product containing both glyphosate and diquat is available
Diflufenican	This is a residual herbicide that can be applied to areas not intended to bear vegetation such as paths and drives
	It can be effective against germinating weeds for up to 6 months.
	All the trade products available with this chemical are combined with glyphosate to kill existing weeds.
2,4-D Mecoprop-P MCPA	All these three are selective herbicides for use on lawns.
	They are called hormone weedkillers because they upset the hormone system of the weeds causing them to grow erratically and die.
	Most proprietary lawn weedkillers contain more than one chemical to cover a wider range of weeds.
Ferrous sulphate	Commonly known as lawn sand and is used as a moss killer
	Often combined with lawn weedkillers.

Insecticides

Insecticides are used for killing pests.

Although we tend to group all small pests together as insects, biologically there are a number of different types. Aphids, springtails, flies, beetles, thrips, earwigs, moths and butterflies are all insects, but woodlice, millipedes, centipedes, mites, slugs and snails are not. From the point of view of controlling pests this distinction is not too important and we will use the word insect to cover them all.

Like herbicides, insecticides can act in different ways:

● **Contact**

These kill by contact with the pest or by coating the foliage which the pest then eats.

One problem with contact insecticides is that many pests live on the underside of leaves and can be difficult to reach with the spray.

An advantage is that they do not enter the plant and cannot therefore contaminate food crops.

Plant problems

- **Systemic**

  These are similar to translocated herbicides as they are absorbed by the plant and move around in the sap. The pests are then killed when they eat the plant or suck the sap.

  Advantages of systemics are that the whole plant does not have to be covered and the effect lasts for a period of time. This last point may be a disadvantage for food crops and, if used, care must be taken not to harvest the crop until the harvest interval has expired.

- **Soil acting**

  These are applied to the soil and control soil borne pests.

- **Selective**

  These are only effective against certain pests.

- **Organic**

  These are derived from naturally occurring substances like plant and animal oils. They break down quickly into harmless substances and are considered more 'green' than man-made chemicals.

The following table lists some of the insecticides available.

Deltamethrin	Kills and protects for up to 4 weeks against attack of greenfly, blackfly, caterpillars, whitefly, beetles and many other pests.
	Can be used on houseplants, roses and other ornamental plants and on selected fruit and vegetables.
	The harvest interval is between 3 and 7 days.
Pyrethrins	A contact insecticide that is included in a number of proprietary products.
	Pyrethrins are natural insecticides produced by certain species of the chrysanthemum plant.
	It is effective against a range of pests including whitefly, small caterpillars, aphids, thrips and leafhoppers. and may be used on both edible and ornamental plants.
	The harvest interval is 1 day
Thiacloprid	A contact and systemic insecticide that can is effective against a range of insects including aphids, mealy bug and scale insects.
	It can be used on indoor and outdoor ornamental plants, on greenhouse tomatoes, aubergines and peppers, and on selected soft fruit and vegetables.
	It is effective for up to 6 weeks.
	The harvest interval is between 3 and 14 days.
Fatty acids	This is a spray based on plant and animal oils and is therefore considered 'green'. It is effective against

	aphids, red spider mite and a number of other insects.
	An advantage is that there is no harvest interval.
Metaldehyde	This is a slug and snail killer usually applied as small granules.
	It can be harmful to small animals and birds and even humans, so should be used with care. It is treated with an animal repellent and coloured blue to make it unattractive to birds.

Fungicides

Fungicides are used to prevent or cure diseases. The diseases may be caused by fungi, bacteria or viruses. In practice most are caused by bacteria and those caused by viruses cannot usually be cured.

Like the other pesticides, fungicides can act in different ways:

● **Preventive**

The fungicide coats the foliage of the plant and prevents the disease from entering. It is obviously important to spray the foliage thoroughly including the underneath of leaves.

Most fungicides are preventive.

● **Systemic**

Like systemic insecticides these are absorbed by the plant and move around in the sap killing the fungal disease within the plant.

The following table lists some of the fungicides available.

Myclobutanil	A systemic fungicide that is effective against mildew, black spot, rust and scab.
	It can be used on roses, ornamental plants and specified fruit trees and bushes.
	The harvest interval is 14 days.
Trifloxystrobin	Protects lawn against lawn diseases such as fusarium patch and red thread.
Copper oxychloride	A preventive fungicide for a number of diseases, including peach leaf curl, potato blight, tomato blight. and canker.
	It can be used on a wide range of vegetables and fruit.
	Also prevents damping off of seedlings.
	There is no specified harvest interval.

Plant problems

Chemicals and trade names

For interest this is a list of some of the trade products that include the chemicals named in this topic. The list is not meant to be complete and in many cases other chemicals are also included in the trade product.

Herbicides

Diquat	Weedol 2 (The Scotts Company (UK))
	Resolva 24H (Westland Horticulture)
Glyphosate	Tumbleweed (The Scotts Company (UK))
	Super Strength Glyphosate (Bayer CropScience)
	Weed Buster (Westland Horticulture)
Diflufenican	Pathclear Weedkiller (The Scotts Company (UK))
Ferrous sulphate	Sold as 'Lawn sand' by many suppliers

Insecticides

Deltamethrin	Greenfly Killer (Bayar CropScience)
Pyrethrins	Bug Gun (The Scotts Company (UK))
	Bug Spray (Doff Portland)
Thiacloprid	Provado Ultimate Bug Killer (Bayar CropScience)
Fatty acids	Organic Pest Control (Bayar CropScience)
	Rose & Flower Pest Spray (Doff Portland)
Metaldehyde	Slug Clear Advanced Pellets (The Scotts Company (UK)
	Eraza Slug and Snail Killer(Westland Horticulture)

Fungicides

Myclobutanil	Systhane Fungus Fighter (Bayar CropScience)
	Doff Systemic Fungus Control (Doff Portland)
Trifloxystrobin	Lawn Disease Control (Bayar CropScience)
Copper oxychloride	Fruit and Vegetable Disease Control (Bayar CropScience)

Common weeds

There is no botanical classification of 'weeds'. It is a name we have chosen to give to plants that we do not want in our garden. Also a plant that may be a weed to one person may be desirable garden plant to another.

Although we tend to think of weeds as small plants, large plants can also be weeds. In parts of the country Rhododendrons have escaped their garden environment and are spreading in the wild with a detrimental effect on the environment. Invasive non-native plants are subject to a voluntary code of practice organised by Defra.

Gardeners have also been guilty of introducing some plants that have turned out to be weeds. Japanese knotweed, which was introduced as a decorative garden plant, has proved to be a most difficult weed to control.

Why are weeds successful

Have you ever wondered why, in spite of spending hours of effort in removing weeds from your garden, they never seem to get any less and may indeed steadily get worse.

In general terms the answer is that the weeds are extremely well adapted to the conditions in which they grow, often more so than our plants which may have evolved in very different environments.

Attempts have been made to count the number of dormant seeds in the soil and figures of 50000 per square metre have been recorded.

In looking at why they are so difficult to eradicate it is worth distinguishing between annual and perennial weeds.

Annual weeds

These weeds complete their life cycle within one year and therefore only survive and muliply through their seeds.

The reasons they are so successful are:

1. They can grow and seed quickly so constant vigilance is needed to spot them.

2. Some grow under or close to other plants and can be difficult to spot.

3. Large numbers of seeds can be produced, eg. groundsel can produce 1000 seeds per plant; greater plantain can produce 14000 per plant.

4. Some can complete up to three life cycles within one year, eg. groundsel and chickweed. These are often called **ephemeral weeds** due to being so short lived. They can be a particular problem as they can grow and seed within a few weeks, and can in theory produce thousands of new weeds per year.

5. Seed can be carried significant distances:
   - By wind, eg. groundsel
   - By being eaten and excreted by animals, eg. fat hen
   - By clinging to animals or clothing, eg. cleavers

➔ By being ejected by the plant from the seedpod, eg. hairy bittercress

6. Many seeds can lie dormant in the soil for many years until the conditions for germination are present. Those conditions can be caused by cultivation bringing the seeds to the surface.

There is a saying **'One year's seed - seven years' weed'**.

Perennial weeds

1. Many spread both by seed and vegetatively. It is the vegetative growth that tends to be the most difficult to control as it is often underground.

2. Some spread by underground stems, eg. ground elder and couch grass, and some by underground roots, eg. creeping thistle.

3. Some have long and deep roots that are difficult to completely remove, eg. bindweed

4. Many will regenerate from small pieces of the plant left in the soil, eg. dandelion and speedwell.

5. Many are resistant to herbicides, eg. ground elder and horsetail.

Weeds Act 1959

This act specifies a number of weeds that are regarded as dangerous and gives powers to control their distribution and growth.

One of the most common is 'ragwort', *(Senecio jacbaea),* which is dangerous to livestock, particularly horses. However, judging by the amount of ragwort that can be seen growing the control measures may not be working as they should.

Annual weeds

Groundsel *(Ephemeral)*

Botanical name	*Senecio vulgaris*
Habitat	Any soil type, prefers sunny position
Form	Height 30 cm
Seeds	Yes - 3 generations per year
Creeping	No
Control	Hand weed, hoe or use diquat or glyphosate

This is a small upright weed with soft stems and ragged oak shaped leaves. The small flowerheads are yellow and produce white seedheads. It can produce three generations a year and its seeds, which are very light and fluffy, can be carried large distances by the wind.

Hairy bittercress *(Ephemeral)*

Botanical name	*Cardamine hirsuta*
Habitat	Any soil type, sun or part shade
Form	Height 15 cm
Seeds	Yes - 2 to 3 generations per year
Creeping	No
Control	Hand weed, hoe or use diquat or glyphosate

This is small weed with white flowers on the end of 15 cm stalks. The leaves form rosettes that are not unattractive. It is is a difficult weed to eradicate because of its multiple generations and its habit of ejecting its seed up to 90 cm when touched. It flowers as early as March and must be caught before it sets seed.

Chickweed *(Ephemeral)*

Botanical name	*Stellaria media*
Habitat	Any soil type, sun to part shade, common in vegetable and flower beds
Form	Prostrate - spread 30 cm
Seeds	Yes - 3 generations per year
Creeping	No
Control	Hand weed, hoe or use diquat or glyphosate

This is a lax, light green weed that has small white flowers that grow in the leaf axils and at the stem tips. It can germinate during winter and flower in early spring. The seeds can remain dormant for up to 40 years.

Cleavers *(goosegrass)*

Botanical name	*Galium aparine*
Habitat	Moist soil, sun to part shade
Form	Flexible stems that can climb a metre or more
Seeds	Yes
Creeping	No
Control	Hand weed (difficult) or use diquat or glyphosate

This weed is easy to identify by its lax stems and narrow leaves arranged in whorls. It flowers between June and August and germinates in autumn so has a head start come spring.It is difficult to control because it scrambles over other plants, particularly hedges, making use of chemicals difficult. All parts of the plant are hairy and stick to animals and clothing thus spreading the seed.

Shepherd's purse *(Ephemeral)*

Botanical name	*Capsella bursa-pastoris*
Habitat	Any soil type, sun, common in vegetable and flower beds
Form	Height 45 cm
Seeds	Yes - 2 or 3 generations per year
Creeping	No
Control	Hand weed, hoe or use diquat or glyphosate

This weed forms a basal rosette of leaves with a flowering stem bearing small white flowers. Can be in flower from late winter through to autumn. The common name is derived from the heart shaped seed pods. The seeds can remain dormant for 30 years.

Plant problems

Perennial weeds

Ground elder

Botanical name	*Aegopodium podagraria*
Habitat	Any soil type, shade
Form	Height 45 cm - spread 1 m per year
Seeds	Yes
Creeping	Yes - by rhizomes
Control	Difficult - hand weed or use glyphosate

This is an invasive garden weed often introduced by being present in the soil of acquired plants. It forms a dense clump that can smother other plants. It is difficult to dig out because it tends to intertwine with other plants, and the roots are brittle.

Stinging nettle

Botanical name	*Urtica dioica*
Habitat	Any soil type. sun or shade, common in hedges and uncultivated ground
Form	Height 1 m - spread 1 m per year
Seeds	Yes
Creeping	Yes - by stolons
Control	Hand weed or use glyphosate

This weed grows in clumps with heart shaped leaves with serrated edges. The stinging is caused by tiny hairs that cover the leaves and stems. Small green flowers are produced between June and September and plants should be dealt with prior to this as many seeds are produced that can remain dormant for several years.

Creeping buttercup

Botanical name	*Ranunculus repens*
Habitat	Prefers moist soil, sun or shade, common in beds and lawns
Form	Height 15-30 cm - spread 1 m per year
Seeds	Yes
Creeping	Yes - by stolons
Control	Hand weed, hoe or use diquat in beds and hormone weedkiller like MCPA or 2,4-D on lawns

This weed produces its distinctive yellow flowers in May to June producing seed that germinates between March and November. Stolons are produced in May and June which spread rapidly.

Greater plantain

Botanical name	*Plantago major*
Habitat	Any soil type, sun to part shade
Form	Broad leaved basal rosette with single stem

Seeds	Yes
Creeping	No
Control	Hand weed or use hormone weedkiller like MCPA or 2,4-D

This weed is quite common in lawns and its low rosette of leaves escapes the mower. It flowers in summer to autumn and needs to be eradicated before it seeds as it can produce 14000 seeds.

Couch grass

Botanical name	*Elymus repens*
Habitat	Well drained soil, sun
Form	A coarse grass up to 1m that emerges in small clumps
Seeds	Sometimes
Creeping	Yes - by rhizomes
Control	Hand weed (can be difficult) or use glyphosate

This weed is very widespread and occurs in all situations. The rhizomes spread rapidly and throw up many shoots. It is difficult to control by hand weeding because the roots are often intertwined with other plants. For severe infestations it may be necessary to dig up the cultivated plants, clean the roots and plant elsewhere.

Common pests

Pests come in many shapes and sizes. Most of the smaller pests are insects which are by far the most numerous species on earth.

The life cycle of insects can vary considerably but many go through a process called metamorphosis and it is worth understanding the principles of this.

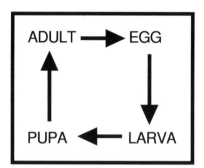

The insects go through a number of stages from egg to adult. The eggs hatch to produce a larva which is completely different to the adult. Grubs, maggots and caterpillars are all forms of larvae.

The larvae feed for a while but then pupate within a cocoon. It is during this stage that the larva changes into the adult form.

There are three reasons for highlighting this cycle. Firstly, it is often the larva rather than the adult that causes the plant damage; secondly, that while in the egg or pupa form insecticides may have no effect, and thirdly eggs can often survive over winter and hatch in the following year.

Birds

The following birds are particularly pests:

- **Bullfinch**

    Bullfinches will systematically eat the buds of fruit and ornamental trees and shrubs, seriously reducing the flowers and subsequent fruit. Plants are most at risk from midwinter until spring.

- **Wood pigeon**

    Wood pigeons will take seeds of peas and beans, young seedlings, and eat the leaves of brassicas. They are most active in spring and early summer.

- **House sparrow**

    House sparrows are a particular nuisance in urban areas. They feed on seeds but will attack and damage all parts of a wide range of plants. They are most active from December to June.

> **Treatment**
>
> Birds are protected by law and cannot therefore be killed. Although damage on ornamental plants may be tolerated, fruit and vegetables need to be protected and the only reliable method is by using a cage.
>
> Other methods like cotton stretched over crops, devices that emit a noise or chemical repellents are partially effective, but do not use repellents on edible crops.

Rabbits

Rabbits will eat most tender parts of plants, and leafy vegetables are particularly at risk. They will also strip the bark from young trees which can cause the tree to die. They are more of a pest in rural areas.

> **Treatment**
>
> Although rabbits can be trapped or gassed this is not practical in a garden environment and the only reliable method of control is by physical protection.
>
> A fence should be made of wire with a 2-3 cm mesh and be about 1 m high with 30 cm buried in the ground.
>
> Individual trees can be protected with a spiral guard round the trunk.

Slugs and snails

Slugs and snails will eat most parts of vegetables and herbaceous plants, with the young growth in spring being particularly vulnerable.

Slugs will also eat seeds and tubers, and maincrop potatoes are often badly damaged.

They are most active at night and in humid conditions.

> **Symptoms**
>
> Irregular holes in leaves and other parts of the plant. Slime trails can be seen on soil and hard surfaces.
>
> **Treatment**
>
> Good hygiene can help to reduce the numbers. Various traps can be used; the best known is the container of beer sunk into the soil.
>
> The most effective control is by the use of slug pellets containing metaldehyde which are scattered around the plants and are effective for up to a week.
>
> There is also a biological control now available in the form of a nematode

Aphids

Aphids are one of the commonest garden pests. There are many different species including greenfly and blackfly. Some species are particular to one plant but others will attack a range of plants. Some are winged and can travel significant distances on the wind.

They feed on the sap of plants by inserting stylets into the plant tissue and sucking out the sap.

In addition to directly attacking plants aphids are also responsible for spreading some viruses.

The breeding potential is enormous. The females give birth to live young which mature in about a week and within a season one female could theoretically have millions of descendants.

> **Symptoms**
>
> The aphids can be seen, usually on the new growth of plants which can be weakened and distorted
>
> They secrete a sticky substance called honeydew which can be infected by sooty mould which is a blackish fungal infection.

> **Treatment**
>
> There are a number of natural predators like ladybirds and lacewings but these are unlikely to keep pace with the rapid build up of the pest.
>
> There are a number of chemicals that can be used:
>
> > Deltamethrin or thiacloprid
> > Pyrethrins
> > Fatty acids
>
> For details of these chemicals see **Topic C-4 'Chemical control'**.

Whitefly

Whiteflies are small, sap sucking insects. There are many species but two of the most troublesome are greenhouse whiteflies and cabbage whiteflies.

Greenhouse whitefly mainly attack glasshouse plants like tomatoes and cucumbers, and can be difficult to control as they breed rapidly in the warm conditions.

Although they are short-lived the females can lay up to 200 eggs. These eggs hatch and pupate as scales before the adult emerges. The reproduction cycle is 3-4 weeks.

The cabbage whitefly is hardier and survives outside on brassicas.

> **Symptoms**
>
> The whitefly can be seen, usually on the underside of leaves. If disturbed they will often fly off the plant in a cloud.
>
> Like aphids they secrete honeydew that can attract sooty mould.
>
> **Treatment**
>
> In a garden environment insecticides such as deltamethrin or thiacloprid can be used. Repeated spraying at frequent intervals may be needed as the eggs are not killed by the spray.
>
> In commercial glasshouses the whitefly are resistant to these chemicals and a biological control is now widely used. This is a parasitic wasp called ***Encarsia formosa*** which can also be used in a garden greenhouse.

Red spider mite

Red spider mites are very small mites that attack a range of plants including fruit (eg. apples, pears, peaches, strawberries), vegetables (eg. cucumbers, tomatoes, beans) and ornamental plants (eg, roses, chrysanthemums, fuchsias).

The glasshouse red spider mite is a particular pest as, like the glasshouse whitefly, it has developed a resistance to insecticides.

The female mite has a life cycle of about a month and can lay up to 200 eggs so the numbers can increase very rapidly.

> **Symptoms**
>
> The upper surface of the leaves develops a yellowish mottling which later turns bronze and the leaf may wither.

The mites develop colonies on the underside of leaves. Individually they are so small they are difficult to see, but they spin a very fine webbing which should be visible.

Treatment

Red spider mite is difficult to control by chemicals but in a garden environment Imidacloprid or fattyacids can be tried.

In commercial glasshouses the mites are resistant to chemicals and a biological control is now widely used. This is a predatory mite called ***Phytoseiulus persimilis*** which can also be used in a garden greenhouse.

Scale insects

Scale insects are small, sap-sucking insects that, in their adult form, tend to stay in one place. They develop a waxy outer coating which gives them some protection from insecticides. They exude honeydew which tends to attract sooty mould.

The females can lay several hundred eggs and the young insects called 'crawlers' move away before settling.

They mainly attack ornamental plants although some fruit trees can also be affected. Plants in glasshouses are particularly susceptible.

Symptoms

The insects are up to 4 mm long, usually brown in colour, and can be seen mainly on stems. The sooty mould they can attract is easily visible.

Treatment

Ensure that new plants are free from infestation as this is often   how the pest is introduced.

Spray with a insecticide such as thiacloprid or fatty acids when the eggs are hatching.

Deciduous trees can be given a tar oil wash in winter.

Caterpillars

Caterpillars are the larvae of moths and butterflies. There are many species, most of which attack a particular plant although some attack a range of plants.

Some of the most common and troublesome are:

> **Winter moth**
> **Codling moth**
> **Noctuid moth (cutworms)**
> **Large white cabbage butterfly**

The plants attacked include fruit (eg. apples, pears, plums, gooseberries), vegetables (eg. brassicas, peas, beans, tomatoes) and ornamental plants (eg. roses, chrysanthemums, carnations).

Females can lay several hundred eggs and there may be several generations within a season. They usually survive over winter by pupating.

Symptoms

Both the caterpillars and the damage they cause can be easily seen. All parts of the plant may be eaten although leaves are the most common and the most obvious.

Plant problems

> Maggot holes in apples are caused by the codling moth larvae.
>
> **Treatment**
>
> Small infestations can be dealt with by picking off the larvae and crushing any eggs.
>
> A contact insecticide such as deltamethrin or pyrethrins can be used.
>
> A grease band can be used on fruit trees which will prevent the female winter moth crawling up the trunk to lay her eggs. Apply the band in October.
>
> A biological control is available in the form of a bacteria called ***Bacillus thuringiensis***. This is mixed with water and applied as a spray.

Flies

There are thousands of fly species, some of which are serious pests in the garden. It is the larvae of the fly that causes the problems rather than the flies themselves.

Some of the most common and troublesome are:

> **Carrot fly**
> **Cabbage root fly**
> **Onion fly**
> **Narcissus fly**

The damage caused by the larvae of these flies is dealt with in later topics when the particular plants are covered.

Eelworms (nematodes)

Although through a microscope these look like eels they are very small and can barely be seen with the naked eye.

There are a number of species and some of the most common and troublesome are:

Stem eelworm	Bulbs are particularly susceptible, both vegetables like onions and leeks and ornamentals like narcissi and tulips.
Chrysanthemum eelworm	
Pea cyst eelworm	
Potato cyst eelworm	

They feed both externally and internally by sucking out the cell contents.

Their life cycle is completed within a month in favourable conditions and the population can increase very rapidly. A badly infested plant may contain thousands of them.

> **Symptoms**
>
> Exact symptoms differ according to the species but in general the plants may discolour, distort and eventually die.
>
> **Treatment**
>
> Good hygiene, including burning infected plants, care when buying new plants, and crop rotation in the vegetable garden will help to avoid this pest.
>
> Soaking bulbs in hot water is used by commercial growers and this can be done by the

amateur. Soak the bulbs for 3 hours at a temperature of 45º C.

Commercial growers also use a chemical which is not available to the amateur.

Vine weevil

The larvae of the vine weevil are a particular pest of house plants, and fushias, cyclamen, polyanthus and begonias are especially vulnerable. They will also damage plants out of doors.

The female lays a large number of eggs which do not need to be fertilised by a male so it is possible for infestations to grow very quickly.

It is possible to introduce this pest through its presence in the compost of purchased plants.

Symptoms

The larvae feed on the roots of plants so the first indication of anything wrong could be the collapse and death of the plant.

Treatment

Good housekeeping should reduce the chances of attack as the adult weevil hides among plant debris.

Spray the plant or drench the soil with a solution of thiacloprid. There is also a biological control that can be used in greenhouses or for house plants. It is a nematode that is watered onto the compost.

New Zealand flatworms

These flatworms do not directly attack plants but they are, nevertheless, a potentially very severe pest. What they do attack is earthworms, killing the worms and completely eliminating them in certain areas.

We have already seen that earthworms are very important to soil structure and fertility, and their elimination may cause a reduction in crop yields, or an increase in costs as soils will have to be more intensively cultivated.

The New Zealand flatworm was first discovered in the UK in the 1960's in Scotland and Northern Ireland and is gradually spreading south. It grows up to 20 cm and is a purple/brown colour. It likes dark, moist conditions, and is likely to be found under cover of stones or paving.

There is also an Australian flatworm that is different in appearance but is also a killer. This appears to be spreading northwards from the south-west.

Symptoms

The symptom will be a lack of earthworms, although this may be so gradual that it is not initially apparent.

Treatment

There is no chemical or biological control although considerable efforts are being made to find one.

The flatworms may be brought into gardens in the compost of purchased plants and pots should be carefully examined for both the worms and their eggs.

Common diseases

Causes of disease

Diseases are caused by fungi, bacteria or viruses, which are collectively known as **pathogens**.

Fungi

Fungi are related to plants but they do not photosynthesise. They derive their food from dead or living organic matter such as other plants. Some fungi are specific to certain plants but others attack a range of plants.

They spread by means of spores which are carried by wind or water, and which can survive in soil, seeds or tubers. Fungicides work by killing the spores or preventing them from germinating.

The damage fungi cause may be localised or it may affect, and eventually kill, the whole plant.

Bacteria

Bacteria are single celled microorganisms that can infect plants through wounds. As we have seen in the section on soil, many bacteria do an essential task in breaking down organic matter.

They reproduce by cell division and the numbers can multiply very quickly under warm conditions.

Bacterial diseases can be difficult to control as fungicides are not always very effective.

Viruses

These are microorganisms that live as parasites in other living tissue. The common cold is a virus affecting humans.

The virus can affect the whole plant and is likely to be transmitted by any vegetative reproduction.

There is usually no cure for a virus infection and the plants affected are best dug up and burned.

Powdery mildew

Powdery mildew is a fungal disease that can affect fruit (eg. apples, plums, peaches), vegetables (eg. peas, turnips) and ornamentals (eg. roses, asters, lupins).

There are a large number of different types of powdery mildew, although the symptoms and treatment for all are basically the same. Some are specific to particular plants while others will attack a range of plants.

The disease is spread by spores that can be carried long distances on the wind. It is worse in warm, dry conditions. The spores survive over the winter on the plant or in the soil and attack the plant again in the next year.

Symptoms

Leaves, stems and buds are coated with a white powdery coating. The leaves may turn yellow and drop prematurely. Growth may be retarded and distorted.

Treatment

The most successful treatment is with a systemic fungicide like myclobutanil. In severe cases spraying may be required at 14 day intervals.

Improving the moisture retention capacity of the soil and removing infected parts of the plant may give some control.

With roses there are some varieties that have some resistance and some varieties that are very susceptible.

Downy mildew

Downy mildew prefers cool, damp conditions. There are a number of species and they are usually restricted to a particular type of plant. The disease occurs on a number of vegetables (eg. brassicas, lettuce) and ornamentals (eg. hellebores, poppies).

In recent years busy Lizzies *(Impatiens walleriana)* have been severely affected, including the plants for sale in garden centres.

The spores survive over the winter on the plant or in the soil and attack the plant again in the next year.

Symptoms

Yellow/brown spots form on the upper surface of leaves while the underneath is covered with a white mould. The leaves may become distorted and wilt.

Treatment

Avoid overcrowding and ensure air circulation and drainage is adequate. Infested plants should be burned.

There are no fungicides available to the amateur for controlling this disease.

Grey mould *(Botrytis)*

This is a widespread fungal disease affecting many varieties of fruit (eg. apples, strawberries), vegetables (eg brassicas, lettuce) and ornamentals (eg. dahlias, pelargoniums). It primarily attacks buds and fruits, rendering the fruit inedible and can also affect stored fruit.

It thrives in damp and overcrowded conditions where it spreads rapidly from plant to plant.

Symptoms

A fluffy grey mould develops on the infected parts which then turn brown and rot.

Treatment

Good hygiene, good ventilation and no overcrowding will reduce the chance of this disease.

There are no fungicides available to the amateur for controlling this disease.

Plant problems

Damping off

Damping off is a general term given to the rotting of seedlings which can be caused by a number of fungi which are usually present in the soil. Most vegetable and bedding plant seedlings are susceptible to damping off.

> **Symptoms**
>
> The seedlings wither at the base and eventually collapse and die.
>
> **Treatment**
>
> Good hygiene is very important. Disinfect seed trays before use. Discard all plants in a seed box if any show signs of infection.
>
> Copper oxychloride watered into the compost at sowing, emergence and transplanting will give some protection

Rust

There are many species of rust which is a fungal infection that attacks a wide range of plants including fruit, vegetables and ornamentals. One of the commonest which most gardeners will be familiar with is rose rust.

Rust takes away nutrients from the host plant causing a general weakening of growth. The spores overwinter on fallen debris.

> **Symptoms**
>
> Orange/brown pustules form on the undersides of leaves and yellowish spots can form on the upper surface. The leaves may wither and fall prematurely.
>
> **Treatment**
>
> Good hygiene is important. Pick off and burn any infected parts of the plant.
>
> Regular spraying with myclobutanil or copper oxychloride should provide control.

Brown rot

This is a common fungal disease particularly affecting fruit. Virtually all tree fruits are susceptible. It usually infects the plant through a wound caused by some other means.

> **Symptoms**
>
> Soft brown patches appear on the fruit, often surrounded by whitish pustules. The disease can spread rapidly and can affect stored fruit. Fruit on the tree may shrivel and become mummified.
>
> **Treatment**
>
> Good hygiene is important. Pick off and burn damaged fruit and in particular do not put any into storage.
>
> There is a fungicide called difenoconazole is claimed to give protection on specified fruits

Honey fungus *(Armillaria)*

This is a very serious disease of trees and other woody plants. Rhododendrons, privet and wisteria are particularly vulnerable.

It is likely to lead to the death of the plant infected. It can spread through the ground to infect other plants and it is very difficult to control. The only consolation is that it is not so common as other diseases.

Symptoms

The foliage may turn yellowish or brown. A white fungal growth develops underneath the bark at the base of the plant. Toadstools up to 15 cm in diameter may appear in autumn around the base of the plant. Black strands of fungus, known as bootlaces, appear in the soil and may infect other plants.

Treatment

The plants must be removed and burned. It is important to remove the roots and any of the 'bootlaces', and it may be prudent to replace the soil.

Do not replant woody plants in the same area.

Use plants that have some resistance to the fungus.

There is no chemical solution available to the amateur.

Canker

There are two types of canker; *Netria* canker which is a fungus and bacterial canker which, as its name indicates, is caused by a bacteria.

Cankers mainly affect trees, and apples and varieties of *Prunus* are particularly vulnerable.

Symptoms

The bark cracks and dies in increasing concentric rings leaving a marked scar. The cambium layer is killed and if the canker encircles the stem then it will cause it to die.

With bacterial canker a gum may seep from the infected area.

Treatment

The canker can be cut out and the area treated with a canker paint but it is probably safer to remove the infected branch cutting well below the infected area.

Copper oxycloride will give some protection against bacterial canker on specified fruit trees.

Some varieties of apples such as Cox's Orange Pippin are very susceptible and should be avoided.

Scab

Scab can occur on most tree fruit, although it is most common and troublesome on apples. Scab also occurs on potatoes but this is caused by a different organism and is covered in the section **'The vegetable garden'**.

The fungus overwinters on fallen leaves and infects new growth in spring.

Symptoms

The leaves and twigs develop greenish-brown blotches or pustules. On the fruit the infection starts as dark spots that grow and develop into a cork-like scar that may then crack.

Treatment

Fallen leaves should be collected and burned.

Regular spraying with myclobutanil should provide control.

Some varieties such as Cox's Orange Pippin are particularly susceptible and some have some resistance.

Viruses

Many plants can be infected with viruses including fruit, vegetables and ornamentals. The virus infects the whole of the plant not just the area where symptoms occur. This means that plants that naturally produce by vegetative means, like bulbs and tubers, are particularly likely to have virus diseases as it is automatically passed to the next generation. The same applies to any form of artificial propagation such as cuttings or grafting. Viruses can also be transmitted via pollen or seed.

Viruses can be carried by other insects, and aphids and eelworms are common carriers.

Micropropagation techniques are now able to produce virus free plants.

Viruses are usually named according to the plant on which they were first identified, although in many cases they are not restricted to that plant, and the effect they have on the plant. Examples are **cucumber mosaic virus** and **potato leaf roll virus**.

Some plant varieties are resistant to virus and some, particularly soft fruits, can be bought certified as virus free.

Symptoms

Symptoms will vary according to the particular virus but common indications include yellowish mottling or streaking of leaves and distortion of foliage by curling or crumpling.

Flower colour can be affected. Some multi-coloured tulips are in fact caused by a virus,

Plants will lose vigour and may eventually die.

Treatment

There is no cure for virus infection. Remove and burn any infected plants. Control aphids which can transmit viruses.

Never propagate from a diseased plant.

Buy plants certified to be virus free wherever possible. This is particularly important for soft fruit.

Common disorders

What is a disorder

Disorders are plant problems that are not caused by pests or diseases but by some problem in the environment in which the plant is being grown. These are called **physiological** disorders.

Disorders can be divided into two groups. The first group are disorders due to lack of the required nutrients. The role of these nutrients in the plant and the effect of them not being available is covered in **Topic A-17 'Plant nutrients'**.

The second group of disorders are those primarily to do with climate and it is these that will be covered in this topic. The following will be discussed.

Frost
Wind
Drought
Waterlogging

Frost

Frost can cause the cell contents to freeze and, as water expands on freezing, the cells can be ruptured and killed. Some plants have ways of combating this as outlined in **Topic A-18 'Adaptations'**.

The main damage from frost occurs either with the first frosts of autumn or the late frosts of spring.

In autumn any non-hardy plants such as many bedding plants will blacken and die in the first frosts. Since this is expected this is not usually a cause of concern.

Much more serious is the damage caused to young shoots, buds and flowers by late spring frosts which can be experienced in May. Particularly at risk are fruit trees where the buds can be killed and the crop ruined, and some early flowering shrubs such as camellia, ceanothos and magnolia. The diagram on the following page shows the latest dates at which frosts may be experienced in different parts of the UK

Damage can also be done by the rapid thawing following a frost. It is for this reason that some plants should not be placed on an east wall where they will get the morning sun.

Symptoms

The foliage is scorched. That is, it turns brown and brittle, particularly at the edges, although the whole leaf may be discoloured and wither. Small plants may be killed.

Buds can be damaged or killed thus reducing the production of flowers and fruit. Blossom and fruitlets may drop. The skin of fruit that is produced may be cracked or russeted.

Treatment

Frost tends to move downhill and therefore any hollow or low lying area is particularly susceptible and should be avoided.

Plant problems

Choose hardy or late flowering varieties of plants. A good plant encyclopedia will indicate the hardiness of plants and varieties.

Provide some form of protection such as hessian, straw, fleece, cloches etc. or bring tender plants under cover over winter.

Plant tender plants in areas where there will be some protection, such as against walls.

Do not plant out seedlings until the danger of frost is past.

It should be borne in mind that although frosts can be bad for plants they can be good for soil, helping to develop a good structure.

Dates of last expected frosts

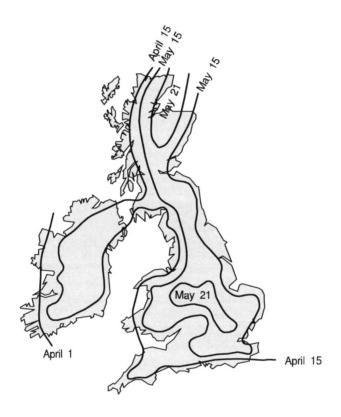

Wind

Wind can adversely affect plants in a number of ways:

- Direct damage by breaking stems and branches, blowing off fruit and damaging flowers.
- Increasing the rate of water loss.
- Lowering the temperature around the plant and causing wind scorch.
- Discouraging pollinating insects.
- Spreading salt damage in coastal areas.

Symptoms

Evidence of strong winds can sometimes be seen in the lopsided growth of trees due to buds being damaged on the windward side.

Physical damage should be self evident.

Lack of pollinating insects will be evident later in the season in the lack of fruit.

The effect of scorch and salt are similar to frost damage.

Treatment

Choice of a sheltered site is best but may not be practical in which case some form of shelter must be provided. Provision of a windbreak or shelter-belt is covered in **Topic G-4 'Hedges and windbreaks'.**

Choose hardy varieties of plants.

Drought

The importance of water to the plant has been emphasised a number of times. It participates directly in chemical reactions within the plant, and provides the vehicle for transporting nutrients and food through the plant.

Water is taken up by the roots and lost by transpiration through the leaves. About 95% of the water taken up is lost by transpiration. To the extent that the loss is greater than the uptake the plant is likely to suffer damage. For short periods such as on a hot day the plant will soon recover but a continuous imbalance will soon cause permanent damage.

Symptoms

The foliage of the plant will start to wilt and turn brown. If not corrected the leaves may fall and the plant may eventually die. Some plants may run to seed. Flowers and fruit may fail to set.

Treatment

Watering the plants regularly or at the critical points in their life is the obvious and immediate treatment. (**See Topic E-6 'Watering**)

Use mulches to reduce the water loss by evaporation. (**See Topic E-9 'Mulching**)

A longer term solution would be to look if there is any way of increasing the moisture retention capacity of the soil. (**See Topic B-6 'Organic matter'**)

Waterlogging

Waterlogging occurs when the pore space within the soil is filled with water. This stops oxygen reaching the roots, which is required for respiration, and prevents the escape of carbon dioxide which is given off by respiration.

In a reasonable soil this should not occur but it is very common with houseplants that are watered to excess.

Symptoms

Leaves may turn yellow and start to wilt. Growth may be stunted. Roots may rot.

On lawns the presence of moss is an indication.

Treatment

Outside, improving the structure of the soil is likely to be sufficient although in some circumstances, as with a high water table, it may be necessary to install some form of drainage. (**See Topic B-11 'Soil Management (2) Drainage'**)

Climate change

This topic is concerned with the impact of long term climate changes and not the normal day to day fluctuations.

At the time of writing there have been no questions in the RHS General Examination questions covering this area. It is included, however, because of increasing concern about the effects which are potentially very serious.

As an indication of the changes taking place, the 1990's was the warmest decade since reliable records started, and in 2006 there were serious concerns of water shortages.

Global warming

Global warming is the term given to the world wide increase in temperature that seems to be taking place. It is thought to be due to what is called the **greenhouse effect**.

Some gases in the atmosphere absorb heat and act as a blanket to keep the earth warmer than it would otherwise be. If this did not happen the earth would not be warm enough to sustain life as we know it.

The main gases involved are carbon dioxide, CFC's (chlorofluorocarbons, used in refrigerators and aerosols), and water vapour. Action has been taken to reduce the use of CFC's, and the major concern is the increase in carbon dioxide. Over the past 100 years the amount of carbon dioxide has increased by 25%. This increase is due mainly to the burning of fossilised fuels (coal, gas and oil) which releases carbon dioxide into the atmosphere. The destruction and burning of the rain forests is also thought to be a factor.

Global warming is recognised as a major concern and summit meetings of the world's leaders have been held to address the problem. The main outcome has been an undertaking on behalf of some countries to reduce energy usage. However this is by no means a universal agreement and a potential problem still remains.

A generally accepted figure is that average temperatures will increase by 2^0 C over the next 100 years.

The effect of this increase is difficult to predict, but it is likely to change the whole pattern of weather. This may benefit some areas, enabling crops to be grown that were not previously possible, but it will certainly be to the detriment of other areas, and is likely to produce more extreme effects, so that hot and wet areas will become even more hot and wet, and dry areas will become even dryer. An even more alarming prospect is that there are indications that the ice at the poles is melting causing a rise in sea levels.

These effects will cause a change in farming and horticulture, possibly causing devastating social and economic changes, and the fact that we may have to change our gardens could be a small problem by comparison.

Pollution

Pollution is caused by many aspects of modern life. The burning of fossilised fuels is again a culprit, releasing sulphur dioxide and nitrogen dioxide into the atmosphere. Another major culprit is the car, where exhaust fumes release carbon monoxide and lead.

All these pollutants can be dangerous to peoples' health. In London in the 1950's and 1960's smoke and fog combined to produce smog which caused the death of many people.

Although steps have been made to create cleaner air, people are still suffering, and the current increase in asthma is blamed on polluted air.

Acid rain

Acid rain is one particular result of pollution which can have serious effects on agriculture and horticulture.

Many of the pollutants, such as sulphur dioxide and nitrogen dioxide, are acidic and when combined with water in the atmosphere form dilute acids which can fall as rain. The damage from this can be extensive:

- Poisons rivers and lakes, killing off fish stocks.
- Washes essential nutrients, such as calcium and magnesium, from the soil.
- Directly damages vegetation, causing crops and forests to be damaged and die.

Depletion of the ozone layer

Ozone is a gas that occurs high in the atmosphere. It has a beneficial effect in that it absorbs ultraviolet radiation from the sun. This radiation can be harmful to people and also has a detrimental effect on plant growth.

The ozone is being depleted by the release of CFC's. These gases have been used in refrigerators and aerosols but they are now banned. However the gases are persistent and may continue to have an effect.

Self test questions

These questions are to enable you to assess how well you have understood and remembered the information in the previous section. No answers are given as these should be apparent from reviewing the relevant topics.

The questions are **not** intended to cover everything you should know.

1   List the types of problem gardeners may face and the types of solution that are available.

2   State the advantages and limitations of the following methods of pest and disease control:
   Cultural
   Biological
   Chemical
   Plant breeding

3   List the reasons for adopting an integrated pest control program, and five factors to be taken into account in planning it.

4   Describe what is meant by cultural control and list four specific ways of controlling weeds and four of controlling pests.

5   Describe what is meant by biological control and list four pests that can be controlled in this way and what the control agent is.

6   List eight safety precautions to be adopted when using chemicals in the garden.

7   Briefly describe the following types of herbicide:
   Contact
   Translocated (or systemic)
   Residual
   Selective

8   Which of the following weeds are annual and which are perennial:
   Stinging nettle
   Groundsel
   Creeping buttercup
   Plantains
   Chickweed

9   Describe the symptoms and treatment of the following pests
   Aphids
   Red spider mite
   Vine weevil

10   Describe the symptoms and treatment of the following diseases:
   Powdery mildew
   Rust
   Scab

11   List three causes of disorders in plants, describe the symptoms and how they can be prevented.

Garden Design

This section covers the principles of garden design from the initial establishment of requirements through to the role of hard and soft landscaping.

Garden style

Introduction

Garden design is a growth industry. Fed by television, magazines, and the opening of many gardens to the public, people are aware of what can be achieved even in the smallest of gardens. This coupled with increased leisure time and a general increase in prosperity has provided the impetus.

There is still however a reluctance to spend on a garden the kind of money spent on things like new kitchens and bathrooms, and it is only when this is overcome and the benefits of an attractive garden, both aesthetically and economically, are realised that a boom is likely to occur.

There are innumerable books on garden design and this section can only touch on the main considerations.

What style

The broadest division in garden style is between formal and informal gardens, although it must be realised that between the extremes of these two there is every possible gradation. In fact most gardens probably fall somewhere between the two.

It is also possible, of course, to have both formal and informal sections within one garden although this option is only practical in a larger garden.

The style adopted will be that wanted by the owner. The reasons will be personal and could be complex. He or she is likely to be influenced by experience, knowledge, nostalgia, fashion, budget, time and family.

Formal gardens

Most people will associate formal gardens with stately homes and indeed the origin of the formal garden goes back to the Renaissance period in Italy and France when it was the chateaux of the wealthy that developed the style. The gardens at Versailles are a good example.

Formal gardens may be characterised by:

- Geometric shapes such as rectangles and circles
- Symmetry of arrangement
- Enclosure by walls or hedges
- Manicured lawns
- Straight paths
- Topiary
- Water features
- Statuary
- Limited range of plants
- Knot gardens and parterres

There is no doubt a formal garden can satisfy people's desire for neatness and order and be very restful.

In current times the use of formal gardens goes best with houses and plots of regular shapes. They would not be out of place with modern town houses.

A very different type of formal garden is the Japanese garden. This does not meet the characteristics outlined above, having many irregular features. Nevertheless it is steeped in tradition, has a largely constant set of features, and is arranged with precision in careful patterns.

Informal gardens

Informal gardens have their origin in the 'natural' gardens designed for the wealthy by people like Capability Brown, and the cottage gardens of the poor.

Informal gardens may be characterised by:

- Curved, flowing lines
- Asymmetrical layout
- Winding paths
- Informal or no hedging
- Profusion of planting

Fashion and public opinion influence the informal garden. In the past, shrub borders and herbaceous borders have been popular; more recently heathers, conifers and ground cover have been used a lot, and at the time of writing this, 'natural' and wildlife gardens are in vogue. This edition of the book includes for the first time a topic on ornamental grasses and bamboos as they seem to be the 'in' plant of the moment.

Example of formal and informal designs

The design on the following page is for a small country house and includes formal, informal, and 'natural' areas.

In front of the house there is a formal garden that matches the symmetry of the house, and is largely enclosed by hedges. To the left of this is an informal garden with asymmetrical beds and an informal pool. At the back of these two gardens is an area of woodland underplanted with bulbs and ground cover plants.

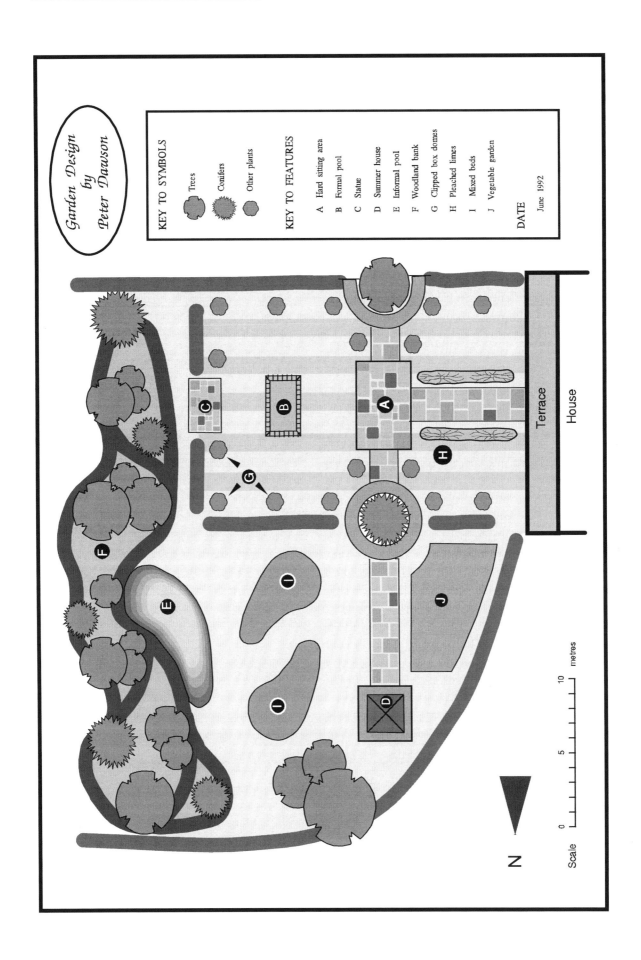

Garden Design
by
Peter Dawson

KEY TO SYMBOLS

- Trees
- Conifers
- Other plants

KEY TO FEATURES

A Hard sitting area
B Formal pool
C Statue
D Summer house
E Informal pool
F Woodland bank
G Clipped box domes
H Pleached limes
I Mixed beds
J Vegetable garden

DATE   June 1992

House

Terrace

Scale   metres

N

Requirements and site analysis

Requirements

The customer is always right - or is he ?

An important part of the designers job is to ensure that the client's requirements are realistic and can be met within the confines of site and budget.

It is of course essential that the designer understands the clients requirements and does his best to incorporate them in his design. The designer should however use his knowledge and expertise to avoid the client making any mistakes that he will later regret. If this is done tactfully the client will think any changes were his idea.

The requirements can be considered under a number of headings:

- **Aesthetic**
  - ➜ Views from within the garden
  - ➜ Views from within the house
  - ➜ Views from outside the property

- **Recreational**
  - ➜ Passive eg. eating or relaxing
  - ➜ Active eg. sports and pastimes

- **Productive**
  - ➜ Fruit and vegetables
  - ➜ Herbs
  - ➜ Cut flowers

- **Useful**
  - ➜ Dustbins
  - ➜ Compost
  - ➜ Clothes drying
  - ➜ Garden shed
  - ➜ Bonfire

- **Personal**
  - ➜ Pet likes and dislikes
  - ➜ Budget
  - ➜ Available time for maintenance
  - ➜ Time scale for effect

Site analysis

A thorough analysis and survey of the site is necessary to establish its potential and its limitations.

- **Size, shape and levels**

➔ This requires a survey of the site which can vary significantly in complexity

➔ Generally speaking the larger and more irregular the site, the more complex will be the survey

➔ The most difficult site to survey is one with slopes and undulations and this may require special surveying equipment

- **House**

  ➔ Views from windows

  ➔ Access to garden

  ➔ Shade cast

- **Aspect and climate**

  ➔ North point

  ➔ Prevailing wind

  ➔ Frost pockets

  ➔ Areas of heavy shade

- **Soil**

  ➔ Depth of topsoil

  ➔ Texture and structure

  ➔ Drainage

  ➔ pH

- **Existing features to be retained**

  ➔ For example, trees, hedges, hardstanding, buildings

- **Existing features to be hidden**

  ➔ These may be inside the garden or outside

- **Services**

  ➔ Establish water, power and drainage routes

Having established the requirements and analysed the site the designer is in a position to start the design process itself.

Basic Surveying Techniques

Introduction

Most gardeners will develop their own gardens in situ without feeling the need to commit the design to paper. However if one is starting with a virgin plot or designing someone else's garden then drawing up a plan will allow different ideas to be explored and discussed. Certainly anybody starting a business as a garden designer will need to be able to accurately measure and draw a clients garden.

In general the following things will need to be accurately measured and drawn:

- The outline of the house
- The outline of the plot and the position of the house within it.
- The outline and position of hard and soft landscaping features within the garden.
- The contours of the plot, ie any rises and falls in level that may influence any design.

Scale considerations

Any plan will need to be drawn to a scale. The two factors that will determine a scale will be the overall size of the plot and the size of the paper on which it is to be drawn, since it is easier to visualise if the whole plan can be seen at the same time.

For example consider .a plot size of 50 metres by 25 metres to be drawn onto a piece of A4 paper, (297 x 210 mm).

On a scale of 1:100 the drawn plot size would be 500 x 250 mm, and would not fit on the A4 paper.

On a scale of 1:1000 the drawn plot size would be 50 x 25 mm, and would not make use of the available space on the paper.

It is apparent that something between these two scales should be chosen and a scale of 1:250 would give a drawn plot size of 200 x 100 mm which would fit comfortably on the paper.

Scale rulers are available which make it easier to draw to scale by having several scales marked on them. For example if you wanted to draw a line of 50 metres at a scale of 1:250 you would use the part of the ruler with this scale marked on it and measure 50 units along it. The use of graph paper may make this easier.

Although many designers seem to use hand drawn plans there is likely to be a move to using personal computers where drawing or design packages can automatically be set to draw at any scale.

Outline of the house

This is probably the easiest task as most houses will have straight walls and right-angled corners.

It is important to mark the position of doors and windows as these may affect the positioning of landscaping features.

Let us take an example using just one house wall.

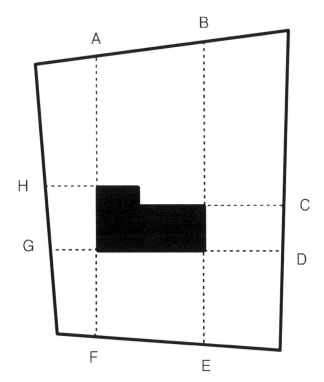

It is easier to fix the measuring tape at one corner and mark off the measurements on a cumulative basis. This will save constant repositioning of the tape.

Outline of the plot

The outline of the house can be used as a base to measure the outline of the plot.

There are basically two methods by which this can be done.

Extensions from the house walls

This is probably the easiest method if the plot consists of four straight sides.

It entails extending a line from the house walls to the boundary and measuring this distance.

Mark points A to H on the plan and draw a line through A-B, C-D, E-F and G-H. Where these lines intersect will be the corners of the plot.

Triangulation method

This method can be used instead of the extension method and will need to be used with many sided or irregular plots.

It is based on the principle that a point can be accurately positioned if it is measured from two fixed points.

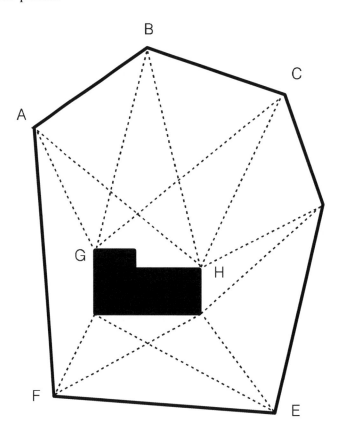

For example the distance of point A is measured from points G and H on the house walls. When drawing the plan if a compass is used to draw arcs to the correct scale and distance from points G and H then where the arcs intersect will be the correct position of point A.

All the other positions on the boundary can be plotted in the same way.

Plotting a curve

Plotting a curve is a little more difficult and may entail taking several measurements.

It is first necessary to establish the start and end points of curve and to lay a line joining these points, (Line A-B on the following diagram). This becomes the base line for the other measurements.

It is then necessary to take regular measurements (called offsets) from the base line to the edge of the curve. The number of measurements will depend on the complexity of the curve.

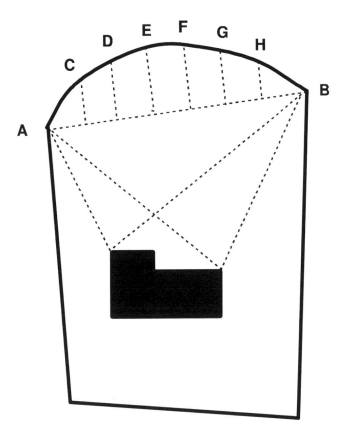

When drawing the plan, points C to H can be plotted using these measurements and a line drawn through them to create the curve.

Outline and position of hard and soft landscaping features

These can be done using any of the methods previously discussed

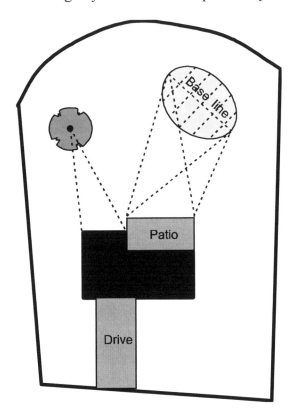

Anything adjacent to the house can be positioned by using the house ouline as a base.

Any individual feature like the tree can be positione by using the triangulation method.

Any irregular feature like a flower bed can be positioned by establishing a base line by the triangulation method, and thn measuring offsets from that line.

Contours of the plot

This is the most difficult thing, both to measure and to indicate on the plan.

It is worth asking the question whether the contours of the plot are such that they will make any difference to the plan. Small undulations can probably be ignored but any significant changes in level that may require special treatment, such as the provision of steps or terraces, obviously need to be noted. To accuratly measure such changes would require special surveying equipment.

Without any special equipment, an estimate of any change in levels can be done by measuring the change over a small length and multiplying that to give the change over the full length. This will only work if the slope is uniform over its whole length.

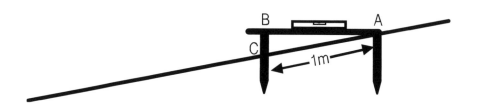

1.   Drive in two short stakes 1m apart.

2.   Set the one highest on the slope at ground level.

3.   Drive in the other until its top is level with the first, using a piece of wood and a spirit level to check the levels are the same.

4.   Measure the distance from the top of the second stake to the ground, (distance B-C). This will be the drop over 1m.

5.   Multiply this drop by the length of the slope to give the overall drop.

In the above diagram, if the drop over 1m is 0.2m and the overall length of the slope is 20m, then the overall drop is 0.2m x 20m = 4m.

Ensuring an area is level

There will times when it is necessary to ensure that an area is level, such as when constructing a path, patio or pool.

This can be done by using short stakes, a length of wood with a straight edge, and a spirit level.

1.   Drive in one stake as a starting point so that its top is at the level required.

2.   Using the length of wood and the spirit level drive in another stake so that its top is level with the first.

3. **Repeat this process from stake to stake until the whole area is covered.**

An alternative method of ensuring levels over a large area is by the use of 'boning rods'. A boning rod consists of a vertical piece of wood with a horizontal piece fixed at right angles to it. The minimum number of boning rods is three and it is essential that the horizontal piece of wood is at the same height on each rod.

The principle behind using the rods is that when viewing along the line of the horizontall, if all rods are in line then they are at the same level.

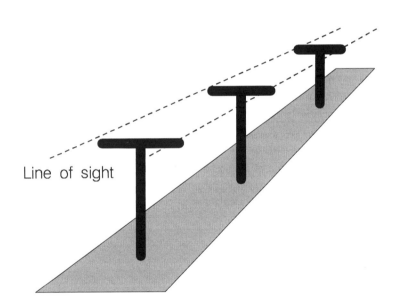

Line of sight

Principles of design

Basic principles

Harmony
Proportion
Balance
Simplicity
Interest

Harmony

My dictionary defines harmony as 'a fitting together of parts so as to form a connected whole'. My thesaurus includes as synonyms 'rapport, compatibility, unity'.

With harmony we are concerned with the overall garden and the way the components are combined to make a pleasing effect. There should be harmony between the house and garden, within the garden and outside the garden. There should be an impression of some purpose and aim behind the design and no jarring of the senses with haphazard layouts or clashing styles.

This is not to say that there cannot be different styles or different features. Some of the most famous gardens such as Bodnant and Sissinghurst successfully combine different styles but in a way that makes the transition from one to another seem natural.

Methods of achieving harmony

- Consider the style and proportions of the house. A formal garden around a country cottage will look out of place, as will a cottage garden around a town house.

- Use materials for hard landscaping that match the house.

- Use the same hedging material all round the house.

- Use hedges to screen areas within the garden such as around a rose or herb garden.

- Use features like hedges, walls, arches and pergolas to lead from one part of the garden to another.

- Use focal points to draw the eye and lead into new areas.

- Use repeating geometric shapes.

- Use repeating plant types including trees, or repeating plant colours, whether of flowers or foliage.

Proportion

Proportion and scale are aspects of harmony dealing with size and shape, and are important to achieve a pleasing effect. I expect everybody has seen small houses dominated by huge trees, or a large expanse of lawn with a tiny flower bed around the perimeter.

The starting point for determining proportion is the house itself. A stately home calls for sweeping lawns and wide paths; a country cottage would look better with a brick path winding through massed beds of cottage garden flowers.

Points to bear in mind

- Take into account ultimate sizes when planting trees and shrubs.

- A lot of small features in a garden can make it look fussy and unrestful.

- Paths generally should be wide enough for two to walk on or to push a wheelbarrow along. Also take into account what it leads to. A large focal point needs a substantial path.

- If a sitting out area is required take into account the number of people to be accommodated together with the size of house and garden.

- In individual beds and borders a guideline is to have plants at the back approximately 1.5 times the width of the border.

- Have some plants higher than eye level and so that they break the skyline.

- Do not be afraid to have large groups of the same plant in a large garden. A large number of different plants can again look fussy and unrestful.

- It is possible to create illusions of size and shape in particular circumstances, such as having a path that narrows in width to make it look longer.

Balance

Balance is related to proportion but it would be possible to have a garden in which all the components were in proportion but because of their positioning the overall effect is unbalanced.

An individual bed can appear unbalanced if a tree or large shrub is positioned at one end. A garden can appear unbalanced if the features tend to be clustered in one area.

Note that balance is not the same as symmetry. A balance can be achieved by using different shapes or densities or even different colours.

Simplicity

We have mentioned already that too many features or too many different plants can make a garden fussy and unrestful.

However it is difficult to achieve simplicity in a small garden where there is a natural desire to have different features, and this is a challenge to the garden designer. How do you convince a client that he cannot have the lawn, patio, sandpit, barbecue, pool, vegetable garden, fruit garden, rock garden, toolshed and greenhouse in his suburban back garden.

How many different types of plant should be used to fill a border of a particular size? I do not know the answer but I think it would be an interesting area for discussion and research.

Interest

It would be possible to meet all the other design principles but end up with a garden without interest or inspiration.

It is in the area of providing interest that skill of the designer comes into its own. The designer is painting a 3-dimensional picture with paints that will change colour, spread and texture through the year. A formidable task for anyone.

The tools the designer has to produce the interest are:

- **Shape and form**

  ➜ Ground shapes can be regular or irregular. Regular shapes tend to be static and restful whereas irregular ones, particularly sweeping curves, give an impression of movement.

  ➜ Plant shapes can be large or small, prostrate, round, upright, conical, spreading, fastigiate and many others.

  ➜ Focal points are features that attract the attention and can be plants such as a tree or large shrub, or a non-living feature such as a seat or statue. The focal point becomes the centre of the picture for the viewer with the surroundings forming the backdrop.

- **Texture**

  ➜ Texture can be reflected in hard or soft landscaping.

  ➜ Hard landscaping can be large (paving) or small (pebble), modern (concrete) or traditional (bricks), reflective or moving (water), solid (fence) or see-through (railings).

  ➜ Soft landscaping texture is dictated by the foliage and can be dense or airy, large or small, shiny or dull.

- **Colours**

  ➜ Colour can be reflected in both hard and soft landscaping.

  ➜ Flowers provide the most dramatic and vibrant colours but only last for a limited time. Foliage provides more subtle colours and lasts for longer. Evergreens have an important role since they provide colour all year round.

- **Combinations**

  ➜ Combinations of plants can be particularly effective, and they can be harmonising or contrasting, and of form, texture or colour.

  ➜ A contrasting combination of form could be a prostrate conifer combined with a fastigiate tree.

  ➜ A harmonious combination of colour could be a border where all plants have the same flower colour.

- **Surprise**

  ➜ A garden is always more interesting if parts of it are hidden from immediate view. Walls, hedges and beds can all be used to hide part of the garden.

  ➜ Sharp contrasts in colour or form can be used to produce a special effect.

Hard landscaping

What is hard landscaping

Hard landscaping is basically any non-living feature in the garden. It will include:

Paths and drives
Patios
Fences
Walls
Steps
Pools
Rock gardens
Arches and pergolas

In this section we will cover paths and drives, patios, fences and walls. Pools and rock gardens will be covered in the relevant topics in the section on ornamental gardening.

The uses of hard landscaping

- It meets practical requirements like access, support and screening.

- It can link different elements of the soft landscaping and be a foil for them.

- It can be decorative in its own right.

- It can enhance either formal or informal designs.

Paths and drives

Paths and drives are basically for carrying traffic, whether pedestrian or motorised. They need to be safe and usable in all conditions.

Materials

- **Tarmac**

  More likely for drives or other large areas than paths. Provides a hardwearing surface that should need little maintenance. Functional rather than decorative.

- **Concrete**

  Hard wearing and maintenance free. Can be moulded to different shapes.

  A recent development is pattern imprinted concrete, where a pattern and colour is pressed into the surface to give the impression of different materials such as stone or bricks.

- **Concrete slabs**

  These come in many shapes, sizes, textures and colours, often made to look like natural stone. They can be used to make geometric patterns.

  They are cheap but may not be strong enough for heavy use.

- **Bricks and blocks**

Bricks are made from clay while blocks are the same or a similar size to bricks but are made from concrete. They are small enough to enable a number of patterns to be constructed.

Bricks can give a cottage garden feel and are suited to older properties.

- **Natural stone**

    This can be in irregular shapes for constructing crazy paving, or regular shapes for a formal look.

    The right thing for a stately home but expensive and heavy to work with.

- **Gravel**

    This is good to cover large areas and give an informal feeling at a cost less than the other materials. Plants can be allowed to seed in it to give a soft, informal look.

    It is not maintenance free. It will need to be weedkilled, raked and periodically topped up.

Styles

Although paths and drives are a functional requirement they can be made to look attractive in ways outlined above.

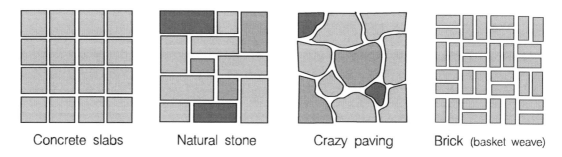

| Concrete slabs | Natural stone | Crazy paving | Brick (basket weave) |

Construction considerations

- **Base**

    It is very important, particularly for drives, that an adequate base is provided. This will entail using hardcore and the use of cement or sand as a bedding layer for slabs, bricks or blocks.

- **Flexible or rigid**

    Bricks and blocks can either be laid adjacent to each other on a bed of sand (flexible) or on a mortar base with pointing between them (rigid).

    The flexible method is easier and is very popular. It is used considerably on public areas like shopping precincts.

Patios

Patios provide a hard area on which to sit and may incorporate things like a barbecue and plants in containers. It is the hub of the outside room.

Materials

- The materials for a patio are largely the same as those for paths and drives although tarmac and gravel would not normally be used.

Styles

- Combination of materials can be used effectively such as bricks and paving slabs.

- Do not have an intricate design surrounded by intricate planting. The two may fight for attention and the effect can be unrestful. It is often better to have a plain patio to act as a foil for the plants.

Construction considerations

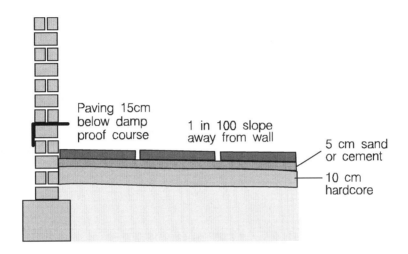

Paving 15cm below damp proof course

1 in 100 slope away from wall

5 cm sand or cement

10 cm hardcore

- Position the patio so that it gets the maximum sunlight if that is what is required.

- If it is not adjacent to a house exit, provide a hard path to it.

- As with paths and drives an adequate base must be provided.

- If the patio is against the house ensure it is 15 cm below the level of the damp proof course, and slope it slightly away from the house to ensure rainwater runs away.

Fences

Fences are primarily used for boundary definition and privacy.

Materials

- A wide variety of woods are used for fencing, from softwood used for the standard type of overlapped fencing panels, to oak that is often used for post and rail fencing.

- The type of wood will have an effect on the life of the fence. Softwood has a limited life although this can be extended by coating it periodically with a preservative.

- Other materials can be used such as iron railings.

Styles

- The standard overlapped or interwoven fencing panel that can be obtained from most garden centres is usually used as a substitute for a wall or hedge to mark a boundary or provide some privacy.

- Post and rail is a traditional country type fencing usually made of oak or chestnut. It is often used as a means of retaining livestock.

- Picket fences have a neat but cottagey look. The appearance can be highlighted by painting them but this will have to be repeated every few years to keep them looking good.

- Iron railings can look very attractive but will also require periodic painting. They will look best with a more formal garden.

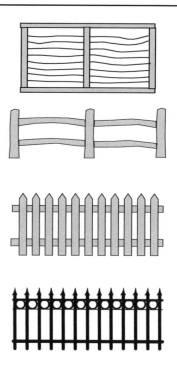

Construction considerations

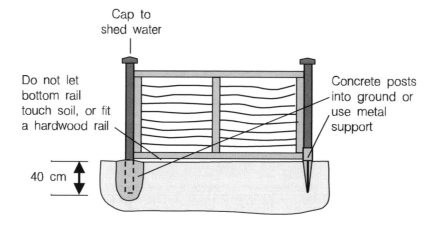

- The weak point of any fence is the posts, which tend to rot at ground level. Concrete posts would overcome this but some people may not like the appearence of these. It is possible to buy metal post supports which are hammered into the ground, and into which the posts are fixed.

- Always ensure that the wood is treated with a preservative, preferably applied under pressure.

- If a high solid fence is erected the wind pressure against it can be considerable and the posts must be very secure.

Walls

Walls provide a permanent and maintenance free structure that can be used for boundary definition, privacy, retention etc.

There are basically three types of wall:

1. **Load bearing as in the case of house walls.**

2. **Free-standing as in boundary walls.**

3.   Retaining as in walls to support the soil in terraced gardens.

Materials

- Walls can be made of brick, concrete blocks, and various natural materials like stone, slate and flints.

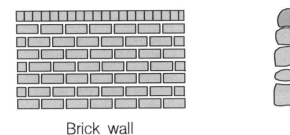

Brick wall   Stone wall

Styles

- Bricks can be laid in a number of ways, including the following:

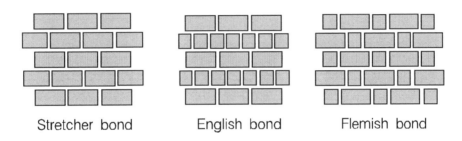

Stretcher bond   English bond   Flemish bond

- Stone walls can be laid with or without mortar.

- Often combinations of materials are used. In my locality of the South Downs brick and flint is commonly used.

- A wall made of stone foreign to the locality such as a slate wall in southern England can jar and look out of place.

Construction considerations

- Good foundations are essential to the stability of a wall.

- The top of a wall should have some form of coping to protect it from rain.

- A retaining wall must have gaps or pipes set in it to allow water to drain out.

- For any wall over say 1 m it is probably better to call in a professional.

Soft landscaping

What is soft landscaping

Soft landscaping comprises all the plants and the ways in which they are used. It includes:

Lawns
Trees and conifers
Shrubs
Hedges and windbreaks
Roses
Climbers
Ground cover
Perennials
Annuals and biennials
Bulbs and corms
Alpines and rock gardens
Herbs
Wild flower gardens
Ornamental grasses and bamboos
Containers
Water gardens

All these are covered in the section **'The Ornamental Garden'**.

Within the soft landscaping features, choices have to be made of what plants to use and what role they are to fulfil.

The role of plants within the design

Most designers deliberately or subconsciously assign a role to plants irrespective of the type of plant. Typical roles are:

1.   **Focal points**

   A tree or shrub which because of its size, shape or colouring will attract and hold the attention of the viewer and automatically define the boundaries of the view.

   A plant used as a focal point is often planted by itself such as in a lawn, or surrounded by plants that emphasise rather than diminish its significance.

   Plants fulfilling this role are sometimes called architectural plants.

2.   **Structural (or skeleton) plants**

   Most people want a garden with some form and colour in it all year round. A garden of annuals will look very colourful in summer but nothing in winter.

   This need is met by trees, conifers and shrubs. Conifers and evergreen shrubs make a particular contribution in the winter with the colour of their foliage. Deciduous trees and shrubs can also contribute to the winter garden by their form or by the colouring of their bark.

3.   **Body plants**

Having established a skeleton plants can be added to make up the body.

Any type of plant can be used for this purpose, and it is primarily at this stage that flower form and colour come into their own.

Decisions will have to be taken about whether to plant primarily for seasonal interest or for year round interest. In a large garden both needs could be satisfied by having seasonal plants in a summer border in a part of the garden that would mainly be used in summer, and having year round interest close to the house.

4.   Decorations

To continue with the body analogy, decorative plants can be considered the clothes and jewellery to complete the picture.

Any plants can fulfil this role although they are likely to be the more showy ones such as annuals, biennials or perennials

These plants can also be used to infill in the early years of a garden while other plants are growing to their mature size.

Attributes of plants

All plants have certain attributes which must be considered in making a choice. The major attributes are:

> **Size**
> **Shape**
> **Texture**
> **Colour**
> **Fragrance**

Size

The range of sizes from small alpines to large trees is enormous. Even within any plant group there is is a wide choice of sizes.

10

Metres

0

Shape

Round   Spreading   Fastigiate   Conical   Weeping   Prostrate

The same basic shapes apply to other types of plants such as shrubs but without the trunk.

Texture

Texture refers to the visual impression of the plant given primarily by its foliage. This can vary in a number of ways:

- **Evergreen or deciduous**

- **Size**

  From the tiny leaves of *Erica carnea* to the huge ones of *Gunnera manicata*.

- **Shape**

  Almost too many shapes to classify but including elliptic, ovate, lobed, palmate and linear.

- **Density**

  Either sparse, giving a light, delicate feel and creating dappled shade, or dense giving a feeling of strength and permanence.

- **Colour**

  All shades of green, yellow, gold, purple and many combinations of these, with tints of red, gold and purple in autumn.

- **Surface**

  Dull or glossy; smooth or hairy

Colour

All parts of the plant contribute to the colour. Stems are mostly brown or green but can also be shades of white, red and silver.

Foliage, as mentioned above, can be of many colours and has an impact over the longest period.

Flowers produce the most spectacular colours but remember that they only last for a limited time.

Fragrance

Fragrance is normally a characteristic of flowers but a number of plants have aromatic foliage. The fragrance is usually there to attract the pollinating insects.

The choice of plants

There are a number of factors that will affect the choice:

1. **Environment**

    The climate and the soil are overriding constraints. It is generally not worth trying to grow plants that are unsuited to the environment.

    Examples are trying to grow slightly tender plants in a cold garden, or trying to grow lime hating plants in an alkaline soil. It is not impossible but is it worth it when there are plants available for any environment.

2. **Function**

Consider the role of the plants as discussed earlier in this topic.

3. Visual quality

This is also connected with the role of the plants but in addition consider:

➔ **Plant attributes**

As discussed earlier.

➔ **Plant associations**

Size, shape, texture and colour should all be taken into account. It is the ability to combine plants effectively that distinguishes the good designer and the successful garden.

➔ **Succession**

Take into account how the garden will look at all seasons of the year and plan for some interest at all times.

4. Personal

Take into account

➔ The individual preferences of the owner
➔ Budget
➔ Time available for maintenance
➔ Time scale, ie. is a quick effect needed

Beds and borders

Plants are usually arranged in some form of bed or border but not necessarily so. Plants used as focal points can stand on their own so there are no surrounding plants to detract from the effect.

The shape of beds can influence the impact of the garden. Regular geometric shapes like squares and circles are static. They hold the eye as there is no implied direction of movement, and are therefore restful. They are suitable for formal gardens. Not all geometric shapes have the same effect; a long thin rectangle will draw the eye along the length. This is the effect of a path. Irregular curved beds give a feeling of movement and attract the viewer along them.

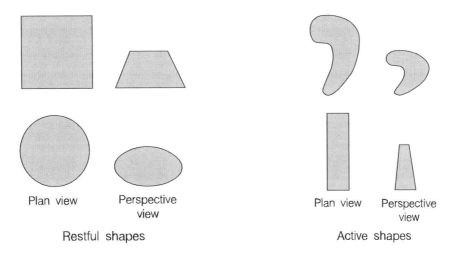

| Plan view | Perspective view | | Plan view | Perspective view |

Restful shapes   Active shapes

Scale and proportion must be applied to both the size of the beds and borders, and to the size of the plants within them. It is difficult to lay down rules, particularly for beds and borders, although ideally there should be enough depth to accommodate at least three tiers of plants.

Within a bed or border a guideline is to have some plants with a height 1.5 times the depth of the border.

A bed or border can be devoted to a particular type of plant, such as an herbaceous border, or even to a particular plant such as a rose bed. With the general reduction in the size of gardens this is not so practical and a better choice for most people is to have a mixed border.

The mixed border

A mixed border is one that contains different types of plants. There is no restriction on what may be included and trees, shrubs, perennials, bulbs, biennials and annuals can all be used.

The advantages of a mixed border are:

- **More suitable to smaller gardens.**

- **A wider variety of plants can be used.**

- **Easier to achieve all year round interest.**

- **Trees and shrubs can provide height and structure; other plants can provide colour and texture.**

- **Trees and shrubs can provide a micro-climate to enable other plants to be grown eg. shade lovers.**

The use of colour

The effective use of colour is extremely important and is a factor that distinguishes the outstanding designer. One of the most famous gardens in France was created by the painter Monet and it reflects his artists eye for colour.

There are books devoted to colour theory and the use of colour in the garden. Here we can cover only some of the basic principles.

There is a concept called the colour wheel where the colours of the spectrum are arranged in a circle.

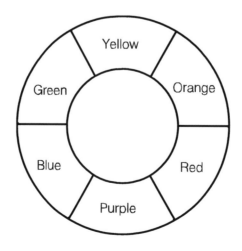

The principle is that adjacent colours harmonise and can be safely used together, while opposite colours complement each other and can be used to create a contrast. Therefore yellow will harmonise with green or orange but contrast with purple. The use of complementary colours can create a dramatic effect but it may be overpowering in a small garden.

Some general points on colour:

- Orange and red colours tend to be warm: blue and green tend to be cool.

- Warm colours tend to appear closer than cool colours.

- Soft colours are more restful than bright colours.

- Patches of bright colours can create interest among a panorama of softer colours.

- Light colours can be used to brighten shady places.

- White and silver can be used to link other colours.

Self test questions

These questions are to enable you to assess how well you have understood and remembered the information in the previous section. No answers are given as these should be apparent from reviewing the relevant topics.

The questions are **not** intended to cover everything you should know.

1   List the factors to be considered in assessing a site for a garden.

2   List five ways in which a designer can add interest to a garden.

3   List four materials that can be used for constructing a path, and the advantages of each.

4   Show by means of a diagram the construction of a patio adjoining a house.

5   List and briefly describe the factors to take into account in choosing plants for a garden.

6   You have been asked to design a back garden for a family of of two adults and two children under five. Indicate on the following plan three hard landscaping features and three soft landscaping features that would be appropriate.

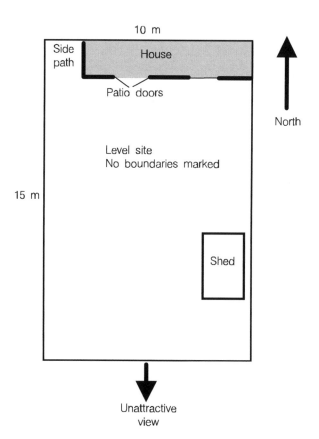

Note: Questions on overall garden design in the RHS General Examination have been few and far between. What is more common are questions requiring the design of a particular type of bed or feature, including the naming of plants. Examples of these are covered in the section **'The ornamental garden'**.

Techniques and procedures

This section covers techniques and procedures that are basically independent from any particular type of plant. For example, raising plants from seed is basically the same irrespective of the type of plant.

The advantage of doing this is that the same information does not have to be repeated in the topics dealing with the various types of plants, and the student only has to learn the information once.

Where there are variations to the basic techniques, as there are for example in pruning, the variations are covered in the topics dealing with the different plants.

Buying plants

Many people will choose to purchase plants rather than try to raise them from seeds or propagate them vegetatively. In some cases this will be the only way to obtain a particular plant.

The other big advantage that buying gives is a saving in growing time and an earlier effect in the garden, since purchased plants will already have had a period of growth. In the case of trees this could be several years.

Sources of supply

1. Garden centres

For many people this will be the main source of supply. Although the garden centres may not have a range of plants to satisfy the expert, they will usually have sufficient for most people.

Purchase from a garden centre has the advantage that the plants can easily be inspected and will probably be of reasonable quality. However surveys have shown that not all centres have good quality plants, and even good centres may have some poor plants, so care must be taken in choosing.

2. Other stores

The major DIY stores usually have a garden section, and so do a few high street stores.

Generally speaking, since selling plants is not their prime business, quality can be very varied, and additional care needs to be taken to ensure good plants are acquired.

3. Nurseries

The nursery that grows and sells its own plants is becoming rare except for some specialist nurseries.

Quality can vary considerably but the good are likely to be of high quality and good value for money.

4. Specialists

Similar to purchase from nurseries. The types of plants available are likely to be very restricted (eg roses), but the range of varieties within each type is likely to be large.

5. Mail order

Purchase by mail order from reputable firms and specialists should be satisfactory although there is the disadvantage of not seeing the plants before purchase. Many specialists, such as rose growers and bulb growers, sell mainly in this way. A reputable firm will replace any plants that fail to survive.

The advantage of mail order is that it is often possible to obtain a much wider range of plants than is available through the garden centres.

Purchase from special newspaper offers is more risky. In general avoid offers that seem to promise miraculous plants but fail to give an accurate name for them.

Techniques and procedures

Method of supply

1. Container grown

Most plants from garden centres will have been grown in containers and have the big advantage that they can be planted at any time when the soil conditions are suitable.

As long as care is taken in choosing individual plants this is a perfectly satisfactory way of buying them.

2. Containerised

This term applies to plants that have been grown in open ground and then transferred to containers for sale.

This is less satisfactory than container grown plants. The plants may suffer a set back when they are transferred. The plants should have been in the container long enough to make some new roots.

3. Bare rooted

Bare rooted plants are dug from the open ground and sold during the dormant season. This can be quite satisfactory although the planting time is obviously restricted. Roses from specialist growers are normally supplied in this form.

Bare rooted plants will tend to be cheaper than container grown ones.

4. Balled plants

These are plants that have been grown in the open ground, but are dug up with the soil around their roots which is kept in place with hessian or a similar material.

This is commonly done for conifers to reduce the shock of transplanting.

What to look for

Whatever the source of the plant, care must be taken in choosing one that is healthy, and the following points should be considered:

Good signs

- ✓ Compact, bushy growth
- ✓ Leaves a healthy colour
- ✓ Roots firm and reach edge of container, if container grown
- ✓ Compost moist
- ✓ No sign of pests or diseases
- ✓ Comprehensive label

Bad signs

- ✗ Weeds growing in container
- ✗ Dry compost
- ✗ Roots matted on the outside of the compost or through the drainage holes
- ✗ Dry and shrivelled roots on bare rooted plants
- ✗ Spindly growth
- ✗ Leaves wilting, yellowing, discoloured or spotted
- ✗ Signs of pest or disease damage
- ✗ Die back on leaves or shoots

Other considerations

- Ensure the plant is suitable for the purpose and environment it is meant for.

- Purchase plants certified to be free of virus where applicable (often on fruit bushes).

- Choose pest and disease resistant cultivars where these are available.

Planting

In **Topic B-13 'Soil - Management (4) Cultivation'** we covered the general cultivation of the soil to get it into a state where planting could take place. In this topic we will consider the actual planting in more detail.

The following general guidelines will apply to most plants planted on an individual basis like trees, shrubs and hardy perennials. Planting of seedlings is covered in **Topic E-3 'Propagation (1) Seed'**.

When to plant

Planting should be done to cause the plant as little disturbance as possible.

- Only plant when the ground conditions are suitable, ie. not frozen, waterlogged or parched.

- Plant bare rooted plants while they are dormant. For most plants this will be in the period October to March. Autumn is preferable because the plant will have a chance to develop some roots before the next growing season.

- Plant evergreen plants in October or March when the soil is likely to be warmer.

- Plant container grown plants at any time of the year.

Ground preparation

Reread **Topic B-13 'Soil - Management (4) Cultivation'**.

The key to getting plants off to a good start is to provide an hospitable environment. We have all probably been guilty of buying a plant in a container, digging a hole a little bigger than the container and dropping the plant in. If the soil is in good condition the plant will grow satisfactorily but if it is not the plant may never realise its potential. I have seen plants dug up after two years where the roots have hardly grown at all.

Plant preparation

- Only plant healthy plants.
- Soak the roots for an hour if they are dry.
- Cut back any long old roots, or any that are damaged.
- Tease out some of the roots of container grown plants.
- In some cases it may be advisable to cut back some of the top growth if the plant is not dormant to reduce the moisture loss by transpiration.

Digging the planting hole

- Dig the hole 2-3 times as wide as the root ball and 1.5 times the depth.

- Dig some well rotted compost or manure into the bottom of the hole if the soil is not already fertile, and also add some to the removed soil. In addition a general fertiliser, such as 'growmore' or 'fish, blood and bone', can be added.

- Ensure the soil removed from the hole is broken down into a good tilth so that it will fill in closely around the roots.
- If the plant is to be staked, drive the stake in just off centre so that the plant roots can be fitted around it. Alternatively the stake can be driven in at an angle of 45⁰ to the trunk so that it is clear of the plant roots. The stake should be on the windward side of the plant.

Planting procedure

- Place the plant in the hole and spread out the roots.
- Ensure the plant will be at the same depth as it was in the nursery or in its container.
- Carefully replace the soil taken from the hole so that it settles closely around the roots. Shaking the plant up and down will help this process.
- Firm the soil down with the foot.
- If staked secure the plant firmly to the stake using a tie with a spacer to avoid chafing.
- Water the plant well.
- Apply a mulch to reduce moisture loss.

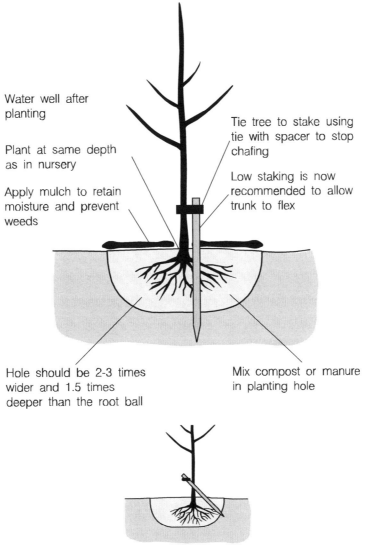

Water well after planting

Plant at same depth as in nursery

Apply mulch to retain moisture and prevent weeds

Tie tree to stake using tie with spacer to stop chafing

Low staking is now recommended to allow trunk to flex

Hole should be 2-3 times wider and 1.5 times deeper than the root ball

Mix compost or manure in planting hole

Alternative staking method avoiding root damage

Aftercare

- For a period after planting ensure the plant is adequately watered. The length of the period will depend on the type of plant.
- Ensure any support ties are slackened as the plant grows.
- Keep an area of 1 m diameter around the plant free of weeds.

Tests have shown that weed control and mulching are very significant in getting plants off to a good start, having more effect in many cases than adding compost, manure or fertilisers.

Heeling in

For a number of reasons it may not be possible to plant new plants in their permanent location. If this is the case they should be heeled in.

This entails digging a shallow trench in a suitable part of the garden and laying the plants in it at an angle so that their roots can be covered. This will ensure that the roots do not dry out which could damage the plant. Plants can be left heeled in for several weeks if necessary.

Propagation (1) Seed

In **Topic A-19 'Types of reproduction'** we looked at how plants reproduce both sexually and vegetatively. The methods discussed occur naturally with no human intervention. It is worth re-reading that topic and **Topics A-20 and A-21**.

In this topic and the next we will see how we can turn Nature's methods to our own advantage to produce new plants under artificial conditions. In this way we can reproduce the number and type of plants we require and almost at any time we require them.

Propagation techniques

We will cover six methods:

> **Seed**
> **Cuttings**
> **Division**
> **Layering**
> **Grafting and budding**
> **Micropropagation**

Propagation by seed will be covered in this topic and the other methods in the next topic.

Only propagation by seed is sexual reproduction; all the others are types of vegetative reproduction.

In any form of propagation hygienic conditions, and sharp and clean tools are important. Emphasise this in any examination question concerned with propagation.

Why use seed

Advantages

1.	Volume	Plants produce large volumes of seeds, several thousands in some cases.
2.	Cost	Seeds are the cheapest way of getting large volumes of plants.
3.	Simplicity	Many plants can easily be raised from seeds and some seeds can be sown directly in the ground.
4.	Choice	A vast choice of seed is available for all kinds of plants.
5.	Reliability	Seed quality is subject to controls under The Seeds Acts and one of the requirements is that a specific germination rate has to be achieved.
6.	Storage	Seeds can be stored for a reasonable length of time and used when required.

Disadvantages

1.	True to type	Some plants will not reproduce the characteristics of their parents. This applies to most cultivars and hybrids.
2.	Sterility	Some plants that have been extensively inbred may lose the capability of producing viable seed.
3.	Time	Some plants may take a long time to reach a reasonable size. Buying young plants may save 2-3 years in reaching maturity.

Collecting seed

The choice and cost of seed is such that most people will purchase their seed from specialised seedsmen.

It is however possible to collect seed from plants in your garden and use them to produce new plants. As you have probably experienced some plants will produce new plants from seed with no encouragement whatsoever. Foxgloves (*Digitalis*) and *Alchemilla mollis* are prolific self-seeders.

There are some points to bear in mind if you are thinking of using your own seed.

- Seed from cultivars or hybrids will not usually come true to type.
- Collect seed when it is ripe - indicated by seed pods or capsules turning brown or fruit changing colour.
- Store pods or capsules in a warm dry place until they split.
- Soak fruits, remove seeds and allow to dry.
- Packet and label the seeds and keep them in a dry, darkened and well ventilated area at a temperature of 1-5^0 C.
- Be aware of any special requirements needed to induce germination.

Trees such as *Sorbus* and *Fagus*, shrubs such as *Camellia* and *Cytisus*, perennials such as *Aquilegia* and *Papaver*, and annuals such as *Calendula* and *Campanula* can all be raised from collected seed.

Buying seed

As a glance through any seed catalogue will show there is a huge number of plants of all different types that can be raised from seed.

The seed for some plants may have been treated in some way to make growing easier.

Primed seed	The seed is treated so that it is close to germination. It is then coated to suspend further germination until it is planted. The result is very quick germination although tests have shown that non-primed seed eventually catches up.
Chitted seed	This is seed that has started to germinate. It is grown on a gel that supplies the moisture and nutrients required and supplied in a sealed plastic container. The seeds should be transferred to trays or modules as soon as possible.

Pelleted seed	Pelleted seed is covered with a coating to make handling and sowing easier. The coating may include a fungicide and nutrients.
	Pelleted seeds need the compost or soil around them to be kept moist if they are to germinate successfully.
Tapes and gels	Tapes are soluble strips with the seeds embedded in them at the correct sowing distance.
	Gels are paste like substances containing the seeds which are squeezed into the drills (fluid sowing)

Most specially prepared seed will be F_1 hybrids which are the first generation offspring of pure bred parents. F_1 seed is more expensive as it has to be produced under controlled conditions, but it has the advantage that all plants grown from the seed will be the same.

A comparatively recent development by the seed companies is the sale of seedlings or plugs. These are obviously more expensive but some of the work of growing has already been carried out. They are ideal if you require a reasonable quantity but have no facilities for growing them from seed. Plants offered in this way are usually F_1 hybrids.

Seedlings	These are supplied at a stage ready to be pricked out. They are supplied in quantities of around 100-250.
Plugs	These are larger than seedlings and come rooted individually in their own 'plug' of compost. They are supplied in quantities of around 20-50.

Requirements for germination

The following table is a copy of that already covered in **Topic A-20 'Sexual reproduction'.**

Water	Seeds hold very little water - about 5% compared to 80-90% in a mature plant. It is one of the reasons that seeds can stay dormant for a long time.
Temperature	The requirements of individual seeds will vary within an overall range of 5-35° C. In our climate 10-20° C is typical.
	Heat will speed up the process which is why we use greenhouses and propagators to assist germination.
Oxygen	A supply of oxygen is necessary for respiration.
Food	A supply of food is necessary to fuel the process until the plant is able to photosynthesise. The food is stored in the seed in the cotyledons or the endosperm.
	If seeds are planted too deep they can die by exhausting their food supply before reaching the point at which they can photosynthesise.
Light	Some seeds require light to germinate.
Time	Some seeds have chemical inhibitors which need to diminish before germination is possible.

Techniques and procedures

Inducing germination

Some seeds are difficult to germinate either because of their tough coat, or because of chemical inhibitors, or because they must be exposed to certain temperatures before germination will occur.

A number of techniques have been developed to overcome these difficulties.

Soaking	Soaking in warm water for 12-24 hours will soften the seed coat and help it to absorb water. This treatment may also remove any chemical inhibitors. The seeds should be planted immediately after soaking.
Scarification	The purpose of this is to weaken the seed coat and allow water to enter. Large seeds such as those of peas or beans (Legume family) may be nicked with a sharp knife. Smaller seeds can be rubbed with an abrasive substance.
Stratification	The purpose of this is to expose the seed to a period of cold such as it would encounter under natural conditions. The most common example is with annuals that produce seed in late summer but which will not germinate until the following spring. Place the seeds in a 50:50 mixture of moist sand and peat, and refrigerate them at a temperature of $1-5^0$ C for 4-12 weeks. Although in our climate exposure to a period of cold is the stratification usually required, some seed requires exposure to a period of high heat. Seed purchased from a seed company will have had this treatment if necessary.
Heat	Most seeds will germinate better with some heat . An ideal temperature for many seeds is $18-21^0$ C. Constant temperature can be provided by using a propagator. These come in all shapes and sizes from ones the size of a seed tray that that can be placed on a windowsill to sophisticated units which control the total environment.

Sowing under cover

This includes sowing in a greenhouse, propagator or in the home.

Greenhouse plants, house plants, tender vegetables and half hardy annuals are plants that need to be sown under cover.

Sowing medium

The best medium is a specially prepared soilless compost. Traditionally these composts have been based on peat but, because of the concern over the depletion of peat, there are now alternatives such as coir which is made from coconut fibres. Under no circumstances use garden soil.

- Fill a seed tray to the top with the compost.

- Firm the compost but do not compress it. Remember there has to be pores for the movement of air and water. The firming is best done with a piece of wood cut to the size of the tray.

- Wet the compost by watering with a fine rose or placing the tray in water. Allow to drain before sowing.

- A fungicide such as Cheshunt Compound may be added to the compost to prevent 'damping off' of the seedlings. This is a fungal infection often caused by sowing the seed too close or keeping the compost too wet.

It is possible to sow seed in individual containers called **modules.** These come in a variety of forms such as inserts to seed trays, polystyrene blocks, compost blocks, or small pots. The advantage of modules is that the plants suffer less disturbance on being transplanted and may reduce the chance of diseases.

Sowing the seed

- Scatter the seed thinly on the surface of the compost. It is better if the seeds do not touch each other. Very small seeds can be mixed with fine sand to get an even distribution.

- Unless the seeds are very small, cover them lightly with compost to a depth of twice the diameter of the seed.

- Firm down the compost again.

- Cover the tray with a sheet of glass and paper and place in a temperature of 18-21^0 C.

Aftercare

- Wipe the glass each day to remove condensation.

- Do not allow the compost to dry out.

- When the seedlings emerge, remove the paper and glass, and move the tray to where it can get the maximum light but not be in direct sunlight.

Pricking out

- When the seedlings have developed their first true leaves prick them out into trays or pots of potting compost.

- Handle the seedlings by their seed leaves if present, or their true leaves if not, but not by the stems.

- Ease them out trying not to damage the roots and place them in a hole made in the potting compost. Place them about 5 cm apart.

- Firm the compost around the seedling.

Hardening off

- If the plants are to go outside, such as half hardy annuals, they need to be gradually exposed to the conditions outside. This enables them to form a stronger epidermis and cuticle and causes changes to the stomata.

- The best way is to move them to a closed cold frame for a few days, followed by an open cold frame, followed by standing them outside during daylight when there is no risk of frost.

- The hardening off should take about 2 weeks after which the plants can be planted outside if the risk of frost has passed.

Techniques and procedures

Planting out

- Prepare the ground to receive the plants. A good tilth is required and the soil should be moist.
- If a support structure is required, as with sweet peas or runner beans, put this in place before transplanting.
- Water the plants before transplanting them.
- Do not plant out in the heat of the sun. The best time is the evening.
- Dig a hole or furrow and place the plants in them. Hold the plants by their leaves. Do not leave the plants with their roots exposed as they will quickly dry out.
- Firm the soil around the plants.
- A mulch can be applied to retain moisture and suppress weeds.

Sowing outside

Many flowers and vegetables can be sown directly outside.

Hardy annuals fall into this category and will be sown in March/April when the soil has started to warm up. If the weather is cold or wet delay the sowing until it improves. Biennials and perennials will be sown later in May/June.

Sowing medium

Seeds sown outside can either be sown directly in their final growing position or they may be sown in seedbeds and later transplanted to their final position. The deciding factors include the size of the seed or the difficulty of transplanting. Peas and beans can be sown in their final positions, and so should root crops like carrots and parsnips that do not transplant easily.

Wherever they are planted it is important to provide conditions as hospitable as possible to the seed.

Preparation of seedbed

A good tilth is essential with a crumb structure of about 0.5-3 mm.

Assuming the basic ground preparation has been done then:

- Rake the bed to break up the soil.
- Remove any stones.
- Firm the soil with the back of the rake. Firming the soil by treading is now not in favour as it may damage the natural structure.
- Repeat the above steps working in opposite directions until the required tilth is achieved.
- It should not be necessary to apply a fertiliser as this may cause too rapid growth. However if it is known that the soil is lacking in nutrients a general fertiliser like Growmore or 'fish, blood and bone' can be applied at a rate of 25-50 g/sq m.
- Water the bed if it is dry and allow to drain before sowing.

Because disturbing the soil is likely to produce a flush of weeds as the seeds are brought to the surface, a useful technique is to prepare the seedbed 3-4 weeks in advance of planting it. This will let the weeds germinate and they can then be hoed or killed with a contact herbicide like paraquat. This is called the **stale seedbed** technique.

Sowing the seed

The seed can be sown in drills which are shallow furrows, or it can be scattered (broadcast) over the sowing area.

- Make drills if required with the edge of a hoe or the handle of a rake or other implement. The depth will depend on the seed being sown but is likely to be about 0.5-1.5 cm.
- Sprinkle the seed thinly in the drill.
- Draw the soil over the seed with the back of a rake.

Aftercare

- Ensure the soil is kept moist.
- When the seedlings emerge and develop their first leaves thin them out to about 10 cm apart.
- If sown in a seedbed transplant to final positions in autumn or when they have 5-6 leaves depending on the type of plant.
- Carry out a final thinning to 15-20 cm depending on the type of plant.

Propagation (2) Vegetative

In the previous topic we looked at propagation by seed. In this topic we will look at propagation by vegetative means. The methods covered will be:

Cuttings
Division
Layering
Grafting and budding
Micropropagation

Why use vegetative propagation

Advantages

1.	True to type	Plants are clones. In some cases this is the only way to preserve the characteristics of cultivars and hybrids.
2.	Uniformity	All clones will have the same characteristics of their parent and siblings
3.	Growth	Some plants will grow better on the rootstock of another plant
4.	Sterility	Intensive breeding has made some plants sterile so that this is the only way they can be propagated.
5.	Natural	Many plants naturally reproduce vegetatively eg. bulbs.

Disadvantages

1.	Volume	Higher volumes are easier with seed.
2.	Time	Each plant has to be individually propagated.
3.	Cost	The first two disadvantages will increase the cost.
4.	Adaptation	Because the new plants are clones there is not the same possibility of producing new varieties, or plants that may be better adapted to changing conditions.

Cuttings

A huge number of plants can be raised from cuttings, including trees, shrubs, conifers, alpines, greenhouse and indoor plants. Some examples will be given of plants that can be raised by each type of cutting but it should be remembered that these are only a few of the possible plants.

Cuttings are the most common method of vegetative propagation. They can be taken from different parts of the plant and we will cover:

> **Stem cuttings**
> **Root cuttings**
> **Leaf cuttings**

Stem cuttings

Softwood cuttings

These cuttings are taken from young current year's growth. Plants that can be propagated by softwood cuttings include trees such as *Betula* and *Acer*, shrubs such as *Calluna* and *Lavatera*, and perennials such as *Diascia* and *Osteospermum*.

- As a guide take softwood cuttings between April and June.

- Chose a young sideshoot and cut it just below a node about 5-10 cm from the tip. A few plants that do not produce sideshoots, like delphiniums and lupins can use new shoots from the base (basal cuttings).

- Ensure the cuttings do not dry out. If necessary place in a sealed polythene bag.

- Remove the bottom leaves so that the lower third of the cutting is free of foliage.

- Immerse the cutting in a fungicide solution to avoid fungal infections.

- Dip the base of the cutting in rooting powder.

- Insert in a pot containing a 50:50 mixture of sand and peat, or a proprietary cutting compost. Several cuttings can be placed around the perimeter of a pot.

- An ideal rooting temperature is $18\text{-}21^0$ C. Either place the cuttings in a greenhouse or propagator, or enclose them in a polythene bag and keep them on a warm windowsill.

- Do not allow the compost to dry out.

- Successful rooting will be indicated by growth at the tips. The cuttings can then be carefully removed and potted individually into 10 cm pots filled with potting compost.

- The plants should be hardened off before being planted out.

Semi-ripe cuttings

These cuttings are taken from current year's growth that has started to ripen. That is when the base of the shoot has started to turn brown and woody.

Examples of plants that can be propagated by semi-ripe cuttings are *Berberis, Erica, Potentilla, Juniper, Abutilon* and *Fuchsia*.

- As a guide take semi-ripe cuttings between June and August.

- Choose a current year's shoot that is soft at the tip but beginning to firm up at the base. Cut just below a node about 10-15 cm from the tip. Some plants will root better if the shoot is pulled off with a little bit of woody tissue (called a heel) attached.

- Immerse the cutting in a fungicide solution to avoid fungal infections.

- Dip the base of the cutting in rooting powder.

- Semi-ripe cuttings do not require so much heat as softwood ones and they can be placed in a cool greenhouse or frame.

- Other care is the same as for softwood cuttings.

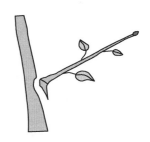

Hardwood cuttings

These cuttings are taken from current year's growth that has turned woody. This means that they are taken at the end of the growing season when the plant is dormant.

Examples of plants that can be propagated in this way are *Berberis, Buddleia, Deutzia, Forsythia,* gooseberries, and red and white currants. Many broad-leaved evergreens, such as *Camellia, Ceanothus* and *Eleagnus,* are also suited to hardwood cuttings.

- As a guide take hardwood cuttings between September and November.

- Choose a stem about the thickness of a pencil.

- Cut a length of stem just above and below a bud and 15-30 cm long. Several cuttings may be taken from the same stem.

- Dip the base of the cutting in rooting powder.

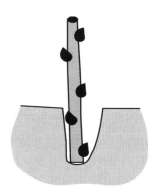

- They can be grown in a cold frame or in the open ground. If in the open choose a sheltered, sunny and well drained position.

- Make a narrow trench about 15-20 cm deep. If the soil is badly drained place some coarse sand in the bottom.

- Insert the cuttings upright in the trench to about half their length and 10-15 cm apart. Firm the soil around them.

- The cuttings should be fully rooted by the following autumn.

- Hardwood cuttings can also be rooted in pots, and if some bottom heat is applied they may be ready for planting out in the following spring.

Root cuttings

Many plants can be propagated from root cuttings including shrubs like *Aralia elata* and *Rhus typhina*, and herbaceous plants like *Papaver orientalis* and *Phlox paniculata.*

- As a guide take root cuttings between September to November.

- Herbaceous plants can be lifted to take the cuttings but shrubs will require the roots to be exposed in situ.

- Select young roots close to the crown of the plant and about the thickness of a pencil.

- Cut a length about 5 cm long. Make a straight cut at the top and a diagonal one at the bottom so that top and bottom can be distinguished.

- Immerse the cutting in a fungicide solution to avoid fungal infections.
- Insert the cuttings in a pot of compost so that the top of the cutting is level with the top of the compost and cover with 0.5 cm layer of compost.
- Some roots which are very fine such as phlox should be laid on the top of the compost in seed trays and lightly covered.
- Place the cuttings in a cold greenhouse or frame.
- Ensure the compost is kept moist.
- Rooting should have taken place by the following spring when they can be carefully lifted and potted on.

Leaf cuttings

Many greenhouse or indoor plants can be propagated from leaves, using either the whole leaf and petiole, the leaf blade or sections from the blade.

Leaf plus petiole

Plants that can be propagated in this way include *Saintpaulia* and *Peperomia*.

- Cut mature leaves complete with petiole.
- Dip petiole in rooting powder.
- Insert in 50:50 peat and sand mixture or in cutting compost so that petiole is buried.
- Place in propagator at temperature of 18-21⁰ C or enclose in a clear polythene bag and place on a warm windowsill.
- When new plants appear at the base of the leaf lift carefully and pot on.

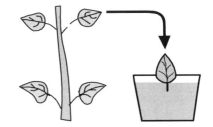

Leaf blade

Plants that can be propagated in this way include *Begonia rex* and *B. masoniana*.

- Cut halfway through the main veins on the reverse of the leaf.
- Place the leaf flat on the surface of the compost with the cut side underneath.
- Place pebbles or small stones on the surface of the leaf to keep it in contact with the compost.
- Place in propagator at temperature of 18-21⁰ C or enclose in a clear polythene bag and place on a warm windowsill.
- New plants will form at the cuts.

Sections of leaf

This method can be used for long leaved plants like *Sanseveria* and *Streptocarpus*.

- Cut the leaves into 5 cm sections.
- Dip bottom end in rooting powder.
- Insert vertically the right way up to half their length.
- Place in propagator at temperature of 18-21⁰ C or enclose in a clear polythene bag and place on a warm windowsill.

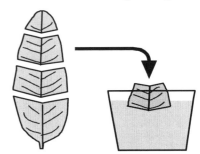

- New plants will form from the base.

Division

Division is the easiest method of propagation. It literally entails dividing the plant into two or more parts.

It can be carried out most readily with clump forming or carpeting plants. This includes alpines such as *Aubrieta* and *Arabis*, and hardy perennials such as *Geranium, Hemerocallis, Aster* and *Doronicum*.

Plants that grow from rhizomes such as irises can be divided and so can some shrubs that spread by suckers such as *Kerria* and *Cornus alba*.

Most perennials need dividing every 3-5 years to retain their vigour.

- Divide in late autumn or early spring when the soil is warm. Spring is probably better, but early flowering plants like *Doronicum* and *Pulmonaria* can be done in autumn or after flowering.
- Lift the plant taking care not to damage the roots and gently shake off the soil.
- Divide the plant with a knife, spade or two forks placed back to back.
- For replanting, select parts of the plant from the edge of the old plant and which have both buds and roots.
- If replanting in the same area add compost or a general fertiliser to the soil.
- Plant new plants as soon as possible to prevent any drying out.

Layering

Layering is a simple method that works well with many woody shrubs and is more successful than cuttings for some shrubs like *Rhododendron, Magnolia, Hamamellis* and *Pieris*.

The principle of layering is to grow a new plant while it is still attached to its parent.

Layering is best carried out between late spring and autumn.

Simple layering

- Use when a stem is flexible enough to be bent to the ground.
- Choose a current or previous year stem.
- Make a diagonal cut about 5 cm long through a node. Rooting powder can be applied to the cut.
- At the point where the node touches the ground dig the soil to create a good tilth, adding compost if the soil is poor.
- Bury the stem 10 cm deep at the node and peg down to keep secure.
- Tie the end of the stem to a support.
- A good root system should be developed in 12-18 months when the plant can be severed from its parent.

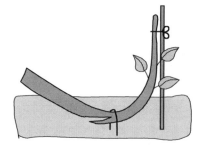

Variations on simple layering

1.   **Serpentine layering**

     This entails pegging the stem down at several nodes to produce more than one new plant. It can be used with plants that produce long flexible stems like *Clematis, Lonicera and Wisteria.*

2.   **Tip layering**

     This entails burying the tip of the plant and is used where this is the natural method of the plant which is the case with the blackberry family.

3.   **Air layering**

     This is based on the principle that if the stem cannot come to the soil then the soil must be taken to the stem. It can be used where the stems are too rigid to bend to the ground.

     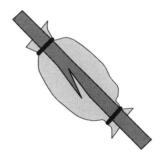

     - Cut a diagonal upwards slit in a young stem.
     - Place some rooting powder on the cut end.
     - Place moist sphagnum moss in the wound and around each end of the stem to an overall length of about 15 cm.
     - Cover the moss with polythene and tape the ends to make it waterproof.
     - A good root system should be developed in 12-18 months.

     Rhododendron and *Magnolia* can be air layered and so can some indoor plants like *Ficus* and *Philodendron.*

Grafting and budding

With grafting and budding part of one plant containing one or more buds is grown on the root and stem of another plant.

The first plant is called the **scion** and the second is called the **rootstock.**

There are four reasons for grafting on to a rootstock:

1.   **For some plants it is the most successful method.**

2.   **Some plants do not grow well on their own roots.**

3.   **Some rootstocks are more resistant to pests and diseases, or will grow better in poor conditions, than the scion.**

4.   **Different rootstocks can be used to control the size of the plant. This is done extensively with fruit trees.**

The rootstocks need to have a close relationship to the scion. Cultivars are usually grown on the species of the same plant. For example *Acer platanoides* 'Crimson King' will be grown on an *Acer platanoides* rootstock. The rootstocks will normally be 1-2 years old.

A sharp flat bladed knife is essential and special grafting knives can be purchased.

Growing plants in this way can be a lengthy process. A tree may take four years to reach a final planting size.

Techniques and procedures

Grafting methods

There are many different grafting methods. Here we will cover three of the more common.

Grafting is usually done in late winter or early spring. It is sometimes called bench grafting as it can be done inside on a work surface.

For any grafting to be successful it is necessary for the cambium tissue on scion and rootstock to come into contact, since it is from this tissue that a junction is formed. A lot of grafting cuts are diagonal so that more cambium tissue can be exposed.

Side veneer graft

This is one of the simplest grafts to do. It can be used for trees such as *Acer* and *Betula*, and shrubs such as *Camellia* and *Magnolia*.

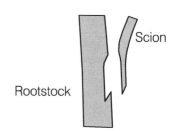

- Choose the scion material from healthy young shoots. Try to match the thickness to the thickness of the rootstock. Trim the shoot to 15-20 cm, cutting above and below a node.

- Cut the scion with a straight cut about 2-5 cm long and one third through the diameter with a backwards slanting cut at the the end.

- Cut the rootstock to match, about 5-10 cm above the soil level.

- Place the scion and rootstock together ensuring as much cambium as possible is in contact.

- Bind and tie the graft. Traditionally this has been done with raffia and sealed with wax, but now it is more usual to use plastic tape to bind and rubber strips to secure.

- Regularly examine the binding and remove when the graft appears to be taken. This time will vary according to the plant and can be up to 3 months.

Whip and tongue graft

This graft can be used for trees such as *Fraxinus* and *Gleditsia* and is commonly used for fruit trees.

- See the diagram for how the wood is cut.
- Other things are as for a side veneer graft.

Apical wedge graft

This graft can be used for trees such as *Catalpa* and *Fagus* and shrubs such as *Daphne* and *Syringa*.

- See the diagram for how the wood is cut.
- Other things are as for a side veneer graft.

Budding methods

The principles of budding are similar to those of grafting but the scion only consists of one bud.

Unlike grafting it is mainly done outside in summer with the rootstocks actually growing. The buds are taken from current year's growth.

Budding is the normal way of propagating roses.

T-budding

- Cut the bud with a sliver of the stem from the scion.
- Cut a shallow T in the bark of the rootstock about 5 cm from the soil surface.
- Ease the bark up to expose the cambium tissue.
- Slip the scion bud under the bark
- Secure the bud in place with a strip of rubber.

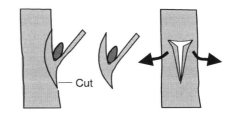

Chip budding

Similar to T-budding but a chip of wood is removed from the rootstock to allow the bud to be bound to it.

Micropropagation

Micropropagation entails taking a very small part of an existing plant and growing it under very carefully controlled conditions to produce a large number of new plants. Micropropagation is used successfully for a wide range of plants including houseplants, cut flowers, ornamental shrubs and herbaceous perennials. The process is also known as **tissue culture**.

The original plant is called the **parent** or **stock** plant and the part taken to propagate from is called the **explant.** The explant can vary; it can be from the apical meristem, from an axillary bud, or from a group of general purpose cells.

Growth has to be carried out under laboratory conditions, and carefully controlled, to ensure there is no contamination of the new plants. The plants are grown in what is called a **culture medium** which must supply all the requirements of the plant, which includes the water and all nutrients. The culture medium will also include hormones to control the growth process.

Advantages of micropropagation	Disadvantages of micropropagation
Large numbers of plants can be raised very quickly.	Laboratory type facilities are required.
Stocks of new cultivars can be built up and made available to the public earlier.	Very costly to set up.
	High skill level required.
Diseases, particularly viruses, can be eliminated.	Possibility of introducing new problems eg. mutations and diseases.
Propagation can take place all year round.	

The cost per plant produced will be the deciding factor in commercial situations this is likely to swing in favour of micropropagation when the required volumes are high.

The process of micropropagation can be divided into four stages:

1. Establishment The stock plant is chosen and the explant taken from it. The explant is treated in a number of ways to ensure it is free of microorganisms or diseases, and is then placed in its culture medium in an aseptic (clean) environment.	**2. Multiplication** The explant is grown to produce new plants. The method of doing this will vary according to the explant material. It could entail taking parts of the explant and growing these in the same way as the original explant material.
3. Pre-transplant This stage gets the plant ready for transplanting and may entail using hormones to encourage the development of roots	**4. Transplant** The plant has to be weaned out of its protected environment and gradually acclimatised to a normal environment. During this stage the plants will be put into a normal rooting medium such as peat.

Pruning

There are complete books written about pruning that detail how to prune any plant you are ever likely to come across.

Such a detailed coverage is beyond the scope of this book. What we will cover in this topic are the principles behind pruning, and some of the practices that are common across many plants. In this way you should be able to determine the requirements for many plants without having to have a detailed knowledge of them.

More detailed information will given in some of the topics dealing with particular types of plant.

It should be borne in mind that many plants will require little or no pruning. In particular trees, conifers and evergreen shrubs should require minimum pruning.

Some new terms

In connection with pruning trees there are some terms that need to be understood.

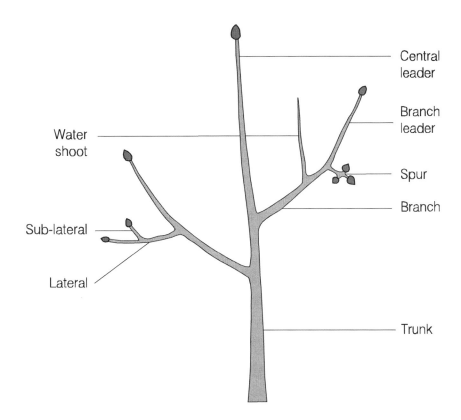

- **Trunk**

  The main stem from the ground up to the first branches.

- **Branch**

  A major stem forming part of the framework of the tree. A distinction is sometimes made between primary branches, which originate from the trunk, and secondary branches, which originate from another branch.

- **Leader**

  The leading shoot of a branch. The central leader is the leader of the dominant branch.

- **Lateral**

  A side-shoot from a branch.

- **Sub-lateral**

  A side-shoot from a lateral.

- **Spur**

  A short branch bearing fruit buds.

- **Water shoot**

  A soft unproductive shoot often caused by hard pruning.

Reasons for pruning

Pruning entails removing part of the growing plant. The part removed can be a shoot, a branch or a root. There are three main reasons for pruning:

1. **To maintain the health of the plant**

2. **To control the shape or size**

3. **To encourage flowers and fruit**

Pruning for health

A healthy plant is one containing no damaged parts, and in which all of the plant has access to the requirements for good growth like light and air.

- **Remove dead, diseased or damaged parts to prevent the spread to healthy parts of the plant.**

- **Remove crossing branches to avoid damage from rubbing.**

- **Remove congested branches to allow light and air into the plant. For many trees and shrubs a goblet shaped structure with an open centre is the best shape.**

- **Remove weak or worn out stems.**

Pruning for shape or size

It is often desirable to train a plant to a particular shape or to restrict it to a particular size. Hedges or topiary are extreme examples of this requirement. However, attempts to grow plants out of their natural size and shape are not always easy or successful.

Pruning will often cause more vigorous growth to occur, so that trying to restrict size by pruning may have the opposite effect. Although it may be difficult to appreciate, if a plant is growing strongly on one side and weakly on another, it is better to prune the weaker side in an attempt to make the growth more balanced.

Restricting the growth of a plant may be easier by **root pruning** (see later in this topic) or **bark ringing**.

Bark ringing entails removing a strip of bark about 1 cm wide from the trunk of the tree. Doing this restricts the movement of food from the leaves to the roots and reduces the vigour of the tree. Bark ring in late spring and cover the area with adhesive tape to avoid infections.

Pruning for flowers or fruit.

Left to grow naturally plants will often produce large quantities of small sized flowers or fruit. In many cases this is not what is required. Whether it is large flowers for decoration or showing, or large fruit and vegetables for eating, increased size may be a strong requirement.

This can be achieved by correct pruning which usually entails restricting the number of flowers and fruits. Techniques like disbudding, fruit thinning and dead heading are based on this principle.

The effect of pruning

Encourage axillary bud development

In the section on the structure of plants we covered a feature called apical dominance. This is where the apical bud produces a hormone called auxin which has the effect of inhibiting the development of axillary buds below it.

A lot of pruning entails cutting back the growing tips of plants and the reason is to remove the effect of apical dominance and allow the axillary buds to develop.

- **To make plants bushy remove growing tips**

Concentrate growth over smaller area

A large tree or shrub that has not been subject to regular pruning will have developed a mass of branches, stems, shoots and buds.

The energy of the plant will go into growth and development of these with the result that it is thinly spread.

Removing some of the old growth will allow the energy of the plant to be concentrated over a smaller area, which will provide stronger growth in that area.

There are many plants that benefit from the regular removal of older growth. Many fruit trees are pruned in this way. Roses are often pruned to within a few inches of the ground so that the new growth consists of a small number of stems and buds and therefore produces larger flowers.

- **To get a large number of small flowers prune lightly or not at all**
- **To get a small number of large flowers prune hard**

Change root/stem balance

Under natural conditions the roots and the above ground organs grow in balance with each other, the roots supplying the rest of the plant with water and nutrients and the leaves supplying the rest of the plant with food in the form of carbohydrates.

Any curtailment of the roots or the above ground growth will have an effect on the overall plant and this is exploited in a number of ways:

Removal of branches and stems bearing leaves reduces the production of carbohydrates and will slow down the growth of the plant. Trained fruit trees are often pruned in summer to maintain them at a manageable size.

Root pruning reduces the supply of water and nutrients and will also slow down the growth of the plant.

- **Prune above ground in summer to reduce growth.**
- **Prune roots in winter to reduce growth.**

Types of pruning

Formative pruning

This is the pruning done in the early years of a plant's life to provide a good framework of branches.

It is most commonly required for trees, particularly fruit trees, but may also be required for shrubs. It may include:

- **Selecting main branches at the right height and angle of growth**
- **Removing lateral growth to provide a clear trunk**
- **Removing leaders to encourage a branching pattern**
- **Tying in growth to a framework if the plant is to be trained to a specific shape such as a fan or espalier**

When trees are purchased the formative pruning may have already been partly or completely carried out.

Pruning back to a bud or lateral (Also called heading back)

This entails cutting back a leader or a lateral to a good bud to encourage the growth of new shoots and make the plant more bushy.

The pruning may be **light**, where only a small part of the shoot is removed, or **hard**, where a significant part is removed. Unfortunately there is no precise definition of **light** and **hard** and it can therefore be very subjective.

In general hard pruning will result in more vigorous new growth than light pruning.

This type of pruning is suitable for a number of deciduous shrubs including *Deutzia, Forsythia, Syringa* and *Weigela*.

Hard pruning

Light pruning

Pruning out a complete shoot or branch (Also called thinning)

This is a more drastic method of pruning. It can be done to remove congestion and make a more open plant, or to remove old and worn out branches, or to make room for new growth.

Many plants benefit from having a proportion of the older growth, typically 1/3 or

1/4, removed each year to allow new growth to take its place. This is called **renewal pruning**.

Spur pruning

Many fruit trees and some shrubs such as *Wisteria* flower on very short stems known as spurs.

Spur pruning entails maintaining a permanent branch framework but cutting back lateral and sub-lateral growth to 2-4 buds.

Spur pruning

Coppicing

This is the cutting back of a tree or shrub to its base. Cut back to within a few inches of the base in early spring.

This will result in new strong shoots growing from the base. Originally this was done to provide a continuous supply of firewood, or young growth suitable for fencing or basket weaving. Now it is probably only done to restrict size or to create a special effect.

Coppicing

It is quite common to do this with shrubs where the decorative effect of the shrub is in the colour of its new stems. Shrubs suitable for this treatment include:

> *Cornus alba*
> *Salix alba*
> *Hydrangea paniculata*

Pollarding

This is similar to coppicing but the plant is cut back to its main trunk or stem or to a framework of short branches.

Pollarding is sometimes seen on street plantings of trees.

Not all trees and shrubs are suitable but some that are include:

> *Corylus avellana*
> *Salix acutifolia*
> *Eucalyptus gunnii*

Pollarding

Pinching out

This is the removal of the growing tip of smaller plants by using the thumb and forefinger. Like other pruning, removal of the growing tip will encourage bushier growth.

This is commonly done for carnations, pinks and sweet peas and may also be done for a number of annuals and indoor plants.

In addition to giving bushier growth it can also be used to control the time of flowering.

This technique is also known as **stopping**.

Disbudding

This is the removal of some buds so that the remaining ones can develop more strongly.

It is often done to produce large flowers for showing as with dahlias and roses.

Dead-heading

This is the removal of flowers as they begin to fade. It prevents the energy of the plant being spent in the production of seeds and encourages new flowering growth.

Once a plant has produced its seed it considers its job is done and little further growth takes place.

Most herbaceous and annual plants will benefit from dead-heading and also some shrubs like roses and lilac.

Root pruning

Root pruning can be used to reduce the vigour and therefore the size of a plant. It can be used with fruit trees, ornamental trees and shrubs

- **Dig a trench around the plant at a radius of 1-1.5 m to expose the roots and sever some of the larger, old roots.**
- **This will reduce the uptake of water and nutrients.**
- **Root prune during the dormant season.**

When to prune

Winter pruning

As a general rule it it is better to prune a plant when it is dormant.

- **It is less of a shock to the plant when it is not actively growing**
- **The plants are less likely to bleed (lose sap)**
- **With deciduous plants the branch structure can be more clearly seen**

Summer pruning

Summer pruning can be done if it is required to reduce the vigour of a plant. This is achieved because the loss of leaves will reduce the supply of food.

Summer pruning of trained fruit trees like cordons and espaliers is the recommended method.

Timing for flowering shrubs

This will depend on whether the shrub flowers on the current year's growth or on previous year's growth. If you get no flowers you may have pruned at the wrong time!

- **Prune shrubs that flower on the previous year's growth after they have flowered.** This then gives them time to make new growth for flowering in the following year. These shrubs are mainly the early flowering ones like *Forsythia, Chaenomeles, Deutzia* and *Ribes.*
- **Prune shrubs that flower on the current year's growth during late winter or**

early spring. They then have time to grow and flower in the same year. These shrubs are mainly the later flowering ones like *Caryopteris*, *Buddleia* and *Spiraea*.

How to prune

All cuts should be done with sharp tools to ensure a clean cut.

Pruning back to a bud

● If the buds are opposite, cut straight across the stem about 0.5 cm above the buds.

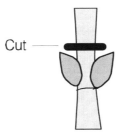

● If the buds are alternate, choose a bud that is pointing in the required direction and cut at an angle pointing in the same direction as the bud and about 0.5 cm above it.

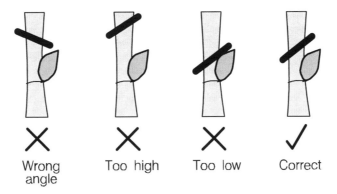

Pruning out a branch

● For a large branch, cut it back in sections to reduce the chance of a split where it joins the trunk or other branch. It may be easier to make a partial cut from the underside of the branch and then make a cut from the top to join up with it.

● Make the final cut just outside the collar that forms where the branch joins the trunk. This can be distinguished by a swelling at the junction.

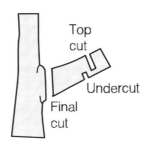

Aftercare

- There is some disagreement about whether the wounds created by heavy pruning should be painted with a fungicidal paint such as Arbrex. This has been done in the past to prevent diseases entering through the wound, but there is some doubt whether this is effective and it may even be harmful.

- A dressing of a general fertiliser such as Growmore will help the plant to grow strongly following the pruning.

Major plant groups

Trees and conifers	see Topic G-2
Shrubs	see Topic G-3
Hedges	see Topic G-4
Roses	see Topic G-5
Climbers	see Topic G-6

Pruning equipment

Secateurs	Use for cuts up to 1 cm diameter.
Loppers	These are like secateurs with long handles.
	They can be used to reach higher parts of the plant and provide increased leverage.
	Use for cuts up to 2 cm diameter.
Pruning saws	A <u>bow saw</u> can be used for thick branches but may be difficult to get in the right position.
	A <u>Grecian saw</u> that has a curved blade which can be used in confined spaces and which cuts on the pull stroke makes it easy to use.

Watering

As we have previously seen water is essential for plants to grow and survive. Re-read **Topic B-9 'Soil water'**.

To the extent that water is not available naturally through rainfall it must be supplied by the grower. It should be appreciated that, in the period from April to September, the water lost by evaporation and transpiration will on average exceed the water supplied by rainfall, and some watering over this period is bound to be necessary.

In this topic we will look at ways of supplying and conserving water in the context of a domestic garden. In a commercial situation the principles will be the same but the need for a properly controlled and monitored system is essential, and the equipment will be more sophisticated. However the combination of dry summers and more expensive water may lead to better controlled systems in the garden.

Watering of plants grown under cover will be dealt with in Topic **E-10 'Greenhouse gardening'**.

Water requirements

The exact requirement will depend on the plants being grown. Large leaved plants will in general require more water than small leaved ones, and shallow rooting plants will require more than deep rooted ones.

For commercial growers tables are available which give the requirement for different crops.

In the garden a rough guide would be that in summer 25 litres per square metre per week is required. This is equivalent to about 3 cm of rainfall.

Plants at risk

Not all plants will have the same need for water. Trees and shrubs that have been established for some time will have extensive and deep root systems that should enable them to survive periods of drought.

The type of plants that are at risk include:

> Newly planted plants of all types, particularly bedding plants and vegetables
> Plants grown in full sun
> Plants growing close to walls
> Plants grown in sandy soils
> Plants grown in containers
> Shallow rooted plants eg. Rhododendrons

When to water

It is much better to water before there are any visible signs of drought.

- Dig down 10-15 cm to see if the soil is moist, or,
- Water after so many days without rain. This may be 1-2 days for seedlings up to 7-10 days for lawns , trees and shrubs.

- Water at sensitive times in the growth cycle:
  - → Seedling stage
  - → Transplanting
  - → When flowering and fruiting
- Water in the early morning or evening when there will be less loss by evaporation.
- Over-watering can also cause some problems:
  - → Leaching of nutrients
  - → Excessive leaf growth
  - → Reduced flavour in some vegetables
  - → Split fruit, eg. tomatoes

How to water

1. **Blanket watering**

   An area is covered evenly by using a sprinkler. It is better to have a fine spray as heavy droplets can compact the surface of the soil.

   Where there are a number of plants in a small area which all require watering this is the easiest method. It is the most suitable method for lawns and vegetable gardens.

2. **Spot watering**

   Water is applied individually to the plants requiring it. It is the most suitable method for larger plants such as trees and shrubs.

   It is more economical than blanket watering although some of the water may be lost before it can reach the plant roots.

   Water is absorbed quite slowly by the soil and the effect of spot watering can be enhanced by making a shallow depression around the stem that will hold the water, or sinking a tube from the surface of the soil to the area of the roots and watering down the tube.

Whichever method is used sufficient water must be applied to wet the soil to the required depth. With blanket watering a container can be placed on the ground to measure the depth of water applied.

Conserving water

Collect rainwater	Devices are available to divert water from drainpipes into water butts
Dig in organic matter	Organic matter in the soil acts like a sponge and holds the water instead of it draining away.
Mulch the soil	A mulch applied to the surface of the soil will reduce moisture loss by evaporation.
Remove weeds	Weeds growing close to the plant will rob it of moisture.
Do not cultivate deeply	Cultivation can bring moisture to the surface where it will evaporate.

Equipment

There are a wide range of watering cans and sprinklers available. Sprinkler systems can be embedded in lawns and pop up when the system is activated.

Less usual equipment includes:

Seep hoses	Hoses that are porous or have holes in them to allow the water to seep out.
	They can be used either on or below the surface of the soil.
	Suitable for the vegetable garden.
Drip feed systems	These are basically hoses that can have small tubes attached which release the water slowly.
	They are common in glasshouses.
Timers and computers	These are more sophisticated devices that allow watering to be done at set times or under certain conditions.

Planning for long term shortages

There is concern that global warming will produce long term changes in our climate and that one result may be regular periods of drought. At the time of writing this in 2006 there are widespread water shortages in the south of England resulting in restrictions and hosepipe bans. Many water authorities are considering the introduction of drought orders which impose even stiffer restrictions.

In these circumstances our approach may need to be:

SAVE MORE - USE LESS

Save more

As much rainfall as possible will need to be saved. Drainage from roofs is the best source, and this could be stored in overground or underground tanks.

Use less

Some plants require less water than others, and these can be introduced. Plants originally from warmer areas, such as *Ceanothus*, *Cistus*, *Hebes*, *Lavandula* and *Phlomis* and succulent plants like *Agave*, *Sedum* and *Sempervivum* would be suitable.

More space could be given to hard landscaping features. Even that symbol of the English garden, the lawn, may need to be reduced or given up.

Spraying

Spraying is the most common way of applying pesticides to the garden. Spraying can also be used for applying fertiliser or, in the greenhouse, for just applying water.

The safe use of chemicals has been covered in **Topic C-4 'Chemical control'**. In this topic we are concerned with the practicalities of spraying.

Types of sprayer

In a garden situation there are four main types of sprayer that can be used, all of which use hand power to operate them. In a commercial situation motor operated ones may be used.

1.   Simple hand sprayer

This usually holds 500 ml of spray and is worked by a simple hand pump incorporated into the handle. The spray can usually be adjusted by tightening or loosening the nozzle cap.

This sprayer is useful in the greenhouse or for spraying individual plants outside, such as the spot treatment of weeds.

2.   Handheld pressure sprayer

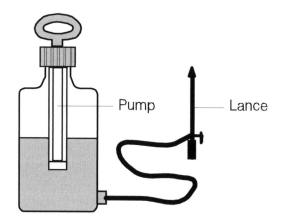

These are available in a variety of sizes typically in the range of 1 - 10 litres. A compression pump is incorporated into the handle that is used to build up the pressure in the container. A trigger on the handle or lance releases the spray under the pressure.

The spray can be adjusted in the same way as with a simple hand sprayer, and by varying the pressure within the container.

The nozzle is usually fitted on a lance which is connected to the container by a short piece of hosing.

3.   Knapsack pressure sprayer

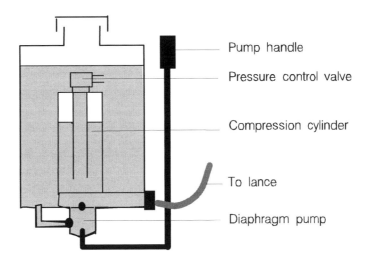

This is a larger and more sophisticated version of the handheld pressure sprayer. The container fits on the back, and the pressure is maintained by a pump action handle located at the side. The capacity is in the order of 15 - 20 litres.

They incorporate a compression chamber within the main container, and a pressure release valve that can be set to different pressures. These enable the spray to be applied at an even rate.

This type of sprayer would only be required in a large garden with a significant number of plants requiring spraying, such as large lawns or an orchard.

4.   Dribble bar

A dribble bar is a horizontal tube with small holes in it that is attached to a watering can or special applicator. The spray is fed by gravity through the holes.

The spray consists of large droplets so that no wind drift occurs and it is a useful way of applying a herbicide among other plants.

All these sprayers can be obtained made of some form of plastic, and some can be obtained in stainless steel which is considerably more expensive.

Nozzles

The more expensive sprayers may have a choice of nozzles which may be plastic, brass or stainless steel. The nozzles differ in the size of droplets and the spray pattern.

There are three basic types.

Techniques and procedures

1.   Cone

This produces a hollow or solid cone pattern of fine droplets. It is suitable for applying insecticides and fungicides. The fine droplets enable the spray to adhere to most surfaces.

2.   Fan

This produces a flat fan pattern of medium sized droplets. It is suitable for liquid fertilisers.

3.   Anvil

This produces a wide band pattern of heavy droplets at low pressure. It is suitable for applying herbicides as the heavy droplets are less likely to drift with the wind and damage other plants.

Calibrating a sprayer

It is important to apply any chemical at the rate recommended by the manufacturer, and if a significant amount of spraying is to be done it is worth checking how much is applied.

The amount applied is dependant on the pressure, the nozzle, the height of the nozzle above the ground and the walking pace of the individual.

A.   Use the nozzle and pressure recommended by the manufacturer.

B.   Fill the sprayer with 1 litre of water.

C.   Spray this over a surface where the ground covered can be seen and measure this area in sq m.

D.   Divide this area into the total area to be covered to give the total volume of spray to be applied.

E.   Calculate the required volume of the chemical for the total area according to the manufacturers instructions.

F.   Dilution rate is the ratio of E to D.

Example

1 litre of water will spray 25 sq m at the walking pace of the operator

The area to be sprayed is 0.25 hectare (2500 sq m)

Total volume of spray = 2500 divided by 25 = 100 litres

The stated application rate of the chemical is 5 litres/hectare

Volume of chemical required = 5 X 0.25 = 1.25 litres

Dilution rate 1.25 : 100 = 1 : 80

Guidelines for spraying

- Review the safety guidelines in **Topic C-4 'Chemical control'**.

- Always comply with the manufacturers instructions.

- Spray when the weather is cool or the spray may be lost by evaporation.

- Do not spray if windy, or rain is likely within 24 hours.

- Use of canes or string to mark out the area will help to ensure the correct amount of spray is applied.

- Ensure all the foliage is covered with contact sprays, including the underside of leaves.

- Thoroughly clean all equipment after spraying.

- For some chemicals available to commercial users a Certificate of Competence is required.

Making garden compost

Why make compost

Making garden compost is useful in two ways. Firstly it is a way of getting rid of garden and kitchen waste, and secondly it produces an extremely useful product that can be used in a number of ways.

The use of garden compost

Garden compost should not be confused with seed and potting composts. It is not suitable for those uses, where a clean and balanced compost is required.

Garden compost can be used for:

1.   A mulch

Spread a 10 cm layer over the soil to suppress weeds and conserve moisture.

2.   A planting medium

Mix with the soil when planting trees, shrubs and perennials.

3.   A soil conditioner

Dig into the vegetable garden or newly cultivated areas.

The compost material

Any organic waste from the garden or kitchen is a candidate, but the following are best avoided:

- Perennial weeds
- Plants with seed heads formed
- Diseased plants
- Woody stems (small stems will breakdown eventually but it might take longer than the rest of the material.)
- Grass cuttings - can be included if mixed with other material but limit it to 25% of the total compost otherwise it will tend to be slimy and smelly.
- Remains of meat or cooked food (will encourage pests)

The compost container

A container that retains heat and protects the compost from rain is required.

Ideal are ones made from bricks, blocks or wood. Plastic or wire mesh is not so effective.

The size needs to be commensurate with the garden but in general the bigger the better (a cubic metre should be the minimum size).

It is better for the container to rest on the soil so that soil organisms can get to the compost.

Having two containers can be useful so that the compost can be used from one while it is being built up in the other.

The process

The conditions required in the compost heap are similar to that required in a well structured soil. That is, it should contain air, water and soil organisms. **It is the soil organisms, particularly the microorganisms, that are responsible for the breakdown of the waste material into the compost**.

As the compost breaks down it heats up, which aids the decomposition process. Weeds will be killed by a temperature of over 70^0 C for 30 minutes and diseases will be killed by a temperature of over 50^0 C for 72 hours.

● Build up the compost heap in layers consisting of 15 cm of compost followed by 3 cm of soil. The soil is important to introduce soil organisms into the compost.

● Do not compress the heap too firmly.

● Keep the heap covered.

● Turning the heap is sometimes recommended and may give more even composting but is not essential and can be impractical with a large heap.

● It is important to keep the carbon/nitrogen balance correct. Since all organic material contains carbon it is more likely that additional nitrogen will be needed. Apply an activator such as Garotta, which is basically nitrogen, if there is a lot of woody material in the compost.

● The compost is ready when it is dark, crumbly and sweet smelling. This can take 3-6 months.

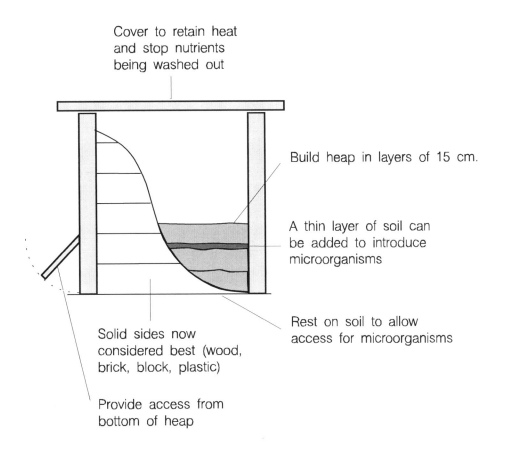

Cover to retain heat and stop nutrients being washed out

Build heap in layers of 15 cm.

A thin layer of soil can be added to introduce microorganisms

Rest on soil to allow access for microorganisms

Solid sides now considered best (wood, brick, block, plastic)

Provide access from bottom of heap

Mulching

What is mulching

Mulching is covering the surface of the soil with an organic or inorganic substance.

Why mulch

Primary benefits
Suppression of weeds
Retention of moisture

Secondary benefits
Provision of organic matter and nutrients (only with some mulches)
Help to maintain an even soil temperature
Prevent capping of the soil surface
Decorative

Mulching material

Organic	
Bark chippings	One of the best mulches as it is long lasting and does not provide a germinating medium for seeds that are blown or dropped on it.
	If the bark is not composted then it may use nitrogen from the soil as it breaks down. Applying a nitrogen fertiliser will prevent this.
	Bark is available in several sizes and is widely used in public planting schemes.
Peat (or substitute)	Good to look at but it quickly gets incorporated into the soil and it allows weed seeds to germinate on it.
	The use of peat in the garden is now generally disapproved of as it is a non-renewable resource.
Garden compost	Similar comments as for peat plus it is likely to contain weed seeds.
	Will supply some organic matter and nutrients to the soil.
Manure	As for garden compost.
	Needs to be well rotted and may be difficult to obtain.

Inorganic	
Black polythene	Effective but not nice to look at and no improvement to the soil.
	Water will not penetrate it so soil must be well wetted before applying and any fertilisers required must be applied in advance.
Woven polypropylene	The advantage of this is that it will suppress weeds but it will also allow air and water through.
	It can also be covered with a thin layer of soil or an organic mulch to give an attractive but low maintenance garden.
Floating mulch	This can be either a thin plastic sheet with small perforations in it or a woven fibre fleece. They are placed over the planting and are so light that they are raised as the plant grows and so act like a cloche.
	The fleeces provide some insulation and protection.
Chippings	These can be used as a decorative mulch and are often seen on rockeries.

Applying the mulch

- In general an organic mulch will be suitable for the ornamental garden and an inorganic one suitable for the fruit and vegetable garden.

- Apply the mulch in spring when the ground is moist. If necessary water the ground beforehand.

- Remove perennial weeds or treat with a glyphosate based weedkiller.

- If necessary apply a fertiliser before applying the mulch.

- Apply the mulch to the complete planting area or selectively around certain plants.

- Organic mulches should be applied evenly over the surface of the soil to a depth of about 10 cm. Avoid the mulch actually touching the stems of plants which might encourage disease.

- An organic mulch will need topping up or renewing about every three years.

- Inorganic mulches should be put down and cuts made where plants are to go. They will also need to be secured by burying the edges or placing some heavier substance on the top.

Greenhouse gardening

Why have a greenhouse

- Some gardening can be done irrespective of the weather conditions.

- A wider range of plants can be grown than is possible outside.

- Earlier fruit and vegetables can be obtained when shop prices are high.

- Half-hardy plants can be raised from seed for planting out when the danger of frost is past.

- Large numbers of plants can be economically raised from seed so that in the longer term the greenhouse becomes an economic investment.

Types of greenhouse

Greenhouses come in all shapes and sizes, from mini ones that have to be tended from outside, to large walk in ones that may house permanent collections of tender plants. Commercial glasshouses that may cover acres are outside the scope of this book.

The framework is either wood, which is usually western red cedar, or aluminium, and the glazing may be with glass or some form of flexible or rigid plastic.

Wood	**Advantages**
	Looks more at home in a garden setting
	Better heat retention
	Less condensation
	Easier to put up hooks, staging and shelving
	Disadvantages
	Expensive
	Requires treating with a preservative every few years
Aluminium	**Advantages**
	Maintenance free
	Light to handle when erecting
	Slightly more light transmission
	Disadvantages
	Functional rather than beautiful
Glass	**Advantages**
	Better light transmission
	Better heat retention
	More permanent
	Disadvantages
	Expensive
	Breakable
Plastic	**Advantages**
	Cheap (in the short term anyway)

Easy to handle

Safe

Disadvantages

Limited life (2 to 5 years depending on type)

Shapes

1.   Traditional span

A good all-round greenhouse. The sides may be of wood, brick, or glazed to the ground The span roof gives good headroom. Heat retention is better if it is not glazed to the ground. This type is suitable if most plants are to be grown in pots.

2.   Dutch light

The sloping sides and glazing down to the bottom gives maximum light transmission and is good for crops grown at soil level like tomatoes.

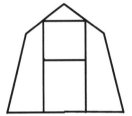

3.   Lean-to

This is made to fit against a wall. The warmth and insulating properties of the wall will help to raise the temperature.

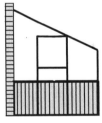

There are many other shapes including domes and polygons, and also some that are part shed and part greenhouse.

Conservatories can also fulfil many of the functions of a greenhouse, particularly the displaying of tender plants.

Choosing a greenhouse

To a large extent it is a question of 'you pay your money and you take your choice'.

There are, however, some factors to take into consideration:

- For most people cost will be a limiting factor. Remember however that a greenhouse can be a lifetime investment and the cheapest to buy may not be the cheapest in the long term.

- In general the bigger the better. Small greenhouses can be subject to rapid changes of temperature and humidity.

- If you cannot 'hide' the greenhouse consider the decorative appearance of it.

- If you want to grow plants in the soil or from the soil level then choose one with glazing to the ground.

- If you want to grow mainly in pots such as alpines or house plants then a traditional design will be suitable.

- If you want to grow plants requiring heat then consider the heating cost in relation to the size.

- Whatever type you choose ensure that it has good ventilation.

- Check whether accessories such as staging and shelving are available.

Siting the greenhouse

- **Open position**

  Avoid positions where the greenhouse is in shade from other buildings or from trees. Consider the position at all seasons. Good light in winter can be very important for some plants.

- **Shelter from wind**

  If the site is not sheltered it will not be pleasant to work in, but worse is that winds can lower the temperature within the greenhouse. In particular avoid positions that may be wind tunnels.

  Windbreaks can be used to provide shelter.

- **Avoid frost pockets**

  Frost will roll downhill so avoid depressions.

- **Access**

  Access by means of a hard path is desirable.

- **Close to water and electricity**

  A water supply will be needed in or near the greenhouse. Electricity may be required for lighting, heating, or running any equipment.

- **Orientation**

  For the most even light distribution it is best to have the length running north to south, although east to west is better for the winter light. Decide on the the basis of the particular use to which it will be put.

Creating the right conditions

The right conditions will depend on what the greenhouse is required for, but in general terms it is getting the right balance of heat, light and humidity.

The following points must be considered:

> **Heating**
> **Insulation**
> **Ventilation**
> **Shading**
> **Humidity**
> **Lighting**

Heating

To heat or not to heat, that is the question. The equation is to balance the cost of heating against the range of plants to be grown. Four different situations can be identified.

Unheated
Not frost free and cannot therefore be used for tender plants.
Extends the growing season with an early spring and late autumn.
Allows half hardy plants to be raised from seed and planted out when the danger of frost is past.
Protects from weather and provides higher temperature in summer that will suit some plants, eg tomatoes.
Hardy plants can be grown over winter, eg bulbs for early flowering.
Suitable for alpines where protection from rain and wind is the prime requirement.

Cool
Day temperature of 5-10^0 C and minimum night temperature of 2^0 C.
Frost free allowing tender plants to be overwintered.
Allows house plants and plants for cut flowers to be grown all year round.

Temperate
Day temperature of 10-13^0 C and minimum night temperature of 7^0 C.
Allows some sub-tropical plants to be grown, eg orchids.

Warm
Day temperature of 13-18^0 C and minimum night temperature of 13^0 C.
Allows sub-tropical and some tropical plants to be grown.
Propagation may be done without additional heat allowing for high volumes.
May require heating all year round.

Methods of heating

Electricity	Advantages
	Most convenient
	Easy automation with thermostats and timing switches
	Cheapest to run if thermostatically controlled

Alternative installations
- Fan heaters
- Convection heaters
- Tubular heaters
- Soil warming cables (may also need air heating)

Little condensation

Disadvantages

Requires an electricity supply to be available

Expensive to install if no supply

Paraffin　　**Advantages**

Portable (no mains supply required)

Cheap to install

Gives off carbon dioxide that may benefit plants

Disadvantages

Not possible to automate

Generally only a low heat output

Produces water vapour and hence condensation

Some ventilation required giving some heat loss

Bottled gas　　Similar advantages and disadvantages to paraffin although it is possible to get thermostatic control.

Tests have shown that there can be safety hazards with all forms of heating and care should be taken with them all.

Mains gas and solid fuel heaters are also available but are unlikely to be used in a garden situation.

It is always possible to heat part of a greenhouse by screening off a section with some insulating material. Alternatively a heated propagator can be used.

The heating requirements can be calculated as follows:

1. Calculate the surface area in square metres.

2. Multiply the square metres by 5.7 (this is the loss in watts per square metre for each degree centigrade that the temperature inside exceeds the temperature outside)

3. Add 25% to the result above to allow for heat loss through leakages.

4. Multiply the result above by the difference between the minimum temperature inside and the minimum temperature outside.

Example
Surface area = 100 sq m
Surface area X 5.7 = 570
Allowance for heat loss = 570 + 25% = 712
Minimum inside temperature required = 10° C
Minimum outside temperature = -5° C
Temperature difference = 15
Heat required in watts = 712 X 15 = 10680 watts = say 10 kilowatts

A thermometer that measures maximum and minimum temperatures is an essential piece of equipment.

Insulation

Insulation will raise the temperature in an unheated greenhouse and reduce the cost of heating in heated ones. Tests have shown that up to 40% of the heating costs can be saved.

The most appropriate insulation is some form of clear or translucent plastic. Bubble plastic in which bubbles of air are held between plastic sheets is particularly effective.

Insulation will cut down the light transmission and should be removed when no longer required.

As stated under **'Heating'** insulating material can be used to section off an area that is to be maintained at a higher temperature.

Ventilation

Ventilation is extremely important to maintain an even temperature and to replace stale air.

A guideline is that the ventilation area in the roof should be one sixth of the floor area and very small greenhouses would benefit from more.

There are two basic types of ventilators;

Hinged - one pane hinged at the edge

Louvre - small, multiple panes that move in unison

The ventilators can be fitted in a number of ways. It should be apparent that as fresh air has to enter and stale air has to leave that one ventilator would not be efficient.

The best arrangements are:

1. To alternate the ventilators on each side of the roof. The air would then enter from one side, be diverted around the greenhouse and expelled from the other side.

2. As warm air rises, an even better arrangement is to have additional ventilators at the floor level. The warm air in the greenhouse would escape through the roof and fresh air would be drawn in from the floor.

Ventilators can be fitted with automatic openers that react to the temperature and unless almost constant supervision is possible these should be used. Some can be set to open at a particular temperature. Extractor fans can also be used.

Shading

Shading can serve two purposes. It can lower the temperature and it can reduce the light intensity. Both of these may be required during periods of hot sunny weather to prevent plants from wilting or scorching.

The traditional method of shading is to paint the outside of the greenhouse with a mixture which used to be lime and water, but is now usually a proprietary product such as PBI Coolglass. Some products turn transparent in rain so letting more light in. The shading will normally be applied at the beginning of the hottest period and removed at the end.

External or internal blinds made of a variety of materials can be used. External blinds are more effective at reducing the temperature. It is also possible to get an automatic control for the blinds.

Humidity

Humidity is a measure of the water vapour in the air. It is expressed as the percent of water vapour present to the maximum possible which will vary according to the temperature. A figure of 50 would therefore mean that half the maximum was present.

The humidity has an impact on the rate of transpiration, with transpiration being reduced by high humidity. Since transpiration has the effect of cooling the plant it may overheat if transpiration is reduced.

There are no simple right and wrong levels. Tropical plants may require high humidity, while desert plants may require low humidity. Seedlings and cuttings require high humidity to avoid loss of water through transpiration. The purpose of mist propagators is to provide a humid atmosphere around seedlings and cuttings.

Although it is possible to buy humidifiers, this should not be necessary in a garden environment unless very specialised plants are being grown.

In very hot weather good ventilation plus **'damping down'** should ensure the humidity is kept within acceptable bounds. Damping down is the practice of splashing water on the floor of the greenhouse where it will evaporate to raise the level of humidity.

Hygrometers are used to measure humidity and an acceptable range for most plants is 40-75.

Lighting

For light to work by any domestic system using bulbs or fluorescent tubes is suitable. However it is also possible to have lighting that will enhance the growing conditions of the plants.

The growth of plants can be effected by light in two ways:

1. Light is essential for photosynthesis

Lights that contain a similar spectrum to natural daylight can augment or even replace natural light.

2. Day length is critical to trigger growth and flowering in some plants

This is called **photoperiodism**. See **Topic A-16 'Control systems'** for plants affected by day length.

Day length can be manipulated to cause growth and flowering at times when it would not naturally occur. The production of chrysanthemums throughout the year uses this technique.

Professional growers make extensive use of artificial lighting.

The types of lights available are:

1.   Mercury-tungsten lamps

These have the advantage of fitting into an ordinary light socket, and being cheap to run. They are satisfactory for seedlings and cuttings and can be used indoors to provide good lighting for house plants.

2.   Mercury lamps

These produce a considerably greater output of light than mercury-tungsten lamps but require special wiring and controls.

One bulb can illuminate an area in the range of 2-5 sq m depending on the wattage of the lamp.

A wide range of plants can be grown under these lamps even in the total absence of natural light.

3.   Metal halide lamps

These are more advanced mercury based lamps that have an even higher output and greater coverage of the light spectrum.

4.   Sodium lamps

These are highly efficient but only cover a narrow part of the spectrum and are therefore usually used in conjunction with mercury lamps.

Watering systems

Because of the higher temperatures more watering will be required than in the open garden.

The traditional method of watering is with a watering can and in many ways this is still the best since each plant can be given the amount it needs, and the plants can be inspected at the same time for signs of any problems like pests and diseases.

There are however an increasing number of automatic watering aids available and aimed at the amateur gardener.

The biggest advantage of an automatic system is that it allows the greenhouse to be left unattended for periods of time that can extend to several days.

A mains supply of water to the greenhouse is extremely useful although some of the watering systems will run from a reservoir held in the greenhouse and which just needs to be topped-up periodically. The advantage of a reservoir is that fertilisers can be added to it.

There are basically four methods of automatic watering:

Capillary system

Spray system

Drip feed system

Seep hose

Capillary system

This system is based on the fact that water will move through a series of fine pores within a substance, including moving upwards.

This is an old method that used sand as the capillary material. A layer of sand about 5 cm thick was held on the bench and kept permanently moist. The drawback was that the sand was very heavy and the benches needed to be strong enough to support the weight. Nowadays capillary matting made from woven polyester is normally used. It is light and easily handled and can hold 2-3 litres per sq m.

Wetting the matting can be easily automated by placing one end in a tray of water.

Spray system

This system involves spraying water from overhead nozzles. It is common in commercial glasshouses where a large number of plants have to be sprayed at regular intervals.

Overall spraying in the small greenhouse is not so practical or necessary, although some of the kits on the market include spray nozzles that spray a limited area.

Drip feed system

This is the basis of the systems that are aimed at the amateur gardener. The principle is to deliver to each plant via some form of hosing a regular supply of water. It is a useful system where plants are grown primarily in pots.

The kits available will consist of a supply of hosing, nozzles and sometimes a pressure regulator to reduce the pressure of the mains water.

The nozzles can usually be adjusted to regulate the supply and some spray nozzles may also be supplied.

A recent development is a ceramic cone attached to the hosing which is pushed into the compost. As the compost dries out it draws water from the cone by the process of osmosis thus supplying the plant with just what it needs.

Seep hose

A seep hose is only really of use if plants are grown in a border within the greenhouse, which will not usually be practical in a small one.

Automatic controls

Irrespective of what system is used further automation is possible with:

1.   Timers that will turn the water supply on or off for a period of time or until a set volume of water has been released.

2.   Sensors that will turn the water supply on or off depending on the compost moisture content or the humidity.

It is worth pointing out that some people who have tested automatic systems have come to the conclusion that they prefer the old fashioned watering can.

I have a vision of an automated greenhouse going berserk with ventilators opening and shutting, blinds being raised and lowered and water spouting from every outlet.

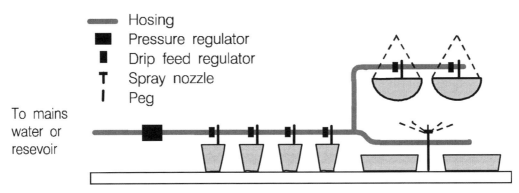

Hosing
Pressure regulator
Drip feed regulator
Spray nozzle
Peg

To mains
water or
resevoir

Automatic watering system for a small greenhouse

Other equipment

In considering the environmental control and watering requirements we have covered most of the equipment that may be needed. There are however a number of other items that may be required.

Staging

Staging is the term given to benches suitable for the greenhouse. If plants are to be maintained in pots, or propagation work is going to be done, some form of staging will be necessary.

It comes in a variety of forms. The greenhouse manufacturer will supply staging to fit and match his products. It can be slatted or solid. Slatted is better for heat and air circulation but if capillary matting or propagation work is required it is better if it is solid. Sometimes it can be folded away so that plants can be grown from ground level.

Many people will opt for staging down one side while the other side is used for growing from ground level.

Shelving

Shelving, which will usually be fitted above the staging, is useful for providing additional storage space and is good for displaying trailing plants.

Take care it does not throw too much shade on the plants below.

Trays, pots and growing bags

Seed trays come in a standard size or half-size. There are a variety of inserts for trays so that each plant can be grown in its own block of compost.

Pots were traditionally made from clay but, although these are still available, most people use plastic pots which are cheaper, lighter and easier to keep clean. They are available in a wide range of sizes.

Growing bags have revolutionised growing in greenhouses and largely replaced the practice of growing in a soil border. Although probably used more for tomatoes than any other plant, they can be used for a wide variety of heat loving vegetables. Growing bags should be used as directed by the manufacturer.

Propagators

Seeds and cuttings grow best in a temperature around 18-21^0 C which will normally be above the overall temperature of the greenhouse at the time they are required. Propagators can be used to provide the required temperature in a restricted area.

The most convenient propagators are portable electric ones with a base unit, containing a heating element, which will take one or more standard seed trays, and covered by a plastic dome to retain the heat and humidity. The dome will usually have some form of ventilation. Most will be thermostatically controlled to conserve energy.

A propagator should be able to maintain a temperature in the range 15-25^0 C.

There are more advanced propagators called propagation boxes or cabinets which are completely self contained and provide heat, water, nutrients and light, but these are more for the professional.

Soil warming cables

An alternative to a propagator is to have soil warming cables. These can be used in the greenhouse soil if it is used, or in containers on the bench top. The cable is laid beneath the surface of the soil in a series of loops.

Misting units

Another propagation aid is a misting unit which throws out a very fine spray, and is used to reduce the transpiration of seedlings and cuttings. It can be open or enclosed and may be incorporated in the more advanced propagators. The misting unit is usually controlled by a sensor, commonly termed an **'electronic leaf'**, that detects when the moisture level has dropped.

Growing media

There are four possibilities:

1. **Border soil**
2. **Soil based composts**
3. **Soilless composts**
4. **Hydroponics**

Border soil

This is standard garden soil within the greenhouse. It has many disadvantages; the quality will be variable, it will contain pests and diseases and, if used for the same crops year after year, it will develop soil sickness.

There are ways of minimising these disadvantages but the widespread use of growing bags has made the use of border soil largely unnecessary and it is not to be recommended.

Soil based composts

In 1939 workers at the John Innes Horticultural Institution produced formulae for seed and potting composts which revolutionised the growing of plants in containers.

These composts are known as John Innes (or JI) composts and are the basis of all soil based composts available today.

The composts consist of one seed compost and three potting composts. The formulae are:

Seed	2 parts sterilised loam (all parts are by volume)
	1 part peat
	1 part coarse sand
	Superphosphate of lime at 1 g per litre
	Ground limestone at 0.5 g per litre
	These rates are direct conversions from the imperial measurements that were originally used.
Potting	7 parts sterilised loam
	3 parts peat
	2 parts coarse sand
	Ground limestone at 0.5 g per litre
	Hoof and horn at 1 g per litre
	Superphosphate of lime at 1 g per litre
	Sulphate of potash at 0.5 g per litre
	These rates of fertiliser are for John Innes No. 1. No. 2 has twice these amounts and No. 3 has three times.

The seed compost has less loam in order to ensure it is free draining, and less fertiliser since the seed contains its own supply of food.

The three potting composts are designed to cope with different sizes and feeding requirements of plants.

Soilless composts

Shortage of good quality loam caused a search for a good substitute, and the best substitute was found to be peat, which has been used for many years and has a number advantages over soil based composts.

There is now a lot of concern about the use of peat, and a search is on to find a further substitute. Experiments have been carried out with a number of products but at this time only two seem to viable. One is **coir** which is a waste product of coconut husks and the other is **composted bark**.

References to peat in other parts of this book should be taken to include peat substitutes.

As with the soil based composts there are formulations for seeds and for potting. A

COIR

Coir appears to be the best alternative to peat. It is made from the remains of coconut fibres which would otherwise be waste and is therefore 'green'.

There is a Coir association that lays down standards for the production and sale of coir products.

Coir has an open and free-draining texture and may require more frequent watering and feeding than peat.

Coir may lock up certain nutrients and it is possible to buy fertilisers specially formulated for use with coir.

---

typical seed compost consists of equal parts of peat and sand and a potting compost consists of 3 parts peat to one of sand. Both have nutrients added.

Multi-purpose composts are available that strike a balance between the requirements and these are quite successful.

Growing bags exclusively use soilless composts.

Comparison of soil and soilless composts

Soil based	Soilless
Better nutrient reserves	Lighter and cleaner to handle
Firmer support for larger plants	Good aeration and water holding capacity
Easy to wet	More feeding necessary
Deteriorates quicker	Difficult to re-wet once dry
Difficult to obtain good loam	

Hydroponics

Hydroponics means growing plants in water, although the term is used to cover growing in all mediums other than soil.

The technique dates back a considerable time, but became popular after a series of experiments in California in 1929/30. In these experiments tomatoes and other plants were grown in water filled troughs and gave yields that were considerably in excess of those grown more conventionally.

Since no soil is used there has to be a way of providing the plants with the nutrients they require. This is done by adding the nutrients to the water to create a **nutrient solution.** The provision and maintenance of a correct nutrient solution is the key to successful growth.

Another problem with water only systems is to ensure that the roots receive the amount of oxygen they require for respiration

A number of different systems have been developed which can be classified as follows:

1. **Water culture**

2. **Substrate culture**

    2a. **Open systems**

    2b. **Closed systems**

Water culture

The original methods of water culture entailed growing plants in water filled troughs with the plants supported by a wire mesh above it.

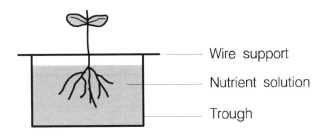

These systems have been refined over a period of time and one that is currently used is called the **nutrient film technique (NFT)**. This technique entails growing the plants in some form of open ended trough or gully through which a thin layer of the nutrient solution is continuously passed.

The key points of this technique are:

● The nutrient solution is continuously circulated, making it economical in water usage. To facilitate this the gullies are on a slight incline (1:100 is sufficient).

● The layer of nutrient is so thin that only parts of the root are submerged thus ensuring that sufficient oxygen is available to them.

● The roots develop as mats in the nutrient solution.

● Because only a small amount of nutrient solution is used, the construction of NFT systems can be from lightweight materials such as plastics.

● The systems are highly automated with all environmental conditions like light, temperature and nutrient levels being continuously monitored and controlled.

The following is a simplified diagram showing the main components of an NFT system.

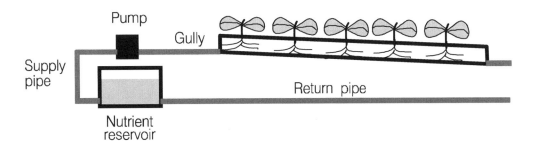

Substrate culture

In substrate culture the plants are rooted in a substance called the substrate or aggregate. Among the substances used are sand, gravel, vermiculite, perlite and rockwool. The latter three substances are derived from natural minerals and rocks.

The advantage of substrate culture is that the substrate provides support for the plant.

Substrate systems can be divided into **open** and **closed** systems. An open system is one where the nutrient solution is allowed to drain away whereas in a closed system it is recirculated. An open system will usually have a fine textured substrate like sand so that the nutrient solution is held in the capillary pores. Closed systems can use a more open substrate.

Why use hydroponics

The use of hydroponics in commercial situations is one of economics. If plants can be produced of better quality, earlier, more quickly or at all times of the year then it will be used. It is successfully used in the commercial production of tomatoes and lettuces.

The other situation in which it will be used is where the environment is unsuitable for other methods. For example, salad crops have been successfully produced in desert areas where the soil conditions are not suitable and the economical use of water is important.

The factors that produce these advantages can be summarised as follows:

1. **Precise control can be obtained over nutrients and other environmental factors.**

2. **Precise control can be obtained over pH.**

3. **Economic on water usage.**

4. **Labour effort and therefore costs are reduced.**

5. **No need for soil sterilisation.**

6. **Crop rotation does not apply.**

7. **No need for weed control.**

8. **Year round cultivation.**

There are however some disadvantages:

1. **Initial costs are high**

2. **A high level of expertise is required**

3. **Constant monitoring is required**

4. **The 'Jurassic Park' factor !**

Pests and diseases

Pests and diseases will flourish in the warm, humid and protected atmosphere of the greenhouse unless adequate steps are taken to control them.

The most common pests are whitefly and red spider mite, and the most common diseases are damping off and grey mould. All these are covered in Topics **C-6 'Common pests'** and **C-7 'Common diseases'**.

In commercial glasshouses extensive use is made of biological controls since many pests have developed resistance to chemicals. See **Topic C-3 'Biological control'**. Many of the biological controls are now available to the amateur gardener.

Hygiene is particularly important, and clean equipment and composts should always be used, and any plant debris should be removed.

Smoke cones are available that when lit give off an insecticide and fungicide, and these should be used in an annual clearing up program.

Organic gardening

This topic is included because of the increasing concerns of growing crops with the extensive aid of chemical fertilisers and pesticides, and without taking steps to conserve the natural structure and fertility of the soil.

The aim is to explain what organic gardening entails and where the organic gardening practice may differ from the non-organic.

It is probably true to say that organic gardening has been viewed with a certain amount of scepticism, but this view is changing. Many people must have been concerned by a Government warning in 1995 that carrots should be topped, tailed and skinned because of the build up of pesticide residues in the crop.

What is organic gardening

For many people 'organic gardening' will mean gardening without the use of chemicals. Although this is an important part of the organic gardeners policy, it does not completely cover the philosophy and aims of the committed organic gardener.

The aims of the organic gardener can be summarised as follows:

● **Maintain an ecological balance**

Ecology is about the relationship of plants and animals with each other and with the environment. The term 'sustainability' is used to mean that practices should be able to be used year after year with no adverse affects.

In nature an ecological balance is maintained as every plant and animal has some natural limiting factor, and everything is recycled. This is not usually the case in the unnatural environment of a garden unless special steps are taken to preserve the balance.

● **Avoid damage to the environment**

There is widespread concern about the extent to which the environment is being damaged. The main concerns are the widespread use of chemical fertilisers and pesticides which can pollute the soil, water and the atmosphere, and the use of non-renewable resources such as peat.

● **Avoid contamination of food crops and water supplies**

Chemicals can get into the food chain and the water supply with potentially very serious results.

Organic gardening is not new. The proliferation of chemicals has occurred largely over the last fifty years, and prior to that much more reliance was put on good cultural practices.

Why garden organically

1. Non-organic gardening can damage the natural structure and fertility of the soil.

2. Non-organic gardening could lead to a loss of wildlife species, many of

which are beneficial in the garden.

3. Pesticide residues in food crops and in water can be damaging to health.

4. Pesticides can lead to the development of resistant strains of pest.

5. In the longer term pesticides can lead an increase in the volume of pests.

6. The handling and application of pesticides can be damaging to health.

7. The use of pesticides is likely to become increasingly expensive.

8. The range of pesticides available to the amateur gardener is reducing.

It may seem odd that the use of pesticides may lead to a greater volume of pests. The reason is that most pesticides are not selective and will kill predators as well as pests. If this happens the pests tend to be the first to recover and therefore have a period when they can breed without the natural control by their predators.

Why doesn't everybody do it ?

You might wonder why, in view of the above, all horticulture is not done organically. In many cases it is probably an unawareness of the implications or an indifference to the effect. It must also be said that there are many gardeners and horticulturists who believe that chemicals are acceptable if used responsibly.

There are however some more specific reasons.

1. **It is not always easy**

   In particular the control of pests and diseases can be difficult without using chemicals. Even organic gardeners will allow some naturally based chemicals to be used.

   For the commercial grower the problem is made more difficult by the fact that they are likely to be growing large volumes of a single crop, giving the pests plenty to feed on, and not having an environment that encourages predators.

2. **For commercial growers larger yields may be obtained with chemical fertilisers**

3. **Some degree of crop damage may have to be expected**

   This is a problem to the commercial grower since buyers expect unblemished crops.

4. **It is easier to pick up a spray than to adopt other methods of control**

5. **For commercial growers the cost of production may be higher.**

It will be appreciated from the above that the problem for the commercial grower is much more difficult than for the amateur gardener. There is in fact very little certified organic fruit production.

Principles of organic gardening

- **Work with nature rather than against it**
- **Feed the soil rather than the plants**
- **Recycle all waste**
- **Encourage natural predators**

- **Avoid the use of chemicals, whether as fertilisers or pesticides**

Organic gardening in action

Throughout this book the emphasis has been on adopting good gardening practices, and most of these would be approved of by organic gardeners. In some areas however the organic gardener will go to greater lengths to achieve his objectives.

In the following paragraphs we will identify where the organic gardener may differ from the non-organic gardener.

Garden design

Most people will not be in a position to start from scratch but, if this is the case, the following points should be considered.

- Plan to provide the best possible growing conditions for all plants as healthy plants are best able to withstand pests and diseases, and chemical 'props' will not be available to help overcome adverse conditions.

- Include features to encourage wildlife since many wildlife creatures are predators of garden pests. A pool, nesting boxes and wild flowers are all possibilities.

- Use hedges rather than walls or fences since these provide a wildlife habitat, and are the best form of windbreak.

- Plan to use a wide range of plants since this again will attract a wider range of wildlife.

- Consider mixing food crops with ornamental plants, such as having vegetables and fruit bushes in the mixed borders.

Soil management

Good soil management is key to successful organic gardening.

The argument is that if the soil is maintained in a fertile and well structured state then there will be little or no need to apply artificial fertilisers to the crops.

On a new site or one where the characteristics of the soil are unknown, it would be advisable to to have the soil analysed. It is possible to get an analysis specifically for the organic garden which will identify nutrient and organic content, and if necessary, recommend what organic fertilisers should be used.

Key points for the organic gardener are:

- Bulky organic matter such as manure or garden compost will be used to feed the soil. If fertilisers are necessary only organic ones, such as fish, blood and bone, bonemeal and seaweed will be used.

  It should be appreciated that in a natural environment the soil does not contain a high nitrogen content. This is because it is taken up by plants, and because it is easily leached. It is added as a fertiliser because it can significantly increase the rate of growth. However this growth can be soft and lush, and is prone to attack by many pests.

- The making of compost is very important since this is one of the primary ways in which the soil can be fed. See **Topic E-8 'Making garden compost'**. In addition to normal garden compost, leaf mould and worm compost may be used.

- Many organic gardeners advocate the use of no-dig bed system of cultivation, although this should not be considered 'mandatory'.

- Green manures are likely to be used, partly to provide nutrients, but also to protect the soil surface and prevent nutrients being washed out of uncovered soil.

- Mulches are likely to be used to protect the soil surface and to suppress weeds. See **Topic E-9 'Mulching'**.

Weed control

Weed control is one of the areas that can be difficult for the organic gardener,

Reread **Topic C-5 'Common weeds'** to understand the characteristics of annual and perennial weeds, and the factors that make them difficult to control.

The following points are key to any program of weed control:

- All plants need light to survive. Depriving them of this will eventually kill them.

- All plants need to photosynthesise to survive. By not allowing the top growth to develop they will be weakened and eventually die.

- It is particularly important to remove all perennial weeds, since they are difficult to eradicate once they start growing among other plants.

- Weeds should never be allowed to seed.

- Seeds can lie dormant in the soil for long periods of time, and cultivating the soil may bring them to the surface where they will germinate

- Some weeds may be attractive to predators, and therefore allowed to grow under 'controlled' conditions. Examples are:

  Stinging nettle (*Urtica dioica*) is attractive to butterflies

  Groundsel (*Senecio vulgaris*) is attractive to bees

- There are no organic chemicals for controlling weeds.

For the options available to the organic gardener reread 'Cultural control of weeds' in **Topic C-2 'Cultural control'**.

Pest and disease control

This is the most difficult problem for the organic gardener. The emphasis should be on preventing problems since this is easier than curing them once they have occurred. It is also important to correctly identify the problem, which is not always easy as the symptoms from some diseases and disorders can look very similar.

Cultural control

This is covered in 'Cultural control of pests and diseases' in **Topic C-2 'Cultural control'**.

Biological control

This is covered in **Topic C-3 'Biological control'**

Chemical Control

There are a few naturally derived chemicals which are acceptable to the organic gardening, but only as a last resort. These include:

- **Insecticides**

    Fatty acids (soap)

- **Fungicides**

    Copper oxychloride

    > Organic farmers growing potatoes have used copper based fungicides to control potato blight as there has been no viable alternative. However the EU is likely nhto ban the use of copper in the next few years.

Garden Organic

This is a charitable organisation, previously known as the Henry Doubleday Research Association (HDRA), whose aim is to promote the ideas of organic gardening. They carry out scientific research, produce publications, run courses and give advice on all aspects of organic gardening.

They also put their principles into practice in Ryton Organic Gardens which consists of ten acres of ornamental and demonstration gardens, and is open to the public all year round.

Membership of Garden Organic is open to the public and provides a variety of benefits including free entry to the garden at Ryton and also to the RHS garden at Wisley.

Their website is '**www.gardenorganic.org.uk**'

Self test questions

These questions are to enable you to assess how well you have understood and remembered the information in the previous section. No answers are given as these should be apparent from reviewing the relevant topics.

The questions are **not** intended to cover everything you should know.

1   In buying a plant from a garden centre list six things you would look for to ascertain whether the plant was healthy.

2   Describe with the aid of a diagram the steps you would take to plant a tree, purchased in a pot, in a lawn.

3   List the advantages and disadvantages of raising plants from seed.

4   What is the difference between scarification and stratification.

5   Describe the procedure for raising a half hardy annual such as*Impatiens* (busy lizzie) from sowing the seed to planting in their flowering position.

6   Describe the steps involved in preparing an outside seed bed.

7   Describe how you would increase your stock of*Potentilla* covering:
    Timing and method of propagation
    Preparation of cutting
    Choice of compost
    Aftercare

8   State three reasons for choosing grafting as a method of propagation. Describe the procedure for propagating a *magnolia* by grafting.

9   List the reasons for pruning a shrub. What is the difference in pruning a shrub that flowers on previous year's growth and one that flowers on current year's growth.

10   Describe with the aid of a diagram the procedure for making garden compost.

11   State four methods of conserving water within a garden.

12   List the benefits of mulching. List three organic and three inorganic materials that can be used for mulching, and the advantages and disadvantages of each.

13   State the importance of ventilation within the greenhouse and describe two methods of supplying it.

14   Distinguish between photosynthetic lighting and photoperiodic lighting.

15   Describe with the aid of a diagram a watering system for a small greenhouse.

16   List the advantages and disadvantages of soilless composts compared to soil based composts.

17   What do you understand by 'hydroponics', when is it likely to be used, and what are the advantages and disadvantages.

18   What steps can the organic gardener take to control:
    Weeds
    Pests and diseases

Equipment and machinery

This section covers the more common power tools that can be used in the garden. It is assumed that students are familiar with hand tools which are not included in the book.

Emphasis is placed on the choices available, the safety precautions needed and the maintenance requirements.

Introduction

We have covered specific items of equipment in other topics where it has been appropriate to do so. The following items have been covered:

Pruning equipment	Topic E-5 'Pruning'
Watering equipment	Topic E-6 'Watering'
Spraying equipment	Topic E-7 'Spraying'
Greenhouse equipment	Topic E-10 'Greenhouse gardening'

In this section we will cover equipment not already covered. It is assumed that students will be familiar with standard hand tools, and this section only includes power tools.

The following are included:

1. **Alternative sources of power**

   ➜ The advantages and disadvantages of each will be discussed but it is outside the scope of this book to cover the internal workings of the power sources in any detail.

   ➜ Routine maintenance.

   ➜ Safety precautions.

2. **Lawnmowers**

3. **Cultivators**

4. **Hedgecutters**

5. **Trimmers and brushcutters**

There are many other kinds of equipment and machinery that can be used particularly in a commercial situation. Among these are:

1. **Garden or mini tractors**

2. **Ploughing, harrowing and rolling equipment**

3. **Seed sowing and transplanting machinery**

4. **Fertiliser distributors**

5. **Turf lifters**

6. **Harvesting machinery**

7. **Soil sterilisers**

8. **Chainsaws**

9. **Shredders.**

Power sources

What type of power

Petrol engine

Mains electricity

Rechargeable battery

Petrol engine

Petrol engines are available on all the machinery covered in this section. The engines will usually be single cylinder, 2 stroke or 4 stroke, and air cooled. Most are started with a manual recoil starter although an increasing number are available with electric starters.

Advantages
More powerful than electric motors
More portable (no mains supply needed)
Can be used in all weathers

Disadvantages
Noisy
Heavier
Petrol needs to be stored
More maintenance required

Major components of a petrol engine

Cylinder block and piston	Small petrol engines have one cylinder and piston. The piston moves up and down in the cylinder and this motion is converted to a rotation that drives the machine.

The power is provided by the ignition of a petrol and air mixture. A spark plug at the top of the cylinder ignites the mixture at the correct time.

The timing of the ignition used to be controlled by contact points but new machines will have an electronic system which is maintenance free. |
| Carburettor | The carburettor controls the flow of petrol and air into the cylinder. There are usually adjustments on the carburettor to set the idling speed of the engine and the ratio of petrol to air.

A 'choke' reduces the volume of air to make it easier to start when cold.

Attached to the carburettor is an air filter which stops any dust or other material being drawn into the carburettor or cylinder. Filters are made of a variety of materials including foam, felt, paper, and gauze.

Where an engine may not always be used in a horizontal position, a special carburettor called a diaphragm carburettor is used which stops petrol from spilling out. |

Clutch	A clutch is used to connect or disconnect the engine from the wheels or cutting mechanism of the piece of equipment.
	There may be more than one clutch so that the wheels can be connected independently from the cutting mechanism.
	A clutch may be manual (controlled by the operator) or automatic (controlled by the speed of the engine). Automatic ones are usually activated by centrifugal force.
Gear box	A petrol engine rotates at high speed and the function of the gear box is to reduce the speed of the engine to the speed required at the wheels or cutting mechanism.
	The gearing is usually fixed on all items in this section other than cultivators. Fixed gearing is usually effected by joining, by a chain or belt, two different sized cogs.

Routine maintenance

The manufacturer's service guide will contain specific instructions which should be followed. They are likely to include the following tasks:

● **Before use**

  → Check supply of petrol

  → Check the oil level if a 4 stroke

  → Check for loose bolts

  → Clear cooling fins of grass and debris

● **Periodic** (depending on usage) **and start of season**

  → Check air filter

  → Change oil

  → Adjust spark plug gap or replace plug.

  → Adjust contact breaker points (not for electronic ignition)

  → Adjust tension of transmission chains or belts

Safety considerations for petrol engines

● Stop the engine and disconnect spark plug cap before touching any part of the cutting mechanism

● Do not refill with petrol while the engine is running

● Do not run the engine in a confined space

● Do not smoke while working on the engine

● Store fuel in a cool place in a proper container

Mains electric

Advantages and disadvantages compared to petrol engines.

Advantages	Disadvantages
Quiet	Requires a mains supply so less portable
Usually cheaper to buy and run	Danger of cutting cable
Easy to handle	Cannot be used in wet conditions
Less maintenance	Not as powerful as petrol engine

Mains electric versions are available for all the machinery covered in this section except for cultivators.

They are generally simpler than petrol engines as there is no gear box, and there is usually no clutch.

Routine maintenance

Electric motors themselves should need no maintenance. If they fail the equipment should be returned to a service centre.

Keeping them out of a dusty atmosphere may extend their life.

● **Before use**

→ Check condition of plugs and cables

→ Check for loose screws or bolts

Safety considerations for electric motors

Electricity can be extremely dangerous and should be used with care.

● It is important to have a Residual Current Device (RCD) fitted somewhere in the electric circuit. These devices cut off the power in a fraction of a second if anything affects the supply like cutting the cable.

They can be fitted at:

1. **The main source of supply to the house, to be effective for any device using that power supply.**

2. **A socket to control devices plugged into that socket.**

3. **A plug which just controls the device attached to that plug.**

● Ensure all plugs and cables are in good condition.

● Use proper weatherproof plugs outside.

● Use the correct fuse for the device. (Divide watts by volts to get the fuse rating in amps).

● Switch the electricity off and unplug before doing any maintenance on the equipment.

● Do not use electric appliances in wet conditions

Rechargeable battery

Advantages and disadvantages compared to mains electric.

Advantages	Disadvantages
Portable (no mains supply required) Light and easy to use Safer than mains electric	Charge only lasts for a limited period. For example a hedgecutter may last 30 minutes Recharging may take some hours although most have a fast recharge facility Not as powerful as mains electric

Rechargeable battery versions are available for all the machinery covered in this section except for cultivators.

It is likely that considerable improvements will be made to rechargeable equipment and it will become increasingly popular.

Routine maintenance

Rechargeable batteries should need no maintenance apart of course from the recharging itself. If they fail the equipment should be returned to a service centre.

Keeping them out of a dusty atmosphere may extend their life.

Safety considerations for rechargeable batteries

These are the safest of all power sources and there are no special safety precautions.

Lawnmowers

Types of mower

Cylinder

Wheeled rotary

Hover rotary

Other mowers are gang mowers and flail mowers but these are outside the scope of this book.

Cylinder mowers

Advantages	Disadvantages
Gives a fine finish, striped if a rear roller is fitted. Easy to mow over edges of lawn	Not good at cutting long or wet grass Cutting mechanism easily damaged by stones or other debris

- **Choice**
  - ➜ A wide variety of cylinder mowers are available ranging from small electrically powered ones with a cutting width of 30 cm, up to large petrol powered ones with a cutting width of 60 cm.

- **Characteristics**
  - ➜ Cuts with a scissors action between a rotating cylinder containing a number of blades and a fixed bottom blade.

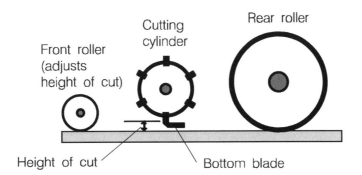

- ➜ Number of blades can vary from about 5 up to about 12. The more blades the finer will be the finish, and it is the mowers used for things like golf greens or tennis courts that will have the larger number. A typical garden mower will have 5 or 6.
- ➜ Normally sold with a grass box to collect the clippings.

- **Adjustments**

  → Distance between blades and bottom plate is critical to performance. Should be able to cut a piece of paper.

  → Height of cut can be adjusted, usually by raising or lowering front wheels or roller.

  → Handlebar height can sometimes be adjusted.

- **Typical uses**

  → Sports turf where a fine finish is essential, eg. golf greens.

  → Domestic lawns where a good finish is required.

Wheeled rotary mowers

Advantages	Disadvantages
Cutting mechanism works reasonably even if not very sharp. In fact some blades on the smaller models are made of plastic Good for long grass	Not as fine a finish as with a cylinder mower Can be heavy to handle

- **Choice**

  → The widest choice is available for these mowers, ranging from small electrically powered ones with a cutting width of 25 cm, up to large petrol powered ones with a cutting width of 60 cm.

  → Available with or without power to the wheels.

- **Characteristics**

  → Cuts with a slicing action relying on the speed of the blade to sever the grass.

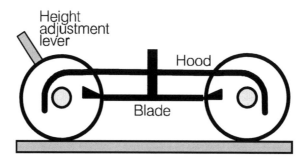

  → Available with 4 wheels, or front wheels and a rear roller to give a striped effect.

  → Normally sold with a grass box to collect the clippings.

- **Adjustments**

  → Height of cut can be adjusted, usually by raising or lowering the wheels.

➔ Handlebar height can sometimes be adjusted.

- **Typical uses**

  ➔ Utility lawns.

  ➔ Small paddocks and orchards.

  ➔ Areas of rough grass.

Hover rotary

Advantages	Disadvantages
Cutting mechanism works reasonably even if not very sharp Light and easy to use. Good for manoeuvring into awkward places Safer to use on banks than other mowers	Not so fine a finish as with a cylinder mower Do not usually collect the clippings Difficult and heavy to carry around unless carriage wheels are supplied

- **Choice**

  ➔ These were pioneered by Flymo but since their patents expired there are a number of other manufacturers.

  ➔ There is less choice with hover rotaries than with wheeled ones, but nevertheless there is a range from small electrically powered ones with a cutting width of about 30 cm, up to large petrol powered ones with a cutting width of about 60 cm.

- **Characteristics**

  ➔ Cuts with a slicing action relying on the speed of the blade to sever the blades of grass.

  ➔ A cushion of air holds the mower just above the surface of the ground.

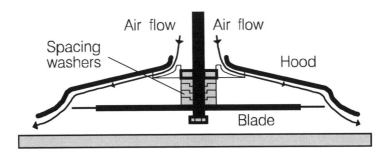

  ➔ Some of the larger ones have wheels which can be used just for transport or to use in conjunction with the hover effect.

  ➔ Some models now also collect the grass.

- **Adjustments**

  ➔ Height of cut can be adjusted, usually by washers fitted underneath the blade. The control is not so precise as with other mowers.

  ➔ Handlebar height can sometimes be adjusted.

- **Typical uses**
    - ➔ Utility lawns.
    - ➔ Banks and awkward areas.

Routine maintenance

- **Pre-use checks**
    - ➔ See **Topic F-2 'Power sources'** for checks relating to the power source.
    - ➔ Check the cutting mechanism is working freely.
    - ➔ Check the blade on a rotary is firmly fixed.

- **Periodic** (depending on usage) **and start of season**
    - ➔ See **Topic F-2 'Power sources'** for maintenance of the power source.
    - ➔ Check the cutting mechanism. On cylinder mowers adjust the distance of the blades from the bottom plate to get a clean cut. On rotary mowers check the blade for sharpness and damage.
    - ➔ Oil the cutting mechanism on cylinder mowers and any other points according to the instruction manual.
    - ➔ Regrind the blades on a cylinder mower (should not be necessary more than once per season), and sharpen and balance the blade on a rotary mower. The balance is important as the speed of rotation will cause vibration if it is not balanced.

Safety considerations for lawnmowers

- See **Topic F-2 'Power sources'** for safety relating to the power source.
- It is desirable that the following safety factors are built into the machine.
    1. **The cutting mechanism should be adequately shielded.**
    2. **A 'dead mans handle' should stop power to the cutting mechanism and to the wheels.**
    3. **There should be a separate lock-off switch on electric models.**
    4. **Blades should not continue to rotate when the power is cut off (electric models) or the engine is idling (petrol models).**
- Ensure the lawn is free of stones or other debris.
- If mowing rough grass where there may be hidden objects wear hard capped boots, gloves and goggles.
- Ensure young children and pets are kept away while the mowing is taking place.
- Never leave the mower running while unattended.
- Always mow by pushing the mower away from you.
- Do not try to clear any clogged grass without stopping the engine.

Cultivators

The object of using a cultivator is to break up the soil into a tilth that is suitable for sowing or planting.

Cultivating equipment includes ploughs, sub-soilers, rotary cultivators, harrows and rollers.

The only one likely to be used in a garden environment is the rotary cultivator and this topic will just cover pedestrian controlled ones. They are usually referred to as rotavators and that is the term we will use.

Pedestrian controlled rotavators

- **Choice**

  → A wide variety of rotavators is available. They will usually be petrol driven 4 stroke engines with a gear box.

  → They come in many shapes and sizes. A typical size would be a working width of 50 cm and a depth of 20 cm.

  → Available with 1, 2 and even no wheels.

- **Characteristics**

  → Usually has a number of forward gears and a reverse gear.

  → The basic tines are L shaped and can be rotated at a speed independent of the forward speed. The faster the speed of the tines relative to the forward speed, the finer will be the tilth.

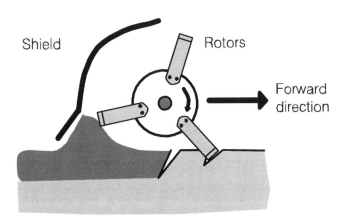

  → On some machines a shield covers the tines. This is partly for safety and partly to help create the tilth by the soil being thrown against it. The fineness of the tilth can sometimes be adjusted by moving the position of the shield.

  → Other fittings are usually available such as a ridger and scarifier.

- **Adjustments**

  → There is usually a 'skid plate' which can be adjusted so that the rotors work at a specific depth.

→ Handlebar height can sometimes be adjusted.

→ On some the handle can be offset to avoid walking on the area being cultivated.

- **Typical uses**

  → Large garden or small estate where there is an ongoing requirement for cultivation such as with a kitchen garden.

  → Commercial enterprise.

Routine maintenance

- **Pre-use checks**

  → See **Topic F-2 'Power sources'** for checks relating to the power source.

  → Check the rotors are able to move freely.

  → Check the bolts are tight, particularly the ones holding the rotors.

- **Periodic** (depending on use) **and start of season**

  → See **Topic F-2 'Power sources'** for maintenance of the power source.

  → Oil or grease moving parts according to the instruction manual.

  → Check oil levels in gear box and chain case.

  → Sharpen the rotors when necessary.

Safety considerations

- See **Topic F-2 'Power sources'** for safety relating to the power source.

- Wear hard capped boots, gloves and goggles.

- Ensure the shield plate is in place.

- Never leave the rotavator running and unattended.

- Never rotavate by pulling the machine towards you.

Hedgecutters

This topic covers hand-held hedgecutters although it is possible to get cutters for attaching to a tractor.

- **Choice**

  → There are a large number of hedgecutters available, driven by petrol, electricity or rechargeable batteries.

  → The length of cut is usually in the range of 30 cm to 75 cm.

- **Characteristics**

  → The cutting mechanism consists either of one blade reciprocating against a fixed blade, or two blades reciprocating against each other.

  → A hand shield protects the operator from the blades.

  → Some models, particularly petrol ones, will have a clutch to enable the engine to run without the blades moving, and this is an additional safety feature.

- **Adjustments**

  → None.

Routine maintenance

- See **Topic F-2 'Power sources'** for maintenance of the power source.

- Periodically oiling the blades and any other moving parts during use will extend the life.

- The blade will require periodic sharpening.

Safety considerations

- See **Topic F-2 'Power sources'** for safety relating to the power source.

- It is desirable that the following safety factors are built into the machine:

  1. **An adequate hand shield in front of the blades.**

  2. **Two switches, one for each hand, that both have to be pressed for the cutter to work. Alternatively a lock-off switch and an operating switch is nearly as good.**

  3. **A brake to stop the blades quickly when the motor is stopped. The blade should stop in less than a second.**

  4. **An extension on the blades to lessen the risk of a finger being trapped.**

- Wear gloves and goggles.

- Ensure the hand shield is in place.

- If using steps to cut a high hedge be sure they are set securely.

Trimmers and brushcutters

These are used for clearing grass or rough vegetation in situations where mowers are not suitable, such as uneven ground, banks, or areas where space is restricted.

Trimmers and brushcutters work on the same principle, but a trimmer refers to a low powered, usually electric, device suitable for the domestic garden whereas a brushcutter refers to a more powerful device, usually petrol driven, that can be used for tougher vegetation.

Trimmers (also called strimmers)

Advantages	Disadvantages
Good for long grass	Power supply needed for most types
Good for difficult places (eg around trees)	Not very powerful
Light and easy to use	

- **Choice**
  - → There are a number of trimmers available usually electric, although there are some rechargeable battery ones. Apart from this they are fairly basic and all very similar.

- **Characteristics**
  - → Cutting mechanism is a rotating nylon line. This wears out in use and a new length is pulled out from a spool either manually or automatically.
  - → A shield protects the operator from the rotating line.

- **Adjustments**
  - → The head on some trimmers can be rotated so that it can cut vertically which is useful for trimming lawn edges.
  - → Some models have a second handle positioned down the shaft that can be adjusted and some have a shaft that can be extended.

- **Typical uses**
  - → Tidying up difficult areas of grass in a domestic garden, such as around trees or fences, or in restricted areas.

Brushcutters

- **Choice**
  - → There are a number of brushcutters available usually powered by 2 stroke petrol engines since these are comparatively light.

Advantages	Disadvantages
Can tackle more difficult areas than a mower or strimmer	Heavy and tiring to use
	Noisy
Portable (no mains supply needed)	Protective clothing advisable

- **Characteristics**

  → Cutting mechanism is a rotating nylon line or a rotating blade. The blade is more efficient than the line but is potentially more dangerous.

  → A centrifugal clutch allows the engine to run without the line or blades rotating.

  → A shield protects the operator from the rotating line or blade.

  → A harness is usually used to help support the weight.

- **Adjustments**

  → The harness and handles can usually be adjusted to give the most comfortable fit.

- **Typical uses**

  → Areas of rough grass, undergrowth and other vegetation.

Routine maintenance

- See **Topic F-2 'Power sources'** for maintenance of the power source.

- Periodically oil all moving parts.

- The nylon line comes on a reel or spool which will need replacing.

- The blade, if used, will require periodic sharpening.

Safety considerations

- See **Topic F-2 'Power sources'** for safety relating to the power source.

- It is desirable that the following safety factors are built into the machine:

  1. **An adequate shield over the cutting head.**

  2. **A lock-off switch.**

  3. **A clutch to ensure the blades do not rotate when the engine is started.**

- Wear hard capped boots, gloves and goggles if using a brushcutter on rough ground.

- Ensure the shield is in place.

- Ensure you have a sound foothold on banks and rough ground.

- Keep children and pets away from the working area.

Self test questions

These questions are to enable you to assess how well you have understood and remembered the information in the previous section. No answers are given as these should be apparent from reviewing the relevant topics.

The questions are **not** intended to cover everything you should know.

1   List four checks you would carry out each time before using a petrol driven piece of equipment.

2   List four checks you would carry out periodically before using a petrol driven piece of equipment.

3   State the major safety precautions to be taken when using a petrol driven lawnmower.

4   List the advantages and disadvantages of the following types of mower and the typical uses of each.

Cylinder

Wheeled rotary

Hover rotary

5   Describe using diagrams the cutting principles of cylinder and rotary mowers (wheeled or hover).

6   List four desirable safety features to be incorporated into a mains electric hedgecutter.

The ornamental garden

This section covers all the different types of plants and features that make up the ornamental garden.

Most of the topics follow a similar format and include:

Uses
Buying
Planting
Initial pruning
Aftercare
Propagation
Problems
Suitability for special purposes
Examples

Lawns

There are very few people who would not want a lawn as part of their garden. Indeed for many people the lawn is the garden with perhaps a few other plants dotted around. Whether this situation will continue if water shortages become a normal part of life remains to be seen. Although it is true that a nicely cut green lawn can add enormously to the attraction of a garden, it is equally true that a brown and patchy lawn can be a depressing sight.

What makes grasses ideal for creating lawns

1. They grow under a wide range of climatic conditions

2. There are many species so that different needs can be met. For example, a bowling green will need a different grass to a children's playground

3. They stand up to constant cutting

4. They grow densely enough to discourage other plants   (weeds)

5. They can look attractive all the year round

6. Grass is the ultimate ground cover plant

Characteristics of grass plants

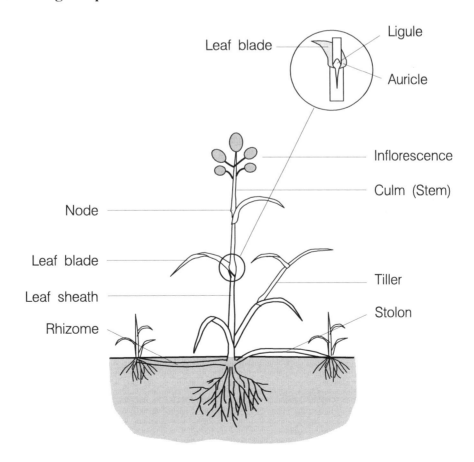

Grasses are in a family called **Poaceae** which worldwide consists of many thousands of species. Most of our agricultural cereal crops such as wheat and barley are in this family. In this topic however we are concerned with the grasses used for creating lawns in domestic gardens. As we will see there are many different species that can be used for this purpose.

- Grass is a monocotyledon. It has the fibrous roots and narrow leaves with parallel veins which characterise monocotyledons.

- The leaf blade (lamina) is attached to a leaf sheath which encircles the stem. If you pull the blade gently then the sheath will peel away from the stem.

- At the top of the leaf sheath is a small flap of tissue called the **ligule,** and at the base of the leaf blade is a small growth called the **auricle**. It is the exact form of these that can be used to distinguish one type of grass from another.

- Grass has the capability of producing new shoots from the base of the plant. These shoots are called **tillers**.

- Some grasses can spread by rhizomes or stolons.

- One of the major things that makes grass so successful for lawns is that there is a meristem at the base of the leaf and therefore the grass continues to grow after the top of the leaf has been cut off. In fact cutting off the top encourages the formation of tillers.

Grass seed mixtures

All turf or seed bought for lawns will be a mixture of different species. This is because no one species has all the characteristics required. Some may be hard wearing, some resistant to disease, some spreading, some drought resistant, so it makes sense to use a mixture.

For the domestic lawn we can broadly identify two requirements:

1. **The luxury lawn**

2. **The utility lawn**

It would be wrong to think that a luxury lawn is automatically better than a utility lawn. A luxury lawn will require more care, more frequent mowing, and be less hardwearing than a utility one. A compromise could be to have a luxury front lawn and a utility back lawn.

Luxury Lawn Seed		
Species	%	Characteristics
Browntop bent (Agrostis tenuis)	20	Tufted Spreads by stolons & rhizomes Hardwearing Good drought resistance Tolerates close mowing
Chewings fescue (Festuca rubra commutata)	80	Densely tufted Quick to establish Good drought resistance Tolerates close mowing

Utility Lawn Seed		
Species	%	Characteristics
Browntop bent (Agrostis tenuis)	10	As above
Creeping red fescue (Festuca rubra rubra)	20	Tufted Spreads by rhizomes Good resistance to drought & cold Will not tolerate close mowing
Smooth stalked meadow grass (Poa pratensis)	30	Major component of many utility mixtures Spreads by rhizomes Tolerates wide range of climatic conditions Will not tolerate close mowing
Perennial ryegrass (Lolium perenne)	40	Tufted Very hardwearing & tolerant Modern varieties of ryegrass are suitable for utility lawns unlike some older ones

Making a new lawn

1. Decide whether to use turf or seed

- Advantages of turf
  → Gives an instant effect
  → Available for use earlier
  → Ground preparation not so important although it will help the turf to establish itself quicker
- Advantages of seed
  → More choice of grass type
  → Much cheaper
  → Easier to cover awkward shapes or undulations

In general seed is more likely in the long run to produce a satisfactory lawn.

A comparatively recent development is the introduction of seeded turf. This is turf grown from seed on a specially prepared base. It is expensive but combines the advantages of turf and seed. It is usually supplied in rolls.

2. Ground preparation

Good ground preparation will pay dividends whether the lawn is being constructed from turf or seed.

Ground preparation can be done at any time when conditions permit (ground not waterlogged or frozen). Ideally the ground should be left after preparation to allow annual weeds to germinate. These can then be weedkilled to avoid competition with the grass seed.

- The site must be free of weeds particularly perennial ones. Either dig out the weeds or apply a translocated weedkiller such as glyphosate.

- Carry out any levelling or changes of gradient that are required. Ensure that in doing this subsoil is not brought to the surface. If necessary remove and stack the topsoil and replace after the levelling has been carried out.

- The minimum depth of topsoil is 15 cm but preferably should be at least 20 cm.

- Decide whether any special drainage needs to be installed. For the domestic garden this should not be necessary except in exceptional conditions.

- Dig or rotavate the soil to create a good tilth.

- Tread the soil to firm it and rake the surface to create a fine tilth.

- Water the soil if necessary, so that it is moist before the turf is laid or the seed is sown.

3. Lay the turf (if turfing)

The best time to do this is September to March. It can in fact be done at any time when the ground conditions are suitable but more aftercare may be required such as watering.

- Apply a general fertiliser to the soil at 25 g/sq m and rake it in.

- Turf can be obtained in sods which are usually 100 x 30 cm or in rolls.

- Sods should be laid in an offset pattern.

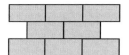   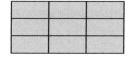

like this   not like this

- Allow the turf to overlap the edges of the lawn, and trim to shape when the complete lawn has been laid.

- Water in with a sprinkler

4. Sow the seed (if seeding)

The best time to do this is either September or April.

- Apply a general fertiliser to the soil at 25 g/sq m and rake it in.

- Sow at the rate recommended by the supplier (likely to be 25-50 g/sq m). To get an even distribution halve the recommended rate and then sow in opposite directions.

- Lightly rake the seed into the surface of the soil.

- Water in with a sprinkler.

- If birds are likely to eat the seed, cotton stretched over the area may be a deterrent.

5. Aftercare

- The main requirement is to ensure that the ground is not allowed to dry out until the grass is established.

- Do not apply a weedkiller within 6 months even though there may be many annual weeds germinate.
- Cut the new grass when it reaches a height of 5 cm.

Routine maintenance

The following tasks make up the routine maintenance. Not all of them will necessarily be needed in a particular situation.

Mowing & trimming
Watering
Feeding
Weed control
Moss control
Scarifying
Aerating
Top dressing

Mowing & trimming

- As a general guide mow once a week during the growing season. A luxury lawn may need to be done more often, and a utility lawn may be done less frequently. The best guide is the length of the grass.
- The choice of mower will depend on the finish required. There are basically three types of mower that can be used for the domestic garden.

Cylinder
Wheeled rotary
Hover rotary

The characteristics of these mowers, and their advantages and disadvantages have been covered in **Topic F-3 'Lawnmowers'**.

- The length of the cut is largely a matter of personal preference. From 1-3 cm is a typical range. In general the grass will be healthier, and less problems of weeds and moss will arise if the grass is at the upper part of this range.
- Opinions differ as to whether clippings should be left on the lawn. The balance is probably in favour of removing them, although if this is done feeding is essential.
- Trim the lawn edges after mowing.

Watering

Watering is essential to retain a green lawn in periods of low or no rainfall.

However, watering lawns has been difficult in recent years because of the widespread water shortages and consequent hosepipe bans. If watering is not possible it is unlikely that the grass will die and it should be rejuvenated with the first significant rainfall.

Keeping the grass longer than normal will help to reduce water loss and keep the grass looking greener.

- Water before the signs of drought are evident in the lawn.
- Water thoroughly. The soil should be moist to a depth of 10 cm.

Feeding

Feeding is very important particularly if the clippings are removed from the lawn.

Lawn fertilisers are normally purchased and applied as a balanced mix of the main nutrients required. These are:

Nitrogen (N)	Required for leaf growth and for a good colour
Phosphorus (P)	Required to build up a healthy root system
Potassium (K)	Required for healthy and disease resistant growth

The relative amount of each nutrient is shown on containers as the NPK ratio, eg.

Scotts Turf Builder	32:0:4
Evergreen Autumn Lawn Care	6:5:10

Some lawn feed mixtures now contain slow release nitrogen fertiliser which should avoid a sudden rush of growth and keep the lawn looking greener over a longer period.

- Apply a high nitrogen fertiliser in spring.
- Apply a high phosphorus fertiliser in autumn.
- Water in if there is no rain within 48 hours.

Weed control

The different weedkillers are covered later in this topic.

- Apply at any time that the weeds are in active growth, although spring is best to give a weed free lawn through the season.
- If applied in granular form water in if there is no rain within 48 hours.

Moss control

The important thing about moss control is to eliminate as far as possible the environmental conditions that give rise to the moss. Typical causes of moss are:

1. **Poor drainage**
2. **Soil compaction**
3. **Shade**
4. **Cutting grass too short**
5. **Poor soil fertility**
6. **High pH value of soil**

The use of mosskillers is the same as weedkillers.

Scarifying

Scarifying is the raking the surface of the lawn with a special rake that has a number of thin sprung tines. There are both hand and powered rakes.

The purpose of scarifying is:

1.   **To remove thatch**

    Thatch is the accumulation of plant and other debris on the surface of the soil. It can impair drainage and encourage fungal diseases. It will be worse if mowing is done without collecting the clippings.

2.   **To remove moss**

3.   **To stimulate the growth of tillers**

Scarifying is best done in the autumn although it can be done at other times during the growing season.

Aerating

Aerating is the making of holes in the lawn to a depth of 8-15 cm.

The purpose of aerating is:

1.   **To allow air to reach the grass roots**

2.   **To improve drainage**

3.   **To relieve compaction**

It is necessary in some cases because with a lot of use the surface of the soil may become compacted and impede the passage of air and water. This is more likely with clay soils.

The holes may be made at intervals of 15 cm using either a garden fork or a special hand or powered tool called an aerator or tiner.

The special tools can have different kinds of tines.

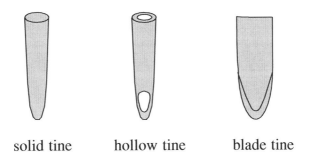

solid tine   hollow tine   blade tine

The solid tine just makes a hole in the lawn; the hollow tine removes a core of soil; the blade tine makes a slit.

The advantage of a hollow tine is that it removes a core of soil whereas the other types, although they make a hole, actually compress the soil around the hole. The use of a hollow tine is particularly useful in conjunction with top dressing.

Aerating should only be necessary once a year and is best done in autumn.

Top dressing

Top dressing is the application of a sand, peat and loam mixture to the surface of the lawn. Note that top dressing does not contain nutrients and does not therefore have a fertilising effect.

The ornamental garden

The advantages of top dressing are:

1. Improves the structure of the soil particularly if applied after aerating.

This aids drainage in clay soils and moisture retention in sandy soils.

2. Fills in small indentations in the lawn.

The actual mix of ingredients can be varied according to the type of soil. On a very heavy soil for example just sand and peat could be applied.

- Apply top dressing in the autumn at a rate of 1-2 kilo/sq m.
- Work into the surface of the lawn with a besom (broom) or a special tool called a loot.

Lawn care timetable

	Jan	Feb	Mar	Apr	May	Jun	Jul	Aug	Sept	Oct	Nov	Dec
Turf	■	■	■						■	■	■	■
Seed				■					■			
Mow			■	■	■	■	■	■	■	■		
Water					■	■	■	■				
Feed			■									
Weedkill			■									
Moss control		■										
Scarify									■	■		
Aerate									■			
Top dress									■			

In practice there is more flexibility in when things should be done than is obvious from the above chart.

Renovating a neglected lawn

A decision has to be taken whether to start again and create a new lawn, or attempt to recover the old one.

This will be largely a question of judgement, but the following steps can be taken to help form a decision:

1. If it is very overgrown cut down with strimmer or shears so that the surface can be seen.

2. Examine the grass that still exists to see if it basically of good quality. If it is all coarse and poor quality then go for a new lawn.

3. Look at a profile of the soil. If it is obviously in bad condition (infertile, compacted, stony) then go for a new lawn.

If the decision is to try to recover the lawn this is best done starting in spring. The tasks are basically the same as for routine maintenance carried out in the following sequence:

1. Cut down top growth, in stages if very overgrown, to a length of 5 cm.
2. Diagnose problems eg.

    Compaction
    Drainage
    pH
    Moss
    Weeds
    Disease

3. Improve environmental conditions (improve drainage, remove causes of excessive shade if possible).
4. Weed and moss kill
5. Scarify to remove dead weeds and moss
6. Aerate if necessary
7. Fertilise and top dress
8. Reseed any bare patches
9. Mow regularly

Chemicals for the lawn

Chemicals for the control of lawn problems have been reduced over recent years, placing increased importance on providing good growing conditions and encouraging healthy growth.

Some chemicals that are suitable for the lawn have already been covered in **Topic C-4 'Chemical control'**. For convenience they are summarised here.

Moss control

Ferrous sulphate	An iron salt that burns the moss. Usually combined with sand and a fertiliser to form 'Lawn Sand'. This is now the only chemical treatment available.

Weedkillers

2, 4 - D Mecoprop-P MCPA	These are selective weedkillers, killing broad leaved weeds but not the grass. They are called hormone weedkillers because they upset the hormone system of the weeds causing them to grow erratically and die. Most proprietary weedkillers contain more than one chemical to cover a wider range of weeds.

Fungicides

Trifloxystrobin	Protects lawn against diseases such as fusarium patch and red thread. Can be applied all year round.

Insecticides

Imidacloprid	Systemic insecticde for the control of chafer grubs and leatherjackets, Provides season long control.

Many lawn products on the market combine weed control chemicals, ferrous sulphate for moss control, and lawn fertilisers to provide a complete treatment in one package.

Weeds

Although a limited number of weeds may be tolerated in lawns they can become unsightly and will gradually take over the grass if no action is taken.

Lawn weeds are not the same as weeds in flower or vegetable beds. Because they have to survive frequent cutting (or grazing in nature), they have developed forms to survive this.

The main forms of grass weed are:

Rosette forming	Leaves lie parallel to the ground to escape mower eg. plantains, daisies, dandelions
Creeping	Spread vegetatively by stolons or rhizomes eg. clover, speedwell
Mat forming	Create a carpet below the level of the grass eg. moss, pearlwort

One of the worst weeds in lawns is grass itself. Coarse forms of grass may develop which spoil the lawn particularly if it is a luxury one. They are difficult because grass weedkillers will not work against them. On sports surfaces like golfing or bowling greens annual meadow grass which seeds prolifically can be a severe problem.

The following table identifies a representative number of lawn weeds:

Plantain (Plantago major)	A rosette forming perennial weed with broad leaves. It is very common in all lawns. It produces large amounts of seed and needs to be dealt with before this sets. Remove by hand weeding or with a selective weedkiller.
Dandelion (Taraxacum officinale)	A rosette forming perennial weed which has a long taproot. It is very common in all lawns. It flowers through the year and produces large numbers of seeds that can be carried long distances by the wind. Hand weeding is unreliable because any root left will regenerate. Treat with a selective weedkiller

Speedwell (Veronica filiformis)	A weed that was originally introduced as a garden plant and has attractive bright blue flowers. It spreads by stolons but can reproduce from small pieces spread by mowing. It does not however produce seed. This is a difficult weed to control. The best weedkiller (ioxynil) is no longer available. Use one of the available selective weedkillers.
Daisy (Bellis perennis) .	A common weed that grows mainly in lawns. It is quite attractive and many people will regard it as acceptable. It spreads slowly by stolons and by seed. Control by hand weeding or with a selective weedkiller.

Pests

Grass is not subject to the same pest problems that can inflict so much damage on flowers, fruit or vegetables.

The following table identifies some of the pest problems that can arise.

Cats and dogs	These can damage newly seeded lawns by disturbing the seed. On established lawns fouling the garden is unsightly and can cause the grass to die. If the animals are not yours the best prevention is to make your garden secure.
Moles	An invasion of moles can be heartbreaking. In addition to the familiar mounds of earth where they come to the surface their runs can collapse leaving depressions all over the lawn which can be difficult to remove. There are various folk remedies that can be tried such as creosote or mothballs placed in the run but it is more reliable to use the services of a professional to trap or poison them.
Leatherjackets	Leatherjackets are the grubs of the cranefly (daddy long legs). They can cause damage by feeding on the roots of the grass. There is a chemical control called imidacloprid or a biological control iin the form of a nematode *Steinernema feltiae*.
Chafer grubs	Chafer grubs also eat the roots of the grass but are in general not much of a problem. Control with imidacloprid or with a biological control in the form of a nematode *Heterorhabditis megidis*.

Diseases

The majority of diseases are caused by fungi. They are most prevalent in spring and autumn when the ground is moist. Leaving clippings or leaves on the lawn may increase the chances of a fungal disease.

The following table identifies some of the diseases that can affect lawns.

Fusarium patch (snow mould)	This is a fungal infection most prevalent in autumn and spring.
	It starts with small patches of yellowing grass which can grow and merge to form a large area in which the grass eventually dies.
	Improve aeration and ensure grass is not walked upon in wet or cold weather.
	The chemical control trifloxystrobin can be used.
Red thread (corticium disease)	This is a fungal infection most prevalent in autumn.
	Although the grass does not die it loses its colour and becomes unsightly.
	The leaves have minute red needles growing from the surface.
	Improve drainage and ensure grass is adequately fertilised.
	The chemical control trifloxystrobin can be used.
Dollar spot	This is a fungal infection mainly affecting fine grasses (creeping red fescue is particularly susceptible)
	The first sign are small circular straw coloured patches which can spread and form larger areas.
	Improve drainage. Avoid the use of *festuca* grasses which are particularly prone.
Toadstools	A few toadstools are not a problem but 'fairy rings', characterised by rings of bright grass can be very difficult to get rid of and may require the soil to be removed to a depth of 30 cm.
	Do not leave clippings on the lawn as this may spread the problem.

Trees and conifers

This topic is concerned with ornamental trees only; fruit trees are covered in the section **'The fruit garden'**.

Reference in this topic to 'trees' includes conifers unless otherwise stated.

What is a tree or conifer

Trees and conifers are distinguished by having a trunk or main stem. In trees this is usually clear of branches up to a certain height, while in conifers the branches may start at the base of the trunk.

As a generalisation it can be said that trees are deciduous and conifers are evergreen but there are exceptions to this.

Uses of trees

- Component of garden design
- Screening of unsightly objects
- Providing shelter and shade
- Preventing soil erosion
- Supporting wildlife
- In public areas for providing shade, increasing humidity, oxygenating the air and improving the appearance

Sizes and shapes

Trees come in many sizes, from ones no more than 2 m high, up to forest trees that may reach 30 m. Conifers have an even wider range with dwarf and prostrate conifers measured in centimetres.

Some small trees suitable for the average garden are:

Acer griseum
Amelanchier lamarkii
Gleditsia triacanthus
Laburnum 'Vossii'
Malus 'Golden Hornet'
Malus tschonoskii
Prunus 'Amanogawa'
Pyrus salicifolia

Some of the more common shapes are:

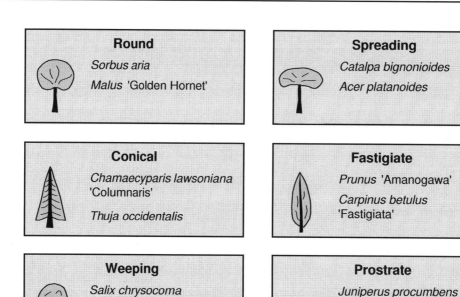

Round	Spreading
Sorbus aria	*Catalpa bignonioides*
Malus 'Golden Hornet'	*Acer platanoides*

Conical	Fastigiate
Chamaecyparis lawsoniana 'Columnaris'	*Prunus* 'Amanogawa'
Thuja occidentalis	*Carpinus betulus* 'Fastigiata'

Weeping	Prostrate
Salix chrysocoma	*Juniperus procumbens*
Fagus sylvatica 'Pendula'	*Picea pungens* 'Prostrata'

Trees in design

Trees make an important contribution to the structure of a garden. They are the biggest and longest-lived of all the plants and therefore should be chosen and positioned with great care. The only solution to a badly chosen or planted tree once it is well established is to remove it.

Trees can contribute to the design by:

- Use as focal points
- Providing contrasting forms, eg. fastigiate and prostrate
- Dividing spaces or framing views
- Providing shelter and shade
- Participating in a mixed border
- Providing year round interest

Trees can be used in formal and informal designs. The more regular shaped ones are more suited to formal designs.

In public areas a combination of trees and ground cover can provide an attractive and low maintenance scheme.

Buying trees

The general rules on buying plants set out in **Topic E-1 'Buying plants'** apply, particularly in view of the expense, significance and permanence of trees.

Find out what the ultimate size of the tree is going to be. In ten years it may have outgrown its space and dominate the garden.

Trees can be bought at many stages of their life from 1 year old whips up to heavy standards. There is also a growing market for mature trees which will make an immediate impact, but these can run into many hundreds of pounds.

The problem of buying a very young tree is that it will take some years before it reaches a significant size and will flower. Most trees bought from garden centres will have been growing for several years.

British Standard 3936 sets out specifications for trees of different sizes. It identifies seven sizes, including the following three:

Half standard	Trunk	125 - 150 cm
	Overall height	175 - 250 cm
	Girth	4 - 6 cm
Standard	Trunk	175 - 200 cm
	Overall height	250 - 300 cm
	Girth	8 - 10 cm
Heavy standard	Trunk	175 - 200 cm
	Overall height	> 350 cm
	Girth	12 - 14 cm

Planting

See **Topic E-2 'Planting'** for general guidance on planting.

Beware of planting trees too close to a house or other building where their roots may cause some damage. As a general guide plant as far away as the mature height of the tree. For some trees such as willows and poplars plant even further away.

The bark of young trees is attractive to rabbits and if these are a nuisance it is possible to buy tubular or spiral guards to place round the base of the trunk.

Initial pruning

Conifers and trees bought as standards will require little or no pruning. Younger trees may require some initial pruning and training to establish a good branch structure.

See **Topic E-5 'Pruning'** for general guidance on pruning.

Aftercare

Watering

For the first 2-3 years trees should be watered in periods of no rain.

Feeding

A general fertiliser in the first 2-3 years will help the tree to establish quickly but once established no feeding should be necessary.

Weed control

The area round the base of the tree should be kept clear while the tree is getting established to ensure it is not robbed of water and nutrients. This is one of the most important factors in getting a tree off to a good start.

Pruning

See **Topic E-5 'Pruning'** for general guidance on pruning.

Established trees should require little or no pruning other than pruning for health.

Propagation

Trees may be grown from seed or propagated vegetatively from cuttings, layering or grafting.

Trees from seed	Trees from cuttings	Trees from layering	Trees from grafting
Aesculus (Horse Chestnut)	*Acer*	*Magnolia*	*Acer*
Fagus (Beech)	*Betula* (Birch)	*Corylus* (Hazel)	*Betula*
Quercus (Oak)	*Prunus* (Cherry)	*Davidia*	*Gleditsia*
Sorbus (Mountain Ash)	*Salix* (Willow)	*Laurus* (Laurel)	*Robinia*

See **Topics E-3 and E-4 'Propagation'** for general guidance on propagation.

Propagation from seed has the disadvantage that it may take several years to reach a reasonable height and to flower. Also remember that cultivars will not come true from seed and have to be propagated vegetatively.

Problems with trees

Trees are generally trouble free and many will grow satisfactorily for many years with no attention whatsoever.

Although they are attacked by pests and diseases just like other plants this is usually of less concern because we are not growing them to provide food.

The most troublesome pests are aphids, and the worst disease is honey fungus.

If a tree is not growing satisfactorily it is quite likely that it is suffering because of poor planting or poor soil, or some other problem with the environment. See **Topic C-8 'Common disorders'** for information on environment problems.

Trees for special purposes

For acid soils	For alkaline soils	For evergreen foliage
Liquidambar styraciflua	*Fraxinus excelsior*	All conifers (except Larch)
Magnolia acuminata	*Juniperus*	*Ilex*
Pinus sylvestris	*Malus*	*Quercus ilex*

For ornamental bark	For coloured foliage	For autumn colour
Acer griseum	*Fagus sylvatica* 'Purpurea'	*Amelanchier lamarkii*
Betula jacquemontii	*Robinia pseudoacacia* 'Frisia'	*Malus tschonoskii*
Eucalyptus dalrympleana	*Thuja plicata* 'Zebrina'	*Prunus sargentii*

For flowers
Catalpa bignonioides
Magnolia grandiflora
Prunus 'Kanzan'

For fruits
Crataegus prunifolia
Malus 'Golden Hornet'
Sorbus hupehensis

For fragrance
Laburnum vossii
Magnolia
Malus coronaria

For focal points
Acer pseudoplatanus
Betula pendula 'Youngii'
Liriodendron tulipifera

For small gardens
Acer griseum
Malus tschonoskii
Pyrus salicifolia

For dwarf conifers
Chamaecyparis obtusa 'Nana'
Picea abies 'Nidiformis'
Thuja orientalis 'Nana'

Some of the best

Trees

Amelanchier lamarkii

A small tree suitable for the small garden. Also known as 'Snowy Mespilus'.

White flowers in spring and apple green foliage that turns red and orange in autumn.

Betula pendula

A fast growing 'Silver Birch' with the characteristic white bark. This species has attractive drooping branchlets.

Good as a focal point or planted in lawns. 'Youngii' is a particularly striking cultivar.

Catalpa bignonioides

A medium to large tree with a spreading habit. Often seen in public places.

Its main feature is its large, heart-shaped leaves although it also has white, yellow and purple flowers in July/August followed by slender seed pods.

Fagus sylvatica

This is our native beech tree. It can grow large but there are cultivars which are smaller.

'Purpurea' is a striking cultivar.

Often used as a hedging plant.

Malus 'Golden Hornet'

A 'crab apple' that is suitable for a small garden and will tolerate most conditions.

White flowers in April followed by large yellow fruits that can smother and bend the branches with their weight.

Robinia pseudoacacia 'Frisia'

A small to medium sized tree that has golden yellow foliage made up of a number of leaflets.

Suitable a a focal point.

Sorbus hupehensis

A small tree with purple/brown branches and blue/green finely divided leaves.

Main attraction is the white, pink tinged fruits which persist well into winter.

Tolerant of most conditions.

Prunus 'Kanzan'

A popular small flowering cherry with upright growth.

In spring it is covered in pink blossom.

Conifers

Chamaecyparis obtusa 'Nana'

A dwarf conifer growing no more than 1 m and therefore suitable for a rockery or small garden.

It grows in tiers of cup shaped branches.

Juniperus horizontalis

A prostrate conifer that can be used as ground cover and is suitable for covering a bank.

There are a number of cultivars some of which have a spread of 4-5 m but do not exceed 1 m in height.

Pinus sylvestris

This is the native 'Scots Pine' which will grow into a large conifer although there are a number of cultivars, some of which are dwarf or medium sized.

The foliage tends to be grey or blue green although some of the cultivars are golden.

Thuja plicata 'Zebrina'

This is 'Western Red Cedar' and this cultivar has attractive foliage of light green striped with yellow. It will eventually make a large conifer.

Thuja plicata stands being cut hard back and is often used for hedges.

Shrubs

This topic covers shrubs other than roses and climbing shrubs which have their own topics.

What is a shrub

A shrub is a woody perennial that has a permanent branch structure. Unlike a tree it is multi-stemmed or with a very short main stem.

Shrubs can be evergreen or deciduous and vary considerably in size and shape.

Uses of shrubs

- Main component of the all year round garden
- Shrub or mixed border
- Hedges (See **Topic G-4 'Hedges and windbreaks'**)
- Covering walls, arches and pergolas (See **Topic G-6 'Climbers'**)
- Ground cover (See **Topic G-7 'Ground cover'**)
- Topiary
- Containers

Sizes and shapes

Shrubs vary considerably in size from a few centimetres like heathers to several metres such as many rhododendrons.

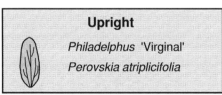

Round

Choisya ternata

Hebe albicans

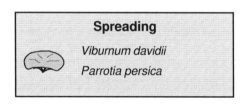

Spreading

Viburnum davidii

Parrotia persica

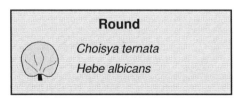

Upright

Philadelphus 'Virginal'

Perovskia atriplicifolia

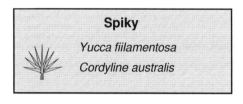

Spiky

Yucca fiilamentosa

Cordyline australis

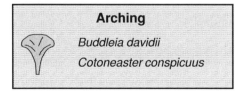

Arching

Buddleia davidii

Cotoneaster conspicuus

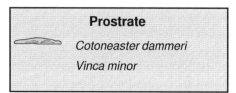

Prostrate

Cotoneaster dammeri

Vinca minor

The ornamental garden

Shrubs in design

The main use of shrubs in the garden is to contribute to the structure, although large shrubs can also be used as focal points.

Because they have a permanent branch structure they contribute to the all year round interest of the garden.

Shrubs can contribute to the design by:

* Use as focal points
* Providing contrasting forms, textures and colours eg. upright and prostrate, small and large leaved, grey and green foliage
* Providing a succession of flower colour through the year
* Making a shrub border or participating in a mixed border
* Providing year round interest

Shrub borders were very popular in Victorian times but are less so now, largely because of the space required. It is more usual now to use shrubs as specimen plants or as part of a mixed border.

Smaller shrubs can look more effective planted in groups rather than singly.

Buying shrubs

See **Topic G-1 'Buying plants'** for general guidance.

As with trees it is important to find out the ultimate size of the shrub.

Nearly all shrubs are now bought in containers and can therefore be planted at any time of the year.

Siting and Planting

There are shrubs available that will suit almost any site and soil. In general it is better to use plants that are suited to the conditions rather than to try and adapt the conditions to the plant.

See **Topic E-2 'Planting'** for general guidance.

If planting a bed or border a decision has to be made about how far apart to plant the shrubs. If they are planted at a distance that reflects their ultimate size they will look a little sparse, and leave a lot of bare ground unless something else is used to cover it. Bare ground is a thing to be avoided since it will be colonised by weeds and the choice comes down to:

1. **Plant the shrubs closer and be prepared to remove some as they mature.**

2. **Fill the ground with other plants like annuals, biennials and perennials.**

3. **Buy mature plants. This is a very expensive option.**

Option 2 is probably better than option 1, partly because it could be cheaper, but mainly because the other plants will cover the bare ground more quickly than the shrubs will.

Initial pruning

Shrubs should require no initial pruning other than trimming back any weak, straggly or damaged stems.

Aftercare

Watering

For the first 1-2 years shrubs should be watered in periods of no rain. Subsequently they should only require watering in extended periods of drought.

Feeding

Plants that are pruned heavily will require an application of general fertiliser in spring at a rate of 25/50 g/sq m. Other shrubs will also benefit from a once a year application at the lower rate.

Weed control

The area round the base of the shrubs should be kept clear to ensure the plants are not robbed of water and nutrients. This can be done by hand weeding or using a weedkiller as long as the spray is kept off the foliage of the shrubs.

Pruning

See **Topic E-5 'Pruning'** for general guidance.

There are four different situations to consider:

1. **Evergreen shrubs**

    These should require very little pruning other than the removal of dead, diseased or damaged wood, or to contain its size and shape. This is best done in spring just before new growth starts.

    eg. *Berberis, Eleagnus, Ilex*

2. **Shrubs that flower on current years growth**

    These should be pruned hard in spring.

    eg. *Buddleia, Caryopteris, Fuschia*

3. **Shrubs that flower on previous years growth**

    These are mainly spring and early summer flowering shrubs and should be pruned after flowering

    eg. *Philadelphus, Syringa, Weigela*

    Cut back the flowering shoots to fresh, young growth.

4. **Shrubs grown for ornamental stems**

    These should be pruned to within a few centimetres of the ground in spring

    eg. *Cornus alba, Rubus cockburnianus, Salix alba*

Propagation

Shrubs may be grown from seed or propagated vegetatively from cuttings, layering or grafting. Evergreen shrubs are particularly suitable for hardwood cuttings.

See **Topics E-3 and E-4 'Propagation'** for general guidance.

Remember that cultivars will not come true from seed and have to be propagated vegetatively.

Shrubs from seed	Shrubs from cuttings	Shrubs from layering	Shrubs from grafting
Arbutus	*Erica*	*Chaenomeles*	*Hamamelis*
Cotoneaster	*Kolkwitzia*	*Kalmia*	*Magnolia*
Daphne	*Lavatera*	*Skimmia*	*Rhododendron*
Euonymus	*Mahonia*	*Syringa*	*Syringa*

In addition shrubs that produce suckers can be propagated by division.

Problems with shrubs

Shrubs are very similar in this respect to trees and most will grow with few problems.

The most troublesome pests are aphids and the worst disease is honey fungus.

If a shrub is not growing satisfactorily it is quite likely that it is suffering because of poor planting or poor soil or some other problem with the environment. See **Topic C-8 'Common disorders'** for information about environment problems.

Shrubs for special purposes

For acid soils	For alkaline soils	For evergreen foliage
Erica	*Buddleia davidii*	*Eleagnus pungens*
Kerria japonica	*Deutzia*	*Euonymus fortunei*
Rhododendron	*Hypericum*	*Mahonia aquifolium*

For ornamental stems	For coloured foliage	For autumn colour
Cornus alba	*Berberis thunbergii* 'Atropurpurea'	*Cotinus coggygria*
Salix alba	*Euonymus fortunei* 'Silver Queen'	*Rhus typhina*
Rubus cockburnianus		*Viburnum opulus*

For flowers	For fruits	For shade
Buddleia davidii	*Chaenomeles x superba*	Euonymus fortunei
Potentilla 'Elizabeth'	*Cotoneaster conspicuus*	Ilex
Rhododendron	*Pyracantha*	Mahonia aquifolium

For focal points	For fragrance	For containers
Camellia japonica	*Daphne odora*	Hebe
Rosa species	*Osmanthus delavayi*	Lavandula
Viburnum plicatum	*Philadelphus* 'Virginal'	Salvia

Some of the best

The shrubs are deciduous unless otherwise stated.

Sizes are given as small, medium or large as applicable to an average garden and mean:

Small	< 1 m
Medium	1 - 2 m
Large	> 2 m

Berberis thunbergii 'Atropurpurea'

Berberis is a genus with many species including both evergreens and deciduous. One thing they all share are sharp thorns.

This particular cultivar is included because of its dark purple foliage that turns red in autumn.

It is a medium sized shrub and will grow in most conditions.

Buddleia davidii

There are a number of cultivars of this species which produce large flower spikes in shades of pink, blue and purple. It is known as the 'Butterfly Bush' because of its attraction for butterfies.

It is a medium sized shrub which produces its best flowers if it is pruned hard in spring.

Cotoneaster conspicuus

This is a large evergreen shrub that has arching branches that are covered in autumn with red berries.

It is an easy shrub to grow, and there are cultivars that are smaller in size if space is limited.

Euonymus fortunei

This shrub is included for its all year round contribution to the garden. It is evergreen and a number of cultivars have attractive variegated foliage such as 'Silver Queen' that is green with creamy white markings.

The cultivars are small or prostrate.

They will grow in most soils and tolerate some shade.

Philadelphus 'Virginal'

This is a large shrub that has arching branches that are covered in early summer with double, white, highly fragrant flowers. Its common name is 'Mock Orange'.

It is an easy shrub to grow, and there are other cultivars that are smaller in size if space is limited.

Potentilla 'Elizabeth'

Potentillas are a very useful group of shrubs.

Most are small to medium in size, easy to grow and flower over a long period.

This particular cultivar has buttercup yellow flowers from May to September.

Rhododendrons

There are so many species and cultivars that it is difficult to single out any particular ones. They are mostly large and evergreen although they include azaleas which are mostly deciduous.

What they all require however is an acid soil (pH < 6.5) and attempts to grow them on an alkaline soil will not be successful.

Viburnum plicatum

This makes a large shrub with the branches arranged attractively in tiers. In May flat flower heads 7-10 cm across of pure white smother the branches.

They will tolerate most soils but prefer a sunny position.

Good cultivars are 'Mariesii' and 'Lanarth'.

Weigela florida

This is a medium sized shrub with arching branches that produces many tubular, pink flowers in May/June.

It is very undemanding and will grow in most soils, and in sun or partial shade.

A good cultivar is 'Variegata' which is more compact and has leaves with white margins.

Yucca filamentosa

This is a small to medium sized shrub which is grown mainly for its strong architectural shape, consisting of sword like leaves growing in a rosette from ground level.

It also has large flower spikes of white. cup shaped flowers in August.

It requires a well drained soil and will grow in sun or partial shade.

A sample shrub border

Planting suitable for a bed approximately 5 m x 3 m, to provide all year round interest.

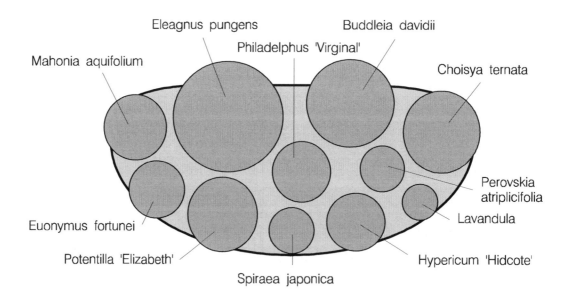

Hedges and windbreaks

What is a hedge

A hedge is a row of plants planted close enough together to create a continuous line. The plants can be trees, conifers or shrubs, and can be evergreen or deciduous.

The plants are usually clipped to restrict their size and to give a uniform appearance.

The use of hedges

● **Boundary definition**

This is the most common use. A large number of houses will have one serving this purpose. It is significantly cheaper than walls and more permanent than fences.

On the other hand it takes time to become established and requires maintenance.

● **Internal partitioning**

Hedges can be used to sub-divide a garden, such as placing one around a vegetable garden or rose garden.

● **Privacy**

As a boundary definition or internal partitioning, a hedge can provide privacy.

● **Shelter**

A hedge can protect areas of the garden from wind. See later under **'Windbreaks'**.

● **Design element**

Hedges can be an integral part of the overall design of the garden.

Formal hedges, particularly the dark, small leaved ones like yew and box, can make an excellent backdrop and foil to other elements in the garden. Dwarf box hedges around beds is a common feature of old gardens. Informal hedges can provide colour in their own right.

Hedges can be used to lead the eye and direct the feet around the garden, and create an element of surprise by hiding something from immediate view.

Types of hedge

Hedges can be broadly divided into formal and informal and can be evergreen or deciduous.

1. Formal

A formal hedge is one that is kept clipped to a regular shape and not allowed to flower. It will require more maintenance than an informal one.

Most formal hedges will be evergreen and include yew, box, privet and leyland cypress. Beech and hornbeam are also used as formal hedges and, although not evergreen, the dead leaves hang on over winter.

2. Informal

An informal hedge is one that is made from flowering shrubs. They are pruned to produce the most flower in the same way as other shrubs.

Informal hedges can be either evergreen or deciduous and include escallonia, lavender, forsythia and rugosa roses.

Plants for hedges

YEW		
Botanical name		
Taxus baccata		
Formal/informal		
Formal		
Evergreen		
Yes		
Planting distance		
60 cm		
Height in 5 years		
1 m		
Clipping		
Spring & autumn		
Initial pruning		
Group 3		

BOX

Botanical name
Buxus sempervirens
Formal/informal
Formal
Evergreen
Yes
Planting distance
30 cm
Height in 5 years
50 cm
Clipping
Minimum twice yearly
Initial pruning
Group 3

PRIVET

Botanical name
Ligustrum ovalifolium
Formal/informal
Formal
Evergreen
Yes
Planting distance
30 cm
Height in 5 years
1.5 m
Clipping
Minimum twice yearly
Initial pruning
Group 1

LEYLAND CYPRESS

Botanical name
Cupressocyparis leylandii
Formal/informal
Formal
Evergreen
Yes
Planting distance
75 cm
Height in 5 years
1.5-3 m
Clipping
Spring & autumn
Initial pruning
Group 3

BEECH

Botanical name
Fagus sylvatica
Formal/informal
Formal
Evergreen
No (but leaves hang on over winter)
Planting distance
30-60 cm
Height in 5 years
2 m
Clipping
Late summer
Initial pruning
Group 2

ESCALLONIA

Botanical name
Escallonia
Formal/informal
Informal
Evergreen
Yes
Planting distance
60 cm
Height in 5 years
1.5-2 m
Clipping
After flowering
Initial pruning
Not necessary

FORSYTHIA	RUGOSA ROSE	LAVENDER
Botanical name *Forsythia x intermedia*	**Botanical name** *Rosa rugosa*	**Botanical name** *Lavandula spica*
Formal/informal Informal	**Formal/informal** Informal	**Formal/informal** Informal
Evergreen No	**Evergreen** No	**Evergreen** Yes
Planting distance 60 cm	**Planting distance** 60 cm	**Planting distance** 30 cm
Height in 5 years 1.5-2 m	**Height in 5 years** 1.5 m	**Height in 5 years** 1 m
Clipping After flowering	**Clipping** Spring	**Clipping** After flowering
Initial pruning Not necessary	**Initial pruning** Not necessary	**Initial pruning** Not necessary

Factors in choosing the right plant

- Formal or informal
- Evergreen or deciduous
- Climate and aspect
- Soil
- Size and shape
- Rate of growth
- Ability to stand clipping
- Cost
- Maintenance

Planting

See **Topic E-2 'Planting'** for general guidance on planting.

Rather than dig individual planting holes it is probably easier to dig a trench. String or canes may be useful to ensure the plants are correctly aligned.

Planting distances are included in the table of hedging plants.

A double row of plants is sometimes recommended but this should not be necessary in a garden environment.

Initial pruning

Group 1	Cut back to 15-30 cm in first year and remove half of the new growth in the second year.
Group 2	Cut back leading shoots and strong laterals by one third.
Group 3	Cut back laterals only until the hedge has reached the required height.

The ultimate shape of the hedge should be wedge shaped with the top narrower than the bottom so that the bottom branches are not in shade. The top can be flat or tapered to stop snow settling on it.

Aftercare

Like any newly planted shrub, a hedge may need to be watered in periods of no rain.

Regular clipping or pruning is the main requirement. The time and frequency is indicated in the table of plants.

The area round the base of the hedge should be kept clear to ensure growth takes place at the base and the plants are not robbed of water and nutrients.

Most hedging plants will respond to hard cutting back in the event of them becoming overgrown. Exceptions are leyland cypress and lavender.

Windbreaks

Strong wind can cause considerable damage to plants (see **Topic C-8 'Common disorders'**) and if these are likely some form of windbreak should be provided.

The best form of windbreak is one that is permeable and reduces the strength of the wind. An impermeable one can cause a lot of turbulence on the leeward side that can cause more damage than the wind. Ideal is one with 50% permeability.

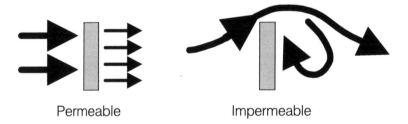

Permeable   Impermeable

A windbreak will provide some protection over an area 10 times the height of the windbreak.

Materials for windbreaks

Plants

Any hedge will provide some protection from the wind, although the dwarf ones will only provide it over a limited area.

In a large garden, or around an orchard, trees can be used for the windbreak. Fastigiate trees are the most suitable and the Lombardy popular (*Populus nigra* 'Italica') is often used. It is a common sight around the apple orchards of Kent.

Advantages	Disadvantages
Automatically provides some permeability. May already be present. Complements the garden	Takes time to establish. Requires maintenance. May take water and nutrients from other plants.

Walls

Advantages	Disadvantages
Permanent. Takes up little space. Maintenance free.	Most walls are not permeable although it would be possible to build one that is. Expensive.

Fences

Fences come in a variety of forms, some of which are more suitable than others for windbreaks. Some of the different types of fences were discussed in **Topic D-4 'Hard landscaping'**. Generally the open ones like the picket fencing are better.

Advantages	Disadvantages
Quick to erect and comparatively cheap. Takes up little space.	Some fences are not permeable. Not permanent.

Other materials

Wire or plastic mesh fencing will provide some protection.

Special windbreak material, which is usually a close woven plastic, can be obtained although this is more suited to providing protection in specific areas like the vegetable garden.

Shelter-belt

A shelter-belt is a group of plants, usually trees, planted more informally and having more depth than a hedge. They are only suitable for a large garden or estate.

Roses

Roses are shrubs but they are treated separately partly because of their popularity and partly because they can require more attention than most shrubs to get good results.

The choice of roses is huge; there are over 100 species and thousands of cultivars.

Types of rose

There are a number of different types of rose. Also, as more and more hybridisation takes place the distinction between them tends to get blurred. This resulted in 1979 in the renaming of the two most popular groups. What had been known as **'hybrid tea'** became **'large flowered bush'**, and what had been known as **'floribunda'** became **'cluster flowered bush'**. Even so many catalogues stick to the old terminology.

A summary of the types is as follows:

Bush varieties

- **Large flowered bush (hybrid tea)**

  Upright growth, with large flowers carried one to a stem or in small clusters. Repeat flowering.

- **Cluster flowered bush (floribunda)**

  Upright growth, with smaller flowers carried on large clusters or trusses. Repeat flowering and often over a longer period than large flowered bush.

- **Dwarf cluster flowered bush (patio)**

  Similar pattern of growth to cluster flowered but on a smaller scale.

Shrub varieties

- **Species roses**

  These are the wild or natural roses native to the country.

- **'Old' roses**

  This is a general name for a number of groups of roses that have existed for many years and from which the modern varieties have been developed. The main groups are:

  Alba
  Bourbon
  China
  Damask
  Gallica
  Moss
  Rugosa

  These roses tend to have smaller flowers, in more pastel shades, and only flower once a year. On the other hand the form of the flowers is very attractive and they are often scented.

- **Modern shrub**

    A general heading for roses that do not fall into other categories. A particular type of modern shrub rose is the 'English' rose bred by David Austin by crossing modern and old varieties. The result has been to produce some attractive roses that have the form and scent of the old varieties and the repeat flowering properties of the modern ones.

- **Ground cover**

    These are a comparatively new development. They are roses with a low spreading habit and can be very vigorous.

Climbers and ramblers

Climbing roses tend to have stiff upright growth with large flowers. Some are repeat flowering.

Rambling roses are more lax and flexible in growth with smaller flowers carried in clusters. They tend to only flower in summer.

Standard roses

A number of roses can be grown as standards by being budded onto a long stem. Standard roses need a stake or some other form of support.

Roses in design

Roses are very versatile plants since they vary in size, shape, flower form, flower colour and flowering period.

Size	From about 30 cm high for some dwarf varieties, up to 2-3 m for some of the shrub roses.
Form	Can be upright as with most large flowered bush, or spreading as with ground cover, or climbing as with climbers and ramblers.
Flower form	From single (4-7 petals), through semi-double (8-14 petals), double (15-20 petals), and fully double (over 30 petals).
Flower colour	From delicate pastel shades through to vibrant reds and yellows.
Flowering period	From once a year usually in early summer, to repeat flowering up until the autumn frosts.

In addition many roses have a scent and some have hips and attractive foliage.

Uses in design

- **As a focal point or structural plant**

    Some of the shrub roses are suitable for this purpose.

- **In a formal bedding scheme**

This is the traditional way of growing roses and large gardens often had a separate rose garden. If growing roses in this way it is more effective to use one variety or a very limited number. A bed containing a large mixture of varieties rarely looks attractive.

A bed growing against the background of a formal hedge can be attractive.

Large flowered bush roses are the most suitable for bedding schemes.

- **In a mixed border**

  Most roses will happily associate with other plants although cluster flowered bush or shrub roses look more at home.

- **Clothing walls, pergolas or other structures**

  Climbing and rambling roses can create interest on vertical structures or help to conceal unattractive sights.

- **As a hedge**

  Rosa rugosa and other shrub roses can be planted to create an informal hedge.

- **In containers**

  Dwarf varieties can be grown in containers on a patio.

Underplanting roses

Beds containing only roses can look a little bare during winter and spring but this can be overcome by underplanting the roses with other plants. These plants will generally be foliage plants or ones that flower in spring or early summer before the roses develop their full canopy of leaves.

Suitable plants are:

Foliage	*Stachys lanata*
	Artemesia gnaphalodes
Flower	*Geranium* species.
	Alchemilla mollis
	Arabis
Bulbs	*Narcissi*
	Galanthus

Buying roses

See **Topic E-1 'Buying plants'** for general guidance.

Roses from specialist growers are still sold bare rooted, while those from garden centres are usually containerised. The specialist growers will usually have a much wider selection of varieties.

Siting and planting

Ideally roses like an open and sunny site with some shelter from the wind. This is why traditional rose gardens were often surrounded by a hedge. The soil should be a well drained loam with a pH of 6.5. Do not despair however if you do not have these conditions as most roses are quite tolerant.

See **Topic E-2 'Planting'** for general guidance.

Nearly all roses are budded on to a rootstock and the union should be 2.5 cm below the soil level.

If planting a climber or rambler against a wall plant it 40 cm from the base of the wall. More information on dealing with climbing plants is in the next topic.

Pruning after planting

Prune large flowered bush varieties hard back to an outward facing bud about 10 cm from the base, and cluster flowered bush varieties to about 15 cm.

Do not prune shrubs, climbers or ramblers other than to remove weak and straggly growth.

Aftercare

Aftercare is the same as with other shrubs with the exception of pruning and feeding. Because roses are grown primarily for their flowers pruning plays a more important role than with many other shrubs. Also because of the pruning feeding is important to encourage the new growth and get the best flowers.

Pruning

See **Topic E-5 'Pruning'** for general guidance.

Pruning for health applies to all roses but other pruning can be different for the different types of rose.

- **Bush roses**

  These roses flower on current year's growth and they are therefore pruned hard during the dormant season. The best time is in spring just as the buds are beginning to break. In addition larger varieties can be trimmed back at the beginning of winter to reduce the danger of them being rocked in the wind.

  On **large flowered bushes** cut back the main stems to 20-25 cm of the base.

  On **cluster flowered bushes** cut back the main stems to 30-40 cm and reduce the length of side shoots by one third.

- **Shrub roses**

  Most of these roses flower on wood that is over one year old, and the pruning has to reflect this otherwise they will never flower.

  Use the renewal method of pruning by removing each year some of the older stems down to the base, which will encourage new young growth.

- **Climbers and ramblers**

  These roses are not self clinging and require some kind of support and training. Climbers are pruned differently to ramblers.

  In the first few years the priority is to develop the structure of the rose so that it covers the desired area. During this time allow the main stems to grow and tie them to their support. Leave sideshoots to grow if required as part of the structure, otherwise shorten them to 15-20 cm

On mature **climbing roses** shorten the sideshoots to 15-20 cm in the autumn when flowering has finished. The base of climbing roses can sometimes become bare and if so cut back some of the main shoots to within 30 cm of the base.

On **mature ramblers** shorten the sideshoots to 2-4 healthy buds in the autumn. New shoots are usually produced freely from the base and they can get congested. Cut back to ground level some of the older shoots if this occurs.

Feeding

Roses require a good supply of the major nutrients, particularly those that are pruned hard. A balanced fertiliser such as Growmore can be used or there are a number of proprietary mixtures.

Apply after pruning in spring at a rate of 25-50 g per plant.

Dead heading

Regular dead heading will encourage the growth of new flowering sideshoots and prevent the plant from putting energy into the development of seedheads.

Cut out the central bloom of a cluster to encourage the other blooms, and cut back to a healthy shoot or bud when the whole truss has flowered.

Removing suckers

Sometimes the rootstock sends up shoots known as suckers. These should be removed as close to the rootstock as possible, preferably by pulling them off.

Propagation

Roses may be propagated by seed, cuttings or budding.

Species roses may be grown from seed but most others will not breed true.

Most shrub roses can be grown from cuttings. However, growing from a cutting will take a number of years to produce a a reasonable size plant and most people would consider it worth buying an older plant to save this time.

The usual way of propagating is by budding on to a rootstock. The rootstocks are selected for their vigour and hardiness and include *Rosa multiflora, R. canina* and *R. laxa.*

The rootstocks are grown independently and are budded in late summer while still growing in the open.

Problems with roses

Why is it that the most popular plants seem to have the most problems? This certainly seems to be the case with roses, that suffer from a number of pests and diseases.

Pests

Aphids	See Topic C-6 'Common pests'
Red spider mite	See Topic C-6 'Common pests'
Leaf-rolling rose sawfly	This is caused by the female sawfly laying eggs in the leaf in May/June. The larvae feed on the leaf tissue. **Symptoms** The leaves roll up tightly along their length and remain rolled up all season. **Treatment** Spray with a contact insecticide in May/June to kill the females before they lay their eggs.

Diseases

Black spot	This is a very common and widespread disease. **Symptoms** Dark brown or black blotches appear on the leaves and they may drop prematurely. If untreated the plant is seriously weakened. **Treatment** Pick and burn infected leaves promptly. Spray with an approved fungicide after spring pruning, and repeat during the season according to instructions.
Powdery mildew	See Topic C-7 'Common diseases'
Rust	See Topic C-7 'Common diseases'

There are also products on the market that combine both insecticides and fungicides, and therefore make spraying much easier.

Some of the best

Large flowered bush

Alec's Red

Large fragrant, red flowers on strong upright stems on a medium sized bush.

Good disease resistance.

Peace

Probably the most famous rose. Introduced in 1945 and a best seller ever since.

Large creamy flowers edged with pink. Very healthy.

Silver Jubilee

Fragrant well formed flowers of apricot and peach on a medium sized bush of mid-green glossy foliage.

Very healthy.

The ornamental garden

Cluster flowered bush

Iceberg

The best white rose in this category. Large, pure white sprays on a medium sized bush.

Queen Elizabeth

Clear pink flowers on a tall (1.5 m), healthy bush.

Flowers tend to be carried at the top of the bush.

Can be used as a hedge.

Pink Parfait

Soft pink, fragrant blooms on a compact bush.

Very healthy.

Old roses

Great Maidens Blush

An 'Alba' rose dating back to the sixteenth century.

An arching habit up to 1.5 m with delicate blush-pink flowers.

Not repeat flowering

Roseraie de l'Hay

A 'Rugosa' rose. Vigorous spreading growth up to 2 m.

Large, fragrant, double blooms of crimson are borne over a long period.

Rosa Mundi

A 'Gallica' rose. A compact rose with flowers that are pale pink striped with crimson and white.

Not repeat flowering.

Climbers and ramblers

Golden Showers

A repeat flowering climber growing to 2 m.

Well shaped blooms of golden yellow are borne in profusion.

Handel

A popular repeat flowering climber with upright growth to 3 m.

Creamy flowers edged with pink.

Albertine

An old but popular, vigorous rambler growing to 4-5 m.

Blooms are prolific and salmon-pink but not repeat flowering.

Others

Nevada

A modern shrub rose growing to 2 m with large cream blooms with golden stamens.

Some repeat flowering.

Graham Thomas

One of the best 'English' roses.

Vigorous upright growth with full, golden yellow blooms over a long period.

Grouse

One of the new ground cover roses.

Growth is prostrate and spreads up to 3 m. Blooms are single, fragrant and pale pink.

Climbers

This section covers climbing plants other than roses which have been covered in the previous topic.

What is a climber

A climber is a plant that has a habit of growth that enables it to grow up a vertical surface or structure. They have developed largely as a result of the plants efforts to reach the light in competition with other plants. For this reason tropical rain forests are home to many climbers.

Most climbers are shrubs but there are some annuals and perennials.

A variety of mechanisms are used to attach to the surface.

- **Adventitious roots**

    These are roots formed at stem nodes that can penetrate other structures, either living like trees or man-made like walls.

    eg. *Hedera* (ivy)
    Hydrangea petiolaris

- **Adhesion**

    Adhesive pads attached to short stems.

    eg. *Parthenocissus quinquefolia* (Virginia creeper)

- **Tendrils**

    Tendrils are modified leaves that twine round their support

    eg. *Vitis* (vines)
    Lathyrus odoratus (Sweet pea)

- **Twining stems or petioles**

    Stems or petioles that naturally coil around other structures.

    eg. *Lonicera periclymenum* (Honeysuckle)
    Wisteria sinensis
    Clematis

In addition to natural climbers there are a number of shrubs, called **wall shrubs,** that are often grown against a wall, either because they look particularly effective that way, or because they benefit from the micro-climate, such as being slightly warmer.

    eg. *Garrya elliptica*
    Ceanothus dentatus

Climbers in design

Climbers can contribute to the design by:

- Provide a vertical element to the planting.

- Disguise unsightly objects.
- Cover house walls thereby linking the house to the garden.
- Climb through other plants like trees to give an extended period of colour.
- Many climbers will grow horizontally for considerable distances in their search for something to climb up. Because of this they can be effectively used as ground cover. Ivy and clematis are among the climbers that can be used in this way.
- Occupy little ground space.

Support for climbers

Climbers that rely on tendrils or twining stems for support require some form of structure that they can attach to. This structure can be:

1. **Wooden trellis**

2. **Wire attached to vine eyes or straining bolts.**

3. **Plastic mesh**

The supports may have to hold a significant weight and it is worth taking the time to make it sturdy.

The supports should protrude as far as possible from any solid structure like a wall so that air can circulate around the plant, otherwise the plant is more susceptible to disease.

Siting and planting

There are climbers that will suit any aspect, including north walls.

Planting should be about 40 cm from the base of a wall with the plant pointing towards the wall. It may be necessary to support the plant initially with canes until it has become attached to the wall.

Initial pruning and training

The objective for the first 2-3 years is to build up a strong framework of branches.

After planting tie in the main stems to the support and cut back sideshoots to 15-30 cm. Subsequently let the main stems, and any sideshoots required for the framework, grow and tie them in the required position.

If the plant is to cover a wide area train some of the stems at a wide angle. Remember that stems grown at an angle towards the horizontal will develop more sideshoots and more flowers.

Aftercare

In general this is the same as with other shrubs but watering may need to be more frequent since the base of walls tends to be dry.

Pruning

The pruning of roses is covered in the previous topic. The pruning of clematis and wisteria are dealt with separately in this section. The pruning of other climbers follows the same rules as other shrubs. That is:

1. **Evergreen climbers**

   These should require very little pruning other than the removal of dead, diseased or damaged wood, or to contain its size and shape.

   eg. *Hedera, Lonicera japonica*

2. **Climbers that flower on current years growth**

   These should be pruned hard in spring

   eg. *Clematis (not all), Solanum crispum*

3. **Climbers that flower on previous years growth**

   These are mainly spring and early summer flowering climbers and should be pruned after flowering

   eg. *Jasminum , Wisteria*

Pruning clematis

The pruning of clematis is complicated by the fact that some flower on the previous year's wood and some on the current year's, and some on both. They can be divided into 3 groups:

1. **Early large flowered cultivars**

   eg. *C.* 'Lasurstern', *C.* 'Nelly Moser'

   These flower on short stems from the previous year's wood but will also produce a second flush later in the year on new growth. Cutting out a proportion of the old growth after flowering will give the best second flush.

2. **Early flowering species**

   eg. *C. montana, C. alpina, C. macropetala*

   These flower on short shoots from the previous year's growth. The flowering shoots can be cut back to the main framework after flowering to allow new shoots to grow and flower in the following year. Alternatively they can be left unpruned for a number of years and cut back hard periodically.

3. **Late flowering species and cultivars**

   eg. *C. orientalis, C. x jackmanii, C. viticella,* C. 'Hagley Hybrid'

   These flower on current year's wood and, to avoid bare stems at the bottom they should be pruned back in January/February to strong buds 15-30 cm from ground level. The new growth will then need to be tied in.

All clematis can be cut back hard if they get out of control although this may result in no flowers for the next year. This is best done in January/February.

Pruning wisteria

Wisteria flowers on spurs of old wood, and the pruning must encourage this growth along the main framework. The framework itself should be trained in horizontal tiers.

After flowering, long flexible stems are produced, and these should be shortened to about 15 cm in June/July unless they are required to extend the framework. This stops the plant putting all its energy into the production of shoots at the expense of flower buds. In winter further shorten these shoots to 7-10 cm to leave 2-3 buds.

Problems with climbers

There are some problems with climbers over and above those for other shrubs.

- Some are extremely vigorous and may get out of hand, particularly as they grow out of reach without a ladder. *Parthenocissus quinquefolia* (Virginia creeper) and *Polygonum baldschuanicum* (Russian vine) are both strong growers.

- The climate and aspect can be extreme. For example a north wall may be cold and get little sun.

- The soil at the base of a wall may be poor, and it can be in a rain shadow so that it is also dry.

- Routine maintenance such as pruning and spraying can be more difficult simply because parts of the plant may be out of reach.

- Climbers growing on a house may interfere with guttering and drainpipes, and make painting of walls and windows difficult.

Climbers for special purposes

For north and east walls	For south and west walls	For evergreens
Hydrangea petiolaris	*Actinidia chinensis*	*Hedera helix*
Jasminum nudiflorum	*Lonicera periclymenum*	*Garrya elliptica*
Hedera helix	*Wisteria sinensis*	*Pyracantha*

For flowers	For berries	Herbaceous climbers
Clematis	*Celastrus scandens*	*Cobaea scandens*
Jasminum officinale	*Chaenomeles*	*Lathyrus odorata*
Lonicera periclymenum	*Pyracantha*	*Tropaeolum speciosum*

For fragrance	For fast growth	For autumn colour
Jasminum officinale	*Parthenocissus quinquefolia*	*Parthenocissus quinquefolia*
Lonicera periclymenum	*Polygonum baldschuanicum*	*Vitis*
Lathyrus odorata	*Wisteria sinensis*	

The ornamental garden

Some of the best

Clematis

There are many species of clematis and many cultivars including both large and small flowered ones.

Clematis montana is a vigorous early flowering species with many small single flowers in shades of white and pink. 'Nelly Moser' is a large flowered cultivar that is suitable for a north wall.

Hedera helix

There are many Hedera species that make good climbing plants, being evergreen, hardy and self clinging. Most will grow on a north wall.

This species is the common English ivy that has dark green leaves and will grow to 10 m x 5 m. There are also a number of less vigorous cultivars.

Hydrangea petiolaris

This is a self clinging climber that can grow up to 20 m. It is very hardy and grows well on a north wall.

It has flat corymbs of creamy white flowers 20-30 cm across in June.

Jasminum officinale

This is a hardy twining climber bearing fragrant white flowers in summer. It can grow to 10 m.

It will grow in most soils and is best in full sun.

Lathyrus odorata (sweet pea)

The sweet pea is a very popular annual climber with very fragrant flowers in shades of pink, blue, purple and white, from summer through to autumn.

They climb by means of tendrils up to a height of 3 m although there are some dwarf cultivars.

Lonicera periclymenum

This native honeysuckle is a hardy, vigorous climber with very fragrant red and yellow tubular flowers.

There are a number of cultivars such as 'Belgica' which is early flowering and 'Serotina' which is late.

Tolerates most soils and some shade.

Wisteria sinensis

This is a vigorous, deciduous climber that attaches itself to its support by twining stems.

This is the most widely grown species and it has long racemes of blue flowers in May/June.

Requires a sunny position. Flowers may be damaged by late frosts.

Garrya elliptica

This is not a true climber but is included here as an example of a wall shrub.

It is evergreen with leathery, dark green leaves, and long catkins in Feb/Mar. Male plants produce the best catkins.

Will grow in most soils and tolerate some shade.

Ground cover

What is ground cover

Ground cover consists of plants that cover the ground so thoroughly that they suppress weeds and require the minimum of maintenance.

Requirements of ground cover plants

- Dense growth
- Quick growth but not too invasive
- Low maintenance
- Hardy
- Tolerant of aspect, soil, and drought
- Disease resistant
- Vandal resistant in public areas, eg. prickly

A number of different types of plants can be used, but shrubs have the advantage of a permanent structure and of some being evergreen. Nevertheless herbaceous perennials can be used where they retain their leaves over winter or make growth early in the year before the weeds germinate.

Plants that spread vegetatively by stolons or rhizomes are particularly useful.

Uses of ground cover

- Create low maintenance area. Particularly useful in public areas
- Solution to problem areas, eg. shade, dry, banks, under trees
- Prevent soil erosion
- Barrier to control foot traffic
- Link elements of design
- Design element in its own right, eg. contrasting groups of plants

Siting and planting

Ensure the plants are suitable for the area being planted, particularly if it is a problem area.

Initial cultivation of the ground is important to ensure it is weed free as subsequent weeding may be difficult.

The planting distance will depend on the particular plants but in general they should be planted more closely than normal so they quickly knit together.

Aftercare

Since the idea is to have low maintenance there should ideally be little aftercare, although during the establishment period the normal requirements of watering and keeping weed free will be required. Once established a periodic clipping over will keep many plants from growing straggly, and an occasional feed will be of benefit.

Types of ground cover plants

- **Prostrate conifers**

Juniperus horizontalis	A number of cultivars with dense growth that hug the ground. They can spread 2-3 m.
Picea abies 'Procumbens'	The only prostrate Picea spreading 2-3 m.

- **Other prostrate plants**

Erica carnea	Evergreen. Suitable for most soils. 'Springwood White' is a good cultivar. Spread 1 m.
Cotoneaster dammeri	Evergreen. Small, dark, glossy leaves and red berries. Spread up to 2 m.

- **Hummock forming plants**

Hebe rakiensis	Evergreen. Hardy rounded shrub with small mid-green leaves. Spread up to 1 m.
Lonicera pileata	Evergreen. Dense shrub with small dark green leaves. Spread up to 2 m.

- **Surface spreaders**

Hedera helix	Evergreen. Common ivy with many cultivars.
Rubus tricolor	Evergreen. A very vigorous and rapid spreader.

- **Underground spreaders**

Gaultheria procumbens	Evergreen. White flowers in summer followed by red berries.
Hypericum calycinum	Semi-evergreen. One of the best. Large yellow flowers in summer. Grows in most conditions.

- **Herbaceous perennials**

Lamium maculatum	Semi-evergreen. Leaves are attractively striped. Can be invasive. Good in shade.
Epimedium x rubrum	Semi-evergreen. Young leaves are tinged red with crimson flowers in May.

Perennials

What is a perennial

A perennial is an herbaceous plant with a life of more than 2 years.

They are sometimes sub-divided into **hardy perennials** that can safely be left in the ground over winter, and **tender perennials** that need some protection.

The above ground growth usually dies back in winter but a few are evergreen which means they retain some leaves over winter.

Uses of perennials

- Herbaceous borders
- Part of mixed borders
- Temporary infill between shrubs
- Some suitable for ground cover
- Containers (particularly tender perennials)
- Cut flowers

Perennials in design

Although many perennials have striking foliage, they are mostly used to provide flower colour over a long period of time. Flowers are available in virtually every shape, size and colour.

Traditionally perennials have been used to construct herbaceous borders which contain only perennials. There is a good example of such a border at the RHS Garden at Wisley.

Comparatively recently there has been a move to plant perennials in island beds. This has a number of advantages:

1. **The plants can be seen from all sides**
2. **All plants get the same amount of light**
3. **Air circulation is better**
4. **There is a lack of competition compared to a border against a hedge**
5. **Maintenance is easier as the plants can be accessed from all sides**

The disadvantage of any bed or border consisting only of perennials is that for a large part of the year it will be bare and uninteresting. Because of this and the general reduction in the size of gardens, perennials are now very often planted as part of a mixed bed where they can add splashes of colour to the overall scheme.

If a traditional border or bed is to be made the plants should be positioned so that they are graded in size from the back of the border or the centre of the bed.

Do not be afraid to plant in large groups. Groups of 3 or 5 are often used and in a large bed this will look better than a large number of different plants. Alternatively plant in drifts for a more informal look.

Tender perennials are often used in containers as they can more easily be protected over winter. They are commonly referred to as **patio plants**.

In choosing plants take into account:

- **Colour**

  The use of colour is largely a matter of personal preference and beds can be attractive with just one, or a small number of basic colours.

- **Seasonal interest**

  There is a choice of having a bed full of colour for a limited period or trying to spread the flowering over as long a period as possible.

- **Form**

  A mixture of sizes and shapes will add to the interest. Some perennials have striking foliage.

Buying perennials

See **Topic E-1 'Buying plants'** for general guidance.

All plants purchased from garden centres will be in containers.

Siting and planting

There is a wide choice of perennials that will suit almost any situation, but the ideal for most is:

> **Sunny**
> **Sheltered**
> **Well drained**
> **Moisture retentive**

There are very few perennials that require an acid soil and most will grow well in one that is neutral or slightly alkaline.

As purchased plants are in containers they can be planted at any time of the year although autumn and spring are the best to get them off to a good start.

Aftercare

Watering

Plants are in general shallow rooting and should be watered in periods of little or no rain.

Some plants such as *Achillea*, *Dianthus* and *Geranium* are able to withstand some degree of drought.

Feeding

Apply a balanced fertiliser such as Growmore in early spring at a rate of 25 g/sq m.

Weed control

Beds need to be kept free of weeds which can get very entangled with the plants and difficult to eradicate.

Applying weedkillers is difficult because of the danger to the perennials, and hand weeding, hoeing or mulching are the best options. Persistent weeds can be painted with a weedkiller gel (eg, Tumbleweed Gel which contains glyphosate).

Staking

Some of the taller growing perennials can easily be blown over and need some form of support. Traditionally pea sticks have been used, but bamboo canes or a number of specialised support systems can be used.

Dead heading

Regular dead heading will keep the plants flowering longer. On some plants like delphiniums and lupins cutting right back to the base after flowering may induce a second flush.

At the end of season all growth can be cut back and the bed weeded and tidied for the winter.

Dividing

Many perennials lose their vigour as they get older and need to be divided and replanted. This is necessary every 3-4 years and is best done in late autumn or early spring.

Dig up the old plant and separate it with a knife, spade or two forks back to back. Replant healthy pieces with a good root structure from the outside of the plant. Take this opportunity to add some organic matter to the soil.

There are some plants like Peonies and Hellebores that are best not disturbed.

Aftercare for tender perennials

Tender perennials differ from hardy perennials in that they must be provided with some protection over winter. Among the options available are:

1. **Move plant into a greenhouse or conservatory**

    eg. Argyranthemums, pelargoniums

2. **Store dry plant in frost-free room**

    eg. New Guinea Impatiens

3. **Protect in situ with straw or fleece**

    eg. Diascias, osteospermums

4. **Take cuttings and grow on for following year**

    eg. Can be done for most tender perennials

Propagation

Perennials may be propagated from seed, from cuttings, or by division.

See **Topics E-4 and E-5 'Propagation'** for general guidance.

Seed can be sown under cover in April/May or in a seed bed in May/June, and the plants thinned or transplanted to a nursery bed when they are large enough to handle. They can be transplanted to their final position in autumn or the following spring.

From seed	From stem cuttings	From root cuttings	By division
Alchemilla mollis (prolific self-seeder) *Aquilegia* *Lupinus*	*Argyranthemum* *Dianthus* *Penstemon*	*Papaver orientalis* *Phlox decussata*	*Chrysanthemum maximum* *Geranium* *Pulmonaria*

Problems with perennials

Perennials do require a certain amount of effort in supporting, dead-heading and dividing. They can be damaged by wind or rain in exposed areas.

Slugs and snails can be a problem, particularly on some plants like hostas where the leaves can be completely shredded. Eelworm can be a problem on phlox and some other plants. Aphids can also be troublesome.

Powdery mildew can affect some plants, particularly asters. Rust also affects a number of plants including aquilegias and chrysanthemums.

Plants for special purposes

For flowers	For foliage	For form
Delphinium *Iris* *Paeonia*	*Hosta* *Heuchera* 'Palace Purple' *Rheum palmatum*	*Acanthus spinosus* *Crambe cordifolia* *Phormium tenax*

For shade	For ground cover	For early flowers
Epimedium x rubra *Helleborus orientalis* *Tellima grandiflora*	*Ajuga reptans* *Houttuynia cordata* *Lamium maculatum*	*Doronicum* *Primula vulgaris* *Pulmonaria*

For winter interest	For cottage gardens	For cut flowers
Helleborus niger *Iris unguicularis*	*Althaea* (Hollyhock) *Dianthus* (Pinks) *Lupinus* (Lupins)	*Gypsophila paniculata* *Helenium autumnale* *Scabiosa caucasica*

Perennials

Some of the best

Hardy perennials

Delphinium

These are stately plants for the back of the border growing to 1.5 m. They have long spikes of flowers in shades of blue, pink and white. May require staking

There are a number of species and cultivars. *D. x belladonna* and New Century hybrids are good choices

---

Gypsophila paniculata

This plant produces a profusion of small white flowers in loose panicles. Its common name is 'Baby's breath'.

It grows to about 75 cm and flowers in summer. It is good for filling gaps left by earlier flowering plants.

Geranium (cranesbill)

These are the native 'Cranesbill'. They are easy to grow and make bushy plants usually no higher tham 50 cm.

Excellent for ground cover.

Flowers are borne over a long period in early summer in shades of white, pink and blue. Good varieties are 'Wargrave Pink' and 'Johnsons Blue'.

Hosta

These are hardy and adaptable plants that will tolerate shade.

They are grown for their foliage which is large leaved and in shades of green, blue and many variegations. Good varieties are *sieboldiana* and 'Francee'

Slugs can badly damage the plants.

Iris

There are a huge variety of irises. They are grown mainly for their flowers in summer although they also have striking strap-like leaves.

They are divided into groups, the most common of which are bearded, beardless and crested. Flower colour is in shades of white, blue and purple.

Lupinus (lupin)

An easily grown cottage garden flower with large flower spikes in many colours including some bi-colours.

Modern varieties are more compact and suitable for the small garden.

They prefer a sunny well drained position.

Paeonia (peony)

A showy plant growing up to 1.5 m with bold foliage and large flowers.

Likes a sunny position but will tolerate light shade.

Good varieties are P. 'Bowl of Beauty' and 'Sarah Bernhardt'

Taller varieties may need support.

Phlox paniculata

An upright plant growing to 1 m. Useful for providing colour in late summer.

There are many cultivars of this species in shades of white, pink, red and purple.

Topic G-8

319

Tender perennials

Argyranthemum

These comprise a large and varied group of which the best known is *A. frutescens* better known as marguerite. This has grey/green foliage and many white daisy like flowers throughout the summer.

There are other varieties with yellow or pink flowers. Most grow to about 75 cm but there are shorter varieties.

Brachycome multifida

Commonly known as Swan River daisy.

These are compact plants growing to about 30 cm. They flower over a long period, usually in shades of blue or lilac.

Impatiens New Guinea' hybrids

These are showy forms of the common busy lizzie but are a much more substantial plant.

They grow up to 50 cm and have larger flowers in many colours including red, pink and white. The foliage is sometimes variegated.

Pelargonium

There are a huge number of cultivars of pelargoniums, mostly in shades of red and pink.

There are a number of groups including zonal pelargoniums that often have attractive variegated foliage, ivy leaved pelargoniums which have a trailing habit, and regal pelargoniums which are more bushy plants with exotic flowers.

A sample island bed

This plan is for a bed with maximum dimensions of 6m x 4m.

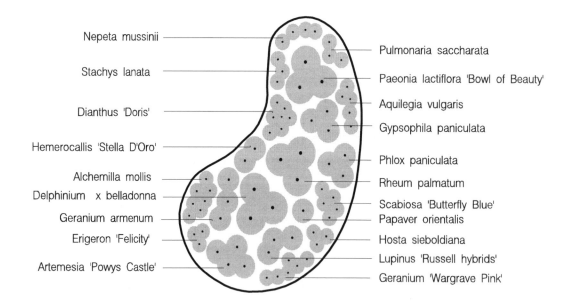

Nepeta mussinii

Stachys lanata

Dianthus 'Doris'

Hemerocallis 'Stella D'Oro'

Alchemilla mollis

Delphinium x belladonna

Geranium armenum

Erigeron 'Felicity'

Artemesia 'Powys Castle'

Pulmonaria saccharata

Paeonia lactiflora 'Bowl of Beauty'

Aquilegia vulgaris

Gypsophila paniculata

Phlox paniculata

Rheum palmatum

Scabiosa 'Butterfly Blue'

Papaver orientalis

Hosta sieboldiana

Lupinus 'Russell hybrids'

Geranium 'Wargrave Pink'

Annuals and biennials

What are annuals and biennials

An annual is a plant that completes its lifecycle in 1 year. They mostly germinate in spring or early summer and die at the start of winter. Even though the plants die they perpetuate themselves by producing seed that germinates in the following year.

Annuals are generally divided into hardy and half hardy groups. A hardy annual is one that will stand frost and is usually sown directly in open ground. A half hardy annual will not stand frost and is usually raised under glass and planted out when the danger of frost is over.

A biennial is a plant that completes its lifecycle in 2 years. In the first year it germinates and makes vegetative growth, and in the second year it flowers. They are useful plants as they tend to flower early in the second year.

Uses of annuals and biennials

- In bedding schemes. Beds can be formal with plants arranged in patterns or informal with plants arranged in drifts
- Part of mixed borders
- Temporary infill between shrubs and perennials
- Create an instant effect in a new garden
- Excellent for tubs, window boxes and hanging baskets
- Cut flowers

Annuals and biennials in design

The main attribute that annuals and biennials bring to a garden is flowers. There are flowers of virtually every shape and colour. In addition some plants have striking form and foliage, and some are scented. There are even some annual climbers.

Traditionally annuals and biennials have been used in formal bedding schemes particularly in public areas. They have been the mainstay of parks and leisure areas. The fact that biennials tend to flower early has enabled two displays a year to occur:

1. **Spring bedding**

    This is made up of biennials such as wallflowers, primulas, and forget-me-nots. The spring bedding is planted in October and removed the following May.

2. **Summer bedding**

    This is made up of annuals. They are planted out in May and removed in October.

Such formal displays date back to Victorian times and are contrary to the current vogue for informal and natural gardens. They are also expensive and, sadly, are subject to increasing vandalism. For these reasons the use of formal schemes may decline.

In private gardens they can still be used to provide colour and interest over a long period, but they are more likely to be used in conjunction with other plants or in containers. If grown from seed they are a cheap and easy way of producing a large number of plants.

At the time of writing this, a replica of the Olympic symbol has been created with bedding plants by Manchester Corporation, who are bidding to hold a future Olympics. It occupies a six acre field and consists of 200,000 plants! It is being submitted to the Guinness Book of Records as the largest ever flower bed.

Buying annuals and biennials

See **Topic E-1 'Buying plants'** for general guidance.

Many people will opt for raising their own plants from seed. This is cheap and easy, and gives a much wider range of plants to choose from. Perusing the seed catalogues in the winter months is a must for the enthusiast.

Nevertheless many people will find it easier to purchase from the garden centre. Do not buy half-hardy annuals until the danger of frost is past.

Many of the seeds and plants are F_1 hybrids and give a reliable and uniform display.

A recent development on the part of the seed companies is to sell seedlings or small rooted plants called plugs. This is much cheaper than buying from the garden centre and avoids the problem of germinating seed. On the other hand the range of plants is very limited and they still need to be grown on before they can be planted out.

In calculating the requirements for a bedding scheme it is necessary to take into account the area and the planting distance for the particular plants. An example is included at the end of this topic.

Siting and planting

Nearly all annuals will grow best in a sunny, sheltered position. In a formal scheme mark out the bed with canes and string or with sand.

See **Topic E-3 'Propagation (1) Seed'** for information on sowing and planting out. If sowing hardy annuals in situ prepare the ground as if it were a seed bed to ensure good germination

Spring bedding will be planted out in October and summer bedding in May.

Aftercare

Watering

Plants generally have low water requirements but should be watered in any lengthy period without rain, particularly just after being planted out.

Feeding

Apply a balanced fertiliser such as Growmore at a rate of 25 g/sq m when the beds are prepared for planting.

Weed control

Beds need to be kept free of weeds. Applying weedkillers is not possible because of the danger to the plants, and hand weeding, hoeing or mulching are the best options.

Dead heading

Regular dead heading will keep the plants flowering longer but is not really practical on large schemes

Propagation

Annuals and biennials are propagated from seed and a large number of plants can be raised for a low cost.

See **Topic E-3 'Propagation (1) Seed'** for general guidance.

A timetable for hardy, half hardy and biennials is as follows:

Hardy	**Half hardy**	**Biennials**
Sow Mar/Apr in flowering position	**Sow** Feb/Mar under glass	**Sow** Apr/May under glass or May/Jun in seed bed
Harden off Not applicable	**Harden off** Apr/May	**Harden off** Not applicable
Plant out Not applicable	**Plant out** After danger of frosts has passed	**Transplant or thin** When 5 cm high
Thin As required	**Some plants** *Antirrhinum* cultivars *Ageratum houstonianum* *Begonia semperflorens* *Impatiens* (Buzy Lizzie) *Lobelia erinus* *Petunia* cultivars	**Plant out** Sept/Oct
Some plants *Lobularia maritima* (Alyssum) *Iberis umbellata* (Candytuft) *Helianthus annuus* (Sunflower) *Helichrysum bracteatum* *Tropaeolum majus* (Nasturtium) *Viola x wittrockiana* (Pansy)		**Some plants** *Campanula medium* (Canterbury bell) *Cheiranthus cheiri* (Wallflower) *Dianthus barbatus* (Sweet William) *Digitalis* (Foxglove) *Lunaria annua* (Honesty) *Myosotis alpestris* (Forget-me-not)

Problems with annuals and biennials

We have already mentioned that annuals and biennials can be time consuming and costly unless plants are raised from seed. Also there is the problem of vandalism in public areas.

From a cultural point of view, if the plants are healthy when planted they should not be too troubled by pests and diseases. Slugs and snails are the worst pest problem particularly with young plants, and aphids and caterpillars can also be troublesome.

Damping off can affect young seedlings, and rust or powdery mildew may affect some plants.

Plants for special purposes

For architecture	**For fragrance**	**For climbing**
Digitalis	*Lathyrus odoratus*	*Cobaea scandens*
Ricinus communis	*Nicotiana affinis*	*Lathyrus odoratus*
Salvia turkestanica	*Matthiola bicornis (Night scented stock)*	*Tropaeoleum majus*

For cutting	**For shade**	**For containers**
Chrysanthemum carinatum	*Begonia semperflorens*	*Petunia*
Nigella damascena	*Impatiens*	*Impatiens*
Zinnia	*Lobelia erinus*	*Osteospermum*

Some of the best

Hardy annuals

Lobularia maritima (Alyssum)

A bushy low growing annual suitable for planting in paving or on the rock garden.

Flowers through the summer in shades of white, pink and purple.

Many cultivars available.

Calendula officinalis (Pot marigold)

A cottage garden plant. Grows up to 50 cm with daisy like flowers up to 10 cm, in shades of yellow and orange. The leaves and stems have a distinctive smell.

Easy to grow and flowers all summer.

Tropaeolum majus (Nasturtium)

A climber that can grow up to 2 m although some cultivars are shorter.

Trumpet shaped flowers up 5 cm in shades of yellow and orange are produced through the summer

Dwarf varieties good for hanging baskets

Lathyrus odoratus (Sweet pea)

A favourite climbing annual with lots of flowers in soft colours, and with a lovely fragrance. Good as cut flowers.

They require good soil and a sunny, sheltered position.

Low growing varieties are available.

Half hardy annuals

Antirrhinum (Snapdragon)

A popular plant with varieties growing from 20 cm up to 80 cm. Flower spikes in shades of white, yellow, pink and red from July to the first frost.

Rust can be a problem although some varieties have some resistance.

Begonia semperflorens

A compact plant growing up to 30 cm, with numerous small flowers all summer in shades of white, pink and red.

The foliage is an attractive green or bronze.

Impatiens (Busy Lizzie)

One of the most popular and adaptable annuals that will stand some shade.

They grow up to 30 cm, and have cup shaped flowers in shades of white, pink and red.

New F_1 hybrids are particularly good.

Petunia

Showy flowers in many colours including bi-colours, on plants growing up to 30cm.

Best in a sunny position and good for containers.

New F_1 hybrids are particularly good.

Biennials

Cheiranthus cheiri (Wallflower)

A popular spring flowering plant growing up to 40 cm, with spikes of flowers in many colours from April to June.

The mainstay of many spring bedding schemes.

Digitalis (Foxglove)

A indispensible cottage garden plant with spires of flowers up to 1.5 m. The native plant has purple flowers but varieties are available in shades of white and pink, and with attractive markings.

Natural habitat is in woodland, and therefore it is good in shade.

Myosotis alpestris (Forget-me-not)

Compact plants with sprays of small flowers in many shades of blue. Flowers in spring, and is often part of spring bedding schemes.

Prolific self-seeder.

Will tolerate some shade.

Campanula medium (Canterbury Bell)

An upright, clump forming plant with cup shaped flowers in shades of white, blue and pink. Cultivars vary in size from 30 cm to 1 m.

Flowers in late spring and early summer.

The ornamental garden

A sample formal bed

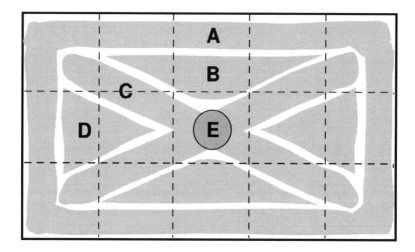

A   Ageratum 'Blue Ribbon'
B   Petunia 'Mirage Rose'
C   Nicotiana 'Crimson'
D   Impatiens 'Accent White'
E   Ricinus communis

Calculate the number of plants required as follows:

A.   Calculate the number of plants required for a square metre. For example if the planting distance is 20 cm then 25 plants/sq m will be required.

B.   Estimate the number of square metres to be covered by drawing a grid on the planting plan. In the above example the grid is drawn at metre intervals and from that it can be estimated that the area for plant A is about 7 sq m. Always estimate on the generous side.

C.   Multiply A by B to get the total number. In this example it is 25 x 7 = 175

Planting distances for common plants:

Alyssum	30 cm
Antirrhinum	30 cm
Ageratum	20 cm
Begonia	15 cm
Cheiranthus	30 cm
Dianthus	20 cm
Digitalis	40 cm
Impatiens	30 cm
Lobelia	20 cm
Myosotis	20 cm
Petunia	30 cm
Polyanthus	20 cm
Viola	20 cm

These are guidelines only as different cultivars have different growth characteristcs.

Bulbs and corms

What are bulbs and corms

Read **Topic A-21 'Vegetative reproduction'** to refresh your memory on the botanical nature of bulbs and corms. Collectively these plants are referred to as **'bulbous'** plants and the word 'bulb' will be used in this topic to cover them both.

Bulbs are mostly monocotyledons from a limited number of families:

Amarillidaceae	Includes *Narcissus* (daffodil). *Galanthus* (snowdrop) and *Nerine*.
Iridaceae	Includes *Iris*, *Crocus* and *Gladiolus*
Liliaceae	Includes *Lilium* (lilies), *Tulipa* (tulips), *Colchicums* (autumn crocus) and *Chionodoxa*.

Uses of bulbs

- Part of mixed borders
- Part of spring bedding schemes
- Naturalising in grass and woodland
- Under trees
- In the rock garden
- In containers
- As indoor plants
- As cut flowers

Bulbs in design

Bulbs are useful for providing colour at times of the year when the garden may otherwise appear dull. The obvious time is late winter and early spring when daffodils, snowdrops and crocus make a big contribution. The reason bulbs flower when they do is because of the conditions in their natural environment. For example, spring flowering bulbs in woodland seize their opportunity when the soil temperature has started to rise, but the trees have not developed their canopy of leaves.

There are are bulbs available for all seasons of the year:

Spring	Summer	Autumn	Winter
Narcissus	*Iris*	*Colchicum*	*Galanthus*
Crocus	*Gladioli*	*Crocus speciosus*	*Chionodoxa*
Tulipa	*Allium*	*Nerine bowdenii*	*Eranthis*

Some bulbs with regular and upright growth like tulips and hyacinths seem more suited to formal bedding schemes, while others like daffodils and snowdrops are more suited to naturalising. To naturalise scatter the bulbs over the area required and plant them where they fall.

If bulbs are grown in grass they must be allowed to die down naturally before the grass is mown. This can leave an untidy looking area if it is in an otherwise immaculate lawn.

Spring flowering bulbs can be lifted, dried and stored for the following year. This enables other plants to be grown in the same ground.

Buying bulbs

Most bulbs are bought **'dry'** in their dormant season. Ensure the bulbs are firm with no signs of pest or disease damage. Some bulbs, notably narcissi, can be bought in different sizes.

There are some bulbs like snowdrops that establish better if bought **'in the green'**. This means after they have flowered and while they still have their leaves.

Siting and planting

Bulbs come from a number of different natural habitats and there are plants for most locations. This aspect is covered later in this topic. The one thing that nearly all of them have in common is that they like a well drained soil. Some, like lilies and gladioli, are particularly susceptible to wet, and in heavy ground should be planted on a bed of sand. The best pH is neutral to slightly alkaline.

As a general guideline plant them at a depth of twice their height and at a distance apart of two to three times their width. Some experiments have taken place with planting deeper to avoid competition with grass and the initial results appear to be good.

They can be planted with a trowel or with a special bulb planter which is easier if planting in turf. For small bulbs the turf can be lifted, the bulbs planted and the turf replaced, or holes can be made in the turf with a fork.

The best time for planting is in autumn for spring flowering plants, in spring for summer flowering ones and in summer for autumn and winter flowering ones.

Aftercare

Watering

Only necessary in prolonged periods without rain.

Feeding

Many bulbs will give a good display for years with no attention. If the quality of flower starts to deteriorate a low nitrogen/high potash fertiliser can be applied after flowering at a rate of 25 g/sq m.

A deterioration in quality may be due to overcrowding and not a shortage of nutrients.

Weed control

Necessary in a bedding scheme but not in naturalised planting.

Dead-heading

Dead-heading will prevent the plants putting energy into the production of seeds.

Lifting

Bulbs can be lifted after flowering so that the ground can be used for other plants. This is normal practice for plants used in spring bedding schemes, but not of course for naturalised plants.

Thinning

Most bulbs will propagate vegetatively and eventually form dense clumps. This can lead to a deterioration in quality, and the bulbs should be periodically lifted and thinned out.

Propagation

Bulbs can be propagated from seed but it may take several years to get flowering plants, and there is also the usual problem of cultivars not coming true from seed.

Propagation is therefore usually done by vegetative means using the natural method of the plant. There are basically three methods that can be used:

1. **Offsets**

   These are naturally produced embryo plants that develop around the bulb or corm. It is through these that clumps of bulbs get denser. Offsets of bulbs are called **bulblets** and those of corms are called **cormlets**.

   The offsets are separated from the parent and can be replanted in pots or in a nursery bed. They should be grown on for a year and can then be planted in their final position.

   The best time for separating offsets is when the plant is dug up for storing or thinning.

   Narcissi, tulips and crocus can be propagated in this way.

2. **Bulbils**

   Bulbils form in the axis of leaves and can be separated from the parent plant and treated as though they were seed.

   Lilies can be propagated in this way.

3. **Scales**

   Scales are the modified leaves that make up the bulb. The scales are attached to the base of the bulb and should be separated with a part of the base attached. The best time to do this is in autumn.

   Plant the scales in compost to half their depth and keep in a greenhouse or cold frame. Within about 6 weeks bulblets should form around the base of the scale. When shoots appear pot up into individual pots and grow on in a frost free place until the following autumn when they can be planted out.

   Lilies and fritillaria can be propagated in this way.

Problems with bulbs

Bulbs are generally easy to grow and trouble free although there are a number of pests and diseases that can give problems.

Of the pests covered in **Topic C-6 'Common pests'**, aphids, slugs and snails, eelworms and vine weevil can be troublesome. In addition the larvae of the **narcissus fly** can cause extensive damage to narcissi, hyacinth and some other bulbs. The larvae burrow into the bulb and feed on it. The symptoms are yellow and distorted leaves, but by the time these appear the damage is done. Affected bulbs should be dug up and burned.

Of the diseases covered in **Topic C-7 'Common diseases'**, grey mould and virus infection can be troublesome. In addition **tulip fire** is a common and serious disease of tulips. The shoots are withered and distorted and may be covered by a grey mould. The flowers may fail to open. Affected bulbs should be dug up and burned, and the remaining bulbs sprayed with carbendazim or mancozeb.

Disorders are most likely to be caused by overcrowding or a wet soil. Overcrowding can cause the bulbs to be 'blind', which means they fail to produce a flower.

Bulbs grown in grass can make the area look untidy since the grass cannot be cut until the bulb foliage has died down.

Bulbs for special purposes

For bedding	For woodland	For grass
Hyacinthus	Eranthis hyemalis	Narcissus
Muscari (Grape hyacinth)	Galanthus nivalis	Crocus
Tulipa	Endymion nonscripta (bluebell)	Galanthus nivalis

For rock gardens	For cutting	For containers
Chionadoxa	Gladiolus	Lilium
Crocus	Narcissus	Narcissus
Scilla	Lilium	Tulipa

Some of the best

Crocus

One of the indispensable plants for spring, although there are also autumn and winter flowering varieties. There are many cultivars.

The flowers are cup shaped in shades of white, yellow, blue and purple.

Crocus speciosus is an autumn variety and *C. crysanthus* is a winter variety.

They are very hardy but prefer a sunny, well drained position.

Hyacinthus (Hyacinth)

These plants produce a large, upright flower spike in many colours and which is also fragrant.

They are often grown as indoor plants and it is possible to force them into flower for Christmas.

In the garden they are best in formal bedding schemes because of their regular and upright growth.

There are many cultivars.

Galanthus nivalis

The common snowdrop makes its appearance at the end of winter and is a sign of spring to come.

They grow up to 15 cm with drooping white flowers with green markings.

They are adaptable plants and will stand some shade.

A number of cultivars are available, some with double flowers.

Gladiolus

This is a showy summer flowering corm but it is not hardy and needs to be lifted.

There are a number of different groups ranging from large flowered hybrids with an overall height of 1.5 m and a flower spike of 60 cm, to species with a height of 50 cm.

The flower is made up of a number of florets arranged alternately along its length. Virtually all colours are represented and some are bi-coloured.

Narcissus

The daffodil must be the most planted of all plants, and is an essential harbinger of spring, flowering in March/April.

There are over 8000 cultivars grouped into a number of divisions depending on form and colour. The central trumpet can vary from being almost flat to exceeding the length of the surrounding petals.

They are hardy and adaptable plants and can be used for most of the purposes set out in 'Uses of bulbs'

Tulipa

Tulips rank second only to daffodils as the most popular spring flowering plant. Most flower in April/May. Each bulb produces one upright flower spike with cup shaped flowers in many colours.

Because of extensive breeding there are many cultivars which are divided into groups. The main groups are Darwin, Kaufmanniana, Parrot, Fosteriana & Lily.

Adaptable to most situations.

Lilium

Lilies are stately summer flowering plants that have large, mainly trumpet shaped flowers in a wide variety of colours, and often with attractive markings.

They can grow from 40 cm to 150 cm and there are varieties to suit most situations.

Famous species are *L. candidum* (madonna lily) and *L. regale* (regal lily) which are both white and fragrant.

Colchicum

These are known as the 'autumn crocus' because of their similarity of flower.

They flower in Sept/Nov in shades of white, pink and lilac, the flower appearing before the foliage.

Good for planting under trees or in grass.

Alpines

What is an alpine

An alpine is not a completely different type of plant. They are mostly small shrubs or perennials which are particularly adapted to growing in mountainous areas. They mainly grow between the tree line and the line of permanent snow and the conditions they are adapted to are:

Altitude
Cold
Wind
Free draining soil
Poor soil
Short growing season

Because of these conditions alpines tend to be low growing and have leaves adapted to reduce moisture loss, such as being small, rolled, hairy or succulent. A number are evergreen which reduces the amount of growth they have to make each season.

It does not necessarily follow that all these conditions have to be replicated in the garden. Alpines are in fact quite adaptable and can be used in a number of situations. Of all the environmental conditions the most important to provide is good drainage.

In addition to true alpines there are number of other plants including dwarf conifers and bulbs that are suitable for growing in a rockery and associate well with alpines.

Uses of alpines

- Rockery or scree bed
- Between paving
- Troughs
- Alpine house
- Front of border plants

Alpines in design

Alpines are associated with rockeries which are an attempt to recreate their natural environment, although this can be difficult to achieve in a small garden.

It is better in my opinion to grow them in the other ways outlined above. In order to provide the good drainage that many require a simple raised bed can be used. On the other hand a rockery may enhance a natural feature of the garden such as a slope or bank.

Growing them in an alpine house is not to provide warmth but to keep them dry. This is a method of growing for the alpine enthusiast rather than the general gardener.

Creating a rockery

In spite of what I have said above there are many people who have the space for a rockery or particularly want one in spite of restricted space. The following are therefore guidelines for creating it:

- **Siting**

  → An open, well drained position is best. Some alpines will stand shadebut most prefer sun.

  → Do not build one against a house wall because damp will penetrate the wall.

  → Do not build beneath trees as the shade, water drip and leaf fall will cause problems.

- **Choosing the rocks**

  → Use rocks such as sandstone or limestone that will weather quickly and look more natural.

  → Do not mix different rocks.

  → Use rocks as large as can be handled.

  → Choose rocks that have similar strata lines.

- **Choosing the style**

  → A number of styles are possible, depending on the preference of the owner and the contours of the land. Some examples are:

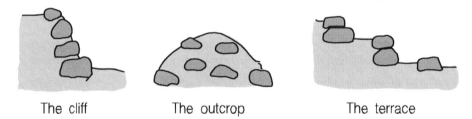

| The cliff | The outcrop | The terrace |

- **Site preparation**

  → Essential to remove all weeds, particularly perennials.

  → Essential to get good drainage. If necessary dig out 30 cm of soil and put in a 15 cm layer of rubble or hardcore. If a heavy clay soil incorporate a good quantity of sharp sand or grit.

  → Alpines are used to growing on poor soil and it should not be necessary to add compost or fertiliser.

- **Placing the rocks**

  → Starting from the front of the rockery, bed the rocks up to one third in the ground and leaning slightly backwards to make them look permanent.

  → Keep the strata lines running horizontally.

  → Fill in and build up the soil behind the rocks and build further levels as required.

  → It will look more natural if the rocks are placed irregularly.

- **Planting**

  → Allow the soil to settle before planting.

  → Plant with a trowel, and use a planting mixture of 1 part topsoil, 1 part peat and 1 part coarse grit.

  → Do not include plants that will look out of place eg. miniature roses!

➔ Planting sparsely with the intervening ground covered with chippings can look more natural than massed plants.

Creating a scree bed

A scree bed is made from stones and small boulders to represent the kind of conditions found at the base of a rock face. It is easier to construct than a rockery since the components are not so heavy.

It can be a separate feature or it could link a rockery to a lawn to make a more natural transition.

Many of the considerations applying to the construction of a rockery also apply to a scree bed. In particular the drainage may need special attention as it may not be so raised or on a slope as a rockery. If necessary dig out the soil to a depth of 30 cm and put in a 15 cm layer of hardcore, rubble or coarse grit.

Plant with space around each plant or group to show the plants to their best advantage.

Creating a alpine trough

This is a traditional way of displaying alpines. It has the advantage that the trough can be raised so that viewing the plants is easier.

The traditional trough is made from stone, but these are very expensive, and concrete or reconstituted stone is cheaper. It is also possible to make a realistic one from an old glazed sink by covering it with a mixture of cement and peat (hypatufa). Whatever kind of trough is used ensure that it has a drainage hole in the bottom.

Put a layer of coarse grit in the bottom of the trough and fill with a proprietary planting compost. Mulch the top of the compost with coarse grit or gravel after planting. Small rocks can be set into the surface if desired.

The plants need to be carefully chosen so that they do not grow too quickly and swamp the others. Some suitable plants are identified later in this topic.

Aftercare

Watering

Alpines are adapted to survive with little water and watering should not be necessary once the plants are established except in prolonged periods of no rain.

Feeding

Alpines are also adapted to poor soils. A light dressing of Growmore in spring is as much as is required.

Weed control

This is an important task although mulching with chippings will help suppress weeds. Because of the delicacy of many alpines they can easily be swamped by weeds. Hand weed for annuals; spot treat any perennials with glyphosate.

Trimming

Trimming some alpines will keep them compact. This should be done as part of an autumn tidy-up.

Problems with alpines

They are generally hardy and not troubled too much by pests and diseases. Of the pests covered in **Topic C-6 'Common pests'**, slugs and snails, aphids, and caterpillars cause the most problems. Of the diseases covered in **Topic C-7 'Common diseases'**, grey mould is the most troublesome.

Disorders are most likely to be caused by poorly drained soil and damp conditions.

Plants for the rockery or scree bed

Alyssum saxatile	*Arabis albida* (rock cress)
A yellow flowered alyssum, growing up to 15 cm, that is covered in flowers in spring.	An evergreen, spreading plant with grey foliage and single or double white flowers in spring.
Needs a sunny, well-drained position.	Needs a sunny, well drained position.
Good for hanging over a wall.	Can be invasive so cut back after flowering

Aubrieta	*Campanula* (bellflower)
A common spring flowering alpine in shades of pink, blue and purple.	There are many campanulas suitable for the rock garden varying from being prostrate, up to 30 cm. The flowers, borne in June/July, are predominantly blue although some are white.
Needs a sunny, well drained position and limey soil.	
Clip after flowering to keep tidy.	Suitable species are *C. carpatica* and *C. garganica.*

Helianthemum nummularium (rock rose)	*Saxifraga moshata* (mossy saxifrage)
A shrubby spreading plant producing a mass of small flowers in June/July in shades of white, pink, yellow and orange.	Delicate flowers in shades of pink and white are carried in spring and early summer on stalks up to 15 cm long, above the evergreen moss-like foliage.
Needs sunny, well drained, limey soil.	There are a number of other saxifrages including *S. urbium* (London pride).

Plants for the alpine trough

The predominant characteristic of these plants is their small size and non-invasive growth.

Armeria caespitosa (thrift)

This species grows no more than 10 cm high with a spread of 20 cm. It has grassy leaves and rounded heads of pink and white flowers.

Dianthus alpinus (rockery pink)

This pink has 2 cm flowers on a neat cushion of evergreen foliage. Height is 10 cm and spread 15 cm.

It flowers between May and August in shades of white, pink and purple.

Sempervivum arachnoideum (houseleek)

This species is grown for its foliage which is fleshy and rosette shaped. The rosettes are covered with fine strands like a cobweb.

Height is 5 cm and spread 30 cm.

Lychnis alpina (dwarf campion)

A small tufted plant with rose coloured flowers in May/July.

Height and spread are 10 cm.

Erinus alpinus (starwort)

This plant produces small flowers in shades of white and pink between April and July.

Height and spread are 10 cm.

Thymus citriodorus (thyme)

This a a slightly larger plant with a height of 30 cm and a spread of 20 cm. Some cultivars are more compact.

It has lemon scented foliage and lilac flowers in May/July.

Other plants for the rockery

There are a number of other plants that associate well with alpines and look at home on a rockery. They fall into three groups:

1. **Dwarf conifers**

   Suitable plants are *Chamaecyparis obtusa* 'Nana', *Juniperus communis* 'Compressa', and *Pinus mugo* 'Gnom'.

2. **Dwarf and low growing shrubs**

   Heathers in particular are suitable, but also some other shrubs like *Hebe pinguifolia* 'Pagei', *Acer palmatum* 'Dissectum', and *Berberis thunbergii atropurpurea* 'Nana'.

3. **Dwarf bulbs**

   Suitable bulbs are snowdrops, crocus, scilla, and dwarf varieties of narcissi.

Herbs

What is a herb

Although the word 'herb' historically means any plant with non-woody growth, (as in herbaceous plants), the current meaning is more restricted. **It includes any plant grown primarily for use in medicine or cooking.**

The grouping of plants as 'herbs' is very much a case of a grouping based on usage since they can include annuals, biennials, perennials, shrubs and even trees. The number of different herbs is very large, and the RHS Encyclopedia of Herbs describes over 1000 species, varieties and cultivars.

The use of plants for medicinal purposes goes back a long way and references can be found in Egyptian and Roman times. 'Physic' gardens were devoted to their growth, and the Chelsea Physic Garden is a surviving example. The march of modern medicine has virtually wiped out this use although some are still used in the production of drugs.

The current use is mainly as an additive to cooking, providing flavour and aroma, and enhancing almost any dish.

Herbs have always tended to be grown in groups, very often in intricate patterns, as many of them are very attractive garden plants, often highly scented. It is for this reason that they are included in this section.

Uses of herbs

In addition to their use in medicine and in cooking, herbs can be used as decorative garden plants.

- In a herb garden
- Part of mixed borders
- For groundcover
- In pots

Types of herbs

Annuals & biennials	Perennials	Shrubs
Angelica (biennial)	Chives	Bay
Basil	Fennel	Lavender
Borage	Hyssop	Rosemary
Caraway	Marjoram	Sage
Chervil	Mint	Thyme
Coriander	Sorrel	
Dill	Tarrogan	
Parsley (biennial)		

Designing a herb garden

A herb garden can be large and complex with the plants arranged in intricate patterns, or it can be tiny and simple with just the minimum of essential plants.

Traditionally herb gardens were laid out in formal patterns, often with an edging of dwarf box.

Key factors are:

- Use plants with similar cultural requirements
- Take account of size, form and colour to create a pleasing effect
- Provide access for picking or cutting
- Avoid very invasive plants or restrict their area of growth

Simple layouts providing easy access

Siting a herb garden

With such a wide botanical range of plants it could be expected that there would be an equally wide range of ideal growing conditions. However, although there are plants to suit most conditions, the majority favour:

- **Aspect**

  Many herbs, such as lavender and rosemary, originate from the Mediterranean area and are adapted to a dry heat. An open, sunny position is therefore required.

  Some herbs are susceptible to frost, particularly the tender annuals, and therefore need to be in a protected position and away from frost pockets.

Tolerant of some shade and moisture
Angelica
Chervil
Chives
Mint
Parsley
Sorrel

- **Soil**

  A well drained soil is important, and a light loam or sandy soil is ideal. In heavier soils making raised beds can help to give the desired drainage.

  Many herbs do not require high nutrient levels and it should not therefore necessary to add manures or fertilisers.

- **pH**

  A slightly alkaline soil with a pH of about 7-7.5 is ideal.

- **Accessibility**

  Although the plants will not mind, it is important for the user that they are easily accessible, and having them near the kitchen door and adjacent to a hard paved area is desirable.

  Many herbs will grow very successfully in pots and this is a way of siting them close to the house. In addition to being useful some herbs, such as lavender and sage, make a fine ornamental display in a pot. Some herbs can even be grown successfully on the kitchen windowsill.

Buying herbs

Most garden centres have a good selection of herbs, very often including collections of popular plants. There are also specialist mail order suppliers.

Plants are usually sold when quite small (eg in 9 cm pots) and are therefore comparatively cheap. Many of the perennials and shrubs however are not long lived and may need to be replaced periodically.

Ground preparation and planting

It is particularly important to remove perennial weeds. Compost can be added to improve the soil structure but it should not be necessary to add manure or fertilisers.

As the plants are sold in pots they can be planted at any time when the ground conditions are suitable, although spring is the ideal time.

If planting to a pattern, lay out the plants to the pattern before actually planting.

Some herbs such as mint spread rapidly by underground runners and can get out of control unless restricted in some way. This can be done by a physical barrier or by planting into a pot or bucket sunk into the ground.

Aftercare

Watering

Annuals and biennials will need watering if there is no rain during their establishment period. Other plants should only need watering in prolonged periods without rain.

Many herbs are of Mediterranean origin and are adapted to dry conditions.

Feeding

As already mentioned herbs do not need large doses of fertiliser, and an application in early spring at 25 g/sq m, of a general fertiliser such as Growmore will be ample. Alternatively the ground could be mulched with compost.

Weed control

As with all planting it is necessary to clear the ground beforehand, particularly of perennial weeds.

After establishment the ground should be kept weed free by hand weeding, hoeing or mulching. Any sprays should be used with care because of the danger of damaging the herbs.

Pruning

Many of the shrubby herbs such as lavender and thyme will need to be trimmed each year to prevent them becoming leggy. Trim after flowering or in early spring.

Other plants can be trimmed during the growing season to produce a supply of new young shoots.

Propagation

Annuals and biennials can be raised from seed, either saved or purchased. Remember that cultivars may not come true from seed.

Many perennials can also be raised easily from seed, and others can be propagated vegetatively by cuttings or by division.

Shrubs will usually be propagated by cuttings.

Harvesting

Either fresh or dried herbs can be used in cooking although fresh ones are usually preferable. Drying is the traditional way of preserving herbs but many can be frozen and stored in the freezer.

- Always pick fresh young growth
- Pick flowers just before they open
- Pick fruits and seeds when they are ripe

Pests and diseases

Herbs are prone to pests and diseases in the same way as other plants. However, as it is usually the foliage rather than the flowers that are used, some degree of damage can be tolerated.

Because the herbs are used in cooking many people will not want to use chemical sprays on them, and the range of protective measures set out in **Topic C-2 'Cultural control'** can be used instead.

Some of the best

Basil	Coriander	Parsley
Type Half hardy annual	**Type** Hardy annual	**Type** Biennial
Botanical name *Ocimum basilicum*	**Botanical name** *Coriandrum sativum*	**Botanical name** *Petroselinum crispum*
Height and spread 30 x 30 cm	**Height and spread** 60 x 30 cm	**Height and spread** 30 x 20 cm
Propagation Seed - tender - sow under glass in spring and plant out after frosts	**Propagation** Seed - sow outside in spring/early summer	**Propagation** Seed - sow at intervals through spring and summer.
Characteristics White fragrant flowers in summer. Leaves are used in cooking, particularly Italian dishes, and in salads.	**Characteristics** White flowers in summer. Leaves are aromatic and both leaves and seeds are used in cooking, particularly curries.	**Characteristics** Bright green crinkled leaves Used as a garnish on many dishes, or included in soups and sauces.

Chives

Type
Perennial

Botanical name
Allium shoenoprasum

Height and spread
20 x 20 cm

Propagation
Seed - sow outside in spring/early summer. Division in spring.

Characteristics
A member of the onion family, with grass like leaves. Leaves can be used in soups and salads.

Fennel

Type
Perennial

Botanical name
Foeniculum vulgare

Height and spread
90 x 60 cm

Propagation
Seed - sow outside in spring/early summer. Division in spring.

Characteristics
Feathery, bright green foliage and yellow flowers in summer. Leaves and seeds taste of aniseed

Mint

Type
Perennial

Botanical name
Mentha spicata

Height and spread
60 cm. Spread indefinite by underground runners.

Propagation
Division in spring.

Characteristics
Probably most widely used of all herbs, particularly as 'mint sauce'. Unlike most it thrives in a damp soil. A rampant spreader.

Rosemary

Type
Evergreen shrub

Botanical name
Rosmarinus officinalis

Height and spread
100 x 60 cm

Propagation
Softwood cutting in spring or semi-ripe in summer

Characteristics
A number of named varieties. Narrow leaves with small blue flowers in summer. Used as a garnish with meats.

Sage

Type
Evergreen sub-shrub

Botanical name
Salvia officinalis

Height and spread
60 x 60 cm.

Propagation
Softwood cutting in spring or semi-ripe in summer

Characteristics
A number of named varieties. Aromatic leaves with blue flowers in summer. Used in stuffings.

Thyme

Type
Evergreen sub-shrub

Botanical name
Thymus vulgare

Height and spread
15 x 30 cm

Propagation
Softwood cuttings in spring or semi-ripe in summer

Characteristics
Many varieties. Evergreen foliage in shades of green, silver and gold. Leaves used for flavouring.

Ornamental grasses and bamboos

In this topic we are concerned with grasses that are suitable for display in the ornamental garden and not lawn grasses which are dealt with in **Topic G-1**. It should also be appreciated that the crops we rely on to survive, such as wheat, oats, barley and rice are all members of the grass family.

There are grasses suitable for a range of purposes and environments, and their popularity has greatly increased over the last few years, particularly in conjunction with the move to more naturalistic forms of planting.

What are grasses and bamboos

Grasses and bamboos are herbaceous plants belonging to the family **Poaceae**.

They are monocotyledons and have the characteristics typical of all monocots:

- One seed leaf
- Narrow strap like leaves with parallel veins
- Fibrous roots
- Wind pollination
- No secondary growth

Grasses can be evergreen or deciduous, although the deciduous ones tend to hang on to their leaves over winter. Bamboos are evergreen, although leaves can be damaged over winter.

Some grasses are annuals and some are tender. Because this restricts their usefulness in the ornamental garden they are not considered any further in this topic.

Grasses can be divided into cool flowering and warm flowering groups. Cool flowering ones, which include *Festuca* and *Milium*, start growth in late winter and start to flower in spring. Warm flowering ones, which include *Cortaderia* and *Miscanthus*, start growth in spring and flower in late summer and autumn. By using the two groups it is possible produce an attactive display over a period of time longer than with other herbaceous plants.

There are some plants that are grass-like in appearance but which do not belong to the same family. The main one is sedges which are in the family **Cyperaceae**, and some of these are included in this topic. Reference to grasses includes sedges unless stated otherwise. The other major group is the rushes which are in the family **Juncaceae**. These are very much moisture loving plants suitable for the edge of ponds or bog gardens, and because of this specialised use they are not considered any further.

Uses of grasses and bamboos

- Grass borders
- Part of mixed borders
- 'Prairie' planting
- Gravel gardens

- Hedges and windbreaks (bamboos only)
- Specimen plants
- Containers

Sizes and shapes

Grasses can come in many sizes from a few centimetres to several metres. Their basic shapes are tufted, arching or upright. The flower heads are often carried well above the foliage.

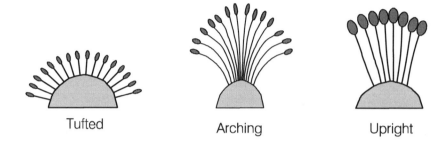

Tufted   Arching   Upright

Bamboos are upright in growth and can vary from dwarf types of around 1m to several metres. Although bamboos are woody they do not make secondary growth and the thickness of the stems does not increase.

Both grasses and bamboos spread by means of rhizomes. These can develop close to the parent plant which gives a clump like growth that steadily increases, or they can run away from the parent and shoot at some distance from it. Some bamboos are particularly likely to spread rapidly and these should be avoided in a small garden.

Grasses and bamboos in design

Grasses can be very attractive in their own right and also be a foil for other plants.

Their regular shape gives them an architectural look, and their form can bring a lightness and grace to the garden. Their leaves can provide a curtain through which other plants can be glimpsed and the slightest wind can bring movement.

Being wind pollinated the flowers tend to be small and lacking in colour, but the whole flower head can be very attractive, and so can the seed heads which can be carried into the winter months.

The foliage, although similar in outline, can vary in colour, with greens, yellows, blues and browns as well as variegated varieties.

Some grasses will tolerate shade and some will tolerate dampness. Sedges and bamboos in particular are suited to damp positions.

Prairie planting

Prairie planting is a style that is currently in vogue, largely due to a Dutch landscape designer called Piet Oudolf. He has won many awards including 'Best Garden in Show' at the 2000 Chelsea Flower Show. There are also beds designed by Oudolf at the RHS Garden at Wisley.

Prairie planting takes its inspiration from the natural prairies of mid America and the steppes of Central Asia. These are largely arid, treeless zones where the predominant vegetation is grasses.

Prairie planting seeks to combine grasses with traditional herbaceous perennials to produce a naturalistic and unstructured form. It could be considered to combine the herbaceous border and the flower meadow.

The style is particularly suited to large areas and once established should be low maintenance.

Plants suitable for prairie planting:

Grasses	Herbaceous
Calamagrostis x acutifolia	*Achillea*
Cortaderia selloana	*Coreopsis*
Miscanthus sinensis	*Kniphofia*
Pennisetum alopecuroides	*Perovskia*
Stipa gigantea	*Rudbeckia*

The plants should be planted in drifts or swathes to avoid the appearance of regular groupings and to blur the transition from one plant group to another.

Bamboos are not suited to prairie planting as they do not grow naturally in that kind of environment.

Buying grasses and bamboos

See **Topic E-1 'Buying plants'** for general guidance.

As with all plants, buying ones that are suitable for the environment in which they will be planted is very important, and the display will be unsatisfactory if this is not done.

Siting and planting

See **Topic E-2 'Planting'** for general guidance.

Although there are grasses and bamboos to suit a range of conditions there are some differences between them:

Grasses

* Open sunny aspect
* Well drained soil
* Tolerates low nutrient soil
* Not fussy about pH

Sedges and bamboos

* Tolerates shade
* Moisture retentive soil
* Prefers high nutrient soil
* Not fussy about pH

It is likely that any purchased plants will be in containers and can therefore be planted at any time of the year although autumn and spring are the best to get them off to a good start.

As a guide to the planting distance use half the ultimate height of the plant.

A mulch around the plants can help to suppress weed growth and help to display the plants to their best advantage. A gravel mulch can be particularly effective.

Many grasses are suitable for planting in containers, either singly or in groups, but do not choose those that tend to spread rapidly. They can be planted in a soil or soilless based compost.

Bamboos can also be grown in containers but will require a large container and will require regular feeding, watering and repotting. Because of their weight and need for nutrients they are best planted in a soil based compost.

Aftercare

Watering

Many grasses originate in areas of low rainfall and plants should not need to be watered once they are established. Anyone who has watched their lawns turn brown in summer only to see them revive in autumn will know how tough grass plants can be. With the increasing shortage of water and likely hosepipe bans this can be significant advantage.

However, watering after planting and during the establishment period may be necessary. Sedges and bamboos grown in pots will require watering in dry weather.

Feeding

Many grasses are tolerant of low nutrient soils and regular feeding should not be necessary. If the plants do not appear to be growing strongly then apply a balanced fertiliser such as Growmore in early spring at a rate of 25 g/sq m.

Bamboos require more nutrients and a dressing of manure or compost in spring will keep them growing strongly.

Weed control

Beds need to be kept free of weeds which can get very entangled with the plants and difficult to eradicate.

Applying weedkillers is difficult because of the danger to the plants, and hand weeding, hoeing or mulching are the best options. Persistent weeds can be painted with a weedkiller gel (eg, Tumbleweed Gel which contains glyphosate).

In prairie planting it is particularly important to start with a weed free area and to keep it weed free during the establishment period. Once established the density of planting should suppress the weeds.

Staking

Plants will not need staking.

Dead heading

Dead heading should not be necessary. Part of the attraction of grasses is their flower heads and seed heads and these should be left on. Of course this may result in you having to weed out many seedlings!

Tidying up

- **Deciduous grasses**

  These may carry their dead leaves over winter but will need to be cut back to ground level in early spring to make way for the new growth.

  Cut with secateurs or shears avoiding damaging any new growth. Clear any debris from around the plant. A mulch or fertiliser could be applied at this time.

- **Evergreen grasses**

  These do not need to be cut back. Tidy by removing spent flowering stalks and any damaged leaves and debris.

- **Bamboos**

  Cut out old or weak canes in spring to keep the plant looking healthy. Remove any damaged foliage.

Dividing

Like other perennials grasses lose their vigour as they get older and need to be divided and replanted. This is necessary every 3-4 years and is best done in late autumn or early spring. Dividing is quite easy due to the fibrous root structure.

Dig up the old plant and separate it with a knife, spade or two forks back to back. Replant healthy pieces with a good root structure from the outside of the plant.

Propagation

See **Topics E-4 and E-5 'Propagation'** for general guidance.

The easiest way to propagate grasses and bamboos is by division.

Grasses can be grown from seed and some seed suppliers have a reasonable selection including mixes. If gathering your own seed remember that cultivars will not come true to type.

Some experiments have taken place with planting ornamental grass seed mixtures in situ, and although it was decided it was possible, better results are likely from sowing in modules.

Bamboos rarely produce seed and need to be propagated by division.

Problems with grasses and bamboos

Once established grasses and bamboos should need little maintenance.

Some varieties, particularly of bamboos, can spread rapidly and these should be avoided.

Pests are not usually a problem. Aphids may attack the young growth, and slugs and snails may attack sedges.

Rust may affect some plants but is not likely to need treating.

Poor growth of plants is more likely to be due to unsatisfactory growing condition, eg. drought for sedges and bamboos, or waterlogging for grasses.

Plants for special purposes

For sun & dry	For shade & moist	For evergreen foliage
Festuca glauca	*Deschampsia cespitosa*	*Carex pendula*
Pennisetum villosum	*Carex (sedges)*	*Cortaderia selloana*
Stipa gigantea	*Milium effusum* 'Aureum'	*All bamboos*

For coloured foliage	For flower heads	For containers
Carex elata 'Aurea'	*Cortaderia selloana*	*Carex elata* 'Aurea'
Festuca glauca	*Deschampsia cespitosa*	*Imperata cylindrica* 'Rubra'
Imperata cylindrica 'Rubra'	*Pennisetum alopecuroides*	*Milium effusum* 'Aureum'

Some of the best

Grasses and sedges

Cortaderia selloana

This is the much over-planted 'pampas grass' and as such it is now very unfashionable.

It is a large evergreen plant with huge plumes of creamy flowers in late summer that can reach to 3m. Beware the sharp edged leaves.

It is very hardy but requires sun and a well drained soil.

'Pumila' is a more compact variety growing to 1.5m.

Deschampsia cespitosa

This is a useful clump forming evergreen grass with arching foliage growing up to 1m.

It has dark green leaves and airy, cloud like flower heads produced in early to mid summer.

It prefers a moist soil and will tolerate some shade.

There are many cultivars. 'Bronze veil' has bronzy red flowers, and 'Golden shower' has golden yellow flowers.

Milium effusum 'Aureum'

The common name of this grass is Bowles' golden grass and is probably the best golden leaved grass. It is short lived but will seed quite freely.

It grows in an arching clump to about 30cm and produces yellow flowers in late spring to early summer.

It will grow in sun or shade but requires a moist soil.

Another good cultivar is 'Yaffle' that grows taller and has a yellow stripe running down the centre of each leaf.

Miscanthus sinensis

These grasses are likely to figure in any grass planting scheme. Although not evergreen the foliage and flowerheads stay into winter extending the season of interest.

They prefer a sunny, well drained position and will form large clumps of bold foliage growing 1.5m to 2m.

There are many cultivars including early and late flowering ones. 'Flamingo' is early flowering with narrow leaves and pinkish flowers. 'Zebrinus' is late flowering growing to 2m, with yellow striped leaves.

Stipa gigantea

This is an evergreen grass with dark green foliage growing to about 75cm but with tall flower stems up to 2m in early summer.

It has large, loose flowers starting golden and fading to golden brown.

It prefers a sunny well drained position but will tolerate dryness and low nutrients.

It is suitable for growing as a specimen plant.

Carex (sedges)

There are many species and varieties of carex. In general they are smaller than grasses, require a moist soil, and will tolerate shade. They are also evergreen.

Becase of their size and attractive foliage they make good container plants.

Good plants are:

Carex elata 'Aurea' which grows to 75cm with arching golden leaves with darker edges.

Carex comans 'Bronze form' which grows to 50cm and has drooping deep bronze leaves.

Bamboos

Fargesia murielae

This is a useful group of clump forming bamboos with narrow canes that turn from brown to yellow. Five thin branches are borne at each node. Varieties can vary from 1-4m

They grow best in a moist position in sun or partial shade.

'Hareward' is a dwarf variety growing to 1m. 'Simba' is compact variety growing to 2m.

They are suitable for hedges or windbreaks, or for specimen planting.

Phyllostachys nigra

This genus includes many easy to grow clump forming bamboos with their coloured canes being the main attraction.

They like full sun and can be tolerant of drought when established.

This species is known as the black bamboo. The canes start green but turn black over 18-24 months.

A large plant in the wild, in cultivation it can reach 4m

Dramatic as a specimen plant,

Wild flowers and meadows

In recent years there has been considerable interest in the use of wild flowers in the garden. This has probably been due to a general move to more natural looking gardens and an increased awareness of the need for conservation since many wild flowers are in danger of extinction.

It is however still possible to see some wild flowers in their natural environment, such as bluebells and foxgloves in woodland, heathers and broom on moorland, and campions and cow parsley in hedgerows and on roadside banks. The area where wild flowers have decreased dramatically is in fields used for grazing or crop production, where they have been virtually eliminated by intensive farming and the widespread use of herbicides.

What is a wild flower

A wild flower can be defined as one that is native to the country, and has not been modified by artificial selection or breeding.

This will include many that we regard as weeds, such as nettles and brambles, that we would not want even in our wild garden.

Most of the desirable wild flowers are annuals, biennials or perennials, although there are also a number of bulbs and some shrubs that would qualify. There are also many native trees that can be used in conjunction with wild flowers to make a woodland garden.

Wild flowers and the law

There are approximately 1500 wild flower species in the UK, and around 100 are officially classified as endangered.

Under the **Wildlife and Countryside Act 1981** wild flowers are protected from being dug up from the wild. For plants on the endangered list even picking the flowers or collecting the seed is not allowed, since this will reduce the extent to which the plants can reproduce.

Reputable retailers of wild flowers will certify that their plants have not been taken from the wild.

Why grow wild flowers

- They are attractive in their own right
- They are in danger of extinction in the wild
- They will attract wildlife into the garden
- Some are particularly useful for growing in difficult places, such as under trees or in wet areas

Wild flowers in design

Wild flowers can be used in a number of different ways:

- In beds and borders
- To solve a problem area
- As a flowering meadow
- As part of a woodland garden
- As part of a natural hedgerow
- Around a pond
- In containers

One characteristic of wild flowers is that they tend to be less showy and more delicate than cultivated varieties, and care needs to be taken that they are not overshadowed or overwhelmed by other plants. It is therefore probably more effective to grow them in an area of their own rather than to mix them with other plants where their impact may be reduced.

In the last few years there have been a number of show gardens at the Chelsea Flower Show that have either incorporated areas of 'natural' garden using wild flowers, or have been completely 'natural'. I use the word 'natural' in inverted commas because it should be realised that such areas are not truly natural and work is entailed in maintaining them. If an area of garden is just left then it is likely to develop into a mass (or mess!) of nettles, brambles, docks, thistles and other plants we would regard as weeds.

A particular variation on the wild flower garden is the wild flower meadow which is a mixture of grass and wild flowers, and is an attempt to recreate the effect of pasture land as it existed before the widespread use of herbicides virtually wiped out the flowers.

A complete wild flower garden may incorporate a meadow, a woodland area, a pool and a rock garden, but would need a large area to look authentic.

It should be realised that some of the plants commonly grown in our gardens are the same as the plants in the wild, such as the common snowdrop (*Galanthus nivalis*) and the common foxglove (*Digitalis purpurea*). Many others are descended from, and closely related to, their wild flower ancestors.

Buying wild flowers

Some wild flower seeds are available from the main seed retailers, but a much wider choice can be obtained from a specialist supplier. In addition to individual varieties most specialists will offer seed mixtures suitable for a number of different environments, including mixtures of grass and flowers suitable for creating a meadow.

Most specialists also sell plants but, compared to seed, the choice is usually restricted. Also to buy plants for anything other than the smallest area would be expensive.

Wild flower bulbs can be obtained from the main bulb retailers or from specialists.

Once some plants are established they can be increased by seed or by vegetative propagation. Many wild flowers will readily self seed.

Remember to buy only from those suppliers who certify that their plants have not been taken from the wild.

Cultivation of wild flowers

In general the cultivation of wild flowers is no different from the cultivation of other plants, and will depend on whether they are annuals, biennials or perennials.

Some specific points:

- The most important thing to get right is to choose the right plant for the right place.

- Seed of individual varieties can be sown directly where they are to grow, in a seed bed, or in trays or modules. With the exception of flowering meadows it is better to grow in a seed bed, trays or modules to avoid the competition from weeds.

- Some seeds may need scarification or stratification.

- The best time to sow the seed is in autumn (August/September), although it can also be done in spring (March/May).

- It is important to ensure the final planting area is weed free. A well prepared and fertile soil will produce the best results.

- Normal aftercare is required:

  → Areas must be kept weed and grass free to avoid the wild flowers being overrun.

  → Watering should only be necessary in prolonged periods without rain.

  → Dead heading will prolong the flowering period and avoid excessive self-seeding.

  → The regular addition of fertiliser should not be necessary.

  → Pests and diseases seem to be less of a problem than with cultivated varieties, and may be more tolerated in a 'natural' environment.

- Special consideration apply to establishing a flowering meadow which are discussed below.

Creating a flowering meadow

Trying to create a flowering meadow by over-sowing an area of existing grass will not be successful. The grass will grow too vigorously to allow the flowers to germinate and grow well. It may be possible to transplant small plants into an existing grassed area but much will depend on the age and quality of the grass. **The most successful method of establishing a meadow will be sowing a mixture of grass and flower seed on a prepared soil.**

The area used should be sunny. Contrary to what has been said above a fertile soil is not required for a meadow since this will encourage the growth of the grasses which may then overwhelm the flowers. The seed mixtures that are available consist of about 80% grasses and 20% flowers. The grasses used are ones that a relatively fine and slow growing. A typical mix for a summer flowering meadow would include:

Grasses	Browntop bent
	Chewings fescue
	Crested dogstail
	Red fescue

Smooth stalked meadow grass

Flowers   Bird's foot trefoil
Buttercup
Cowslip
Field scabious
Daisy
Meadow crane's bill
Oxeye daisy
Selfheal

The steps required are as follows:

- Prepare the area as a seed bed, making sure all weeds are removed. If necessary the area could be treated with the weedkiller **glyphosate** for perennial weeds, or **diquat** for annual weeds. If the soil is particularly fertile consider removing some of the topsoil, down to a depth of 5 cm, to reduce fertility.

- The best time to sow the seed is in August or September:
  - ➜   This is when it would naturally be shed
  - ➜   Winter frost will help to breakdown the dormancy of some seeds
  - ➜   The soil temperature will be higher than in spring
  - ➜   Bird damage may be less as more alternative food sources are available

- Sow the seed at the recommended rate. This is likely to be about 3-5 g/sq m. The seed can be mixed with sharp sand to ensure a more even spread. Rake the seed in lightly and water with a fine spray, avoiding capping the soil surface.

- Keep the area watered during dry weather, and remove or treat any weeds that germinate.

- For the first year after germination cut the meadow to a length of 5 cm whenever the grass reaches a height of 10 cm. This is to prevent the grasses growing too strongly to overwhelm the flowers. **Always remove the cuttings after mowing**.

- After the first year the mowing must be dictated by the need to allow the flowers to grow, flower and set seed. There is likely to be a period of up to 12 weeks when no mowing will take place, the exact timing of which will be dictated by whether the flowers are predominately spring or summer flowering.

- Apart from mowing and keeping weeds under control the area should require little maintenance.

Plants for special purposes

Flower borders (sunny)

Bellflower *Campanula glomerata*	Perennial	Clusters of purple/blue flowers from May to September on erect stems growing up to 45 cm. Can be invasive.
Cornflower *Centaurea cyanus*	Annual	Bright blue flowers from June to August on plants growing to 60 cm. Dislikes alkaline soil.
Corn marigold *Chrysanthemum segetum*	Annual	Golden yellow daisy-like flowers 5 cm across from June to September on plants growing to 45 cm.
Meadow crane's-bill *Geranium pratense*	Perennial	Blue flowers throughout summer on plants growing to 60 cm.
Rock rose *Helianthemum nummularium*	Shrub	Masses of yellow flowers from May to August on a low growing, spreading plant.

Meadow

Bird's foot trefoil *Lotus corniculatus*	Perennial	Yellow/orange flowers on a low spreading plant from May to September. Also known as 'eggs and bacon'.
Cornflower *Centaurea cyanus*	Annual	See description under 'Borders' above.
Cowslip *Primula veris*	Perennial	Yellow drooping flowers borne in clusters in April/May on stems growing to 20 cm. Dislikes acid soil but tolerates some shade. Becoming scarce in the wild.
Field scabious *Knautia arvensis*	Perennial	Pin-cushion like flowerheads of lilac/blue flowerheads from July to September on plants growing to 90 cm.
Field poppy *Papaver rhoeas*	Annual	The common red poppy flowering in June/July on stems up to 60 cm. Prolific self seeder.
Oxeye daisy *Leucanthemum vulgaris*	Perennial	White daisy flowers up to 5 cm across from May to August on plants growing to 60 cm.

The inclusion of annuals makes the timing of mowing more critical since it is essential to allow the seeds to develop and be shed.

Woodland (shady)		
Bluebell *Endymion non-scriptus*	Bulb	Nodding blue flowers in clusters from April to June on 30 cm stems. Tolerant of soil and site but best in deciduous woodland.
Foxglove *Digitalis purpurea*	Biennial	Pink/purple flowers from June to Sept along stems growing to 1.5 m. Prefers a moist, acid soil in partial shade.
Primrose *Primula vulgaris*	Perennial	Pale yellow flowers with darker centre from March to May on separate stems up to 15 cm. Prefers neutral/acid soil in moist shade.
Lily of the valley *Convallaria majalis*	Perennial	Small fragrant white flowers from May to June on plants growing to 15 cm. Good in heavy shade.
Snowdrop *Galanthus nivalis*	Bulb	Nodding white flowers from January to March on plants growing to 20 cm. Prefers a moist soil in partial shade.

Containers

This topic covers gardening in containers, where the container is kept outside for all, or for a significant part of, the year. It therefore does not include indoor, conservatory or greenhouse plants, which are covered in **Topic G-17 'Houseplants'**. Neither does it include alpine troughs which are included in **Topic G-11 'Alpines'**.

Many vegetables and fruits can be grown in containers, but these are outside the scope of this book.

Container gardening has increased greatly in popularity in recent years. This must be partly due to the easy availability and affordability of both containers and plants to put in them, and the way in which they have been promoted by garden centres, but there is also something appealing about being able to create a dramatic effect in a small space and with limited effort.

Most displays are limited to the summer months, but it is also possible to have permanent displays and displays for each season.

Why use containers

- **Enhance garden design**

  → Focal points

  → Framing a doorway, arch or view

  → Soften hard landscaping

  → Brighten dull areas

  → Disguise unattractive features

  → Provide year round display

- **Growing plants that will not thrive in garden soil**

  → Where the pH of the garden soil is unsuited to the plants, such as growing rhododendrons and camellias where the garden soil is alkaline

  → Where the soil contains persistent diseases that attack the plants required, such as clubroot with brassicas and white rot with onions

- **No soil available**

  → Balconies or courtyards

- **Growing tender plants**

  → These are plants that require protection over winter. If they are in containers then they can stand outside during the summer and be brought into the greenhouse or conservatory during winter

What containers

Types

1. Pots

This term is used here to cover all free-standing containers, and includes ones that may more accurately be called tubs, bowls, urns or vases.

2. **Window boxes**

In addition to being used under windows, window boxes can also be used to brighten up areas of blank wall.

3. **Hanging baskets**

Materials

	Advantages	Disadvantages
Terracotta	Attractive Huge range of shapes and sizes Good heat insulation Breathes Wide range of prices	Not all are frost resistant Breakable
Plastic	Low priced Clean Light to handle	Poor heat insulation Not as attractive or authentic
Reconstituted stone	Attractive Authentic when weathered Good heat insulation	Expensive Heavy
Wood	Attractive Good heat insulation	Must be treated to avoid rotting

There are other materials such as lead, iron and fibre glass but these are not so common. Anything which is a genuine antique will be very expensive.

Hanging baskets are usually made out of plastic covered wire or solid plastic, and it is also possible to get attractive wrought iron ones.

Shapes and sizes

Pots are available in all kinds of shapes and sizes from the traditional flower pot to ornamental urns. They can be attractive in their own right and are sometimes used as decoration without being planted. Some of the shapes available are:

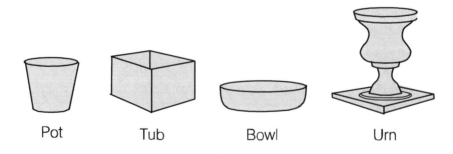

Pot   Tub   Bowl   Urn

The shape and size chosen will obviously depend on what it is intended to grow, but as a general guide it is better to avoid shallow containers since there may not be enough compost for the plant roots to develop properly.

Some pots are adapted to particular purposes, such as a parsley pot or strawberry pot which both have holes in the sides of the pot into which the plants are planted.

Wooden containers, by the nature of the material tend to be square or rectangular, and window boxes are often wooden since a rectangular shape is required.

Designing a container

You may think that it is not necessary to 'design' a container as long as the plants are suitable for the purpose, and a random mixture of plants can indeed provide a colourful and attractive display.

Over recent years however there has been a move towards applying some of the same principles that are applied to the design of the garden as a whole and the results can be quite spectacular. The Chelsea Flower Show usually contains many examples and for a number of years has had a competition for hanging baskets and window boxes that has been open to amateur Horticultural Societies.

There are no fixed rules and each individual will have their own preferences, but some of the things to consider are:

- **Plant types**

    Most summer displays will consist of annuals but most types of plants can be used. It is even possible to get a 5 m tree in a container, but it may weigh over a tonne, cost over £1000 and look out of place on the patio! More suitable plants are:

    Annuals
    Biennials
    Perennials
    Bulbs
    Alpines
    Shrubs
    Conifers

    Alpines, shrubs and conifers are more likely to be used in permanent containers, although other plants can be added to give seasonal colour. Permanent containers are also likely to contain a number of evergreen plants.

    A basic choice to make is whether to have a mixture of plants or just one variety. One variety can make a bigger visual impact than a mixture. A popular hanging basket can be made from just busy lizzies *(Impatiens)*, which form a nearly perfect ball shape.

    Invasive plants should be used with care as they may take over and smother the others.

    Whatever plants are used they need to be suitable for the site.

- **Form**

    The size and shape of the plants in relation to the container and to each other needs to be considered. A tall thin container probably needs bushy plants to balance it. A tall plant could be offset by a prostrate one.

    For hanging baskets and window boxes trailing plants are required to hide the container.

- **Colour**

    Another basic choice is whether to have one colour or multiple colours and, if multiple colours, whether these should be harmonious or contrasting.

Preparing the container

Any examination question is likely to ask about preparing the container, planting the plants, aftercare, and selection of suitable plants, and the rest of this topic covers these points.

Preparing the container is basically the same whether it is a pot, window box or hanging baskets. Where there is a difference it is identified in the following list.

1. Ensure the container is clean.

2. Ensure the container has adequate drainage holes.

3. Decide on the compost to be used. The basic choice is between soilless and soil based composts. For a comparison of these see **Topic E-10 'Greenhouse gardening'**. On no account use ordinary garden soil.

    For hanging baskets and window boxes use a soilless compost because it is much lighter. For pots either can be used, although for permanent planting a soil based compost is marginally better as it will retain nutrients and provide firmer support for larger plants.

    Mix some slow release fertiliser with the compost to avoid having to feed frequently. A slow release fertiliser should last up to 6 months.

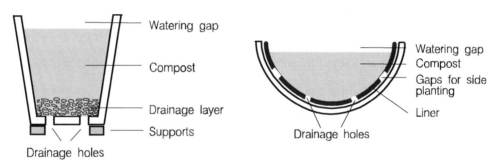

4. If preparing a hanging basket made from wire then it needs to be lined to retain the compost and moisture. The traditional material is moss, but this will not be available to most people, although it can be bought from the garden centre. Many alternatives are available such as plastic, fibre etc.

    If moss is used this is very porous and a less porous liner can be used inside the moss. If a solid plastic sheet is used as a liner then it must have some drainage holes made in it.

5. If a soil based compost is used, or if there are few drainage holes, place a 3-5 cm layer of gravel or grit in the bottom of the container to help it to drain easily.

6. Fill the container with the compost. For hanging baskets do not fill it initially above the point at which plants may be inserted in the side of the container. For other containers fill them to within 3-5 cm of the top, allowing for any compost that is attached to the plants. The gap at the top is to allow for watering.

7. The container can be supported off the ground to ensure it drains freely.

Planting

1. Generally speaking plants are placed much closer together in a container. A40 cm hanging basket may have 15-20 plants in it.

---

2. If the plants are dry water them and allow the excess water to drain off.

3. In a hanging basket it is important to plant through the sides of the basket to ensure it is completely covered. Holes or gaps will have to be made in the liner to enable this to be done. The plants can be inserted from the inside or the outside whichever is easier and likely to cause least damage to the plant.

4. Having inserted all the plants in the side the basket can be topped up with compost and plants planted in the top.

5. After planting firm the compost around the plants.

6. Water the plants in when all have been planted.

7. In order to get the longest period of display it is worth starting off containers with tender plants in a protected environment, such as a greenhouse or conservatory, and moving them outside when the danger of frosts is over. This could add a month to the period of effective display.

Aftercare

Aftercare for containers is not difficult, but it is essential, particularly watering and feeding.

Watering

Containers can dry out very quickly, and in hot weather they may need to be watered daily or even more often. Hanging baskets are the most critical as they are exposed to sun and drying winds, and contain the least compost. At the end of a season a basket can be just a mass of roots with the original compost barely visible.

It is possible to get automatic watering systems that will provide water for a number of days without intervention.

It is also possible to add water retaining gel to baskets which should reduce the need for watering, but there is some doubt about how effective this is.

Feeding

Feeding is also essential since the plants are tightly packed and will soon exhaust the nutrients contained in the compost.

The use of slow release fertilisers has made this a comparatively simple task and if they are incorporated in the compost they should last 6 months.

If slow release fertilisers are not used then the containers will require feeding about every 2 weeks during the growing season, starting 4-6 weeks after planting. A liquid feed applied when watering is probably the easiest method, although a foliar feed can be used to give a quick result.

For permanent containers the top 3-5 cm of compost should be replaced each spring.

Pinching out

Pinching out the growing tips of young plants like fuchsias will make them grow more bushy.

Dead-heading

Regular dead-heading the flowers will keep the container looking tidy and prolong the flowering period.

Weeding

Any weeds that manage to take root can be removed by hand.

Pest and disease control

Treatment of pests and diseases has been covered in other topics and should be dealt with accordingly. The most likely problems are aphids, caterpillars, and slugs and snails.

Plants for containers

Because there are so many plants that can be used it is impossible to produce a recommended list, but in order to provide information for examination purposes the following tables include some of the possibilities.

Permanent planting

Plant	Type	Characteristics
Juniperus communis 'Compressa'	Dwarf conifer	Erect growth with light green foliage
Erica carnea 'Aurea'	Shrub	Golden leaved heather
Euonymus fortunei 'Silver Queen'	Shrub	Small evergreen shrub with variegated foliage
Hebe 'Bowles' Hybrid'	Shrub	Small evergreen shrub with purple flowers from May to Sept
Hedera helix 'Glacier'	Shrub	Evergreen climber with small variegated leaves that will trail over the container
Bergenia cordifolia 'Purpurea'	Perennial	Evergreen perennial with large purple tinged leaves

Spring container

Plant	Type	Characteristics
Crocus 'Joan of Arc'	Bulb	Large flowered white crocus
Narcissus 'Minnow'	Bulb	Miniature multi-flowered narcissus with yellow blooms
Tulipa kaufmanniana 'Heart's Delight'	Bulb	Early flowering compact tulip with red flowers edged with pink
Polyanthus variabilis 'Pacific Giants'	Perennial	Large flowered polyanthus in many colours
Arabis albida 'Snowflake'	Alpine	Evergreen alpine with small white flowers

Aubrieta deltoidia	Alpine	Evergreen alpine with small flowers in shades of blue and purple

Summer container

Plant	Type	Characteristics
Fuchsia hybrids	Shrub	Many varieties, colours and shapes, including trailing
Impatiens hybrids	Half hardy annual	Very popular 'Busy Lizzie'. Many colours, long flowering
Petunia 'Surfinia'	Half hardy annual	Large flowered trailing petunia in many colours
Canna 'President'	Tender perennial	Striking plant with broad leaves and scarlet flowers. Suitable as centrepiece of display
Helichrysum petiolatum	Tender perennial	Prostrate plant with grey felted leaves. Good foil for other plants
Pelargonium hybrids (geraniums)	Tender perennial	Many varieties, colours and shapes, including trailing

Water gardens

Water has long been a part of gardens, from the Egyptians and Romans, through the Renaissance in Italy and France, through the 'natural' gardens of Capability Brown, and up to the present day.

Although at one time the province of the wealthy, new materials and construction methods have brought the possibility of a water feature to everyone.

In this topic the use, construction and planting of water gardens will be covered but the stocking and care of fish is outside the scope of this book.

The value of water

- **Visual impact**

  Like the garden itself, a water feature can be formal or informal. Do not mix garden and water styles, ie. in a formal garden have a formal water feature and vice versa.

  Water can be soothing and restful as with a still pool, or invigorating and refreshing as with a waterfall or fountain.

  The impact can be heightened by the reflective nature of water.

- **Sound and movement**

  Moving water provides a background of sound and movement that can range from a gentle trickle to a forceful gushing.

- **Increased range of plants**

  Plants are available that will grow in the water, or along the edges of a pool where the water content of the soil is high.

- **Wildlife**

  Fish can be kept in a pool and birds and insects attracted to it.

Siting a pool

- An open and sunny position is best. In particular avoid overhanging trees as fallen leaves can be harmful to fish.

- A formal pool will often be incorporated in a patio or terrace, and will look better surrounded by paving or other formal features.

- An informal pool should be in a place where it looks most natural such as in a dell or at the foot of a slope.

- A feature like a fountain should be visible from the house or sitting out area.

- Ensure access can be controlled if there are going to be young children about

- Consider the need to provide for topping up the pool (necessary because water will be lost by evaporation) and for some form of overflow.

- Consider the need for electricity if a fountain or watercourse is used.

Formal pools

Formal pools go with a formal garden and will in general reflect the geometric shapes of the existing house or garden. They are therefore likely to be square, rectangular or perhaps round and may form a focal point within the garden.

The edges are likely to be hard and well defined. A raised pool with a wide edge to sit on would be appropriate, and the edging could be the same as the surrounding area.

Still water will enhance the restful atmosphere of a formal garden, although a central fountain to provide some sound and movement looks good and may appeal more to some people.

The planting should be restrained and just having waterlilies will look right.

A formal pool needs to be constructed of a hard and rigid material, and bricks or concrete are the most appropriate materials.

A formal pool with ledges for marginal plants

Informal pool

An informal pool should be used in an informal garden, and should mirror the shapes used in the garden. Therefore if the garden has beds of sweeping curves the pool should have similar curves.

The objective of an informal pool is to make it look a natural part of the landscape and it will therefore usually have a mixture of plants both within the pool and around the edges. If done well a gradual transition can be made from plants in the pool, to bog plants at the edges, and moisture loving plants around the periphery leading directly on to turf. Although a hard edging is practical the pool will look more natural without it.

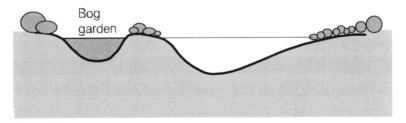

An informal pool with bog garden

An informal pool should be made from a flexible butyl liner which will mould itself to the shape required. It is strong and has a life up to 50 years. Polythene or PVC could be used but are not nearly so strong and durable, and are not recommended. Concrete could be used but is considerably more difficult to construct.

The only viable alternative to a butyl liner is a preformed pool made from fibre glass. These come in many shapes and sizes but all are quite small and can be difficult to make look natural.

Other water features

In addition to pools there are a number of other water features that can be used.

Fountains

We have already mentioned that a fountain can enhance a formal pool although it would look out of place in an informal one.

There are many to choose from that will give a different size and spray pattern. For a small pool a submersible pump will be satisfactory.

Waterfalls and watercourses

These can be used in conjunction with an informal pool to give more interest and movement, and can be combined with a rock garden. Done well the effect can be stunning as anyone who has seen the rock gardens constructed for the RHS Chelsea Show will confirm.

The construction can be done using a butyl liner or using rigid components.

One concern with these features, and indeed with any feature that requires power, is that they are not 'green' (unless driven by wind power!). Also when they are not working they are not so attractive.

Bog garden

Bog plants are those that will grow in a very moist soil although it cannot be constantly waterlogged.

They are the plants that will grow around the edges of a natural pond. However it must be realised that with a man-made pool the edges will not naturally be moist unless it is built in a wet part of the garden. Therefore, in most cases the bog garden must also be artificially created, which can also be done with a butyl liner. See the earlier illustration of an informal pool.

Safe features

There is an inherent danger with pools and they should be inaccessible to young children. There are however a number of water features that are comparatively safe.

These have water that is pumped up from a hidden reservoir through a rock or a stone that is surrounded by small boulders or stones. The water drains through the stones back into the reservoir. There is therefore no depth of water to be a danger.

Pool construction

We will consider a formal pool made from concrete and an informal one made with a butyl liner. There are some considerations that are the same whatever type of construction is used:

- The depth should be between 50-60 cm if fish are to be kept and even deeper if those fish are koi.

- A shallower shelf should be included in the pool if marginal plants are to be grown.

●   It is essential that all the edges of the pool are at the same level.

A formal concrete pool

1.   Excavate the ground to the shape of the pool. Allow an additional 15 cm for the thickness of the concrete. Remove any stones or protrusions.

2.   Line the hole with polythene as a damp-proof membrane.

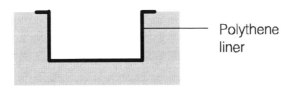

Polythene liner

3.   Lay the base between 10 and 15 cm thick. If the area is over 10 sq m use the larger thickness and place chicken wire in the middle of the concrete to reinforce it.

4.   Build shuttering to contain the concrete at the sides, and pour in the concrete. The sides should also be reinforced in a large pool.

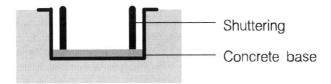

Shuttering

Concrete base

5.   Lay paving around the edges of the pool.

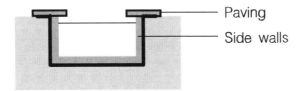

Paving

Side walls

6.   Paint the inside of the pool with a pool sealant.

An informal pool using a butyl liner

1.   The size of the liner should be the maximum dimensions of the pool plus twice the depth.

eg.

> Maximum length = 4 m
> Maximum breadth = 3 m
> Maximum depth = 0.5 m
>
> Size of liner = 4 + 1 by 3 + 1 = 5 by 4 = 20 sq m

2. Excavate the ground to the shape of the pool. Remove any stones or protrusions and line the hole with sand or a thick layer of newspapers to protect the liner.

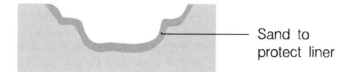

Sand to protect liner

3. Place the liner over the hole and secure it around the edges with bricks or stones.

4. Run water into the liner which will stretch and to a degree mould itself to the shape of the hole. Release more liner from the edges as required.

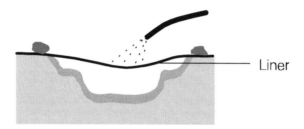

Liner

5. Trim the liner and cover the edge with paving or turf.

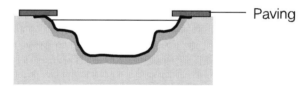

Paving

Plants for the water garden

There are a number of different types of plant that can be grown, and a number that need to be.

Water garden plants (aquatics) have a number of adaptations to enable them to survive. These are called **hydrophytic** adaptations:

- Submerged leaves can photosynthesise in low light
- Submerged leaves are finely divided to give increased surface area
- Floating leaves have stomata on their upper surface
- Some plants do not need to root into soil (free floaters)
- Seeds have high reserves of food to allow plant to grow to the surface of the water

The different groups of plants are:

Oxygenators

These are submerged plants that are not grown for their appearance but because they compete with algae for minerals and carbon dioxide, and thus help to keep the water clear. They also produce oxygen from photosynthesis which is vital if fish are to be kept.

Ceratophyllum demersum (Hornwort)	Will grow in sun and shade and is easy to keep under control.
Myriophyllum spicatum (Milfoil)	A plant with long trailing stems with feathery foliage. Suitable for a small pool.

<u>*Deep-water aquatics*</u>

These root in soil at the bottom of the pool but have leaves and flowers on the surface. The depth of water can be around 30-90 cm. These plants are often decorative, particularly the water lilies (*Nymphaea*) but they also serve a useful purpose in covering part of the water surface, which reduces the build up of algae and provides shade for fish.

Nymphaea species (Water lily)	An indispensable plant both for its decorative appeal and the shading it provides. They are available in a range of sizes from ones requiring a depth of only 10-30 cm, up to ones requiring 50-100 cm. The amount of cover they provide varies correspondingly. They bloom in succession from June until September in many different flower colours.
Nymphoides peltata (Water fringe)	A rapid growing plant producing yellow flowers up to 3 cm across, with crinkly edges.

<u>*Free floaters*</u>

These are the plants that do not need their roots in soil; they can just be placed on the surface of the pool. They are useful in providing cover on the surface of the pool while waiting for the deep water aquatics to get established.

Hydrocharis morsus ranea (Frogbit)	This is a good choice for a small pool as growth is compact. It has small white flowers in summer and autumn.
Trapa natans (Water chestnut)	This is an annual plant that will propagate itself from seed that overwinter at the bottom of the pool. It has attractive dark green serrated foliage and small white flowers.

<u>*Marginals*</u>

These are plants that grow in water but not at the same depth as the deep-water aquatics. They require a water depth of 10-20 cm, and it is common to provide a ledge around the edge of the pool to accommodate them.

Their purpose is decorative and they can link the pool to the garden.

Caltha palustris (Marsh marigold)	A popular marginal that will also grow in the bog garden. Bright yellow flowers in spring.
Iris laevigata (Water iris)	Large blooms in shades of blue and white are borne on 50 cm stems in June.
Zantedeschia aethiopica (Arum lily)	This is a tender plant but worth trying for its dazzling white flowers borne on 60 cm stems.

Bog plants

These are not aquatics in the same sense as the others. They like a moist soil but most will not tolerate continuous waterlogging. They include a number of plants that will grow quite happily in the herbaceous border.

Gunnera manicata (Prickly rhubarb)	Only for the largest of gardens. This is the largest perennial in the UK with giant rhubarb like leaves.
Ligularia dentata (Golden rays)	This plant has handsome, purplish, heart shaped leaves and yellow/orange flowers in summer.
Mimulus cupreus (Monkey flower)	This is a small plant forming mounds up to 20 cm and having flowers in shades of red in summer.

Planting

Plants should be obtained from a reputable nursery, a specialist grower or specialist mail order company.

Unlike most plants, aquatics are planted in the growing season, say from April to September.

It is possible to place soil at the bottom of the pool and plant directly into it, but this can make subsequent maintenance more difficult and most people will use mesh baskets that can be pulled out for maintenance.

With deep-water aquatics the planting basket may need to be lowered in stages by initially standing it on bricks and lowering it as the plant grows.

A good topsoil can be used as the planting medium, or special composts can be used. Do not use a normal garden compost as it is likely to contain too many nutrients. Use baskets with a fine mesh, and place pebbles on the surface of the soil to stop it being disturbed by fish.

Routine maintenance

Spring and summer

- Plant new plants
- Lift and divide existing plants if necessary
- Remove any fallen organic matter
- Remove blanket weed if this is a problem
- Top up the water level if necessary

- Hand weed the bog garden

- Dead-head any spent flowers

- Insert special fertiliser tablets in the planting baskets

Autumn and Winter

- If necessary net the pool to catch falling leaves

- Remove dying foliage

- Cut back oxygenators if necessary

- Remove and service any pump

- If fish are kept ensure the pool does not freeze over. Special pool heaters can be obtained, or in a small pool a ball floating on the surface will suffice.

Problems with pools

The biggest problem is to keep the water clear. Algae will quickly grow and turn the water green. Some forms of algae (*Spirogyra*) form threads that grouped together form blanket weed, and this must be removed.

In order to maintain clear water it is necessary to have some oxygenators in the pool and to ensure that about 50% of the surface is covered by plant leaves.

Pests and diseases are not usually a problem with water plants, but remember you cannot use pesticides if you have fish. Aphids may infest some of the surface leaves and the best way of dealing with these and other pests is to hose the leaves, or weight the plants so that they are under water for a period.

Houseplants

There are many plants that will not survive in the outside garden but which can be grown in the more protective environment of the home. This is because many houseplants originate in tropical or sub-tropical climates and need the warmth provided by the indoor environment.

Most plants covered in this topic would also be suitable for the conservatory or cool greenhouse.

The value of houseplants

- **Decoration**

    This is the prime reason why houseplants are grown. They can bring a room to life with the freshness of their foliage and colour of their flowers. They can lighten up dark and shady areas and bring an impression of coolness to hot and sunny ones. Some are large with dramatic foliage and can be used alone as specimen plants; others can be grouped to form attractive contrasts.

    There are a wide range of plants to choose from and it should be possible to find some for almost any situation.

- **Function**

    In the home plants can be used to create a division within a room. For example climbing plants could be grown up trellis that separates a living area from a dining area. Plants arranged around a window may draw attention away from a dull view.

    In a working environment plants can also be used to create areas of privacy, dampen sound, and generally provide more attractive areas in which to work. They also perform a useful function in helping to oxygenate the air.

- **Hobby**

    For people without a garden, growing houseplants can provide an alternative to outdoor gardening. In this case it is the actual growing of the plants rather than their decorative effect that is the attraction.

Providing the right conditions

This is not necessarily so easy as different plants may have very different requirements. For example sub-tropical and tropical plants require a warm and moist environment, while desert plants like cactus also require warmth but need it to be dry.

It may be obvious to say but our houseplants are outdoor plants in their natural environment, and in determining the right conditions for any plant it helps to know its natural environment, eg. rain forest, desert, swamp, mountain etc.

The requirements for growth are the same as all plants, but in growing them indoors special consideration should be given to the following:

- **Light**

    All plants require light to photosynthesise but actual requirements can differ considerably from plant to plant. The light available is greatest close to a window and diminishes with the distance from it.

Note that light does not necessarily mean sun, and most plants are happier out of direct sunlight.

Artificial lighting which was covered in **Topic E-10 'Greenhouse gardening'** can be successfully used with houseplants.

- **Heat**

Heat is the main reason that plants are grown indoors although this does not mean that a hot-house atmosphere has to be maintained. Most plants will grow well at a temperature around 18-20^0 C, which is a comfortable temperature for us, and with a minimum temperature of about 10^0.

The more demanding plants should be placed in the warmer areas like a living room or kitchen, while those that prefer it a little cooler can go in the bedroom or bathroom.

Fluctuating heat may cause problems with some of the more sensitive plants, and the fact that we tend to heat our houses in the day but not at night should be taken into account in choosing plants. In the same way temperatures in a conservatory may vary widely between day and night.

- **Humidity**

This is probably the most difficult environmental factor to get right. Many plants require the atmosphere to be humid, but our houses, with central heating, tend to be dry.

It is possible to use humidifiers to raise the humidity although to do this too much can make it uncomfortable for us. After all, who wants to live in the atmosphere of the Amazonian rain forest! The best plan if you want to grow the plants that require this environment is to provide it around the plants with a simple water sprayer, or by burying the pots in a container of moist peat, or by having a container of water with a large surface area from which the water can evaporate.

Buying houseplants

In view of the above comments on growing conditions ensure that any plant is suitable for its location. This is particularly important if you are going to group a number of plants together.

Take care to protect the plant from the environment on its journey from shop or garden centre to home.

Aftercare

In practice the requirements for individual plants will vary and a detailed book on houseplants should be consulted.

Summer and winter care

With outdoor plants the growth pattern between summer and winter is obvious and most plants survive the winter with little attention. With houseplants the difference may not seem so obvious, but the plants do react differently and require different treatment.

In general plants require less light, less water and less feeding during the winter period, and like outdoor plants will survive with less attention.

Watering

This apparently simple requirement can in fact be the cause of many plant problems.

It is usually over-watering that is the culprit, depriving the roots of oxygen, discouraging beneficial bacteria, and eventually causing the roots to rot. Many plants only require the compost to be moist and a number prefer it to be nearly dry. This is particularly true during the plant's dormant season.

A moisture meter can be used to detect when a plant needs water. Large leaved plants are likely to need more water that small leaved ones. Succulent plants store water in their leaves and do not need watering so often. Plants at the stage of producing flowers require more water.

Watering can be done from above or from below. In the case of plants with dense or delicate foliage it is better to water from below. To do this stand the pot up to its rim in water until the compost is wet on top, then allow excess water to drain off. It is better to use tepid water rather than cold.

'Little and often' is **not** the right approach to watering. Wait until the compost is nearly dry and then water it well so that all the compost is wetted. If drip trays are used then, when water starts to accumulate in them, the compost is sufficiently wet. Do not however let the plant stand in a pool of water as this will lead to the roots rotting.

There are a number of self-watering pots and systems available to make watering less of a chore and to allow the plants to be left unattended for a period of time.

Feeding

Balanced fertilisers are produced for houseplants. Foliage plants require one with a high nitrogen content, and flowering plants one with a high potash content.

Fertilisers should be applied regularly through the growing season and once a week may be necessary for some plants at critical times of their growth.

Fertiliser sticks or pellets can be used which release nutrients over a period of time

Cleaning

Leaves of houseplants may get covered in dust which blocks the stomata, since there is no rain to wash it off. Regularly spraying the plants with water or wiping the leaves with a proprietary cleaner will prevent this and keep the plant looking healthy. Do not use a cleaner on very young growth or on hairy leaves.

Dead-heading

Regular dead-heading of flowering plants may keep them flowering longer and looking neat. Some of the larger plants may on occasions need pruning to maintain their shape or contain their size.

Potting on

As plants grow bigger they will need to be transferred to a larger pot. This can be judged by the roots filling the old pot.

Supporting

Climbing plants and taller plants will require some form of support and a number of different types are available, from a simple cane to a miniature trellis.

Propagation

Houseplants may be grown from seed or propagated vegetatively from cuttings.

See **Topics E-3 and E-4 'Propagation'** for general guidance.

From seed	From stem cuttings	From leaf cuttings
Begonia rex	Coleus blumei	Peperomia
Calceolaria	Ficus benjamina	Saintpaulia
Cyclamen persica	Kalanchoe	Streptocarpus

In addition bulbous plants can be propagated by offsets and some plants can be propagated by division (eg, *Aspidistra*) or air layering (eg. *Ficus*).

Problems with houseplants

With the combination of growing in containers and growing indoors it is more likely that problems will be physiological rather than due to pests and diseases.

The following chart can be used as a guideline for diagnosing problems but consult a specialised houseplant book to be sure.

	More water	Less water	Feed	Repot	Change position	Check for pests & diseases
Slow growing			■	■		
Spindly growth			■		■	
Wilting	■		■			
Pale leaves			■		■	
Brow leaf margins		■			■	
Mottled leaves						■
Falling leaves		■			■	
Holes in leaves						■
Stem rotting		■				■

Pests

Red spider mite can be a serious pest since they thrive in a warm dry atmosphere, and are difficult to spot early. Aphids, particularly whitefly, can also be troublesome and so can vine weevil, which may be present when the plant is purchased. These pests are covered in **Topic C-6 'Common pests'**.

Diseases

Powdery mildew and grey mould are the most likely diseases and these are covered in **Topic C-7 'Common diseases'**.

Plants for special purposes

For a specimen	For foliage	For flowers
Fatsia japonica	Begonia rex	Azalea indica
Ficus elastica	Coleus blumei	Chrysanthemum
Monstera deliciosa	Peperomia	Kalanchoe

For sun	For shade	For winter interest
Coleus blumei	Aspidistra	Capsicum annuum
Kalanchoe	Hedera canariensis	Cyclamen persicum
Pelargonium hortorum	Philodendron hastatum	Euphorbia pulcherrima (Poinsettia)

Some of the best

Azalea indica

This is included since it is one of the most frequently purchased houseplants and is a splendid sight when in flower. It grows to about 30 cm and has single or double flowers in shades of white, pink and red above neat evergreen foliage.

However many people never get it to flower as well in subsequent years which is probably due to neglect. It requires a cool position out of direct sunlight and the compost must be kept moist at all times, Move the plant outside in late spring and bring it back in before the first frost.

Begonia rex

This is a foliage plant that grows to about 30 cm. It has large, heart shaped leaves in some dramatic colours and patterns. The predominant colours are green, pink, red and purple.

It requires a well lit position but out of direct sun. It likes a moist atmosphere which can be provided by standing it on a gravel tray.

Chrysanthemum

Like the azalea this plant is included because it is so popular, but it is specially treated by the grower to have compact growth and flower out of season. It is therefore difficult to keep and is best treated as a temporary plant and discarded after flowering.

Place it in a well lit position out of direct sunlight and water well while it is flowering.

Cyclamen persicum

This is an autumn and winter flowering plant with heart shaped leaves with silver marbling. The flowers in shades of white pink and mauve are carried well above the foliage.

It likes a cool well lit position and a moderately moist atmosphere.

After flowering the foliage dies down, and it can be kept in a dark, frost free position until new growth starts in the summer.

Fatsia japonica (Castor oil plant)

This is a striking foliage plant with large, glossy. lobed leaves.

It is an easy plant to grow and prefers a a cool, well ventilated position. It will tolerate some shade.

Ficus elastica (Rubber plant)

This is a popular and quite easy plant to grow. It is suitable as a specimen plant.

It can grow up to 3 m and has glossy, oval, dark green leaves that grow from a central stem.

It likes a well lit position away from direct sun.

Kalanchoe blossfeldiana

This is a compact succulent plant with round, slightly serrated leaves. Clusters of small tubular flowers of red, yellow or orange are borne in February.

It is possible to bring it into flower for Christmas by limiting the amount of daylight it receives.

It will flourish on a sunny windowsill and will also tolerate some shade.

Trim the plant after flowering.

Philodendron hastatum

The common name for this plant is 'Elephant's ear', due to its large glossy leaves which can be 15 cm long.

It is a climbing plant with aerial roots and needs a moss pole to grow up.

It grows best in a lightly shaded position and with a humid atmosphere.

Self test questions

These questions are to enable you to assess how well you have understood and remembered the information in the previous section. No answers are given as these should be apparent from reviewing the relevant topics.

The questions are **not** intended to cover everything you should know.

1　What are the advantages and disadvantages of creating a lawn from turf compared to seed?

2　Describe the steps involved in establishing a lawn from seed, covering ground preparation, sowing and aftercare.

3　List and briefly describe the tasks involved in maintaining an established lawn.

4　List five ways in which trees can contribute to the design of a garden, and suggest three trees suitable for a small garden.

5　Design a small shrub border, 5 m x 3 m, planted for year round interest, using at least six different plants from separate genera. Describe the main attributes of each plant.

6　List five hedging plants suitable for a formal hedge. Describe the ground preparation, planting and aftercare required.

7　List four methods by which climbing plants support themselves and name one plant for each method. Describe the procedure for pruning a wisteria.

8　List five desirable qualities of ground cover plants. List five suitable plants and describe their main characteristics.

9　List four tender perennials and specify how they can be protected over winter.

10　Design a small herbaceous border, 3 m x 2 m, planted for summer interest, using at least six different plants from separate genera. Describe the main attributes of each plant.

11　List four hardy annuals suitable for planting in a border. Describe the ideal site, ground preparation, sowing and aftercare required.

12　Describe three bulbs or corms suitable for naturalising in grass, and the method of planting them.

13　Specify the factors to take into account when siting a rock garden. List four suitable plants and describe the decorative attributes of each.

14　Describe the steps required to establish a wild flower meadow, covering choice of site, ground preparation, planting and aftercare. Name and describe four suitable plants.

15　Describe the preparation of a hanging basket for a summer display. Name and describe four suitable plants.

16　With the aid of diagrams show the steps in the construction of a pool from a flexible liner, and incorporating a bog garden. State how to calculate the size of the liner.

17　For a named houseplant specify a suitable method of propagation, the type of position required and the program of aftercare.

The vegetable garden

This section covers the general principles of growing vegetables, and in detail with the following:

Cabbages
Brussels sprouts
Beetroot
Carrots
Runner beans
Peas
Onions
Leeks
Potatoes
Lettuce
Tomatoes (indoor and outdoor)
Cucumbers

For each vegetable three of the most common pests and diseases are identified, but it should be appreciated that there can be many more.

General principles

Is it worthwhile

With the large range of vegetables now available from supermarkets or greengrocers, most of which is of high quality, it could be expected that production of vegetables in the garden might be in danger of dying out. However this does not seem to be the case and some of the reasons may be:

- Most people find fresh vegetables from the garden superior in taste.

- Many people do not like the idea of eating vegetables that have been produced with the aid of chemicals.

- Old-fashioned or unusual varieties may not be available from the shops.

- Cost savings can be made by growing your own.

Vegetable groups

It is convenient to group vegetables into broad categories because some are closely related and have similar cultivation requirements, which are different from other groups.

We can identify five groups:

1. **Permanent plants**

   Most vegetables are grown as annual plants. That is, we plant and harvest them within one year. There are however some that are perennial such as rhubarb and asparagus. These plants need to be assigned a permanent position in the vegetable garden.

2. **Brassicas**

   Brassicas come from the genus *Brassica* and include cabbage, cauliflower, broccoli, brussels sprouts, swedes and turnips.

3. **Legumes**

   Legumes come from the family *Leguminosae* and include beans and peas. Legume actually means a pod and a characteristic of the family is that the seeds are contained in a pod which is the fruit.

   Another characteristic of legumes is that they have a symbiotic relationship with the bacteria *rhizobium*, which results in nitrogen being fixed in nodules on the roots of the plants.

4. **Alliums**

   Alliums are bulbs and come from the family *Alliacaea,* and include onions, leeks, garlic and shallots.

5. **Root crops**

   This group includes those plants with swollen tap roots such as beetroot, carrots and parsnips.

There are some vegetables that do not fit into the above categories and will be covered separately. These are potatoes, which are stem tubers, and salad crops like lettuce, tomato and cucumber.

Principles of crop rotation

One reason for dividing the vegetables into groups is because it is beneficial to grow the groups on different pieces of land each year.

This process is called crop rotation and is usually done on a three or four year cycle. The longer the cycle the better.

The reasons for crop rotation are:

1. **To minimise plant problems**

    If crops are grown in the same area each year this can lead to a build up in the soil of harmful pests and diseases, and to a depletion of the nutrients required by the crop.

    This is given the general name of 'soil sickness' and it can cause the yield from the crop to deteriorate.

2. **One crop can benefit from the previous one**

    - Legumes fix nitrogen in the soil which can then be utilised by brassicas which require a good supply of nitrogen.

    - Potatoes help to suppress weeds because of their dense foliage, which can then be followed by alliums which are poor weed suppressors.

A traditional three year cycle

	YEAR 1	YEAR 2	YEAR 3
PLOT 1	BRASSICAS	ROOTS	LEGUMES
PLOT 2	ROOTS	LEGUMES	BRASSICAS
PLOT 3	LEGUMES	BRASSICAS	ROOTS

Alliums and salad crops should be included with the legumes, and potatoes with the roots.

A four year cycle could be created by treating alliums or potatoes as a separate group.

The following charts show how crop rotation would work for the crops that are dealt with in detail later in this section.

When we discuss ground preparation we will see that the preparation for each group

BRASSICAS

Cabbages
Brussels Sprouts

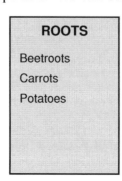

ROOTS

Beetroots
Carrots
Potatoes

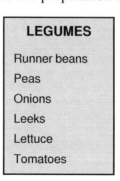

LEGUMES

Runner beans
Peas
Onions
Leeks
Lettuce
Tomatoes

is different.

Limitations of crop rotation

In a commercial situation, and particularly in agriculture, there is no doubt that crop rotation is important. However in a garden situation it must be said that it is not always easy, since the personal preference of the grower will dictate what he grows, which could be all of one group.

Also the argument about pests and diseases is not so relevant since they are mobile over a small area, and some can survive several years in the soil.

However, it is better to do it as far as possible, and certainly to avoid growing the same crop in the same place year after year. This, together with providing good growing conditions, should minimise the problems.

Siting the vegetable garden

If one has the choice, choose a site taking into account the following factors. For most of us the choice will be restricted by the size of our gardens. But do not despair - if you cannot choose the site to suit the vegetables, then choose the vegetables to suit the site.

- **Aspect**
  - → An open but sheltered site is required.
  - → Avoid frost pockets. A number of vegetables are tender, such as runner beans and tomatoes, and cannot be planted outside until the danger of frosts has passed.
  - → Avoid a sloping site if possible since this may lead to soil erosion. If it cannot be avoided plant across the slope or consider forming flat terraces.
  - → Avoid overhanging trees.
  - → Ensure there is reasonable access for wheelbarrows or other equipment, or for deliveries of manure.

- **Sun**
  - → In general, although vegetables vary considerably in their requirements for sun, a sunny site is really required, so the best is likely to be south, south-east or south-west facing.
  - → All vegetables grown from seed will germinate better in a warm soil.

- **Protection**
  - → Shelter from the wind is important, particularly with tall crops and those requiring support. Wind can directly damage the plants but also can reduce the activity of pollinating insects.
  - → Protection for the whole vegetable garden can be provided by a windbreak (see **Topic G-4 'Hedges and windbreaks'**).
  - → Protection for individual crops can be provided in a number of ways which are covered in **Topic H-3 'Protected growing'** later in this section.

- **Soil**
  - → A fertile well drained loam is ideal, with a topsoil of at least 30 cm.

➡ Soil fertility is of great importance as vegetables, more than anything else, take nutrients from the soil. Organic matter is of particular importance especially if the deep bed system of cultivation is used.

➡ An ideal pH is 6.5-7.0 although many vegetables will tolerate a wider range than this.

Planning the layout

Traditionally vegetable gardens have consisted of a few beds that can accommodate a large number of vegetables arranged in rows across the bed. To cultivate such a bed necessitated walking on it and so there were fairly large gaps between the rows.

A more modern approach is to have what is called a **bed** system, where the garden is divided into a number of narrow beds separated by paths, so that the beds can be cultivated without the need to walk on them. Once the beds have been created they can be managed as no-dig beds.

Advantages of a bed system
1. Planting can be denser since there is no need to walk between the rows. Even allowing for the paths overall productivity should be higher.
2. Cultivation can be carried out in all weather conditions.
3. Crop rotation is easier.
4. If raised beds are used a greater depth of topsoil and better drainage can be achieved.
5. Crop protection with cloches or crop covers is easier.
6. Compost, manures and fertilisers can be applied to just the areas in which the crops are to grow.
Additional advantages of a no-dig bed system
7. The natural structure of the soil is preserved.
8. Soil organisms are not disturbed.
9. Weed seeds are not brought to the surface.
10. Moisture loss is reduced.
11. Less hard work and time is required.

Disadvantages of a bed system
1. It is not so suitable for cultivation on a large scale since it does not lend itself to the use of machinery for cultivation, sowing or harvesting.
Additional disadvantages of no-dig bed system
2. Pests may build up in the soil
3. It may be difficult to maintain humus levels since organic matter can only be added as a mulch.
4. Fertility and structure may be reduced in the long term.
5. A compromise would be to re-dig the bed every few years.

Constructing a bed system

The beds should be 1-1.25m wide to allow cultivation from the paths, but they need not be rectangular. Any form is acceptable as long as it can be reached from the paths. Examples are:

Assuming basic ground preparation has been done:

● Mark out the layout. If possible the beds should run north/south so all plants receive the same amount of sun.

● Double dig the beds incorporating compost or manure at the rate of 5 kg/sq m to provide a reservoir of nutrients and humus.

● If the beds are to be raised add some form of edging to contain the soil. The edging can be anything which will do the job. Examples are wood, bricks, or concrete blocks.

● Make the paths wide enough to take a wheelbarrow. The paths can be left as earth but can be of any suitable material. Examples are grass, bark, bricks, paving slabs or concrete.

Physical protection from pests

In this context protection means protection of the whole or significant parts of the vegetable garden. Protection of specific crops is covered in a later topic in this section.

Protection may be required against birds or larger animals such as rabbits, cats or dogs.

Some protection against birds can be provided by 'buzz lines'. This is a form of tape that is stretched tightly across the garden and gives off a noise when moved by the wind. Better protection would be provided by growing all vegetables within a cage as is often done with fruit. The vegetables and fruit could be grown in the same cage.

Protection from rabbits, cats and dogs can only be achieved by some form of fencing which could be solid, such as wooden panel fencing, or open such as chicken wire. Rabbits are one of the worst pests in rural areas and the fence should be buried 15 cm. in the ground to prevent burrowing.

Sowing, planting and aftercare

Ground preparation

Re-read **Topic B-13 'Soil - Management (4) Cultivation'**.

If there are distinct beds and a formal crop rotation plan is to be followed, the preparation of the soil for each group of plants can be tailored to those plants.

BRASSICAS	**ROOTS**	**LEGUMES etc**
Lime the soil during winter if necessary. The pH should be 6.5-7.0. Rake in a general fertiliser 2 weeks before sowing or planting at 25-50 gm/sq m.	Rake in a general fertiliser 2 weeks before sowing or planting at 25-50 gm/sq m.	Add manure or compost when digging Rake in a general fertiliser 2 weeks before sowing or planting at 25-50 gm/sq m.

Sowing and planting

See **Topic E-3 'Propagation (1) Seed'** for general guidance.

Vegetables can be sown under cover, in a seed bed, or in situ.

- **Under cover**

  → Some vegetables, such as tomatoes or cucumbers, may be grown under cover for the whole of their life.

  → Some may be started under cover because they are tender, such as runner beans, and cannot be planted out until the danger of frost has passed.

  → Some may be started under cover to give them a longer growing season or to obtain an earlier crop.

- **In a seed bed**

  → A seed bed is used for the initial growth of plants while the space they will eventually occupy contains another crop.

  → It also makes it easier to care for the plants during a critical part of their growth.

- **In situ**

  → Plants are sown in situ where the seeds are large and easy to handle, such as peas and beans, or where they would not transplant easily, such as with root crops.

Planting density

If a bed system is used planting can be done at a higher density than with conventional gardens since there is no necessity to allow for walking on the beds.

The plants should be grown at an equal distance in all directions in an offset pattern.

If the planting recommendation is given as a distance between plants in the same row, and a distance between rows, then use the first distance or an average of the two. For example, if the recommendation is 30 cm between plants and 40 cm between rows then plant all at 30 cm or 35 cm (30 + 40 divided by 2). The objective is to just have the plants meeting at maturity, and experience will tell which is the best distance.

The dotted lines represent the size at maturity

Row layout   Offset bed layout

Planting for continuity

To derive the maximum benefit from the vegetable garden it is desirable to utilise all the space and have crops for harvesting all year round. Some techniques for achieving this are:

- **Successional sowing**

  This is either:

  1. Sowing the same variety at intervals of time so that the whole crop does not reach maturity together. The use of F_1 seed aggravates this situation since all plants will grow at the same rate.

  2. Sowing different varieties of the same crop. Many crops have early and late varieties.

- **Intercropping**

  This is the practice of growing a quick maturing crop in the space between slower growing plants, eg.

  Lettuce between brassicas
  Radishes between parsnips
  Spring onions between sweetcorn

  The intercrop should not deprive the main crop of water or nutrients, and it may be advisable to space the main crop a little further apart.

- **Catch crops**

  This is a quick maturing crop that is planted in an area that will be required later for a main crop. Plants suitable for intercropping are also suitable for catch crops.

Aftercare

The following tasks may be required:

Watering
Feeding
Weed control
Mulching
Thinning

Earthing up
Pest and disease control

Watering

See **Topic E-6 'Watering'** for general guidance.

For vegetables the critical times for watering are:

1.   **At the seedling stage**

2.   **At transplanting**

3.   **At flowering, and during fruit development when the vegetable is a fruit or seed such as tomatoes, cucumbers, peas and beans**

4.   **At regular intervals for leafy and root vegetables**

Seep hoses and automatic watering systems are particularly useful in the vegetable garden.

Feeding

Like all plants, the main nutrients required for vegetables are nitrogen, phosphorus and potassium.

If organic matter and fertiliser are applied as part of the ground preparation it should not be necessary to feed any further, with the exception of nitrogen.

Because some vegetables have a high requirement for nitrogen and it is easily lost by leaching, a top dressing or liquid feed during the growing season will be beneficial. If sulphate of ammonia (21% N) is used apply 50-100 g/sq m to the following crops:

Potatoes
Brussels sprouts
Cabbage
Leeks
Beetroot
Rhubarb

Adjust the rate of application for other nitrogen fertilisers, or follow manufacturers instructions.

Liquid or foliar feeds will give the quickest effect while organic fertilisers like hoof and horn will give the slowest. Controlled release fertilisers can also be used.

Green manures can also be effectively used in the vegetable garden, both to keep the surface of the soil covered and provide a source of nutrients and organic matter.

Weed control

Weeds and weed control are covered in some detail in the Section **'Plant problems'**.

Weed control is important in the vegetable garden, particularly among seedlings and young plants, as they compete for water, nutrients and light.

Mulching, hoeing or hand weeding are the best methods of control.

Use of chemical sprays is not recommended as it is too easy to damage the vegetables. Spot treatment with a herbicide can be used for perennial weeds. If a chemical is used it should be one that is deactivated on contact with the soil like

The vegetable garden

diquat, and be applied through a dribble bar to avoid drift.

Mulching

See **Topic E-9 'Mulching'** for general guidance.

Black polythene mulches or floating mulches are particularly useful in the vegetable garden.

Floating mulches allow plants to be planted out earlier, and will provide a degree of protection against pests and diseases.

Thinning

This is the removal of overcrowded seedlings to give the remainder the space they need to develop to maturity.

Earthing up

This is the practice of drawing up the soil around the base of a plant. It can be done to keep the plant firmly anchored in the soil, to blanch the stems or to encourage stem rooting.

Leeks are often earthed up to blanch the stems, and potatoes are earthed up to prevent the tubers turning green.

Pest and disease control

Pests and diseases and their control are covered in some detail in the Section **'Plant problems'**.

The following are some specific points relating to vegetables.

- **Good hygiene is essential**
- **Crop rotation will help**
- **Physical protection may be needed against larger animals and birds**
- **Floating mulches may be effective against some insects**
- **Some biological controls are available for use in the greenhouse.** *Bacillus thuringiensis* **can be used outside to control caterpillars**
- **There are a number of chemical controls available including some organic ones**

Specific pests and diseases are covered in the details for particular vegetables.

There is a school of thought that some pests and diseases can be deterred by what is known as **companion planting**. This entails planting some other plant alongside the crop, which will stop the crop being attacked. Examples are:

> **French marigolds in a greenhouse to deter whitefly**
> **Garlic under roses to prevent blackspot**
> **Mint around brassicas to deter the cabbage white butterfly**

It is important to remember that poor results may be due to unsatisfactory **growing** conditions and not pests and diseases.

Protected growing

Protected from what

Protected in this context means protected against the weather, although a degree of protection against pests is sometimes also provided.

The effect of the protection is that the air and soil temperature is raised, and the plants are not directly subjected to the weather.

Protection can be provided in a number of ways and can be either for the life of the plant or for the most vulnerable parts of its life cycle. For example, tomatoes may be grown exclusively within a greenhouse, whereas lettuce plants may be grown under a cloche for a limited time after being sown or transplanted.

Advantages of protected growing

1. Crops can be sown or planted earlier, which means they can be harvested earlier when shop prices are probably high.

    Some crops can be sown or planted in the autumn and protected through the winter to give even earlier crops in the following spring.

2. The effective growing season for some crops can be extended if they are started off under protection.

    This is important for half hardy crops, like runner beans, that cannot be planted in the open until the danger of frost has passed.

3. Plants get off to a good start and are better able to withstand pests and diseases.

4. Some winter crops will stay more tender if protection is provided.

5. Some physical protection from pests and diseases is provided.

Forms of protection

The following all provide a means of protection:

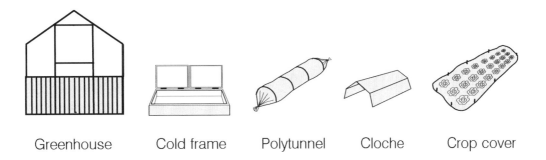

Greenhouse   Cold frame   Polytunnel   Cloche   Crop cover

Greenhouse

A greenhouse is the traditional means of providing protection. It may be heated to allow growing of tender plants all year round. It will usually contain both plants grown to maturity such as tomatoes, and plants for transplanting in the open when conditions permit such as lettuces.

Greenhouse gardening is covered in **Topic E-10**.

Cold frame

A cold frame is often used as an intermediate stage between the greenhouse and the open in order to gradually harden plants off.

It can be used to raise many seeds that do not require the extra warmth of a greenhouse.

Polytunnel

Polytunnels consist of a sheet of polythene stretched over semi-circular hoops. They come in many shapes and sizes, from walk-in versions that are typically 3-4 m long and 2 m high, to low ones 30-40 cm high.

They are the cheapest form of protection to buy, but like all plastic products have a limited life, and the cover may need replacing after 3-5 years. The cover should be treated with an ultra violet inhibitor (UVI) to prolong its life.

Cloche

Cloches come in many shapes and sizes. Unlike greenhouses and walk-in polytunnels they are easily portable and are used to protect different crops at critical stages of their growth.

Cloches can be made of glass or some form of plastic which can be either rigid or flexible.

Glass	**Advantages**
	Better light transmission
	Better heat retention
	More permanent
	Stable
	Disadvantages
	Expensive
	Breakable
Plastic	**Advantages**
	Cheap (in the short term anyway)
	Easy to handle
	Safe
	Disadvantages
	Limited life (2 to 5 years depending on type)
	May need securing to ground

Crop cover (floating mulch or cloche)

These have already been discussed in **Topic E-9 'Mulching'**, and they are indeed a cross between a mulch and cloche.

Crop covers are laid on top of the crop, or can be stretched over hoops to form a low polytunnel. They have the following advantages:

- They are cheap to buy although they do not have a life of more than 2-3 years.

- They are so light that they are pushed up as the plants grow, and can remain on the crop for several weeks, or in some cases until the crop matures.

- They are permeable, so the plants can be watered without the need to remove them.

- They provide some (although not much) protection from frost.

- They protect the crop against larger pests like birds and rabbits and some insect pests. Some of the most troublesome pests like carrot fly, cabbage root fly and onion fly are controlled.

They can also be used for other purposes like protecting tender shrubs against late frosts, and adding an additional level of insulation in the greenhouse.

There are two basic types. One is called a fleece and is made of fibres of polypropylene. It is very light and gives the best protection against frost, but may provide too humid an atmosphere in hot weather. The other is a very fine net which is stronger than the fleece and will last longer. The ventilation is better than the fleece and it can be kept on the crops longer.

Success factors for protected growing

- In general the larger the protected area the better. Small areas can be subject to rapid temperature changes.

- Ventilation is critical whatever the form of protection.

- Watering is critical. This may entail removing the protection. Seep hoses and drip feed systems are particularly useful.

- Avoid wind tunnels. Use end pieces on cloches to prevent this.

- Ensure the soil is free of weeds because they will also like the protection.

- If crops that need pollination like tomatoes or courgettes are grown, the protection must be removed sufficiently to allow the pollinating insects to do their work.

Brassicas

Brassicas are one of the mainstays of the vegetable garden and include the following:

Broccoli
Brussels sprouts
Cabbage
Cauliflower
Kale
Kohl Rabi
Turnips
Swedes

In this section we will look at the things that tend to apply to all brassicas, and at cabbage and brussels sprouts in detail.

General cultivation

- Brassicas are usually sown in a seed bed although they can also be sown in modules.

- It is particularly important to rotate brassicas because of the danger of the disease clubroot.

- Because clubroot likes an acid soil, maintain the pH at 6.5-7.0, liming if necessary.

- Do not manure the soil before planting, although this can be done in the previous autumn.

- Brassicas like to be planted in a firm soil and it is better not to dig it before planting.

- The leafy brassicas will benefit from a nitrogen fertiliser during their growing period. Foliar feeds are suitable.

Pests

Cabbage root fly	The larvae feed on the roots of all brassicas and can kill young plants. Transplants are particularly liable to attack.
	Symptoms
	Leaves develop a blue/red tinge and wilt.
	Treatment
	Place cardboard or plastic collars round the base of young plants or use a crop cover.
	There is no approved chemical control.
Caterpillars	See Topic C-6 'Common pests'
Slugs and snails	See Topic C-6 'Common pests'

Diseases

Clubroot	This is the most serious disease of brassicas and can persist in the soil for up to 20 years.
	Symptoms
	The roots are swollen and distorted. Above ground the leaves may wilt and have a red/purple tint.
	Treatment
	There is no effective treatment so it is important to try and prevent the disease getting into the garden.
	To reduce the risk maintain a soil pH of 7.0, and lift and burn any diseased plants.
Downy mildew	See Topic C-7 'Common diseases'
Damping off	See Topic C-7 'Common diseases'

Key to symbols

In the sections dealing with individual vegetables there is a timetable for sowing, transplanting and harvesting. The symbols used for these activities are:

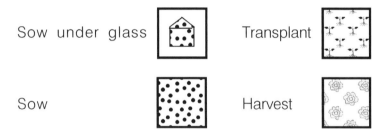

Sow under glass

Transplant

Sow

Harvest

Cabbage

General

There are cabbages for harvesting in spring, summer and winter, and it is therefore possible to have them available at nearly all times of the year.

Timetable

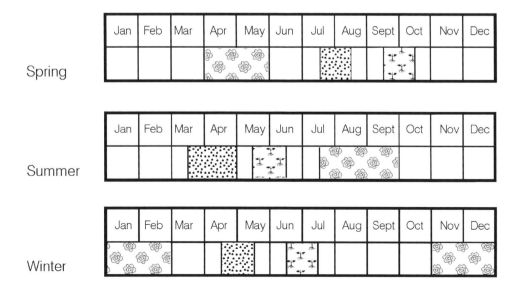

Spring

Summer

Winter

The vegetable garden

Sowing

Sow in a seed bed in drills 15 cm apart and thin seedlings to 8 cm.

Transplanting

Transplant when seedlings have 6 leaves. Plant 30-40 cm apart depending on variety.

Ground occupancy

20-35 weeks depending on variety.

Harvesting

Cut with a sharp knife close to ground level. With spring and summer varieties a second crop can be obtained if a 2 cm vertical cut is made into the stump.

Varieties

Double Early	Spring variety.
Spring Hero (F_1)	Spring variety. Sow in August to avoid bolting.
Hispi	Summer variety. High quality and early.
Minicole (F_1)	Summer variety. Compact and can be left in ground for up to 3 months.
Celtic (F_1)	Winter variety. Hybrid of a savoy and winter white. Can be left in ground until March.
January King	Winter variety. Hardy.

Brussels sprouts

General

These are a winter vegetable that is available from October to February. F_1 hybrids produce compact plants which stand up to winter weather well.

Timetable

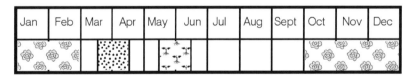

Jan	Feb	Mar	Apr	May	Jun	Jul	Aug	Sept	Oct	Nov	Dec

Sowing

Sow in a seed bed in drills 15 cm apart and thin seedlings to 8 cm. A very early crop can be obtained by sowing under glass in February, or in August of the previous year.

Transplanting

Transplant when seedlings are 15-20 cm high. Dip roots in a solution of thiophanate-methyl to help prevent clubroot. Plant 60-75 cm apart depending on variety.

Ground occupancy

30-35 weeks

Special requirements

In autumn stake tall varieties and draw the earth up around the stems to keep them secure. Pinching out the growing tip of sprouts is no longer recommended.

Harvesting

Pick the sprouts with a downward pull starting at the base of the plant when the sprouts are about the size of a walnut.

Varieties (all F₁)

Peer Gynt	An popular early variety (October) with medium sized sprouts.
Widgeon	A maincrop variety (October/December) with some disease resistance and a good flavour.
Fortress	A late variety (January/February). A very hardy variety with firm sprouts.

Root crops

Root crops include the following:

Beetroot
Carrots
Parsnip
Radish
Salsify

In this topic we will look at the things that tend to apply to all root crops, and at beetroot and carrots in detail.

General cultivation

- Root crops are usually grown in situ as they do not transplant easily.

- They grow best in a deep, fertile and sandy soil, where the roots can easily penetrate downwards. In heavy soils they are likely to be stunted and forked.

- They grow best in a soil with a pH of 6.5-7.0 and liming may be necessary to achieve this.

- Do not manure the soil before planting although this can be done in the previous autumn.

- The soil should not be allowed to completely dry out as heavy rain or watering after dryness can split the roots.

Pests

Carrot fly	This is a serious pest of carrots and parsnips. The adult female lays eggs in the soil in May/June and August/September. The larvae eat the roots and tunnel into them and can cause them to rot.
	Symptoms
	Leaves develop a reddish tinge and can wilt in sunny weather.
	Treatment
	Sowing seed in June will avoid attack from the first generation of larvae. Sowing under a crop cover will give some protection.
	Do not leave carrots in the ground once they are mature.
	There is no approved chemical control.
Aphids	See Topic C-6 'Common pests'
Cutworms	See Topic C-6 'Common pests' under 'Caterpillars'

Diseases

Violet root rot	This is a fungal disease of beetroot, carrots and parsnips.
	Symptoms
	Above ground the growth may be stunted and yellowish. Below ground the base of the stump is covered with purplish strands.
	Treatment
	There is no effective treatment. Burn any diseased plants and do not re-grow the crops on the same ground for 3-4 years
Downy mildew	See Topic C-7 'Common diseases'
Powdery mildew	See Topic C-7 'Common diseases'

Beetroot

General

Most varieties are round and deep red in colour, but cylindrical and tapered ones can be obtained, and so can some that are coloured yellow or white.

Beetroot can be picked fresh from late spring to autumn and can also be stored for use during the winter.

Timetable

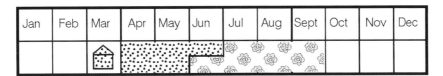

Jan	Feb	Mar	Apr	May	Jun	Jul	Aug	Sept	Oct	Nov	Dec

Sowing

Sow in situ 2 cm deep in drills 30 cm apart. Thin seedlings to 10-20 cm apart.

For an early crop sow in March in modules, or outside under a cloche or crop cover.

Because they are quick to grow they can be grown as a catch crop.

Ground occupancy

12-15 weeks

Harvesting

Pull or gently fork up while they are still young. Lift plants for storage in October

Storage

Place undamaged roots between layers of moist peat or sand and keep in a cool, frost free place. They should last until March.

Varieties

Boltardy	An round, red, early variety that is bolt resistant.
Detroit	A round, red, maincrop variety with good flavour. Good for storage.
Furono	A cylindrical, red variety. Good for storage.

Carrots

General

Carrots are available in many shapes and sizes, from short stumpy ones to long tapering ones. The short ones can be grown in most soils but the long ones need a deep, sandy soil free of stones to grow successfully.

Timetable

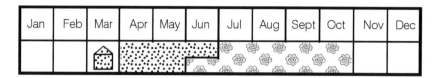

Jan	Feb	Mar	Apr	May	Jun	Jul	Aug	Sept	Oct	Nov	Dec

Sowing

Sow in situ 1 cm deep in drills 15 cm apart. Thin seedlings to 4-6 cm apart.

Thin carefully as the carrot root fly can be attracted by the smell of bruised foliage.

For an early crop (June) sow in March under a cloche or crop cover. The crop cover can be left on until maturity.

An even earlier crop can be obtained by sowing in autumn and overwintering under a cloche.

Ground occupancy

12-15 weeks.

Harvesting

Pull or gently fork up while they are still young. Lift plants for storage in October

Storage

Place undamaged roots between layers of moist peat or sand and keep in a cool, frost free place. They should last until March.

Varieties

Tiana	An early, short rooted variety.
Chanteney Red Cored - Supreme	A popular, medium sized, stump rooted variety.
St. Valery	A long rooted variety, often grown for showing.

Legumes

Legumes are plants that produce their seeds in pods and we eat the seed, or the pod, or both. Legumes include:

Broad beans
French beans
Runner beans
Peas

In this section we will look at the things that tend to apply to all legumes, and at runner beans and peas in detail.

General cultivation

- Legumes are usually grown in situ as the seed tends to be large and easily handled. They can however be started off under glass to give an earlier crop.

- They grow best in a fertile and well drained soil, to which compost should have been added in the previous autumn.

- They grow best in a soil with a pH of 6.5-7.0 and liming may be necessary to achieve this.

- They need a warm soil to germinate successfully. Covering the soil with cloches prior to sowing can achieve this.

- Many varieties require some form of support for them to grow up.

- Legumes have the ability to fix nitrogen in their roots and do not therefore need a nitrogen fertiliser during their growth. After harvesting, the roots should be dug into the soil to provide nitrogen for the next crop.

Pests

Mice	Field mice will eat newly planted bean and pea seeds.
	Symptoms
	Seeds disappear.
	Treatment
	Traps can be set in outbuildings that tend to harbour the mice.
	Seed can be dressed with a repellent.
Bean seed fly	The larvae of the bean seed fly attack the seed and seedlings.
	Symptoms
	Seeds fail to germinate or become distorted. Parts of the seedling may be eaten.
	Treatment
	Flies are attracted to newly disturbed earth so sow in a stale seed bed, ie. one prepared 10 days earlier.

	Cover the seed bed with fine netting.
	There is no approved chemical control.
Slugs and snails	See Topic C-6 'Common pests'

Diseases

Downy mildew	See Topic C-7 'Common diseases'
Powdery mildew	See Topic C-7 'Common diseases'
Grey mould	See Topic C-7 'Common diseases'

Runner beans (scarlet runners)

General

Runner beans are a particularly good crop for a small garden as they produce a heavy crop from a small area. 10 kg can be obtained from a 3 m row.

Older varieties can be stringy but modern ones tend to be stringless.

Timetable

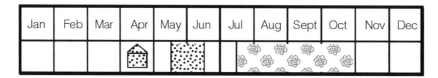

Jan	Feb	Mar	Apr	May	Jun	Jul	Aug	Sept	Oct	Nov	Dec

Sowing

They are usually grown as double rows because of the requirement for support.

Sow in situ 5 cm deep and 20 cm apart, in drills 50 cm apart. It is usual to sow 2 seeds at each point to allow for any losses.

They are not hardy and cannot be grown outside until the danger of frost is past, but for an earlier crop they can be started under glass in April.

Ground occupancy

12-15 weeks.

Special requirements

Most varieties are tall growing and need a substantial support. The traditional method is to support with two rows of poles or canes sloping inwards with a horizontal support where they cross. A wigwam of poles or some form of netting can also be used. Once started off the plants are self clinging. The support needs to be about 2.5 m high.

Pinch out the growing tip when the plant reaches the top of the support.

The old practice of spraying the flowers with water to help them set is now considered to be of no benefit.

Harvesting

Start harvesting when the pods are young and tender. It is important to keep picking and not let the pods reach maturity otherwise the production of pods will cease.

Storage

The normal method is to freeze them.

Varieties

Enorma	A non-stringless variety with long straight pods with a

	good flavour	
Butler	A stringless and vigorous variety.	
Gulliver	A dwarf variety growing to about 40 cm. It produces an early, heavy crop of stringless pods.	

Peas

General

There are many different types of pea. Some are wrinkled and some are round; some are small (petit pois); some are eaten complete with pod.

They are not the easiest crop to grow and results can be disappointing unless care is taken.

Compared with runner beans the yield is low (4 kg from a 3 m row).

Most varieties require some support.

Timetable

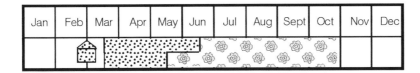

Jan	Feb	Mar	Apr	May	Jun	Jul	Aug	Sept	Oct	Nov	Dec

Sowing

Sow in situ 5 cm deep and 5 cm apart, in drills as far apart as the height of the crop.

Alternatively sow in three staggered rows in a wide drill of 20 cm.

For an early crop (June) sow an early variety in February/March under a cloche or crop cover.

An even earlier crop can be obtained by sowing in autumn and wintering under a cloche.

Ground occupancy

12-15 weeks.

Special requirements

Protection from birds is required after the seed has been sown.

Support should be provided from an early stage. Traditionally the support has been with pea sticks, but wire or plastic netting can be used. Place the support along the side of the row or down the centre if a wide drill is used.

Harvesting

Start harvesting when the pods are young and tender. It is important to keep picking and not let the pods reach maturity otherwise the production of pods will cease.

Storage

Peas can be dried or frozen.

Varieties

Kelvedon Wonder	An early heavy cropping variety that can be sown in succession. Some resistance to mildew.
Alderman	A maincrop variety producing a heavy crop with 11 peas per pod.
Waverex	A petit pois that is sweet and can be eaten raw or cooked.

Alliums

Alliums are bulbs and include:

Onions
Shallots
Leeks
Garlic

In this topic we will look at the things that tend to apply to all alliums, and at onions and leeks in detail.

General cultivation

- Alliums are hardy and generally easy to grow. They can be grown from seed or, in the case of onions and shallots, from sets (immature bulbs).

  The advantages of using sets are:

  → **They are more successful in cold areas**
  → **They will tolerate a poorer soil**
  → **They reach maturity more quickly**
  → **They are not attacked by onion fly**

- They grow best in a fertile and well drained soil, to which compost should have been added in the previous autumn.

- They grow best in a soil with a pH of 6.5-7.0 and liming may be necessary to achieve this.

- Weed control is particularly important as they do not have the above ground growth to suppress weeds.

Pests

Onion fly	The larvae of the onion fly feed on the stems and bulbs.
	Symptoms
	Foliage will wilt and turn yellow. Young plants may die. Roots and stems will be tunnelled.
	Treatment
	Flies are attracted to newly disturbed earth so sow in a stale seed bed, ie. one prepared 10 days earlier.
	Cover the seed bed with fine netting.
	There is no approved chemical control.
Stem and bulb eelworm	See Topic C-6 'Common pests'
Slugs and snails	See Topic C-6 'Common pests'

Diseases

White rot	This is a common and serious fungal disease. It can survive in the soil for many years and can move through the soil to infect new plants. It is particularly bad on salad onions. **Symptoms** The foliage turns yellow and wilts. White mould containing small black bodies appears at the base of the bulb. **Treatment** The chemical that used to be available to treat this (mercurous chloride, sold as Calomel Dust), is now banned and there is no effective alternative. Dig up and burn infected plants.
Downy mildew	See Topic C-7 'Common diseases'
Rust	See Topic C-7 'Common diseases'

Onions

General

Most onions have a typical bulb shape but there are some varieties, usually called salad or spring onions, that have small elongated bulbs.

They can be grown from seeds or sets.

Timetable

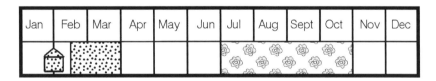

Sowing

Sow in situ 1-2 cm deep in drills 30 cm apart (bulb varieties) or 10 cm apart (salad varieties).

Thin the seedlings in stages to 10 cm (bulb varieties) or 3 cm (salad varieties).

For an earlier crop seed can be sown under glass in January/February and transplanted in April.

They can also be sown in August and overwintered to provide an even earlier crop.

Planting sets

Plant sets from mid-February to mid-April, 5-10 cm apart in drills 30 cm apart, so that the nose of the bulb is just showing.

Ground occupancy

25 weeks (spring sown) 45 weeks (overwintered) .

Harvesting

Bulbs can be pulled for immediate use at any time during the growing period.

When the bulbs are mature the foliage falls over. They can be left for about two weeks after this before lifting.

Storage

They can be dried and will keep up to the following April. They can also be sliced and frozen.

Varieties

Ailsa Craig	An old favourite, good for general use. Large and globe shaped. Limited keeping quality.
Hygro	An F_1 hybrid producing a heavy crop. Globe shaped. Good keeper.
White Lisbon	A quick growing salad variety. Mild flavour.

Leeks

General

These are an easy, undemanding vegetable to grow. They are hardy and will tolerate a less fertile soil than onions. They are not too troubled by pests and diseases.

One drawback is the length of time they occupy the ground.

Timetable

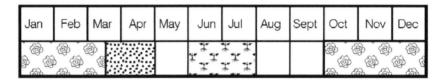

Jan	Feb	Mar	Apr	May	Jun	Jul	Aug	Sept	Oct	Nov	Dec

Sowing

Sow in a seed bed 2 cm deep and thin to 3 cm apart.

Transplant when the leeks are about 20 cm high. Make a hole 15 cm deep and drop the leek into it. This will ensure that the stem is blanched (kept white). Plant 15 cm apart in rows 30 cm apart.

For an early crop sow an early variety under glass in February and plant out in May.

Ground occupancy

35-45 weeks.

Special requirements

As the plants grow draw up the soil around the stem to keep it blanched.

Harvesting

Start harvesting when the leeks are still young.

Storage

They can be left in the ground until required or they can be frozen.

Varieties

Walton Mammoth	Early. One of a strain called Autumn Mammoth. Good all round.
King Richard	Mid-season. Longer stems than average.
Catalina	Late. One of a strain called Giant Winter. Thick stems that keep well in the ground.

Potatoes

Potatoes are dealt with individually, partly because of their importance as our basic vegetable, and partly because they differ botanically from the vegetables we have so far considered.

Although generally regarded as a root vegetable, the potato is in fact a stem tuber. (See **Topic A-21 'Vegetative reproduction'**). It belongs to the family *Solanaceae*.

Potatoes can be broadly divided into two classes:

1. **Earlies**

   These are harvested in June/July to provide 'new' potatoes. Earlies are sometimes divided into first and second earlies.

2. **Maincrop**

   These are harvested from August to October and can be stored to provide potatoes through the winter.

If space necessitates a choice having to be made then go for earlies. The crop takes up less room, is less subject to diseases, and will be available at a time when shop prices are high.

If a three year crop rotation scheme is used then include potatoes with the roots. However, because of the space they occupy they can be grown by themselves in a four year rotation.

General cultivation

- Potatoes are half hardy, and their growth above ground is restricted to a period from the last frosts of spring to the first frosts of autumn.

- Potatoes are grown from **'seed'** potatoes which are not really seed but small tubers. It is important to buy certified seed because of the danger of virus disease.

- The seed potatoes should be **chitted**, which means the development of shoots, before being planted. This is to give them a longer growing season, and is more important with earlies.

  Stand the potatoes in boxes or trays with the **rose** end (end with most eyes) facing upwards and store them in a light, frost free place. Leave them until the shoots are 2-3 cm long which will take about six weeks.

- Potatoes will grow in most soil types and are a good first crop for a newly cultivated area since they suppress weeds and help to improve the soil structure.

- Manure or compost can be dug into the soil if it is not very fertile but do not add lime as a slightly acid soil is preferred (pH 5-6).

The vegetable garden

Pests

Wireworms	Wireworms are the larvae of click beetles, and feed on the tubers. They are more prevalent in newly cultivated ground. **Symptoms** Tubers are tunnelled and larvae may be seen in soil or on tubers. **Treatment** Harvest the crop as early as possible. There is no approved chemical control.
Potato cyst eelworm	See Topic C-6 'Common pests'
Slugs and snails	See Topic C-6 'Common pests'

Diseases

Potato blight	This is the most serious disease of potatoes and was responsible for the potato famine in Ireland in the 1840's. It is more likely in wet seasons. **Symptoms** Dark brown or black blotches on leaves sometimes fringed with white fungus. The disease may quickly spread and cause the whole foliage to collapse. **Treatment** Always start with new certified seed potatoes and ensure no tubers are left in the ground after harvesting. Spray with a copper based fungicide like copper oxychloride.
Scab	This affects the skin of the potato. It is more likely in dry conditions and on light, alkaline soils. **Symptoms** Brown corky spots appear on the surface of the potato and may spread all over it. **Treatment** Always start with new certified seed potatoes and ensure no tubers are left in the ground after harvesting. Improve the organic matter in the soil and water regularly. Do not lime the soil. Buy resistant varieties. There is no approved chemical control.
Virus	See Topic C-7 'Common diseases'

Timetable

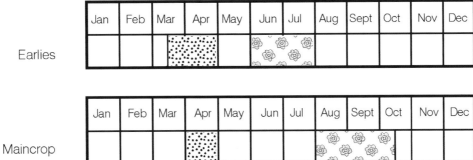

	Jan	Feb	Mar	Apr	May	Jun	Jul	Aug	Sept	Oct	Nov	Dec
Earlies			░	░		❀	❀					

	Jan	Feb	Mar	Apr	May	Jun	Jul	Aug	Sept	Oct	Nov	Dec
Maincrop				░				❀	❀			

Planting

Plant the tubers 10-15 cm deep and 30-40 cm apart in rows 50 cm apart. The smaller distances are applicable to earlies.

Crop covers can be used with earlies to get an earlier crop and provide some protection against late frosts.

Ground occupancy

15 weeks (earlies) 20 weeks (maincrop).

Special requirements

When the haulm (stems and leaves) are about 30 cm high draw the earth up 10-15 cm around the plants. This is necessary to prevent the potatoes being green, as green potatoes are poisonous.

Earthing up can be avoided if the ground is mulched with black polythene.

Regular watering is necessary as the new potatoes develop.

Potatoes require considerable nitrogen so a feed during growth is beneficial.

Harvesting

Harvest earlies when they are about the size of a chicken's egg.

Harvest maincrops after the haulm has turned brown and withered.

Storage

Earlies are not suitable for storing.

Let maincrops dry thoroughly and store in trays or bags in a dark frost free place.

Varieties

Arran Pilot	Early. An old variety producing a heavy crop of white potatoes.
Wilja	Early. High yield, reliable and good cooking qualities.
Maris Piper	Maincrop. High yield and very flavoursome but susceptible to disease.
Pentland Crown	Maincrop. A late variety producing a large crop of white, oval potatoes. Good disease resistance but not a good keeper.

Salad crops

In this topic we will cover two of the most popular salad crops, lettuce and tomatoes.

General cultivation

- Many salad crops have a short growing period and are suitable for intercropping or as a catch crop.

- As far as a crop rotation plan is concerned salad crops do not fall into any of the main categories and the best plan is to fit them in wherever there is space.

  Nevertheless they should not be grown in the same soil two years running.

Lettuce

General

There are many different types of lettuce that can be planted to give a succession of plants almost all the year round. The main types are:

Cos	Long, loosely packed leaves
Butterhead	Round and compact
Crisphead (Iceberg)	Tightly packed giving a good heart
Loose-leaf	No heart

Timetable

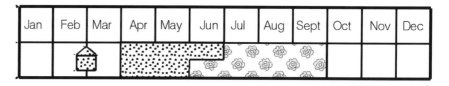

Summer/autumn

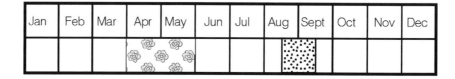

Spring

Sowing

Seed is best sown in situ, or in modules for transplanting, although they can also be sown in a seed bed.

Sow 1 cm deep and thin seedlings, or transplant to 15-20 cm apart in rows 30 cm apart.

For an early spring crop sow in autumn and overwinter under cloches or a crop cover. A hardy variety should be chosen.

To avoid a glut sow a small number at fortnightly intervals.

Transplanting

Transplant, if sown in modules or a seed bed, when there are 5-6 leaves. To avoid wilting water the planting position and transplant in the evening when it is cooler.

Ground occupancy

6-14 weeks depending on type.

Special requirements

The seedlings will need protection from slugs and snails.

Harvesting

Cut early or when mature to avoid bolting (running to seed).

Some types will regrow if the stump is left in the ground.

Storage

Storage is limited to a few days in a refrigerator.

Varieties

Little Gem	Cos. Quick to grow with small and compact heads. Excellent flavour.
All The Year Round	Butterhead. A reliable medium sized lettuce that can be sown in spring, summer or autumn.
Webb's Wonderful	Crisphead. Strong growing with a tight head.
Salad Bowl	Loose-leaf. The premier loose-leaf variety with attractive curled leaves. Individual leaves can be picked over a period of several weeks.

Pests

Slugs and snails	See Topic C-6 'Common pests'
Aphids	See Topic C-6 'Common pests'
Cutworms (caterpillars)	See Topic C-6 'Common pests'

Diseases

Mosaic virus	This can be present in seed or transmitted by aphids and is likely to be worse on overwintered plants **Symptoms** Growth is stunted and the leaves can be mottled and blistered. **Treatment** There is no cure but buying certified seed and control of aphids may help to prevent it. Burn infected plants.
Downy mildew	See Topic C-7 'Common diseases'
Grey Mould	See Topic C-7 'Common diseases'

The vegetable garden

Tomatoes (outdoor)

General

Tomatoes are tender and cannot be grown outside until all danger of frosts has passed. Even then they need to be grown in a sheltered and warm place, such as against a south facing wall.

Outdoor varieties are not necessarily the same as indoor ones, so ensure the correct type is grown. The outdoor varieties can be suitable for growing as a cordon (restricted to one stem and requiring support) or as a bush.

A recent development has been the availabilty to the amateur gardener of grafted tomato plants. These provide higher yields, earlier crops and improved disease resistance.

Ground preparation

Dig over winter and incorporate compost.

Rake in a general fertiliser 2 weeks before planting.

Timetable

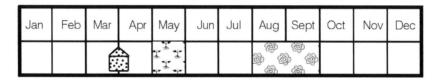

Jan	Feb	Mar	Apr	May	Jun	Jul	Aug	Sept	Oct	Nov	Dec

Sowing

Seed can be sown in trays, but if only a few plants are required it is better to sow in small pots. Sow 2 seeds in each pot and subsequently remove the weakest.

If only a few are required they can also be purchased. Look for pot grown, stocky, dark green plants. Do not buy until danger of frost is passed.

Transplanting

Transplant when the seedlings are 15-20 cm high, and the flowers of the first truss are showing.

Transplant into the open soil, or into growbags or in 20 cm pots. In the open plant 40 cm apart.

Ground occupancy

20 weeks.

Special requirements

Special attention should be paid to watering. Watering heavily after a spell of dryness can cause the fruit to split. Plants grown in growbags or pots will need frequent watering.

Cordon varieties should be tied to a cane at 15 cm intervals. Remove sideshoots when they are 2-3 cm and remove growing tip after the 4th truss.

Feed with a high potash fertiliser every 2 weeks from when the fruit starts to swell.

Harvesting

Pick when the tomatoes are ripe. This can be judged from the firmness and colour of the fruit.

If green tomatoes are left at the end of the season they can be brought inside and will ripen on a windowsill.

Storing

They can be stored for a few days in a refrigerator.

Varieties

Gardener's Delight	Cordon. An old variety giving a heavy crop of small tomatoes. Good flavour.
Red Alert	Bush. A recent variety which produces an early crop of small tomatoes. Good flavour.
Totem	Dwarf bush. An F_1 hybrid that grows to 40-90 cm and is very suited to growing in a pot on the patio.

Pests

Whitefly	See Topic C-6 'Common pests'. Mainly on greenhouse tomatoes.
Red spider mite	See Topic C-6 'Common pests'. Mainly on greenhouse tomatoes.
Aphids	See Topic C-6 'Common pests'

Diseases

Blight	This is the same disease that attacks potatoes. It is more likely in wet seasons.
	Symptoms
	Dark brown or black blotches on leaves sometimes fringed with white fungus. The disease may quickly spread and cause the whole foliage to collapse.
	Treatment
	Spray with copper oxychloride.
Tobacco mosaic virus	This is the most common of the virus diseases that can affect tomatoes. It can be present in seed and is easily spread by physical contact. Unlike some virus diseases it is not spread by aphids.
	Symptoms
	Leaves may be mottled in yellow and green. and may wilt on hot days. Fruit may have brown patches near the calyx.
	Treatment
	There is no cure but it is possible to buy heat treated seed. Good hygiene is important. Some varieties have some resistance.
Grey Mould	See Topic C-7 'Common diseases'

Greenhouse vegetables

The principles of greenhouse gardening are covered in **Topic E-10 'Greenhouse gardening'**.

In this topic we will cover the growing of tomatoes and cucumbers.

Tomatoes

General

Ensure the variety is suitable for growing under glass. Greenhouse varieties are nearly all grown as cordons.

Although tomatoes can be grown in soil or in pots in the greenhouse, the most common method for both amateur and professional is to use growbags.

Tomatoes can be grown in a unheated greenhouse although earlier crops can be obtained in a heated one.

Timetable

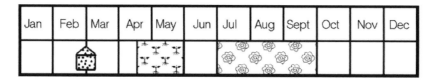

Jan	Feb	Mar	Apr	May	Jun	Jul	Aug	Sept	Oct	Nov	Dec

Sowing

Seed can be sown in trays but if only a few plants are required it is better to sow in small pots. Sow 2 seeds in each pot and subsequently remove the weakest.

If only a few are required they can also be purchased. Look for pot grown, stocky, dark green plants.

Transplanting

Transplant when the seedlings are 15-20 cm high, and the flowers of the first truss are showing.

Growbags will take 2-4 plants.

Special requirements

Special attention should be paid to watering. Watering irregularly can cause the fruit to split. Plants grown in growbags or pots will need frequent watering.

Tie the main stem to a cane at 15 cm intervals. Remove sideshoots when they are 2-3 cm and remove growing tip after the 7th truss.

Plants may need shading in very hot weather.

Feed with a high potash fertiliser every 2 weeks from when the fruit starts to swell.

Harvesting

Pick when the tomatoes are ripe. This can be judged from the firmness and colour of the fruit.

Storing

They can be stored for a few days in a refrigerator.

Varieties

Ailsa Craig	A popular and reliable variety producing an early, medium sized crop. Good flavour.
Typhoon	A new F$_1$ variety producing an early, heavy crop of medium sized fruit. Excellent disease resistance.
Big Boy	An F$_1$ variety producing large 'beefsteak' fruits. Limit the trusses to 4 and the fruits per truss to 3.

Pest and diseases

See outdoor tomatoes in previous topic.

Cucumbers

General

Cucumbers can be grown inside or outside. They are not an easy crop to grow but the rewards can be high. One plant can yield up to 25 cucumbers.

Cucumbers can be grown in 25 cm pots or in growbags.

They can be grown in a unheated greenhouse although earlier crops can be obtained in a heated one.

Although they are often grown with tomatoes they are not that compatible. Cucumbers prefer a more warm and humid atmosphere.

Timetable

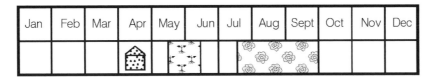

Jan	Feb	Mar	Apr	May	Jun	Jul	Aug	Sept	Oct	Nov	Dec

Sowing

As only a few plants are required it is better to sow in small pots. Sow 2 seeds in each pot and subsequently remove the weakest.

If only a few are required they can also be purchased. Look for pot grown, stocky, dark green plants.

Transplanting

Transplant when the seedlings have produced their first true leaves.

Growbags will take 2 plants.

Special requirements

Special attention should be paid to watering. The compost should be kept moist but not waterlogged.

Tie the main stem to a cane or wire at 30 cm intervals and pinch out the growing point when the stem reaches the roof.

Both male and female flowers can be produced although many F$_1$ hybrids produce only female flowers. The female flower can be identified by a miniature cucumber growing behind it. Pinch out as follows:

Male flowers - remove

Female flowers - pinch out 2 leaves beyond flower

Feed with a high potash fertiliser every 2 weeks when the fruits start to swell.

Harvesting

Cut the cucumbers from the plant when they are a reasonable size, which will be about 12 weeks from sowing. Do not allow them to grow to maturity else cropping will cease.

Storing

They can be stored for a few days in a refrigerator.

Varieties

Telegraph	An old variety but still popular. It produces long, straight, smooth cucumbers.
Conqueror	A hardy variety that is good for a cold greenhouse. Good flavour.
Petita	This is an all female F_1 variety. It produces a large crop of smallish cucumbers. Good disease resistance

Pests

Whitefly	See Topic C-6 'Common pests'
Red spider mite	See Topic C-6 'Common pests'
Aphids	See Topic C-6 'Common pests'

Diseases

Cucumber mosaic virus	This is a very common and serious disease, not only of cucumbers but also of a wide range of other plant. The disease is spread mainly by aphids. **Symptoms** Leaves may be mottled in yellow and green. and the surface may be crinkled. The whole plant is likely to be stunted. **Treatment** There is no cure. Burn infected plants. Maintain good hygiene and in particular keep aphids under control.
Powdery mildew	See Topic C-7 'Common diseases'
Grey Mould	See Topic C-7 'Common diseases'

Self test questions

These questions are to enable you to assess how well you have understood and remembered the information in the previous section. No answers are given as these should be apparent from reviewing the relevant topics.

The questions are **not** intended to cover everything you should know.

1   List the advantages of a crop rotation plan. Describe a three year rotation plan, and name three vegetables from each of the groups involved in the rotation.

2   List the advantages and disadvantages of the 'bed' system of vegetable production.

3   Define the following terms and briefly describe the reasons for each:
      Intercropping
      Catch crops
      Earthing up
      Thinning

4   List five advantages of protected growing, and five structures that can be used to provide protection.

5   Describe the production of a cabbage crop for summer harvesting under the following headings:
      Sowing
      Transplanting
      Pest and disease control
      Harvesting

6   Describe the production of a crop of runner beans under the following headings:
      Ground preparation
      Sowing
      Aftercare
      Harvesting
      Storing

7   Describe the steps involved in the production of a crop of early potatoes.

8   Describe the production of a crop of greenhouse tomatoes, from purchased plants, under the following headings:
      Choice of cultivars
      Planting
      Supporting
      Pest and disease control
      Harvesting

9   Describe the symptoms and method of treatment of the following pests and diseases:
      Clubroot on brassicas
      Carrot fly on root crops
      White rot on alliums
      Blight on potatoes
      Whitefly on greenhouse tomatoes

The fruit garden

This section covers the general principles of growing fruit, and in detail with a number of the more popular ones.

For each fruit three of the most common pests and diseases are identified, but it should be appreciated that there can be many more.

The fruit garden

General principles

In many gardens the growing of fruit probably takes third place behind the ornamental garden and the vegetable garden. One reason for this may be that, with small gardens, people feel that fruit takes up too much space. While this may once have been the case it is now possible to get very dwarf and compact varieties that can be squeezed into the smallest corner, or even grown in a pot on the patio or balcony.

Unlike the vegetable garden, the fruit garden can make a contribution to the ornamental garden since most fruits have a permanent branch structure. An apple tree in the lawn can be as attractive as the common ornamental cherry.

Types of fruit

Tree fruit (also called top fruit)	Unrestricted	Trees are grown in open ground in a basically natural way.
		Trees can be different sizes by growing on different rootstocks.
		Examples are apples, pears, plums.
	Restricted	Trees are trained in particular forms to make them even more compact.
Soft fruit	Bush fruit	Fruit grows on bushes (shrubs).
		Examples are gooseberries, black, red and white currants.
	Cane fruit	Fruit grows on lax stems called canes that require support.
		Examples are raspberries, blackberries.
	Strawberries	Unlike the other fruits, strawberries are herbaceous and short-lived. .
		They are more suited to growing in the vegetable garden.

Ideal growing environment

Most fruits are quite hardy and will tolerate a range of conditions . However for the best results the following should be considered.

- **Soil**

  A fertile, well drained loam is ideal. Preferably it should be 60 cm deep for top fruit and 45 cm for soft fruit.

  Badly drained soils can lead to poor root growth and can encourage diseases.

  A satisfactory pH for most fruits is 6.0-7.0. Changing the pH over a large area is not easy, particularly reducing it in an alkaline soil. Raising the level of an acid soil can be achieved to an extent by liming.

- **Sun**

  All fruits require sun to ripen the fruit and produce a good crop. Some shade is acceptable but not for more than 25% of the time.

- **Shelter**

  Shelter from the wind is very important. Excessive wind can cause the following damage:

  → **Damage fruit buds**

  → **Restrict the activity of pollinating insects**

  → **Blow the fruits off the tree**

  → **Cause excessive water loss from the plant**

  In order to give the necessary shelter it may be necessary to provide some sort of windbreak.

- **Frost protection**

  Late frosts are one of the major causes of poor yields.

  Frost can cause the following damage:

  → **Kill the emerging fruit buds causing them to drop**

  → **Scorching of new growth**

  → **Deformed fruits with russeting on apples and pears**

  In an area susceptible to frosts choose fruit varieties that are late flowering or ones that are naturally more hardy.

Siting the fruit garden

In small gardens a fruit garden as a separate entity may not be practical. The fruit can be incorporated into the total garden. For example:

- **An apple tree may be grown as a specimen tree in the lawn**

- **Currant bushes may be included in a shrub or mixed border**

- **Strawberries may be grown a edging to a path or bed, or grown in a container on the patio**

Where there is sufficient space for a separate fruit garden the site should be chosen by reference to the ideal growing environment above.

Siting all the fruit in one place has advantages as far as the care of the fruit is concerned. Such things as weeding, feeding, watering, and pest and disease control are easier when the plants are together.

The best site is likely to be south, south-east or south-west facing, and level or with a slight slope.

Beware of frost pockets (cold air is heavier than warm air and therefore moves by gravity into low areas).

If necessary provide shelter from the wind. This can be done with a living or a man-made windbreak (See **Topic G-4 'Hedges and windbreaks'**). An man-made one can be a solid, permanent feature like a wall or a fence, although it is better to have one that is permeable as this creates less turbulence. There are various wooden or plastic products available that have this permeability.

A windbreak is effective over an area approximately 10 times the height of the windbreak.

Living windbreaks should be planted far enough away from the fruit to avoid competition for water and nutrients, or excessive shade.

Choosing the plants

In addition to the siting of the fruit garden consideration has to be given to the number, species and varieties of fruit to grow. Personal preference will pay a large part here but also take into account:

- **Number of plants**
  - ➔ If space is not a constraint estimate the number of plants required to produce the volume of fruit required.
  - ➔ Take into account the storage and freezing capabilities of the crop.

- **Space available**
  - ➔ Some varieties are naturally smaller and more compact than others.
  - ➔ Some varieties are more easy to train in restricted forms.

- **Site**
  - ➔ Some varieties are hardier than others.

- **Protection**
  - ➔ If walls or fences are available then forms like fans and espaliers may be grown.

- **Pollination requirements**
  - ➔ Most top fruits are not self-fertile and need another variety of the same species to ensure pollination. This is considered in more detail later in this section.

- **Cropping time**
  - ➔ Within any particular type of fruit there are likely to be varieties that crop at different times. It should therefore be possible to plan for fruits over an extended period of time

- **Pest and disease resistance**
  - ➔ Some plants have a better natural, or bred, resistance than others
  - ➔ Many soft fruits can be bought certified to be virus free and it is important to only buy these.

Planning the layout

As a general guide plants should be arranged to provide each with the maximum amount of sun, eg. on a south facing site place the smallest plants at the southern end.

Ensure the planting distance between plants is sufficient to meet their requirements at maturity.

Physical protection

Birds can cause considerable damage in the fruit garden by eating the buds or the fruit

For this reason it is preferable to grow the fruit within a fruit cage. With the restricted forms of tree fruits now available it is possible to contain all fruit plants within a cage.

At the time of pollination the sides of the cage should be raised to allow easy access for the pollinating insects.

Planting and aftercare

Ground preparation

Re-read **Topic B-13 'Soil - Management (4) Cultivation'**.

- Carry out the final preparation for planting at least two months in advance.

- Ensure all weeds are removed, particularly perennial ones.

- Add compost or manure if planting soft fruits to improve the structure and fertility of the soil. Only do this for tree fruits if the soil is very poor, otherwise it may cause too much vegetative growth.

- Add a balanced fertiliser like Growmore at 25-50 g/sq m.

Planting

See **Topic E-2 'Planting'** for general guidance.

Most fruit plants are purchased bare rooted, and planting will therefore take place during the dormant season.

Restricted forms will require a support structure of some kind. These will be covered in **Topic I-3 'Tree fruits'**.

Aftercare

The following tasks may be required:

Watering
Feeding
Weed control
Mulching
Pest and disease control
Pruning
Fruit thinning

Watering

See **Topic E-6 'Watering'** for general guidance.

Tree fruits should not need to be watered after they are established, except in prolonged periods without rain.

Watering of soft fruits is more important since their roots are nearer the surface. As a guideline water if there is a week without rain.

In both cases the more critical times are when the fruits are being formed.

Feeding

Fruits require feeding with nitrogen, phosphorus and potassium on a regular basis, and may require magnesium, calcium and some of the trace elements periodically.

Apply a balanced fertiliser such as Growmore in spring at a rate of 25-50 g/sq m. Alternatively straight fertilisers can be used such as:

Nitrogen	Sulphate of ammonia (21%N) Dried blood (12%N)
Phosphorus	Superphosphate (18%P) Bonemeal (20%P)
Potassium	Sulphate of potash (50%K) Wood ash (5%K)

Do not overfeed with nitrogen as it can cause vegetative growth at the expense of fruit, and only apply it in spring.

Potassium is particularly important in order to get good, healthy fruit.

For tree fruits apply the fertilisers over the area covered by the tree canopy.

Weed control

Weeds and weed control are covered in some detail in the section **'Plant problems'**

Weed control is important in the fruit garden, particularly in the establishment stage, as they compete for water and nutrients.

In this context grass is considered a weed, and should never be allowed to grow up to the trunk of fruit trees as, in addition to competing for water and nutrients, it can be the cause of fungal infections like collar rot and botrytis. Ensure there is a circle of at least 50 cm around the base of the tree.

As with any program of weed control the alternative methods are:

1. **Cultivation**

   Hoeing or hand weeding

2. **Mulching**

   See later paragraph

3. **Chemicals**

   It is easier to use chemicals in the fruit garden than in the vegetable garden as most of the plants are woody, and as long as the chemical is kept off the foliage no damage should occur. Either of the following can be used:

CHEMICAL	APPLY	
Diquat	Any time	Contact weedkiller effective against annual weeds
Glyphosate	Apr/May	Translocated weedkiller effective against all weeds

As with all spraying ensure that there is no drift on to the fruit plants.

Mulching

See **Topic E-9 'Mulching'** for general guidance.

Any of the mulching materials should be suitable. Black polythene is particularly good for strawberries as it also helps to keep the fruit clean.

Pest and disease control

Pests and diseases and their control are covered in some detail in the section **'Plant problems'.** Additional pests and diseases relating to particular fruits are covered in the details for those fruits.

As with all plants good cultivation and housekeeping is one of the best ways of avoiding problems.

- **Avoid overcrowding when planting**
- **Continuously monitor the plants for signs of problems**
- **Remove dead, diseased or damaged wood when pruning**
- **Ensure routine maintenance tasks are carried out**
- **Remove fallen fruit and leaves**

Fruits can be sprayed with chemicals to combat pests or diseases. Commercial growers will have a regular spraying program as they have to ensure they get unblemished fruit.

In a domestic situation most people would prefer not to spray at all, or only when problems are apparent. The problem with this is that by the time a problem is apparent the damage has been done. Also most fungicides are better at preventing than they are at curing. If spraying is considered necessary then bifenthrin is a suitable contact insecticide for apples and pears and myclobutanil is a suitable fungicide.

Do not spray when the fruit is in blossom as this may kill pollinating insects.

The need for physical protection against larger pests such as birds has already been mentioned. In addition there are some other non-chemical methods of reducing pest and disease problems:

- **Place grease bands round the trunk of trees in August to prevent insects crawling up the trunk to lay their eggs in the foliage**
- **Spray trees with a tar oil wash in winter to kill over-wintering eggs of aphids**
- **Use pheromone traps for monitoring and limiting the male codling moths**

Fruit thinning

Tree fruits can produce so many fruits that they tend to be small and misshapen. Also a heavy crop in one year may cause a poor crop in the following year, since energy has been used to produce the fruit rather than to grow vegetatively.

Thinning should be done in late June or early July after the fruits have naturally shed some of their fruitlets.

Details of the thinning is given in the topic for each fruit.

Pruning

Pruning is dealt with separately in the topics for tree and soft fruits.

Harvesting

- Pick fruits for immediate consumption when they are ripe
- Pick fruits for storage just before full ripeness
- Test apples and pears for ripeness by holding the fruit and twisting it slightly. If ripe it will come away with its stalk
- Test other fruits for ripeness by colour, firmness or taste
- If picking for storage discard any damaged or diseased fruits as they will spoil the other fruit
- Avoid damaging the plant while picking

Storing

Only apples and pears can be stored for any length of time in their natural form, and even then only certain varieties are suitable.

Ideal storage conditions are:

Dark
Cool, constant temperature (5-10° C ideal)
Moist
Some air circulation
Frost proof

Apples

Traditionally these are stored in slatted trays with the fruits not touching to allow the maximum air circulation. Wrapping in greaseproof paper may extend the period they can be stored.

Alternatively they can be placed in unsealed plastic bags with a few holes made in them.

The later varieties tend to keep longer in storage.

Pears

As for apples but do not wrap

Other fruits

Other fruits cannot be stored for any length of time in their natural state, but most of them can be frozen and kept in a freezer, and some are suitable for preserving.

Tree fruit

Types of tree fruit

Apples
Pears
Plums
Cherries
Peaches and nectarines
Apricots

This is not an exhaustive list but these are the most common.

Tree forms (unrestricted)

Unrestricted tree forms are those that are grown in open ground in a basically natural way.

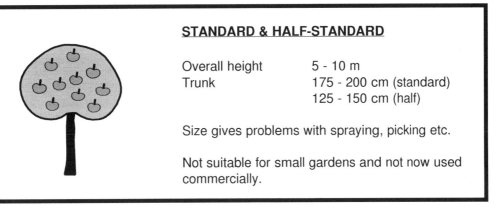

STANDARD & HALF-STANDARD

Overall height   5 - 10 m
Trunk   175 - 200 cm (standard)
     125 - 150 cm (half)

Size gives problems with spraying, picking etc.

Not suitable for small gardens and not now used commercially.

BUSH

Overall height   2 - 5 m
Trunk   50 - 90 cm

Most suitable for for the garden.

Bushes are available in a wide range of sizes depending on the rootstock.

Tree forms (restricted)

CORDON

Height   2 - 2.5 m

Cordons consist of a single stem with spurs on which the fruit is borne.

They can be grown upright but are more usually grown at an angle as this reduces vegetative growth and increases fruiting.

ESPALIER

Height   2 - 2.5 m
Spread   up to 3 m

Espaliers consist of parallel stems trained horizontally from the central stem.

An espalier can be limited to one tier and is called a step-over tree. Useful for edging a path.

FAN

Height   2 - 2.5 m
Spread   up to 3 m

The stems in a fan are trained in an arc from a short trunk.

Fans require the support of a wall or a fence.

COLUMN

Height   2 - 4 m

These are a comparatively recent introduction and are sold under the name of 'Ballerina' trees. The range of cultivars is very limited.

They are similar to a cordon but they naturally do not produce laterals and therefore require no pruning.

Rootstocks

Tree fruits are grown on rootstocks (the roots of another plant). The tree fruit plant is called the **scion** and it is grafted to the rootstock about 15-20 cm from the ground. The graft can usually be seen as it leaves a kink in the trunk.

There are four possible reasons for using a rootstock:

1. **Most fruit trees are cultivars and therefore some means of vegetative reproduction must be used**

2. **Some cultivars may not grow well on their own roots**

3. **Some rootstocks are more resistant to pests and diseases, or will grow better in poor conditions**

4. **Different rootstocks can be used to control the size of the tree. For fruit trees this is the prime reason for using rootstocks**

Different rootstocks are used for different types of tree. The best choice is available for apples as this is by far the most popular tree fruit. The different rootstocks are identified by 'M' or 'MM' numbers which stand for Malling and Malling Merton, which were the Fruit Research establishments where they were developed.

The following diagram gives some idea of the effect that the rootstock can have.

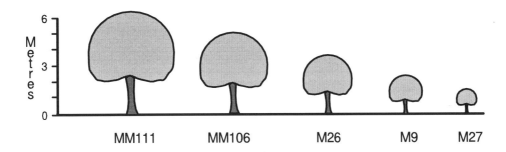

The yield of course will differ according to the size of the tree. For example a standard apple tree on MM111 will produce 75-150 kg of fruit, whereas a cordon on M27 will produce only 2-4 kg.

However as it is possible to get about 60 cordons in the same space as one standard the amount of fruit produced per area can be higher with the restricted forms.

Most commercial apple orchards are grown on M9 rootstocks.

Advantages of dwarf and restricted forms

1. Will fit into small areas

2. Easier to cultivate, eg. spray, water, harvest

3. Easier to protect - growing within a cage is feasible

4. Fruit is produced earlier in the life of the tree

5. A number of different cultivars may be grown in the same space as one larger cultivar

6. Fruit yield per unit of area is increased

Planting distances

	Distance between trees	Distance between rows	Years to fruiting
Standard	10	10	6-7
Half-standard	6	6	5-6
Bush	4-5	4-5	3-5
Espalier	4-5	2	3-5
Fan	4-5	-	3-5
Cordon	0.75-1	2	2-4
Column	0.75-1	2	2-4

All distances are in metres.

Buying fruit trees

Fruit trees can be bought at various stages in their life.

The youngest are one year old trees, which are called **maidens.**

There are two types of maiden:

1.   **Whip**   This is a maiden without side shoots

2.   **Feathered**   This is a maiden with side shoots (laterals)

For most people it is probably better to buy a two or three year old tree in which the initial training has been carried out by the grower.

Bare rooted trees are available from November to March and should be planted as soon as possible. Container grown trees can be obtained and planted at any time of the year when ground conditions are suitable.

Planting, training and initial pruning

See **Topic E-2 'Planting'** and **Topic E-5 'Pruning'** for general guidance.

In the first 2-3 years of the life of the tree, training and pruning is carried out to achieve the shape and form required.

Remember that leading shoots produce a hormone called auxin that inhibits the growth of side-shoots. This is one reason why in the formative years of a tree the leaders are cut back.

Also remember that if something is pruned hard the subsequent growth will be stronger. Therefore strong growth should be pruned lightly and weak growth should be pruned harder.

Unrestricted forms

The objective is to produce an open, goblet shaped tree.

- **At planting**

    If planting a maiden cut back the central leader to a healthy bud or lateral, and where there are three to five buds or laterals below it. These buds or laterals will form the primary branches of the tree.

    The height at which the central leader is cut will determine the height of the trunk, and will vary according to the form of the tree and the rootstock. On a bush it is likely to be 60-90 cm, and on half standards and standards it will be correspondingly higher.

    Prune the laterals required for the primary branches by two thirds, and remove any laterals below them to give a clear trunk.

- **At the end of year 1**

    Cut back the leaders by half to one third which will result in secondary branches being formed in the following year.

- **At the end of year 2**

    The primary and secondary branch structure is now established. Pruning can continue as for an established tree.

Cordons

Cordons are usually grown in rows at an angle of 45^0. They need support which is usually provided with upright posts with wires strained between them, or by a wall.

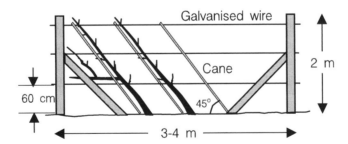

- Plant cordons 0.75-1 m apart and 2 m between rows.
- If possible have the rows running north to south, and point trees to north with the union uppermost.
- If grown against against a wall try to ensure the wires are as far as possible from the wall so that air can circulate, and plant the tree 40 cm away from the wall.
- Tie canes at an angle of 45^0 to the wires, and tie the cordon to the cane.
- Cut back any laterals to 3-4 buds from the base of the lateral.
- Cut back the central leader when it reaches the required height.

Espaliers

- Espaliers require a support structure similar to that for cordons.

- Depending on the rootstock plant espaliers 4-5 m apart.

- If grown against against a wall try to ensure the wires are as far as possible from the wall so that air can circulate, and plant the tree 40 cm away from the wall.

- The supporting wires should be the same distance apart as the tiers of the tree.

- If the tree is already partially trained, tie the branches to the supporting wires

- If the tree is not trained, prune to a healthy bud or lateral 5 cm above the lower support wire, and where there are at least two healthy buds or laterals below the cut. In following years these buds will grow and be tied in to the supporting wires to form the first tiers.

- The above procedure is repeated in subsequent years until the required number of tiers is reached.

Fans

Although apples and pears can be grown as fans, it is more usual for plums, and fruits that require the protection of a wall like peaches and nectarines.

- Fans require a support structure similar to that for cordons with the wires strained horizontally at intervals of 30 cm.

- Depending on the rootstock fans should be planted 4-5 m apart.

- If grown against a wall try to ensure the wires are as far as possible from the wall so that air can circulate, and plant the tree 40 cm from the wall.

- If the tree is already partially trained, tie canes at the appropriate angle to the wires and tie the branches to the canes.

- If the tree is a maiden prune to a healthy bud or lateral about 60 cm from the ground, and where there are at least two healthy buds or laterals below the cut. These laterals will form the initial branches of the fan which should be set at an angle of 45^0.

- In subsequent years laterals from the two main branches are used to form the other branches of the fan

Pruning established trees

See **Topic E-5 'Pruning'** for general guidance.

Let's review the general reasons for pruning that apply to all plants.

1. **To maintain the health of the plant**

2. **To control the shape or size**

3. **To encourage flowers and fruit**

In the case of fruit trees we are concerned primarily with the production of fruit, and the pruning is therefore biased towards this.

General guidelines are contained in the following paragraphs. Any significant difference for a particular fruit is covered in the topic for that fruit.

We can start with a general rule:

> **Unrestricted forms are pruned in winter (November - March)**
>
> **Restricted forms are pruned in summer (July/August)**

Pruning the restricted forms in summer reduces the vegetative growth of the tree by restricting the supply of food through photosynthesis.

Unrestricted forms

Trees differ in where the fruit is formed. They can be:

Spur fruiting

Fruit is formed on spurs of wood which are 2 years or more old.

The objective of pruning is to build up a structure of fruiting spurs.

- Prune new growth on branch leaders by one third to an outward facing bud
- Prune laterals to 3-4 buds from the base of the lateral
- Prune sub-laterals to 1 bud
- If the spurs get too congested they can be thinned to 3-4 buds

Tip fruiting

Fruit is formed at or near the tip of the previous year's wood and therefore a proportion of the shoots must be retained otherwise no fruit will be produced. At the same time new growth must be encouraged to produce the shoots on which future years fruit will be borne.

- Prune new growth on branch leaders by one third to an outward facing bud. This is still necessary to enourage the growth of laterals and to contain the size of the tree.
- Leave laterals that have a fruit bud at the tip, since these will produce the fruit for the current year. Remember that fruit buds can be distinguished by being fatter than shoot buds.
- Cut back other laterals to a fruit bud or to 3-4 buds from the base. This will encourage the new growth which will produce fruit in the following year.

Restricted forms

Trees grown in restricted forms should always be spur fruiting varieties.

- Prune in July/August
- Shorten leaders to 2-3 cm of previous year's growth
- Prune laterals to 3 buds from the base of the lateral
- Prune sub-laterals to 1 bud from the base of the sub-lateral

This method of summer pruning is called the **'Modified Lorette System'**.

If the spurs get too congested they can be thinned to 3-4 fruit buds in the winter.

Reducing excess vigour

If trees grow very vigorously it is likely to be at the expense of fruiting, because the energy of the tree is used for the vegetative growth.

The choice of an appropriate variety and rootstock, and whether one of the restricted forms of growth is to be used, are the main factors in determining how vigorous growth will be.

There are also some other ways that can be used to reduce vigour in existing trees.

1. Grassing	Grass the ground underneath the tree. The grass will rob the tree of some water and nutrients.
2. Root pruning	Dig a trench around the tree at a radius of 1-1.5 m to expose the roots, and sever some of the larger, old roots. This will reduce the uptake of water and nutrients.
	Root prune during the dormant season.
3. Bark ringing	Remove a ring of bark about 1 cm wide from the trunk of the tree in late spring. Cover this area with tape.
	By removing the phloem the flow of food to the roots is prevented.
	Only suitable for apples and pears.

Pollination

Tree fruits are insect pollinated. Most are not self-fertile and require another plant of the same species to be planted reasonably close.

For successful pollination the trees must be in flower at the same time, and for this purpose trees are divided into pollination groups. Apples, for example, are divided into 7 groups. For reliable pollination trees from the same group should be chosen, although those from the groups either side will probably also pollinate successfully.

There are a number of other points to be aware of:

- Some varieties are better pollinators than others.
- Some varieties, although in the same group, are incompatible with each other and need some other variety as pollinator.
- Triploid varieties are not successful as pollinators of other varieties. Therefore it is necessary to plant two other varieties so that they pollinate the triploid and each other.

Propagation

Tree fruits are propagated by grafting or budding (see **Topic E-4 'Propagation (2) Vegetative**).

Apples

General

Apples are the most widely grown tree fruit. They are hardy and have the widest choice of varieties and sizes.

Different varieties fruit at different times of the year and it is possible to have apples from August to November.

Rootstocks

MM111	Vigorous
MM106	Semi-dwarfing
M26	Dwarfing - for average soils
M9	Very dwarfing - for good soils - requires permanent staking
M27	Extremely dwarfing - for very fertile soils or containers - requires permanent staking

Forms & rootstocks

Standard	MM111
Half-standard	MM111
Bush	MM106, M26, M9, M27
Espalier	MM106, M26
Fan	MM106, M26
Cordon	M26, M9, M27
Column	MM106

Pollination

Not self-fertile - pollinators required from same or adjacent group.

Some triploids like Bramley's Seedling will require two pollinators.

Pruning established trees

Apples can be either spur fruiting or tip fruiting and should be pruned accordingly.

Fruit thinning

Dessert   - 10-15 cm apart

Cooking - 15-20 cm apart

Some varieties

Dessert	
Fiesta (spur fruiting)	This is a new late season variety that has Cox's Orange Pippin as one of its parents. For the amateur it is a better choice than Cox's as it is easier to grow.
	It produces a heavy crop of medium to large fruit that have excellent flavour. Also keeps very well.
Worcester Pearman (tip fruiting)	This is a hardy and reliable variety but is susceptible to scab and canker. It produces medium sized fruit that are firm and sweet.
Cooking	
Bramley's Seedling (tip fruiting)	Produces a good crop of flavoursome, juicy apples. A triploid, it is very vigorous and needs to be on a dwarfing rootstock.
Bountiful (spur fruiting)	A good alternative to Bramley's Seedling if space is restricted. Produces large fruits on a compact tree.

Pests

Codling moth	The codling moth lays its eggs in the leaves in June/July and the caterpillars hatch in about 2 weeks. They tunnel into the fruit rendering it inedible.
	Symptoms
	The maggot holes can usually be seen although they are often in the calyx and not obvious. The holes extend to the core of the apple.
	Treatment
	Control is difficult, since the timing is critical, but spraying with deltamethrin after petal fall will reduce damage.
	Pheromone traps can be used to capture male moths.
Apple sawfly	Females lay eggs in April/May and larvae hatch 2 weeks later and tunnel into fruit.
	Symptoms
	Similar to codling moth. Fruitlets may fall in June/July.
	Treatment
	Control is difficult, since the timing is critical, but spraying with deltamethrin after petal fall will reduce damage.
	Pick off and destroy any fruitlets showing signs of damage.
Aphids	See Topic C-6 'Common pests'

Diseases

Canker	See Topic C-7 'Common diseases'
Brown rot	See Topic C-7 'Common diseases'
Mildew	See Topic C-7 'Common diseases'

Pears

General

Pears grow successfully in a wide range of conditions, but compared to apples they flower earlier and therefore need more frost protection.

They also require more sun and warmth during the growing season.

Rootstocks

Quince A	Semi-vigorous
Quince C	Dwarfing

Forms & rootstocks

Bush	Quince A
Dwarf bush	Quince C
Espalier	Quince A
Cordon	Quince C

Pollination

Not self-fertile - pollinators required from same or adjacent group.

Some cultivars are incompatible.

Pruning established trees

Most pears are spur bearing, but there are a few tip bearing, and they should be pruned accordingly.

Fruit thinning

1 fruit per cluster

Some varieties

Conference	A very reliable variety producing a regular and heavy crop. The fruit is juicy and sweet with a pleasant flavour.
Concorde	A comparatively new variety with 'Conference' as one of its parents. It gives a heavy yield of high quality, well flavoured fruit.
Packham's Triumph	A late fruiting variety with good keeping qualities. It can be susceptible to frost in cold areas.

Pests

Pear leaf blister mite	The mites overwinter on dormant buds, and increase during the summer, feeding on the young leaves.
	Symptoms
	Green pustules on the leaves in May, turning brown and black during the summer. Premature leaf fall may occur and severely infected young plants can die.
	Treatment
	There is no good pesticide control. Hand pick and destroy infected leaves as soon as they are seen.
Birds	See Topic C-6 'Common pests'.
	Bullfinches destroy fruit buds in winter and tits peck the ripening fruit.
	The fruits can be protected with netting or individual bags.
Aphids	See Topic C-6 'Common pests'.

Diseases

Fireblight	This is a comparatively new bacterial disease, brought into the UK in 1957. It is a serious disease of pears and can kill mature trees. It used to be a notifiable disease but is not any longer.
	Symptoms
	Flowers and leaves shrivel and die, looking as though they have been burnt. Underneath the bark the wood may have a reddish tinge. Slime may exude from the infected parts.
	Treatment
	There is no approved chemical control. Cut out the infected wood 60 cm below the signs of infection and burn it.
Canker	See Topic C-7 'Common diseases'
Brown rot	See Topic C-7 'Common diseases'

Plums

General

Most plums flower early in the year and are therefore subject to frost damage. It is partly for this reason that they are often grown as fans against a south or west wall

Rootstocks

St Julien A	Semi-vigorous
Pixy	Dwarfing

Forms & rootstocks

Bush	Either
Fan	St Julien A

Pollination

Many plums are self-fertile, but some require pollinators, and some cultivars are incompatible.

Pruning established trees

Plums fruit at the base of 1 year old wood and on spurs of older wood.

Because of the danger of silver leaf infection plums are pruned in June/July.

Little pruning is necessary. Use the **renewal** method to keep the tree productive.

Fruit thinning

5-10 cm apart

Some varieties

Dessert	
Victoria	The best known variety. It is self-fertile and produces heavy crop of large well flavoured fruit. Can also be used as a cooking plum.
Avalon	A new variety producing an early crop of large well flavoured fruit.
Cooking	
Czar	A reliable self-fertile variety that produces a large crop of medium sized fruit.
Marjorie's Seedling	A late season self-fertile variety producing a heavy crop of high quality fruit. Can also be used as a dessert plum.

Pests

Plum sawfly	Females lay eggs in April/May and the larvae hatch in about a week and tunnel into fruit. **Symptoms** Entry holes in the fruit. Fruit may fall prematurely. 'Victoria' and 'Czar' are particularly vulnerable. **Treatment** Control is difficult since the timing is critical, but spraying with deltamethrin after petal fall will reduce damage. Pick off and destroy any fruitlets showing signs of damage.
Aphids	See Topic C-6 'Common pests'
Red spider mite	See Topic C-6 'Common pests'

Diseases

Silver leaf	This is a fungal infection which is the most serious disease of plums. **Symptoms** Leaves show silver discoloration and can cause die-back of the shoots and eventually the whole tree if not treated. Affected branches may be stained dark brown. **Treatment** There is no chemical control available Cut out diseased branches 50 cm below signs of infection. Plants may sometimes recover spontaneously.
Canker	See Topic C-7 'Common diseases'
Brown rot	See Topic C-7 'Common diseases'

Peaches

General

Peaches flower very early in the year (starting in February) and there is therefore a high risk of frost damage. For this reason the only practical way of growing them out of doors is against a south or west facing wall.

Rootstocks

Brompton	Vigorous
St Julien A	Semi-vigorous

Form & rootstocks

Bush	Either
Fan	Either

Pollination

Self-fertile. Hand pollination may be desirable because of shortage of pollinating insects at flowering time.

Hand pollinate using cotton wool or a soft brush to gently dab the flowers. To be sure do this each day while the plant is flowering.

Pruning established trees

Peaches produce fruit on shoots formed in the previous year.

- In spring cut laterals back to three buds.
- After fruiting cut out shoots that have fruited and tie in some of the new year's growth that will fruit in the following year.

Fruit thinning

15-20 cm apart

Some varieties

Peregrine	The best garden variety producing large, firm fruits in August.
Rochester	Produces good-sized , well flavoured fruits in August.
Garden Lady	This is a naturally dwarf variety that can be grown in a container and will produce fruit in July.

Pests

Brown scale	This is a small sap feeding insect that is a serious pest of peaches. The females can lay up to 2000 eggs in May-July which hatch in about a month and further infect the plant. **Symptoms** The insects infest leaves, stems and flowers. They exude honeydew that can attract sooty mould. The vigour of the tree can be significantly weakened. **Treatment** Newly hatched insects can be killed a fatty acid insecticide.
Aphids	See Topic C-6 'Common pests'
Red spider mite	See Topic C-6 'Common pests'

Diseases

Peach leaf curl	This is a fungal infection common on peaches. **Symptoms** Leaves are covered with red blisters and they curl and may drop. Young shoots may be distorted. **Treatment** Spray with oxychloride in autumn just before leaf fall and twice, two weeks apart, in late January and early February.
Canker	See Topic C-7 'Common diseases'
Brown rot	See Topic C-7 'Common diseases'

Soft fruit

Types of soft fruit

Bush fruit

Gooseberries
Redcurrants and whitecurrants
Blackcurrants

Cane fruit

Raspberries
Blackberries
Hybrid berries

Other

Strawberries

Comparison with tree fruit

There are some general differences between the soft fruits and tree fruits.

- **The life of soft fruits is less than that of tree fruits. Strawberries have a life of about three years, and the other fruits about 10-15 years.**
- **Soft fruits are grown on their own roots.**
- **Not all soft fruits have a permanent branch structure. Because of this there is not the same variety of forms as with tree fruit.**
- **Soft fruits are self pollinating.**
- **Irrigation is more critical to soft fruits since their rooting systems are shallower.**

Pests and diseases

Common pests and diseases and their control are covered in some detail in the section **'Plant problems'**. Other pests and diseases affecting only specific fruits are covered under those fruits.

There are however two important problem areas that apply to all soft fruit.

1. Birds

Birds can seriously affect the yield by destroying the fruit buds and the fruit itself. The only satisfactory answer to this is to net the fruits, either with a permanent cage or at the critical stages of growth.

2. Virus infection

This is a severe problem for which there is no cure. Infected plants must be dug up and burned and the site should not be replanted with the same fruit for 3 years.

The best way of avoiding virus problems is to buy certified plants.

Defra Certification scheme

The Department for Environment, Food and Rural Aaffairs has a scheme called Plant Health Propagation Scheme (PHPS), whereby some fruits are certified to be raised under specified conditions and should meet certain health standards. Assurances can also be given about plants being true to type.

The grower is required to conform with certain conditions and these are inspected each year by Defra inspectors. If the conditions are satisfied then a certificate is issued.

There are a number of different levels of certification depending on how stringent the growing condition have been.

It is important to buy certified plants where these are available.

Gooseberries and redcurrants

General

Gooseberries and redcurrants are treated together as the cultivation of the two is basically the same. Whitecurrants, which are a sport of redcurrants, are also the same.

They are both easy fruits to grow. They are very hardy and will tolerate a reasonable degree of shade. There are both cooking and dessert varieties.

They are not so subject to virus infection as other soft fruits, and some cultivars are mildew resistant. There is a limited certification scheme.

Forms

These fruits are the ones that have a permanent branch structure. They are most usually grown as bushes, but it is also possible to grow them as cordons, or even fans. The cordons can be single, double or triple stem, and will require support.

Single   Double   Triple

Planting and initial pruning

The pruning in the first two years is designed to create the required form.

Bush

- Plant bushes 1.5 m apart and 1.5 m between rows.

- Bushes grow on a short main stem (or 'leg') of 10-15 cm. Remove any branches below this height.

- The objective of pruning is to create a bowl shaped bush with an open centre. Shorten leaders by one half to one third until about 8-10 good branches have formed.

Cordon

- Plant cordons 50 cm apart and 1.5 m between rows.

- Shorten the main leader by one half to one third. Shorten laterals to 3 buds.

Pruning established plants

The fruit is carried on spurs of old wood, and the pruning must encourage this formation.

Bush

- Prune in winter (or spring to avoid losing too many buds to the birds).
- Cut back new growth on the leaders by half to a third, and cut back laterals to 2 buds.

Cordon

In summer (July/August)

- Cut back new laterals to 5 leaves from their origin

In winter

- Cut back leader to 1 bud above the previous year's growth when required height has been reached. Until then cut back leader by half to a third.
- Prune laterals to 1 bud.

Propagation

Can be propagated from hardwood cuttings in autumn but, because of the risk of passing on virus infection, it is better to purchase new plants.

Some varieties

Gooseberries

Careless	An established and reliable cooking variety producing large fruits with a good flavour. Does well in most soils.
Invicta	A new cooking variety that produces a heavier crop than Careless, of large well flavoured fruit. It has good resistance to mildew.
Leveller	A dessert variety that produces a heavy crop with an excellent flavour. It does however require good growing conditions.

Redcurrants

Laxton No. 1	An old and reliable variety which produces strong growth and a consistent crop.
Rovada	A new variety that produces an exceptionally large crop.
Redstart	A new variety producing a regular and heavy crop of medium sized fruit with a good flavour.

Pests

Birds	As previously discussed birds, particularly bullfinches, can seriously reduce the yield.
Gooseberry sawfly	Females lay eggs on the underside of leaves adjacent to the leaf veins. Eggs hatch in about one week and larvae eat the leaves. There can be 3 generations within a year. **Symptoms** The larvae can completely defoliate the leaves leaving just a network of veins and seriously affecting the yield if not controlled. **Treatment** Spray with thiacloprid at first sign of attack.
Aphids	See Topic C-6 'Common pests'

Diseases

American gooseberry mildew	A widespread disease of both gooseberries and currants, brought into the UK from North America. **Symptoms** Leaves, shoots and fruits have the typical white powdery coating, and the shoots become distorted. **Treatment** Use plants that have some degree of resistance Ensure plants have adequate space and good air circulation. Control with myclobutanil.
Leaf spot	A fungal disease affecting gooseberries and currants. **Symptoms** Small dark brown spots appear on leaves in May/June, and can lead to defoliation and a reduced yield. **Treatment** Pick off and burn infected leaves. There is no chemical control available to the amateur gardener.
Grey mould	See Topic C-7 'Common diseases'

Blackcurrants

General

Blackcurrants are quite easy to grow. Some varieties flower early and are suspect to frost damage unless protected, but the newer varieties flower later and are therefore not so susceptible.

By choice of varieties it is possible to have fruit from June to September.

There is a certification scheme for blackcurrants and only certified plants should be purchased.

Forms

Blackcurrants fruit mainly on one year old wood and their pruning entails cutting back a proportion of the branches to ground level each year. Because of this they are only grown as bushes.

Planting and initial pruning

- Most plants are sold bare rooted and will therefore need to be planted during the dormant season (November to March).
- Plant 1.5 m apart and about 5 cm lower than in the nursery to encourage the formation of shoots from the base.
- After planting cut the shoots down to one bud from the base.

Pruning established plants

After the third year cut one third of the wood back to one bud. In this way a constant supply of new growth is maintained.

Propagation

Can be propagated from hardwood cuttings in autumn but, because of the risk of passing on infections, it is better to purchase new plants.

Some varieties

Baldwin	This is a popular variety producing a heavy crop of medium to large sized fruit on compact bushes.
Ben Sarek	This is a compact new variety that can be planted as close as 1 m. It produces a very large crop of large fruits with a good flavour. It has some resistance to mildew and is the best garden variety.
Goliath	This is an old variety (pre 1847!) The bushes are medium sized with upright growth and produce large fruit with excellent flavour.

The fruit garden

Pests

Birds	As previously discussed birds, particularly bullfinches, can seriously reduce the crop. The best solution is to grow in a cage or net the crop.
Big bud gall mite	This is a serious disease of blackcurrants. The mites feed and breed within the buds and can cause reversion disease.
	Symptoms
	Swollen buds appear in early spring and may later die.
	Treatment
	It is not easy to control. The infected buds should be picked off and burned.
	There is no approved chemical control.
	Badly infected bushes should be dug up and burned.
Aphids	See Topic C-6 'Common pests'

Diseases

Reversion	This is a virus disease spread by aphids and gall mites.
	Symptoms
	The plant loses its vigour and produces a poor crop.
	Treatment
	There is no effective remedy. The plant will need to be destroyed.
American gooseberry mildew	See Topic I-9 'Gooseberries and redcurrants'
Grey mould	See Topic C-7 'Common diseases'

Raspberries

General

Raspberries are easy to grow and, because of their upright growth, can produce a large crop from a small area. They flower later than some other fruits and therefore are not usually damaged by frost.

There are summer fruiting varieties that produce their fruit in July/August, and autumn fruiting varieties that produce their fruit from late August to the first frosts.

There is a certification scheme for raspberries and only certified plants should be purchased.

Forms

Summer fruiting varieties produce fruit on canes grown the previous year. Autumn fruiting varieties fruit on canes grown in the same year.

A support system is needed for the summer fruiting varieties. There are a number of support methods but the simplest is a post and wire system.

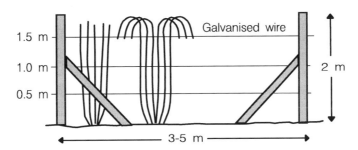

Planting and initial pruning

- Most plants are sold bare rooted and therefore need to be planted during the dormant season (November to March).
- It is easier to dig a trench rather than individual planting holes.
- Plant 40 cm apart in rows 1.5 m apart.
- After planting cut canes back to 30 cm.

Pruning established plants

Summer fruiting

- After fruiting, cut out fruited canes to ground level.
- Retain 5-8 of the strongest new canes and tie these to the support wires at 5-10 cm intervals. Cut the tops to 15 cm above the top wire.
- Alternatively, long canes can be bent over in an arch at the top and tied back to the top wire.

Autumn fruiting

- Cut back all the canes to ground level in late winter.

Propagation

Suckers can be removed and replanted although, because of the risk of passing on infections, it is better to purchase new plants.

Some varieties

Summer fruiting

Glen Moy	This is an early variety which has strong, upright canes and produces a heavy crop of large, well flavoured fruits over an extended period. It has some resistance to aphids.
Augusta	This is a new late season variety which produces a heavy crop of firm fruit.

Autumn fruiting

Autumn Bliss	This is an exceptional recent variety that has sturdy short canes that do not require any support. It produces a very heavy crop from August to September and has some resistance to aphids.

Pests

Birds	Birds can eat the ripening fruit and seriously deplete the crop. The best solution is to grow in a cage or net the crop.
Raspberry beetle	Adults overwinter in the soil and lay eggs in the blossom in June/July. Larvae hatch in 2 weeks. **Symptoms** The larvae eat the developing fruits and can be seen in the picked fruit. **Treatment** Spray with deltamethrin when the fruitlets turn pink.
Aphids	See Topic C-6 'Common pests'

Diseases

Virus	See Topic C-7 'Common diseases'
Grey mould	See Topic C-7 'Common diseases'
Rust	See Topic C-7 'Common diseases'

Blackberries

General

Many people probably regard blackberries as a wild plant, growing in hedgerows, and presenting a challenge to pick because of its thorny stems.

However they can be grown successfully as a garden plant as varieties are available that are more compact than the native species and are also thornless. They are more adaptable than many soft fruits and will grow quite happily in some shade.

Hybrid berries are crosses between species within the *Rubus* genus, usually between raspberries and blackberries. For example, both loganberries and tayberries are crosses between raspberries and blackberries. The hybrids tend to be more compact than the species but their cultivation is the same as blackberries.

There is limited a certification scheme for blackberries and only certified plants should be purchased.

Forms

Like raspberries, blackberries grow on canes and need the same kind of support structure. They can also be grown successfully against walls or over arches.

Blackberries fruit on one year old wood and therefore for most of the time the plant will have both previous year's and current year's canes, and the training must accommodate this.

The easiest method of training is as a **fan**, where previous year's canes are tied to the lower wires of the support structure, while the current year's canes are allowed to grow up vertically and may be tied to the top wire. After fruiting the old canes are removed and the new canes are tied to the lower wires.

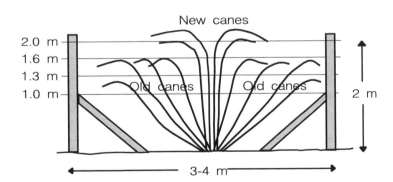

Alternatively one year's canes can be tied to one side of the plant and the next year's to the other side, so that the fruiting alternates from side to side. This is called the **alternate bay** system. There are also a number of other systems.

Planting and initial pruning

- Most plants are sold bare rooted and therefore need to be planted during the dormant season (November to March).

- Plant 2-4 m apart in rows 1.5 m apart.
- After planting cut canes back to 30 cm.

Pruning established plants

After fruiting cut down the fruited canes to ground level.

Propagation

Plants can be propagated by tip layering although, because of the risk of passing on infections, it is better to purchase new plants.

Some varieties

Ashton Cross	This is a moderately vigorous, heavy cropping variety noted for its excellent flavour.
Loch Ness	This is a new compact variety with upright thornless stems and is suitable for the small garden. The fruits are large with a good flavour.
Bedford Giant	This is an early variety with vigorous growth. It produces a large crop of sweet fruit that is particularly good for freezing.

Pests

Birds	Birds can eat the ripening fruit and seriously deplete the crop. The best solution is to grow in a cage or net the crop.
Raspberry beetle	Adults overwinter in the soil and lay eggs in the blossom in June/July. Larvae hatch in 2 weeks. **Symptoms** The larvae eat the developing fruits and can be seen in the picked fruit. **Treatment** Spray with deltamethrin when the fruitlets turn pink.
Aphids	See Topic C-6 'Common pests'

Diseases

Virus	See Topic C-7 'Common diseases'
Grey mould	See Topic C-7 'Common diseases'
Rust	See Topic C-7 'Common diseases'

Strawberries

General

Strawberries are different from the other fruits in that they are herbaceous plants with a short useful life. It is usual to grow them for no more than 3 years before being replaced.

They are suitable for growing in containers or growbags.

It is possible, with the use of cloches or tunnels, to have fruit from May until the first frosts.

There is a certification scheme for strawberries and only certified plants should be purchased.

Forms

There are summer fruiting varieties that produce fruit in June/July, and autumn fruiting varieties that fruit from July to the first frosts.

Strawberries produce runners which will root if left attached to the plant.

Planting

- Because of the need to replace the plants periodically they are better to grow in the vegetable garden.
- Plant in July-September, 40-50 cm apart in rows 75 cm apart.
- New plants can be obtained in pots which are planted complete with pot, which the roots then penetrate. If these are used a crop can be obtained the year after planting. If runners are planted it is better to remove the flowers in the following year to allow the plant to grow stronger.
- The plants can be planted through black polythene which forms an effective mulch and helps to keep the fruit clean and less likely to rot.

Aftercare

- A very early crop (May) can be obtained if the plants are grown under cloches or in a tunnel. Cover the plants in February.
- Remove runners unless required for propagation.
- The fruits have to be protected from splashes from the soil. This is traditionally done with straw, but can be done with polythene or special strawberry mats.
- After the fruits have been picked the foliage should be cut back to 10 cm from the crown and burned, together with any straw and other debris.
- Fertilise after cutting back with a high potash fertiliser or with Growmore.

Propagation

Runners can be removed in July/August and replanted although, because of the risk off passing on infections, it is better to buy new certified plants.

The fruit garden

Some varieties

Summer fruiting

Cambridge Favourite	This is a mid-season variety producing a heavy crop with a good flavour. It is the standard against which other varieties are judged.
Honeoye	This is a new early variety producing a large crop of firm well flavoured fruits.

Autumn fruiting

Aromel	This variety has a superb flavour and will crop twice a year. For the best autumn fruits remove the flowers in May to avoid the first crop.

Pests

Birds	Birds can eat the ripening fruit and seriously deplete the crop. Growing in a cage or netting is the best solution.
Aphids	See Topic C-6 'Common pests'
Slugs and snails	See Topic C-6 'Common pests'

Diseases

Virus	See Topic C-7 'Common diseases'
Powdery mildew	See Topic C-7 'Common diseases'
Grey mould	See Topic C-7 'Common diseases'

Self test questions

These questions are to enable you to assess how well you have understood and remembered the information in the previous section. No answers are given as these should be apparent from reviewing the relevant topics.

The questions are **not** intended to cover everything you should know.

1   List five factors to take into account when choosing plants for a fruit garden.

2   Describe with the aid of diagrams the following forms of fruit trees:
      Cordon
      Espalier
      Fan

3   List four reasons for growing fruit trees on rootstocks.

4   List the advantages of growing restricted forms of fruit trees.

5   Describe the cultivation of cordon apple trees under the following headings:
      Choice of rootstock
      Support structure
      Planting
      Pruning established cordons

6   Write notes on the following:
      The pollination of apples
      Pruning an apple tree for the first two years after planting
      Summer pruning of espalier pears
      The need for physical protection in the fruit garden

7   Describe the cultivation of bush gooseberries under the following headings:
      Choice of site
      Ground preparation
      Planting
      Aftercare
      Suitable cultivars

8   Describe the cultivation of summer fruiting raspberries under the following headings:
      Planting
      Training
      Pruning
      Pest and disease control
      Suitable cultivars
      Harvesting

9   Describe the symptoms and method of treatment of the following pests and diseases:
      Codling moth on apples
      Fireblight on pears
      American gooseberry mildew on gooseberries
      Big bud gall mite on blackcurrants
      Raspberry beetle on raspberries

Metric conversions

This section contains the equivalent imperial measurements for the metric measurements used in this book.

Lengths and heights
1 cm = 0.4 in
5 cm = 2 in
10 cm = 4 in
30 cm = 12 in (1 ft)
60 cm = 24 in (2 ft)
90 cm = 36 in (3 ft)
1 m = 3.3 ft

Surface area
1 sq m = 1.2 sq yds
1 hectare = 2.5 acres

Capacity
1 litre = 0.22 gall
4.5 litre = 1 gall
1 cu m = 1.3 cu yds

Weight
1 g = 0.04 oz
25 g = 1 oz
50 g = 2 oz
1 kg = 2.2 lb

Temperature
-10 C = 14 F
-5 C = 23 F
0 C = 32 F
5 C = 41 F
10 C = 50 F
20 C = 68 F
30 C = 86 F
5-35 C = 40-95 F
18-21 C = 65-70 F

Application rates
25 g/sq m = 1 oz/sq yd
50 g/sq m = 2 oz/sq yd
4.5 litres/sq m = 1 gall/sq yd

Horticultural organisations

There are many different types of horticultural organisations ranging from local societies to national and government bodies. This section just includes those that the student might find of interest.

Royal Horticultural Society (RHS)

Since this book is written to cover the syllabus of one of the RHS's examinations it is only proper to give this organisation pride of place.

Established in 1804 the RHS is the UK's leading gardening charity, dedicated to advancing horticulture and promoting good gardening. Its goal is to help people share a passion for plants, to encourage excellence in horticulture, and inspire all those with an interest in gardening.

The Society is an independant body and does not rely on any government funding. The funding comes from members subscriptions, donations, legacies, and the income from its gardens, shows, bookshops and plant sales.

There is an RHS website, '**www.rhs.org.uk**', and this contains a huge amount of information about the Society and its activities, and includes access to its plant and plant finder databases. The website is open to anyone with access to the web.

Membership of the Society is open to anyone and gives the following advantages:

- Free entry to the RHS Gardens and many other gardens
- Free advisory service
- Free monthly magazine '**The Garden**'
- Reduced price tickets for RHS Shows and other events
- Oppotunity to obtain seeds harvested from RHS Gardens

At the time of writing membership is over 360000.

The activities of the Society are many and varied and can be grouped into:

- Gardens
- Advice
- Plants
- Education
- Publications
- Science and research
- Flower shows

Gardens

The main garden of the Society is at Wisley in Surrey, and for a long time this was the only garden. There are now three further gardens: Harlow Carr in North Yorkshire, Rosemoor in North Devon and Hyde Hall in Essex.

All these gardens are open to the public and are primarily show gardens. However much serious work goes on in the areas of research and experimentation. Trials are carried out of new plant varieties and national collections of some plants are held.

All the gardens run education and training programs in the form of courses, workshops or practical demonstrations.

Advice

The Societies staff includes botanists, entymologists, plant pathologists, plant physiologists and soil scientists who work in conjunction with a team of horticultural advisors.

Advice is available free to members of the society. This can be in the form of face to face discussions, or via telephone, post or email. There is usually an advisory desk at the major shows organised by the society and there is a desk at the Plant Center at Wisley.

For a fee a soil analysis can be obtained, and at Wisley there is a Personal Shopping Service whereby an advisor will help you to select plants to meet your requirements.

Plants

The Society has a huge amount of information relating to plants:

- Plant database accessible from the RHS website giving descriptive and cultural information on a huge range of plants.

- Plant finder database accessible from the RHS website giving information about where to obtain particular plants.

The Society is part of the **International Cultivar Registration Authorities (ICRA)** who are concerned with the correct naming of plants.

There is a plant sales area at each of the RHS Gardens.

One of the most important activities of the Society is to carry out trials of new and existing plants to assess their performance. Those that reach demanding levels of horticultural merit are awarded the **RHS Award of Garden Merit (AGM)**. This means that they may be relied upon to perform well in the garden and it is always worth looking for plants that have this award. There are currently over 6000 plants with this award.

Education

Education is one of the Society's core objectives, particularly to encourage young people to take an interest in gardening.

Every RHS garden has a program of educational activities and they also directly employ students to work in the gardens.

The Society runs a number of examinations which are recognised nationally and internationally as benchmarks in horticultural education. These examinations are primarily aimed at people intent on pursuing a career in horticulture but can also appeal to the enthusiastic amateur wishing to test their knowledge for personal satisfaction.

The Examinations are:

Level 1

The RHS Level 1 Award in Practical Horticulture is aimed at anyone who has an interest in plants and gardening.

Level 2

The RHS Level 2 qualifications can provide a route into the horticultural profession, they can support career development for those already working in the field of horticulture or they can provide a foundation for further learning or training.

There are both theory-based and practical-based qualifications at Level 2.

Level 3

The Level 3 qualifications not only offer opportunities for employment, but also enable you to begin to specialise in your area of interest. They can offer proficiency for those looking for employment in horticulture, they can support further career and professional development for those already working in the field, or they can provide a basis for continued learning or training.

There are both theory-based and practical- based qualifications at Level 3.

The Master of Horticulture (RHS)

TheMaster of Horticulture (RHS) Award is the Society's most prestigious professional horticultural qualification. It is of degree level. Designed primarily for those already working within the profession, the modular structure allows for flexible self-study over a period of three years or more.

The syllabuses for these examinations are available through the website.

This book is written to cover the syllabus of the RHS Level 2 theory-based qualifications.

Publications

The Society publishes a number of books covering many different aspects of gardening and aimed at both amateur and professional gardeners.

They also publish regular journals, one of which, '**The Garden**' is free to members of the Society.

Science & Research

The Society is concerned with the advancement of horticultural knowledge and employs a number of scientists at the laboratory based at the RHS Garden at Wisley. The activities are wide ranging and include:

- Advisory services
- Research projects
- Environmental policies
- Plant naming and the registration of cultivar names
- Plant trials

- Plant collections

The departments produce many advisory leaflets which are available to the public.

Flower shows

The Society organise a number of major flower shows across the country of which the most famous is the **Chelsea Flower Show** which is held in London in May of each year. Any keen gardener should try to visit this show at least once.

A number of more specialised shows are held throughout the year in the exhibition hall at the London headquarters in Vincent Square.

Defra (Department for Environment, Food and Rural Affairs)

Defra is the government department responsible for legislation and guidance on, among other things, horticultural matters.Level 2

Our Level 2 qualifications can provide a route into the horticultural profession, they can support career development for those already working in the field of horticulture or they can provide a foundation for further learning or training.Level 2

Our Level 2 qualifications can provide a route into the horticultural profession, they can support career development for those already working in the field of horticulture or they can provide a foundation for further learning or training.

The following text is taken from the defra website, '**www.defra.gov.uk**'

Defra's core purpose is to improve the current and future quality of life.

For the first time one department has brought together the interests of farmers and the countryside; the environment and the rural economy; the food we eat, the air we breathe and the water we drink.

We do all this by integrating environmental, social and economic objectives - putting sustainable development into practice every day, and by championing sustainable development as the way forward for Government.

Strategic priorities:

- Climate change and energy
- Sustainable consumption and production
- Protecting the countryside and natural rexsources
- Sustainable rural communities
- A sustainable farming and food sector including animal health and welfare

Horticultural responsibilities

Defra has policy responsibility for work on horticultural production and marketing.

This is primarily of concern to commercial growers, where Defra is involved in the Common Agricultural Policy (CAP) within the EU.

Defra is responsible for many aspects of plant health including propagation, marketing and the import and export of plants. Certain pests and deseases are closely monitored and if suspected must be reported to the local Plant Health and Seeds Inspector.

One area where the work of Defra will have an inpact on the amateur gardener is in the licensing of pesticides for use in a garden environment. This is done by the **Chemicals Regulation Directorate (CRD)** which is an agency of Defra. See **Topic C-4 'Chemical Control'** for more informayion.

Defra sponsors other horticultural bodies including:

- The Horticultural Development Council
- The British Potato Council
- The Covent Garden Marketing Authority

Horticultural Development Council (HDC)

The HDC was established in 1986 with an objective to carry out research and development (R&D) on behalf of commercial growers. Up to this date R&D had mainly been funded by the government. The funding is now met by a levy made on the growers.

The needs and priorities of the growers are established by representatives of the growers who are grouped into sectors depending on the type of crop. For example there are sectors for field vegetables and soft fruit.

Aim and Objectives

This information is taken from the HDC website, '**www.hdc.org.uk**'.

Aim

> To serve British growers by being a top class, efficient and progressive facilitator of near-market horticultural research and development and the associated technology transfer. It should provide clear value for money and be respected as making a major contribution to the profitability of the British horticultural industry.

Objectives

- Within the levy budget, identify the most profit enhancing issues and commission relevant R&D, taking account of the varying needs of individual sectors.

- Actively work with the Department for Environment, Food and Rural Affairs (Defra), the Scottish Executive Environment and Rural Affairs Department (SEERAD) and other funding bodies in such a way as to maximise the overall amount and relevance of horticultural research and development.

- Establish and maintain two-way communications with growers to ensure that all HDC and other funded research and development is put into profitable practice wherever relevant, taking due account of the disparate needs of the industry.

- Where specifically identified as being appropriate, sponsor targeted market research and product promotional activities.

- Actively manage the levy collection process and ensure maximum levy collection.

- Ensure that all activities, both internal and external are undertaken in a focused and cost effective manner.

Plant Heritage

This is the new name for what has been known as **'The National Council for the Conservation of Plants and Gardens (NCCPG)'**

The NCCPG had its origins in a meeting organised by the RHS in 1978. The meeting was called because of concern about the loss of plant variety within the horticultural world. This loss was largely due to changes in commercial horticulture whereby large scale production of plants did not lend itself to supporting a wide range of different plants, and financial constraints on government and educational organisations resulting in cut-backs in research and development.

The oucome of the meeting was that a fledgling organisation was formed and aims and objectives agreed. The aims can be summarised as:

- Encourage the conservation and propagation of endangered plants in the British Isles
- Encourage and conduct research into cultivated plants, their origins and their historical and cultural importance
- Encourage the education of the public in garden plant conservation

Plant Heritage is a registered charity, supported by membership fees, donations, legacies and some commercial operations. The current patron is The Prince of Wales.

The website of Plant Heritage is **'www.nccpg.com'**

National Plant Collections

Right from the start the concept of National Plant Collections was established as a mechanism for preserving plants. Under this scheme an individual or organisation undertakes to document, develop and preserve a comprehensive collection of one group of plants. A plant group usually comprises one genus and the collection would include all species and varieties within the genus. There are currently over 500 collections.

The holders of the collections come from a wide spectrum and include individuals, commercial organisations, local authorities, nurseries, botanic gardens and educational bodies. They all commit to the scheme's ideals and stringent regulations. They can make available or sell plants to the public or other collectors.

The collections are open to viewing at specified dates in the year. Details of the collections and the open days are available through the website.

If you wish to establish a collection there is still a huge number of genera that are not covered by the scheme!

The importance of the plant collections cannot be over-emphasised. With a simple concept that distributes the responsibility and workload into manageable units we have a national living database to safeguard our heritage.

The Soil Association

The Soil Association was founded in 1946 by a group of farmers, scientists and nutritionists who were concerned with the link between farming methods and plant, animal, human and environmental health. The overriding aim of the Association is to promote organic agriculture as a sustainable alternative to intensive farming methods.

The Association is active in the following areas:

- Building public awareness to influence government and industry attitudes to things like:
  - → Genetic engineering
  - → Pesticides
  - → Intensive farming
- Setting standards to ensure the integrity of organic food.
- Certifying organic producers. One of the most important functions of the Association. It means that consumers can rely on produce carrying the Soil Association symbol to be genuinely organic.
- Promoting organic food.
- Providing information and education relating to the Association's work.
- Providing an advisory service to growers.

The Association's website is '**www.soilassociation.org**'

Garden Organic

This is a charitable organisation, previously known as the **Henry Doubleday Research Association (HDRA)**, whose aim is to promote the ideas of organic gardening. They carry out scientific research, produce publications, run courses and give advice on all aspects of organic gardening.

They also put their principles into practice in Ryton Organic Gardens which consists of ten acres of ornamental and demonstration gardens, and is open to the public all year round.

They also maintain the **Heritage Seed Library** which aims to conserve and make available vegetable varieties that are not readily available from any other source.

Membership of Garden Organic is open to the public and provides a variety of benefits including free entry to the garden at Ryton and also to the RHS garden at Wisley.

Their website is '**www.gardenorganic.org.uk**'

RHS Level 2 Qualification

Since this book is written to meet the requirements of the RHS Level 2 Examinations it is appropriate to include some information relating to those examination.

The information is taken from the published syllabus which can be obtained from:

> RHS Qualifications
> RHS Garden Wisley
> Woking
> Surrey
> GU23 6QB

The syllabus is also accessible through the RHS website **'www.rhs.org.uk'**.

The syllabus was revised in 2010 as part of the Government reform of qualifications and a new structure was introduced called the Qualifications and Credit Framework or QCF.

The full Level 2 syllabus is now made up of 16 units each of which has a credit value, and may be taken as separate examinations. Examinations are held in February and June.

Certain combinations of the units allow the student to gain a Level 2 Certificate covering those units. These are shown on the following page.

The syllabus is cross referenced to topics in the book. In some cases no specific cross reference is possible because the relevant information is spread through the book.

Students and tutors should satisfy themselves that the information published here represents the latest situation.

Introduction

This qualification provides a route to employment in professional horticulture by assessing knowledge of the principles underpinning horticultural practices, and a range of essential practical skills in horticulture.

It supports career development for those already working in professional horticulture by assessing knowledge of the principles underpinning horticultural practices and a range of essential practical skills in horticulture.

It provides a foundation for further learning or training in the field of horticulture

There are no pre-requisites for entry to the qualification.

The qualification is accredited within the Qualifications and Credit Framework.

Accreditation Number: 501/0208/4

Credit Value

The full 16 units have a credit value of 43.

This equates to 430 learning hours. Learning time is defined as the time taken by learners at the level of the qualification, on average, to complete the learning outcomes of the units to the standard determined by the assessment criteria.

Unit		Credits	Level
1	Plant classification, structure, and function	5	2
2	Plant nutrition and the root environment	3	2
3	Maintaining plant health	3	2
4	Understanding plant propagation	3	2
5	Understanding garden features, plant selection and planning	5	2
6	Understanding the choice, establishment and maintenance of garden plants and lawns	3	2
7	Understanding the production of outdoor vegetables and fruit	3	2
8	Understanding protected environments and their use in plant cultivation	3	2
9	Testing Soil	1	2
10	Sowing seeds and vegetative propagation techniques	2	2
11	Practical skills in ground preparation for seeding and planting	2	2
12	Practical skills in establishing seeds and plants in soil	2	2
13	Care and pruning of plants	3	2
14	Identification of a range of common garden plants, weeds,pests, diseases, disorders and benefical organisms	3	2
	Optional Units (credit value 2)		
15	Sustainable garden practice	2	2
16	Safe operation of powered garden machinery	2	2

Candidates who successfully achieve units 1 – 4 meet the requirements for the **RHS Level 2 Certificate in the Principles of Plant Growth, Propagation and Development**.

Candidates who successfully achieve units 5 – 8 meet the requirements for the **RHS Level 2 Certificate in the Principles of Garden Planning, Establishment and Maintenance.**

Candidates who successfully achieve units 1 – 8 meet the requirements for the **RHS Level 2 Certificate in the Principles of Horticulture**.

Candidates who successfully achieve units 9 – 16 meet the requirements for the **RHS Level 2 Certificate in Practical Horticulture.**

Candidates who successfully achieve units 1 – 16 meet the requirements for the **RHS Level 2 Diploma in the Principles and Practices of Horticulture**.

Units 9 -16 are practical examinations and are not covered any further in this section.

Plant classification, structure and function

Unit 1 - Code:H/601/0307

Unit Level: Level 2

Credit Value: 5

This unit will enable candidates to develop an understanding of the basis on which higher plants are classified and named, and to appreciate the role and function of morphological and anatomical features in higher plants. The unit will ensure that the fundamental physiological processes within the plant are understood including photosynthesis, respiration and water movement. Additionally students will understand the mechanisms of pollination, fertilisation, seed formation and subsequent germination.

		Topic
1.	**Know the basic classification and taxonomy of plants.**	**A-2 A-3 A11**
	1.1 Identify the basic differences between gymnosperms and angiosperms	
	1.2 Describe differences between the monocotyledon and dicotyledon divisions of the angiosperms, including the external features of root type, leaf shape and venation, and internal differences in the distribution of vascular bundles, lignification, and secondary growth.	
	1.3 State the reasons why a universal system of plant names is important.	
	1.4 Describe the use of the terms 'genus', 'species, and 'cultivar'.	
2.	**Know the stages of development and life cycles**	**A-1**
	2.1 Describe the five stages of the life cycle of plants: seed, juvenile, adult, senescent, death.	
	2.2 Define the terms: 'annual', 'ephemeral', 'biennial' and 'perennial'.	
	2.3 Define the terms: 'tender', 'half-hardy' and 'hardy' as applied to annuals.	
	2.4 Define the terms: 'tender', 'half-hardy', 'hardy', 'herbaceous' and 'woody' in relation to perennials, including the process of lignification.	
	2.5 State the meaning of the terms 'evergreen', 'semievergreen' and 'deciduous'.	
3	**Know the structure and function of plant cells and tissues**	**A-4 A-5**
	3.1 Describe the structure of the basic plant cell and state the function of the basic components, including the cell wall, cell membrane, nucleus, vacuole, cytoplasm, chloroplasts & mitochondria.	
	3.2 State where active cell division is located within the plant (apical and lateral meristems).	
	3.3 Define the term: 'plant tissue'.	
	3.4 Describe the basic characteristics and role of the tissues found in flowering plants, identifying protective, meristematic, transport, packing, strengthening, and support functions.	
4	**Know the function of the external vegetative parts of the plant.**	**A-6 to A-8 A-11 A-17**
	4.1 Define: 'primary', 'secondary', 'tap', 'lateral', 'fibrous', and 'adventitious' roots.	
	4.2 Describe the external structure of the root tip and the role of the root cap and root hairs.	

4.3	Describe how the root is adapted in order to perform specific functions, including storage (e.g. tap root, tuber); and climbing.	
4.4	Describe the external structure of the stem.	
4.5	Describe how the stem is adapted in order to perform specific functions, including protection; storage (e.g. corms, tubers, rhizomes); climbing; natural vegetative reproduction (e.g.stolons, rhizomes, tubers, runners).	
4.6	Describe the external structure of the leaf, including the petiole, lamina, and midrib; its shape and colour, and arrangement on the stem.	
4.7	Describe how leaves are adapted to perform other functions including storage (eg bulbs); protection; climbing; and attraction of pollinators.	
4.8	Describe transverse sections of the young dicotyledon root, stem, and leaf; these should include the location of the following: epidermis, cortex, xylem,phloem, pith, cambium, vascular bundles, endodermis, pericycle, palisade & spongy mesophyll, cuticle, stomata.	

5.	**Know the function of the reproductive parts of the plant**	**A-9 A-19 A-20**
5.1	Describe the structure of a typical dicotyledon flower, including sepals, petals, tepals, calyx, corolla, nectaries, anther, filament, stigma, style, ovary and ovule.	
5.2	State the role of each component of the flower listed in 5.1	
5.3	State the meaning of the terms: 'monoecious', 'dioecious' and 'hermaphrodite'.	
5.4	Describe the process of pollination, including self-pollination and cross-pollination.	
5.5	Compare the characteristics of wind and animal pollinated plants including the exposure of reproductive structures, pollen surface roughness, and quantity of pollen	
5.6	Describe the process of fertilisation, including the meaning of the terms 'gametes', 'zygote', 'incompatible', and 'compatible'.	

6.	**Know the function of fruits and seeds.**	**A-10 A-20**
6.1	Define the term 'fruit' and state the role of the fruit in plant reproduction.	
6.2	State that fruits can be divided into dry types (dehiscent and indehiscent) and fleshy (succulent) types (true and false); and that these can be distributed by wind, water, animals (externally), and animals (internally).	
6.3	Name one example of each type of fruit listed in 6.2, and one example for each distribution method.	
6.4	Describe the internal and external structure of the seed of a monocotyledon (examples to include maize, Zea mays) and a dicotyledon (examples to include French bean, Phaseolus vulgaris and broad bean, Vicia faba).	
6.5	Describe the behaviour of French bean (Phaseolus vulgaris), and broad bean (Vicia faba) as examples of epigeal and hypogeal germination.	

7.	**Understand the importance of photosynthesis and respiration.**	**A-14**
7.1	State the basic equation for photosynthesis in words.	
7.2	Describe how levels of temperature, light, carbon dioxide water and mineral nutrients determine the efficiency of photosynthesis.	
7.3	State the basic equations for aerobic and anaerobic respiration in words.	
7.4	Describe how levels of oxygen and temperature determine the	

efficiency of respiration

8.	**Understand the movement of water and minerals through the plant.**	**A-15**
	8.1 Define the term: 'transpiration', and describe how water and minerals move through the plant.	
	8.2 Describe diffusion and osmosis and their roles within the plant, including gaseous and liquid diffusion, transpiration, and water uptake.	
	8.3 Describe how the plant may limit water loss, including the action of stomata and specific leaf adaptations (hairs, thick cuticle, needles).	
	8.4 Describe the effects of relative humidity and temperature on transpiration.	
9.	**Understand plant growth and development relationships**	**A-13 A-16**
	9.1 Describe the stages of growth and development during the life cycle of a plant.	
	9.2 Describe how simple cell division and enlargement produces growth and results in an increase in size of plants	
	9.3 Describe how competition for water, nutrients, light and space influences the growth of plants.	
	9.4 Describe the role of auxin in plant development (influencing shoot and roots), and in phototropic responses.	

Plant nutrition and the root environment

Unit 2 - Code: A/601/0314

Unit Level: Level 2

Credit Value: 3

This unit will enable candidates to develop an understanding of the constituents, properties and management of soils and growing media.

1.	**Understand the importance of using safe, healthy and environmentally sustainable practices.**	
	1.1 Describe how horticultural practices can affect the environment, including examples of: soil cultivations; irrigation and drainage; soil improvement; composting; choice of growing media.	
	1.2 Explain how the practices listed in 1.1 can be adapted to reduce the impact on the environment.	
2.	**Know the main horizons found in soil profiles.**	**B-1 B-2**
	2.1 Name the main horizons found in a typical soil profile, including the organic horizon, topsoil, subsoil, and parent material (rock).	
	2.2 Describe the typical characteristics of each horizon, in terms of: the presence of organic matter; soil organisms; pore space; products of leaching and deposition such as nutrients (iron), clay and stones.	
	2.3 Describe the properties of top soil that contribute to the healthy growth of plants, in terms of: the presence of organic matter; soil organisms; soil structure; air content; water content; nutrient content.	
	2.4 State the purposes of primary and secondary soil cultivations, including the addition of soil conditioners.	
3.	**Know the physical properties of soil.**	**B-3 B-9**
	3.1 Explain what is meant by 'soil texture'.	
	3.2 Describe the physical characteristics of the soil particles sand, silt and clay.	
	3.3 Describe how the characteristics of each of the soil particles listed in 3.2 affect soils and their suitability for horticultural use.	

3.4 Explain what is meant by 'soil structure' (soil aggregates) and state how root establishment and growth are affected by different soil structures.

3.5 State that a crumb soil is the ideal structure for horticultural use.

3.6 Describe two methods by which soil structure can be improved and two practices which damage soil structure, to include: incorporation of organic matter; addition of inorganic soil improvers; compaction; and cultivation techniques.

3.7 State what is meant by 'surface capping'; explain how it may happen and what effects it can have on plant establishment and growth.

3.8 Describe how a cultivation pan can be formed, what effect it has

4. Understand the factors that determine the water status in the soil. | **B-4 B-11**

4.1 Describe the relationship between air and water content in the pore space of soils and growing media.

4.2 Explain the importance of an appropriate balance between air and water for the healthy growth of plants.

4.3 Identify the surface symptoms of poor drainage, to include: standing water, surface run-off and indicator plant species.

5. Understand the importance of organic matter and living soil organisms in the root environment. | **B-6 B-7**

5.1 State the main sources of organic matter in the soil, to include: recycling of natural resources (plant and animal remains); incorporation of imported resources, e.g. farm-yard manure and garden compost; incorporation of crop debris.

5.2 Describe TWO beneficial effects and TWO limitations of organic matter in the soil.

5.3 List four bulky organic materials that can be used for soil improvement in a garden, including farmyard manures; garden compost; mushroom compost; composted municipal waste.

5.4 Compare the benefits and limitations of each of the materials listed in 5.3 for soil improvement.

5.5 List FOUR bulky organic materials used as organic soil mulches, including chipped bark products, leaf mould, composted straw products, cocoa shell.

5.6 Compare the benefits and limitations of each of the materials listed in 5.5 for use as a mulch.

5.7 Describe FOUR methods of composting garden waste, including aerobic and anaerobic methods, production of leaf mould and the use of wormeries.

5.8 Describe the contribution made by earthworms, bacteria and fungi to the organic matter content of the soil.

5.9 State the importance of the ratio of 'green' to 'woody' material in the breakdown of organic matter, and the importance of lime to the composting process.

5.10 Describe what is meant by the term 'green manure' and name TWO plant species that can be grown for this purpose.

5.11 State TWO benefits and TWO limitations of using green manures.

6. Understand the importance of soil pH. | **B-8**

6.1 Describe the pH scale and state the pH range that normally supports healthy plant growth.

6.2 Explain the effect that soil pH has on plant selection.

6.3 Describe what is meant by 'lime-induced chlorosis'.

6.4 Name TWO plants that require an acid soil.

6.5 State TWO methods by which soil pH can be raised, including the application of garden lime, use of composted green waste and wood ash.

6.6 State TWO methods by which soil pH can be lowered, including the application of Sulphur and use of an acidic form of organic matter.

7.   Understand plant nutrition provided by soil and growing media.   A-17 B-12

7.1 List the major and minor (trace) nutrients required for plant growth and development, to include: Major nutrients: Nitrogen, Phosphorus, Potassium, Magnesium, Calcium, Sulphur. Minor (trace) nutrients: Iron, Manganese, Boron, Copper, Zinc, Molybdenum. (Chemical symbols are not required for minor nutrients)

7.2 Describe the typical effects of a deficiency of Nitrogen, Iron, Magnesium and Calcium.

7.3 State what is meant by the terms 'organic fertiliser' and 'inorganic fertiliser' and list TWO examples of EACH.

7.4 State TWO benefits and TWO limitations of using organic fertilisers and inorganic fertilisers.

7.5 State what is meant by: single or straight fertilisers; compound fertilisers. List TWO examples of EACH.

7.6 State what is meant by the terms 'Base dressing', 'Top dressing', 'Liquid feed' and 'Foliar feed'. Describe ONE situation where EACH type of fertiliser application would be appropriate.

7.7 Describe the use of Controlled Release Fertiliser (CRF) granules and state TWO benefits and TWO limitations of their use in growing media.

8.   Understand the uses of alternative growing media   E-10

8.1 Describe the range of compost types available, and the use of EACH of these growing media as alternatives to growing in soil: including peatbased, loam-based, peat-free, multipurpose, ericaceous, seed and cutting and container composts.

8.2 Describe the environmental implications of the use of peat, coir and municipal green

Maintaining plant health

Unit 3 - Code: K/601/0342

Unit level: Level 2

Credit Value: 3

This unit will enable candidates to develop an understanding of pest, disease cycles including modes of infestation. Cultural, biological, chemical and integrated systems are explored.

1.   Understand the importance of using safe, healthy and sustainable practices for the maintenance of plant health.   C-1 to C-4

1.1 State what is meant by biological, chemical, physical (or cultural) and integrated methods of pest and disease control.

1.2 Describe ONE example of each type of control named in 1.1.

1.3 State the benefits and limitations of using each of the types of control named in 1.1.

1.4 Describe how risks to people and the environment can be minimised when using the control methods stated in 1.1.

1.5 State the importance of natural balances in plant protection and describe how garden practices can disturb this balance.

1.6 Describe methods which can be used to restore and maintain these natural balances to minimise the need for pesticides.

1.7   Describe how the selection of plants can help to avoid plant health problems, including the choice of resistant cultivars and growing plants appropriate to a situation and soil.

2.   Understand the problems posed by weeds in horticulture and how these problems can be minimised.   `C-1 to C-5`

2.1   Describe what is meant by a weed.

2.2   Describe how weeds reduce crop productivity and reduce the visual appeal of plantings for display.

2.3   Describe the role of weeds as alternative hosts for plant pathogens.

2.4   Describe the biology of ephemeral, annual and perennial weeds.

2.5   State the botanical names of TWO examples of EACH of the types described in 2.4.

2.6   Describe how the types of weed described in 2.4 relate to horticultural situations, including recently cultivated soil; herbaceous perennial borders; woody perennial plantings; and lawns.

2.7   State the botanical names of TWO weeds associated with EACH of the situations described in 2.6.

2.8   State what is meant by contact, residual, translocated and selective herbicides, and describe ONE situation where EACH type would be used appropriately.

2.9   State the active ingredient of ONE example of EACH type of herbicide described in 2.8.

3.   Know the problems posed by pests in horticulture and ways in which these can be minimised.   `C-6`

3.1   Define 'plant pest'.

3.2   Describe the damage caused by rabbits, cabbage white butterfly larva, black bean aphid, two-spotted spider mite, glasshouse whitefly, vine weevil, slugs, snails, and stem (or bulb) eelworm.

3.3   Describe in outline the life-cycles of cabbage white butterfly, black bean aphid, glasshouse whitefly and vine weevil.

3.4   Describe TWO different methods of reducing the effects of EACH of the plant pests named in 3.2; methods should be selected from more than one of the control options (chemical, physical, cultural or biological) available.

3.5   Describe how a knowledge of the life cycles of the cabbage white butterfly, black bean aphid, glasshouse whitefly and vine weevil contribute to the success of their control.

4.   Know the problems posed by diseases in horticulture and ways in which these can be minimised.   `C-7`

4.1   Define 'plant disease'.

4.2   Describe the damage caused by grey mould, powdery mildew, damping off, honey fungus, rose black spot, potato blight and clubroot.

4.3   Describe TWO different methods of reducing the effects of EACH of the diseases stated in 4.2; methods should be selected from more than one of the control options (chemical, physical, cultural or biological) available.

4.4   Describe the damage caused by fire blight and describe TWO methods used to limit the spread of the disease.

4.5   Describe the damage caused by TWO named plant viruses.

4.6   Describe TWO methods by which viruses can be spread.

4.7   Describe TWO methods of avoiding the spread of plant viruses

5.	**Know the problems posed by plant disorders in horticulture and ways in which these can be minimised.**	C-8

5.1   Define 'plant physiological disorder'.

5.2   Describe the symptoms of lime-induced chlorosis, and how plants and their growth are affected by frost; shade; drought; and water-logging.

5.3   State ONE method of avoiding EACH of the problems described in 5.2.which these can be minimised.

Understanding plant propagation

Unit 4 - Code: M/601/0343

Unit level: Level 2

Credit Value: 3

This unit will enable candidates to develop an understanding of the principles and main practices of plant propagation in horticulture.

1.	**Understand how plant physiology affects the ways in which plants can be propagated.**	A-19 E-3 E-4

1.1   Describe the characteristics of plants that can be propagated from seed.

1.2   State FIVE benefits of propagating plants from seed.

1.3   State FIVE limitations of propagating plants from seed.

1.4   Describe the characteristics of plants requiring propagation by vegetative means.

1.5   State FIVE benefits of propagating plants by vegetative means.

1.6   State FIVE limitations of propagating plants by vegetative means.

1.7   State FIVE examples of plants that are propagated from seed.

1.8   State FIVE examples of plants that are propagated by vegetative means.

2	**Understand the appropriate methods of harvesting and storing different types of seed.**	E-3

2.1   Describe the preparation of fleshy berries for seed storage, under the following headings: harvesting; maceration; separation; cleaning and drying.

2.2   State FOUR NAMED examples of seeds requiring cool dry storage.

2.3   State FOUR NAMED examples of seeds requiring cool moist storage.

2.4   State the effect that storage has on the viability and germination potential of seed.

3.	**Understand the conditions required for successful plant propagation from seed.**	A-10 E-3

3.1   State the environmental requirements for seeds to germinate successfully: light levels; moisture; temperature; oxygen

3.2   State the meaning of the term 'seed dormancy'

3.3   Describe methods of overcoming seed dormancy, including soaking; hot water treatment; nicking (chipping); abrasion; and warm and cold treatments; stating an appropriate plant example for EACH.

3.4   Describe the changes that take place in a germinating seed, including taking in water; rising respiration rate; rapid cell division; and the splitting of the seed coat.

3.5   Describe the preparation of suitable containers and growing media for sowing the following types of seed: fine, medium and large.

3.6   Describe the preparation of a seedbed on an outdoor site

3.7   Describe appropriate methods of sowing seed in containers and in the openground, including broadcast, sowing in drills and station sowing.

3.8   Describe the care of seedlings to include: provision of the most suitable environmental conditions; watering; the avoidance of pests and diseases; the control of THREE commonly encountered pests and THREE commonly encountered diseases.

3.9   Describe the pricking out into containers, thinning out, or transplanting of seedlings to a new site.

4.   Understand the conditions required for successful plant propagation from cuttings.   **E-4**

4.1   Describe the effects of juvenility and plant health on the ability of a section of plant to produce roots/shoots.

4.2   Describe how to collect and prepare the following types of cutting: 'soft tip' (deciduous with leaves); 'semi-ripe' (green wood deciduous with leaves); small hairy or grey-leaved semi-evergreen with leaves; hardwood evergreen with leaves; hardwood deciduous without leaves; and conifers.

4.3   State FOUR NAMED plant examples for EACH type of cutting material described in 4.2.

4.4   State a propagation facility that provides the best possible conditions for rooting EACH of the types of cutting described in 4.2. (Examples to include a propagator, mist bench, cold frame, and the open ground).

4.5   State the environmental conditions required by EACH of the types of cutting described in 4.2.

4.6   Describe how to manage the environment (temperature, moisture, airflow) to encourage the rooting process and help to avoid THREE NAMED pests and THREE NAMED diseases.

4.7   Describe the aftercare of cuttings, including the removal of diseased, dying or dead material; feeding; and hardening off in preparation for potting off.

5   Understand how to propagate specific plants using appropriate vegetative techniques.   **E-4**

5.1   Describe how to propagate by division ONE NAMED plant of EACH of the following types: a suckering shrub; a fibrous-rooted perennial; a perennial with distinct buds (eyes).

5.2   Describe how to propagate ONE NAMED plant for EACH of the following types of leaf cutting: leaf petiole; leaf lamina; leaf squares; midrib; and chevrons.

5.3   Describe how to propagate ONE NAMED plant by leaf bud cuttings.

5.4   Describe how to propagate ONE NAMED plant for EACH of the following sizes of root cutting: thick (over 2mm diameter); and thin (less than 2mm diameter).

5.5   Describe how to propagate ONE NAMED plant for EACH of the following types of layering: air; simple; and serpentine.

5.6   State the meaning of the terms 'budding' and 'grafting'.

5.7   State FOUR reasons why budding and grafting are carried out.

5.8   State TWO benefits and TWO limitations of grafting.

5.9   Describe how to propagate ONE NAMED plant by EACH of the following types of budding: 'T'; and 'Chip'.

5.10   Describe how to propagate ONE NAMED plant by EACH of the following types of grafting: 'whip and tongue' (in the field); 'side veneer graft' (bench grafting).

5.11   For EACH method of propagation specified in 5.1 to 5.8, state what aftercare is required to ensure success.

Understanding garden features, plant selection and planning

Unit 5 - Code: F/601/0251

Unit Level: Level 2

Credit Value: 5

This unit will enable candidates to develop an understanding of basic surveying and design principlesand to apply them to basic garden design and planning requirements. Additionally, the unit willenable candidates to develop an understanding of plant selection for soft landscaping

1.	**Know how to carry out and record a garden survey.**	**D-2 D-3**
1.1	Describe how to identify potential hazards and risks on a site, including overhead and underground hazards (eg electric cables); unsafe buildings, features and trees; topography and existing features, e.g. watercourses and ponds.	
1.2	Describe potential restrictions which may limit work on the site, including financial constraints; difficulties with access for plant, equipment and materials; topography (degree and extent of slopes); boundary constraints; and restrictions on the time the works can be carried out.	
1.3	State what existing garden features need to be identified, including buildings, hard landscape features, and the trees and plants that are to be retained.	
1.4	State why it is necessary to identify the existence of overhead and underground services.	
1.5	Describe how to carry out basic linear surveying techniques, including the use of tapes, offsets and triangulation.	
2	**Know how to carry out a site appraisal and record essential data.**	**D-2**
2.1	State what needs to be recorded when carrying out a site appraisal, including soil type, contour, aspect, microclimate, exposure and drainage.	
3	**Understand basic garden planning principles and the elements that contribute to a good design.**	**D-4**
3.1	Describe the relevance of garden planning principles to the production of a garden design that 'works', - one that follows accepted 'rules' or 'conventions', and which is pleasing to the eye.	
3.2	State the meaning of the following terms: symmetry; asymmetry; colour; focal points.	
4	**Understand the characteristics of accepted garden design styles.**	**D-1**
4.1	Describe the difference between formality and informality in garden design.	
4.2	Describe the main characteristics of a knot garden, a landscape garden and a cottage garden.	
5	**Understand the effective and appropriate use of hard landscaping materials.**	**D-5**
5.1	Describe a range of horizontal elements: paths, steps, patios and decking. Compare the benefits and limitations of a range of materials for each of the above, including concrete, paving and wood.	
5.2	Describe a range of vertical elements: wall fences, screens, pergolas,furniture, statuary. For each of the above, compare TWO examples of natural and man-made materials used in their manufacture.	

5.3 Describe rock gardens and water features. State TWO examples ofmanufactured and TWO of natural materials for EACH element

6 **Understand the effective use of soft landscaping elements.**	**D-6 G-2 to G-15**

6.1 Name appropriate grass species for the following types of lawn: hard wearing utility; high quality ornamental; shade tolerant.

6.2 Name FIVE evergreen and FIVE deciduous trees (large shrubs), suitable for planting in a domestic garden. State details of their decorative merits, height and spread and site requirements; describe a situation where each could be used effectively.

6.3 Name FIVE evergreen and FIVE deciduous plant species, suitable forhedging or screening (including formal or informal use). State details of their decorative merits, height and spread and site requirements; describe a situation where each could be used effectively.

6.4 Name TEN deciduous and TEN evergreen shrubs suitable for planting in a variety of garden situations. State details of their decorative merits, height and spread and site requirements; describe a situation where each could be used effectively.

6.5 Name TEN herbaceous perennials suitable for planting in a variety of garden situations. State details of their decorative merits, height and spread and site requirements; describe a situation where each could be used effectively.

6.6 Name TEN Alpine or Rock garden plants suitable for planting in a variety of garden situations. State details of their decorative merits, height and spread and site requirements; describe a situation where each could be used effectively.

6.7 Name FIVE plants grown as biennials, which are suitable for planting in a variety of garden situations. State details of their decorative merits, height and spread and site requirements; describe a situation where each could be used effectively.

6.8 Name TEN hardy plants grown as annuals, suitable for planting in a variety of garden situations. State details of their decorative merits, height and spread and site requirements; describe a situation where each could be used effectively.nm

6.9 Name TEN half-hardy plants suitable for seasonal bedding. State details of their decorative merits, height and spread and site requirements and describe a situation where each could be used effectively.

6.10 Name TEN patio or basket plants suitable for planting in a variety of garden situations. State details of their decorative merits, height and spread and site requirements; describe a situation where each could be used effectively.

6.11 Name FIVE bulbs, corms or tuberous plants used for winter or spring interest, and FIVE for summer or autumn interest, in a variety of garden situations. State details of their decorative merits, height and spread and site requirements; describe a situation where each could be used effectively.

7. **Understand how to incorporate key elements into a cohesive design**	**D-4 to D-6**

7.1 Understand how elements of hard landscaping should be selected and used to ensure that a design. is cohesive.

7.2 Describe how elements of soft landscaping should be selected and used to ensure that a design is cohesive.

7.3 Describe how other materials and items (e.g. garden furniture) should be selected and used to ensure that a design is cohesive.

8. **Understand the importance of safe, healthy, environmentally**

sensitive and sustainable development of garden sites.-

8.1 Describe TWO hazards associated with EACH of the following: access; slope; location of features; water; electricity; materials; plants.

8.2 State how the risks related to the hazards identified in 8.1 can be minimised by careful planning during the planning and design stage.

8.3 Describe how the environmental sustainability of landscaping materials may affect choices made during the planning and design stage.

8.4 State how sustainable practices in the maintenance of a garden can be integrated successfully during the planning and design stage.

8.5 State how sustainable practices can be undertaken during the construction

Understand the choice, establishmentand maintenance of garden plants and lawns

Unit 6 - Code: T/601/0263

Unit Level: Level 2

Credit Value: 3

This unit will enable candidates to develop an understanding of plant selection, establishment and maintenance of a range of ornamental plants.

		G-9 G-15
1.	**Understand the choice of plants for seasonal display and their establishmenti and maintenance.**	

1.1 Describe, in the context of seasonal displays, what is meant by the terms: bedding, hardy, half-hardy, tropical, edging, groundwork (infill) and dot plant; give TWO plant examples of EACH

1.2 Explain the importance of F1 hybrid plants and the term 'hybrid vigour'. State FOUR specific plant examples.

1.3 Name TEN plants suitable for growing in an annual border.

1.4 Name TEN plants suitable for summer bedding displays.

1.5 Name FIVE plants suitable for spring bedding displays, including TWO bulbs (or corms or tubers).

1.6 Name TEN plants suitable for summer display in containers or hanging baskets.

1.7 Name FIVE plants suitable for winter display in containers or hanging baskets.

1.8 Describe the soil or growing media preparation, sowing or planting out of plants for seasonal display for the situations listed in 1.3 – 1.7.

1.9 Describe the routine maintenance of seasonal bedding, including control of weeds and common pests and diseases (aphids, slugs and snails, vine weevil, grey mould, powdery mildew) for the situations listed in 1.3-1.7.

		G-8 G-10
2.	**Understand the choice of herbaceous perennial plants and 'bulbs' for display, and how to grow them**	

2.1 Name TEN herbaceous perennial plants suitable for growing in an herbaceous border.

2.2 Name FIVE herbaceous perennials suitable for growing in shade and FIVE suitable for use as ground cover.

2.3 Name TEN bulbs or corms or tubers, of which FOUR should be suitable for growing in the border, FOUR for containers and FOUR for naturalizing.

2.4 Describe the soil preparation, planting, routine maintenance and control of weeds, pests and diseases (aphids, slugs and snails, vine weevil, grey mould, powdery mildew ,stem or bulb eelworm) required for growing herbaceous perennials and bulbs, corms or tubers.

3. Understand the choice of woody plants for display and their establishment and maintenance | G-2 to G-7

3.1. Name TEN trees suitable for growing in a domestic garden.

3.2 Name TEN shrubs suitable for growing in a domestic garden.

3.3 Name FIVE trees grown for winter interest and FIVE grown for autumn display.

3.4 Name FIVE shrubs grown for winter interest and FIVE grown for autumn display.

3.5 Name FIVE lime-hating trees or shrubs.

3.6 Name FIVE bush roses suitable for growing in a rose bed, including cluster-flowered (floribunda) and large-flowered (hybrid tea) examples.

3.7 Name FIVE climbers and FIVE wall shrubs suitable for a variety of garden situations including shaded and north-facing.

3.8 Describe the soil preparation and planting for trees and woody shrubs.

3.9 Describe the routine maintenance for trees and woody shrubs, to include pruning and the control of weeds and common pests and diseases(aphids, powdery mildew, black spot of roses, canker, coral spot, honey fungus).

4. Understand the choice of alpine and rock garden plants and how to grow them | G-11

4.1 Name FIVE alpine or rock garden plants for spring display and FIVE for summer display.

4.2 Describe soil characteristics, soil preparation and routine maintenance for the display of alpine or rock garden plants in open soil.

4.3. Describe choice of container, the characteristics and preparation of the growing medium, and the routine maintenance required for an alpine or rock garden display in containers.

5. Understand the planting and maintenance of a garden pool. | G-16

5.2 Name TWO AQUATIC plants from each of the following groups: floating, deep-water, marginal and bog plants.

5.2 Describe the planting and establishment of aquatic plants in a garden pool.

5.3. Describe the annual maintenance of a garden pool, including possible controls for algae including blanket weed.

6. Understand the establishment and maintenance of lawns. | G-1 F-3

6.1. State appropriate grass mixtures for the establishment of a high quality ornamental lawn and for a hard-wearing utility lawn.

6.2 State the benefits and limitations of establishing lawns from seed.

6.3 Describe the procedure for establishing a lawn from seed.

6.4 State the benefits and limitations of establishing a lawn from turf.

6.5 Describe the procedure for establishing a lawn from turf.

6.6 Describe the annual maintenance programme for quality ornamental and for hard-wearing utility lawns.

6.7 Describe the range of equipment used for mowing, feeding, scarifying and aerating lawns.

6.8 Describe the symptoms of a range of common lawn pests and diseases, including red thread, Fusarium patch, fairy rings, leatherjackets and moles; state an appropriate control measure for

EACH.

Understanding the production of outdoor vegetables and fruit

Unit 7 - Code: A/601/0264

Unit Level: Level 2

Credit Value: 3

This unit will enable candidates to develop an understanding of basic cultural operations and production methods necessary to obtain outdoor vegetable and fruit crops.

1	**Know the importance of site selection for outdoor food production in a garden or allotment**	**H-1 G-4**
	1.1 State the factors to be considered when selecting a site: including soil depth, texture and structure, drainage, pH, aspect, slope, susceptibility to frost and wind, area of land available and availability of water.	
	1.2 Describe the reasons for providing shelter for an outdoor food production area, including the effects of wind reduction, frost potential and influences upon pollination.	
	1.3 State the benefits and limitations of living and non-living windbreaks.	
	1.4 Name FOUR plant species suitable for a living windbreak.	
	1.5 Name FOUR types of non-living permeable windbreak.	
	2. Understand the cultural operations used to produce outdoor food H-1 H-2 crops in a garden or allotment. B-13 2.1 Describe a range of soil cultivation techniques suitable for the vegetable garden: including digging rotary cultivation, consolidation and tilth production.	
	2.2 Describe how the timing of soil cultivations will be influenced by soil texture, structure, weather and climate.	
	2.3 Describe what is meant by the bed system for growing vegetables. Compare this with open ground production.	
	2.4 Describe what is meant by a raised bed, giving a specification for a typical raised bed and paths	
	2.5 Explain the no-dig system of managing raised beds.	
	2.6 State the methods used to advance and extend the productiveseason of outdoor food crops, including the use of polythene, mulches, fleece, 'enviromesh', low tunnels, cloches and cold frames.	
	2.7. Describe propagation methods used in the production of vegetable crops, including direct sowing and raising plants in seed beds, blocks and modules.	
3.	**Understand the principles of vegetable crop production**	**H-2 to H-10**
	3.1. Describe the individual production of vegetable crops including runner beans, winter cabbage, Brussels sprouts, carrots, courgettes, onions, leeks, beetroot, potatoes and salad crops to include lettuce and radish.	
	3.2 Describe how quality and yield may be determined by the following: base and top dressings, thinning, weed control, crop support, irrigation and pest and disease control.	
	3.3 Describe how EACH of the vegetables in 3.1 may be harvested and stored successfully.	
	3.4 State ONE common pest and ONE common disease of the vegetables named in 3.1, describing symptoms and control measures.	

3.5   State the benefits and limitations of crop rotation.

4. Understand the production of top and soft fruit. top and soft fruit for a garden or allotment	I-1 to i-13

4.1   Distinguish between top and soft fruit.

4.2   List the types of top fruit (including apples, pears, plums and cherries) and factors for their selection, to include dessert and culinary cultivars; harvesting season; and storage capability.

4.3   List the major types of soft fruit (strawberries, raspberries, blackcurrants, gooseberries, blueberries and grapes) and factors to be considered when choosing suitable cultivars, to include the fruit type; choice of early, mid and late season cultivars; flavour; and freezing capability.

4.4   Describe the production of top fruit (apples and plums) and state the factors to be considered when choosing plants, including fruit type; plant quality; rootstock choice; size of tree; training style; pollination compatibility; and cultural requirements.

4.5   Describe the production of soft fruit, including raspberries, blackcurrants and strawberries.

4.6   State the advantages of purchasing certified stock.

4.7   Describe how quality and yield can be determined by the following: planting; base and top dressings; mulching; weed control; irrigation; training systems; appropriate pruning; and pest and disease control.

4.8   Describe the importance of formative and maintenance pruning for tree shape and yield.

4.9   Explain the importance of cross pollination and fertilisation in top fruit, including flowering periods, compatibility, diploid and triploid cultivars.

4.10   State four methods of ensuring effective pollination in fruit production.

4.11   Describe the harvesting and storage of the fruit crops named in 4.4 and 4.5.

4.12   State ONE common pest and ONE common disease of the fruits named in 4.4 and 4.5, describing symptoms and control measures.

Understanding Protected Environments and their use in plant Cultivation

Unit 8 - Code: L/601/0267

Unit Level: Level 2

Credit Value: 3

This unit will enable candidates to develop an understanding of control of the environment in greenhouses, frames, polythene tunnels and cloches; the horticultural uses of protected environments; the production of a range of plants in greenhouses and tunnels; and the care of plants in the house and conservatory.

1. Know a range of types of protected structure, and their use in growing plants.	H-3

1.1   Describe a range of protected structures, to include greenhouses, cold frames, polythene tunnels, cloches and conservatories.

1.2   Describe horticultural uses for each of the structures listed in 1.1, including plant propagation, crop production, and decorative display.

2. Know the environment provided by a range of the protected structures	H-3 E-10

2.1   Describe the environmental differences between the protected environment and outdoors, including temperature; humidity; light; concentration of atmospheric gases; air movement; and irrigation requirements.

2.2 State the benefits and limitations of using protected structures for growing plants, (for example tomato, Lycopersicon esculentum) compared with growing the same plants outdoors.

2.3 Describe the effect of the environmental factors listed in 2.1 on plants in a protected environment.

3. Know the structural and cladding materials used for a range of protected structures.   H-3 E-10

3.1 List and describe the characteristics of a range of materials used for framework construction, including steel, aluminium, wood, and plastics. State the benefits and limitations of EACH.

3.2 Describe the properties of different cladding materials which can be used for structures, including glass; polyethylene film; polycarbonate; acrylic sheets; shade netting; and horticultural fleece. State the benefits and limitations of EACH.

4. Understand the control of the environment in protected protected structures   H-3 E-10

4.1 Describe the factors that affect light levels in protected structures, including shape of structure; site factors; orientation; type and condition of cladding materials.

4.2 Describe how the temperature can be maintained in structures, including heating by gas, oil or electricity; heat distribution using circulating water and air; cooling by forced or natural ventilation; evaporation; and shading.

4.3 Describe methods of changing the relative humidity (RH) in a protected environment, including the effects of 'damping down', ventilation and temperature changes.

4.4 Describe manual and automated methods of irrigation, including the use of watering cans, hose pipes, capillary systems and 'drip' systems.

4.5 Describe how light levels can be manipulated, by the use of supplementary lighting and shading, including blinds and shading paints.

4.6 Describe the importance of cultural and biological controls to limit the damage caused by plant pests and diseases.

5 Know the types of container growing media used for materials used for the production and display in protected environments.   E-10

5.1 Compare the propeties and characteristics of materials used in the manufacture of plant containers including terracotta, plastic, polystyrene, peat, paper, natural and reconstituted stone, and recycled materials.

5.2 Describe the factors that should be considered when choosing containers for the display of plants in greenhouses and interior displays, including management considerations and visual appeal.

6. Understand the horticultural uses of the protected environment.   H-3 H-10 E-10

6.1 Describe the use of protected environments for the over-wintering, production and display of plants.

6.2 Describe the production of a range of plants which can be grown in a protected environment in a garden situation under the following headings: propagation and establishment; maintenance; control of pests, diseases and disorders. Examples should include one decorative pot plant (Cyclamen persicum), one salad crop (Lycopersicon esculentum), one cut flower (Chrysanthemum x morifolium), one bedding plant (Impatiens walleriana) and one bulb for forcing (Narcissus 'Tete a Tete').

7. **Understand the care of plants in an interior situation.**

G-17

7.1 Describe the environmental factors that must be taken into account when displaying plants inside domestic buildings.

7.2 Describe the choice of suitable containers and growing media for houseplants.

7.2 Describe the management of one fern (Adiantum raddianum), one foliage (Ficus benjamina) and three seasonal flowering plants (Euphorbia pulcherrima, Kalanchoe blossfeldiana, and Saintpaulia ionantha) under the following headings: potting; feeding; watering; deadheading; re-potting; pest and disease identification and control.

Top terms

This section contains brief definitions of the terms that you should know. Page references are included so that the use of the term in the correct context can be seen, and because more detailed information is often available in the main text.

A

Angiosperms	11	Flowering plants that produce seeds within an ovary. Now called anthophytes
Annual	315	Plant that completes its life cycle in 1 year.
Anther	30	Part of the stamen of a flower, in which pollen is produced
Apical bud	14	The bud at the end of a stem.
Apical dominance	14	The effect of a hormone produced by the apical bud, that inhibits the growth of axillary buds.
Apical meristem	18	An area at the end of stems and roots, where new cells are produced.
Available water content (AWC)	89	Difference between the water held at field capacity (FC), and the water held at permanent wilting point (PWP).
Axil	14	The upper angle between stem and leaf.
Axillary bud	14	The bud formed in the axis between stems and leaves.

B

Bark	24	Outer part of stem comprising cork, cork cambium and phloem.
Biennial	321	Plant that completes its life cycle in 2 years.
Bract	29	A leaf like structure at the base of a flower.
Bud	14	An undeveloped stem or flower.
Budding	208	Vegetative propagation using bud only from the scion.
Bulb	66	Plant consisting of compact stem with fleshy leaves attached to it, in which food is stored .

C

Calyx	30	Part of the flower. The collective name for all the sepals.
Cambium (vascular)	21	A layer of cells between the phloem and xylem, that produces new phloem and xylem cells.
Carpel	30	Part of the flower. The female sex organ.
Catch crop	388	Quick maturing crop that is planted in an area that will be required later by a main crop.
Cell	15	The basic building block of all animal and vegetable life.
Chloroplast	16	Component of cells containing chlorophyll, and is where photosynthesis takes place.
Chromosomes	69	Component of cell nucleus responsible for determining heredity.
Clone	60	Genetically identical. Produced by vegetative propagation.

Top terms

Cold hardening	56	The adaptation of a plant to cold weather by increasing the sugar content of cells.
Composite flower	31	Inflorescence with many small flowers grouped together giving the impression of one.
Conifer	283	Form of gymnosperm. Woody perennial, usually evergreen.
Cork	23	Dead cells protecting the stem of woody perennials.
Cork cambium	23	Layer of cells that produces new cork cells.
Corm	66	Plant consisting primarily of a swollen stem in which food is stored
Corolla	30	Part of the flower. The collective name for all the petals.
Cortex	20	A layer of cells in roots and stems, often used for storing food.
Corymb	31	Inflorescence with flowers on stalks of different lengths, resulting in flowers at the same level.
Cotyledon	34	A seed leaf within a seed, providing a store of food.
Cultivar	7	Cultivated variety.
Cuticle	23	A protective layer on the surface of leaves and stems.
Cytoplasm	16	Jelly like substance that fills the cell and surrounds the other contents of the cell.

D

Dehiscent	32	Seeds that burst or split open to release their seeds.
Dicotyledon	12,35	A plant with two seed leaves in each seed.
Dioecious	29	Male and female organs on different plants.
Diploid	69	A cell with two sets of chromosomes.
Disbudding	216	Removing some flower buds to encourage larger flowers on others.
Division	206	Vegetative propagation by dividing existing plants.
Dormancy	56	The reduction in growth to cope with cold conditions, often accompanied by the shedding of leaves.

E

Earthing up	390	The practice of drawing the soil up around the base of the plant.
Embryo	61	Developing plant within the seed.
Endodermis	21	A layer of cells that controls the movement of water and nutrients from the cortex into the phloem and xylem.
Epigeal germination	65	Cotyledons emerge above the soil.
Epidermis	20,23,27	The outer layer of cells on roots, stems and leaves.

F

F_1 hybrids	71	The first generation of plants from pure bred parents.
False fruit	33	Fruit not formed from the ovary but from the receptacle.
Family	9	A group of plants with common characteristics, made up of more than one genus.
Fertilisation	63	Fusion of the male and female gamete.
Fibrous root	19	Fine root originating at base of stem.
Field capacity (FC)	89	Water that remains in the soil after gravitational water has

drained off.

| Filament | 30 | Part of the stamen of a flower, that connects the anther to the receptacle. |

G

Gamete	61	A sex cell. The female gamete is an ovum (egg) and the male gamete is a sperm.
Gene	69	Part of a chromosome that determines inherited characteristics.
Genus	6	A group of plants with common characteristics, made up of more than one species.
Geotropism	65	The tendency to grow downwards under the effect of gravity.
Germination	64	The growth of a plant from its seed to appearing above ground.
Grafting	207	Vegetative propagation entailing attaching part of scion to rootstock of another plant.
Green manure	110	Plants grown in order to be incorporated into soil to provide nutrients.
Guard cells	28	Cells either side of the stomata that control opening and closing.
Gymnosperms	11	Plants that produce seeds not protected by an ovary. Now called coniferophytes

H

Haploid	69	A cell with one set of chromosomes.
Hardening off	199	Gradually exposing plants to colder conditions in order for them to adapt.
Heeling in	194	Covering the roots of plants for temporary protection.
Heredity	69	The inheritance of characteristics from a parent.
Hermaphrodite	29	Male and female organs on the same flower.
Humus	92	Substance remaining after organic matter has been decomposed.
Hybrid	8	Plant produced by sexual reproduction between different species or genera.
Hydroponics	242	Growing plants in water or other artificial medium.
Hypocotyl	34	Part of seed connecting plumule to radicle.
Hypogeal germination	65	Cotyledons remain in the soil.

I

Inflorescence	31	Cluster of flowers attached to one stem.
Integrated pest control (IPC)	121	Planned program of control using variety of methods.
Intercropping	388	Practice of growing a quick maturing crop in the space between slower growing plants.
Internode	14	Space between two nodes.

L

Lamina	25	Leaf blade.
Lateral	212	Side shoot from a branch.
Lateral meristem	18	Meristem running through roots and stems that produces new

phloem and xylem cells.

Leader	212	The leading shoot on a branch.
Leaf - simple	26	Leaf not divided into leaflets.
Leaf - compound	26	Leaf made up of a number of leaflets.
Lenticel	24	A pore in a stem through which gases can be exchanged.

M

Medullary ray	24	Group of cells transporting water and nutrients across stem.
Meiosis	69	Cell division producing gamete with one set of chromosomes.
Meristem	17	An area of active cell division.
Mesophyll	27	Cells within a leaf blade.
Micropropagation	209	Vegetative propagation using a very small part of existing plant.
Micropyle	34	Hole in seed coat where pollen tube entered the ovule.
Mitochondria	16	Part of a cell where respiration takes place.
Mitosis	69	Cell division producing two new diploid cells.
Monocotyledon	12,35	A plant with one seed leaf in each seed.
Monoecious	29	Male and female organs on different flowers on the same plant.

N

Node	14	Point on a stem from which a leaf grows.
Nucleus	16	Part of a cell containing chromosomes.
Nutrients	52	Chemicals required by the plant in order to grow and develop.

O

Osmosis	39	Process by which water moves across a semi-permeable membrane, from a solution with a higher concentration of water molecules to a solution with a lower concentration.
Ovary	30	Part of the female sex organ that contains the ovules. After fertilisation it develops into the fruit.
Ovule	30	Part of the ovary that contains the female sex cells (eggs). When fertilised these develop into seeds.

P

Palisade cells	27	Cells in the upper part of a leaf blade, specially adapted for photosynthesis.
Parthenocarpic	33	Fruits that develop without seeds.
Panicle	31	Inflorescence with many stalks, each in the form of a raceme.
Pedicel	29	Flower stalk.
Perennial	315	Herbaceous plant with a life of more than two years.
Pericarp	33	Fruit wall formed from wall of ovary.
Pericycle	21	Band of cells in root from which new roots are formed.
Permanent wilting point (PWP)	89	Point at which plants wilt because there is no more water available in the soil.
Petal	30	Part of the flower. A thin leaf like organ that surrounds and partially protects the sexual organs.

Petiole	25	Leaf stalk.
pH	97	Measure of acidity or alkalinity of a soil.
Phloem	21	Part of the plant tissue that transfers food to other parts.
Photoperiodism	48	Reaction of a plant to day length.
Photosynthesis	42	The process by which plants use the energy from light to produce food for the plant.
Phototropism	65	The tendency to grow upwards towards the light.
Pinching out	215	Removing the growing tip of plants to encourage bushier growth.
Pith	23	Loosely packed cells in the centre of herbaceous stems.
Plasmodesmata	16	Threads of cytoplasm that connect adjacent cells.
Plasmolysis	45	Process where water is lost from cells due to lower concentration of water within the cell.
Plumule	34	Part of seed that will form first shoot.
Pollen	61	Small grains containing the male gamete.
Pollen tube	63	Access made by pollen grain to ovule.
Pollination	61	The process by which pollen from the anther of the male flower is brought into contact with the stigma of the female flower.
Primary growth	18	Growth at the apical meristem.
Protoplasm	15	All the contents of a cell.

R

Raceme	31	Inflorescence with flowers attached by short stalks to a central stem.
Radicle	34	Part of seed that will form the first root.
Receptacle	29	Part of the flower. The top of the pedicel, that supports other parts.
Respiration	43	Process by which cells release energy to fuel the growth of the plant.
Rhizome	67	An underground stem, often used to store food.
Rootstock	207	Roots of one plant used in grafting scion from another plant

S

Saturation point	89	Soil with all pores filled with water.
Scarification	198	Weakening the seed coat to aid germination.
Scarifying	276	Raking the surface of the lawn to remove thatch and moss.
Secondary growth	18	Growth at the lateral meristem.
Sepal	29	Part of the flower. A leaf like organ that protects the flower bud.
Scion	207	Plant from which material is taken to graft or bud to a rootstock.
Soil Moisture deficit (SMD)	90	The water that needs to be added to restore soil to field capacity.
Soil structure	100	The way in which the individual components of the soil are combined together.
Soil texture	83	The composition of the soil in terms of particle size.
Species	6	A group of plants with common characteristics, that can reproduce sexually among themselves.
Spike (flower)	31	Inflorescence with flowers attached to stem without stalks.
Spur	212	A short branch structure bearing fruit buds.

Stamen	30	Part of the flower. The male sex organ.
Stem tubers	67	Organs formed at the end of rhizomes, which store food and from which new plants can grow.
Stem	13,22	The above ground support for the plant, to which leaves and flowers are attached.
Stigma	30	Part of the female sex organ that receives the pollen.
Stolon	67	A stem that grows horizontally close to the ground.
Stomata	27	A pore in a leaf through which gases can be exchanged.
Stratification	198	Exposing a seed to a period of cold to aid germination.
Style	30	Part of the female sex organ that joins the stigma to the ovary.
Successional sowing	374	Sowing the same crop at intervals of time to prevent the whole crop maturing at the same time

T

Tap root	19	The main root of a branching root system.
Testa	34	Seed coat.
Thinning (seedlings)	390	The removal of overcrowded seedlings to provide space for others to develop.
Thinning (fruit)	427	Removal of small fruits to provide space for others to develop.
Tilth	100	The physical state of the soil in relation to plant growth.
Trace elements	52	Another name for minor nutrients.
Transpiration	46	The loss of water from the plant, mainly through the stomata.
Triploid	69	A cell with three sets of chromosomes.

U

| Umbel | 31 | Inflorescence with flower stalks originating at one point, and all of the same length. |

V

Vacuole	16	A sac within the cell containing water, minerals, and waste products.
Vascular cambium	23	A layer of cells between the phloem and xylem, that produces new phloem and xylem cells.
Variety	7	A sub-division of a species.
Vernalisation	49	A period of cold required to induce flowering.

X

| Xylem | 21,23 | Part of the plant tissue that transfers water and nutrients to other parts. |

Z

| Zygote | 61 | Diploid cell formed by fusion of male and female gametes. |

Index

Index

D

Index

Index